# SUMMER JOBS ABROAD 2007

# SUMMER JOBS ABROAD 2007

EDITORS

## David Woodworth
## Victoria Pybus

**Assisted by Rebecca Donnelly**

Distributed in the USA by
The Globe Pequot Press, Guilford, Connecticut

Published annually by
Vacation Work, 9 Park End Street, Oxford
www.vacationwork.co.uk

Thirty-eighth edition 2007

SUMMER JOBS ABROAD 2007
By David Woodworth and Victoria Pybus

ISBN 13: 978-1-85458-364-2 (hardback)
ISBN 10: 1-85458-364-6 (hardback)

ISBN 13: 978-1-85458-363-5 (softback)
ISBN 10: 1-85458-363-8 (softback)

ISSN 0308 7123

Statement for the purposes of
The Employment Agencies Act 1973:
The price of the Directory of Summer Jobs Abroad is £16.95 (hardback)
or £10.99 (softback) and is for the book and the information contained
therein; it is not refundable.

Cover design by mccdesign ltd

Typeset by Brendan Cole

Printed and bound in Italy by Legoprint, SpA, Trento

# Contents

## Summer Jobs Available

## Country-Specific Vacancies

## CENTRAL AND EASTERN EUROPE

## AFRICA AND THE MIDDLE EAST

## THE AMERICAS

## ASIA

---

**THIS EDITION IS VALID FOR
THE 2007 SUMMER SEASON ONLY.**

N.B. The author and publishers have every reason to believe in the accuracy of the information given in this book and the authenticity and correct practices of all organisations, companies, agencies etc. mentioned: however, situations may change and telephone numbers etc. can alter, and readers are strongly advised to check facts and credentials for themselves.

We have made every effort to make this book as useful as possible for you. We would appreciate any comments that you may have concerning the employers listed. Any comments will be treated in strict confidence.

# Preface

There is no doubt that the prevalence of cheap air travel means that students and others no longer have to restrict themselves, for reasons of economy, to working in Britain. There is a wealth of skill enhancing job possibilities attainable especially throughout Europe, but also further afield. The listings of *Summer Jobs Abroad 2007* are as disparate geographically and occupationally as ever. They range from the practical (building, restoration work, organic farming) to the cerebral (writing reviews for a campsite guide), and from the artistic (theatrical animator, painting teacher) to the compassionate (working with the disabled) as well as an impressive array of workcamps, hotels, campsites, harvests, couriers etc.

The bulk of the individual opportunities in this book are in western Europe. There are also sections for each of the other main geographical areas (The Americas, Asia etc). Entries covering opportunities in a wide distribution of countries or continents are in the *Worldwide* chapter at the beginning of the book; while those with a distribution in three or more European countries are in the *Organisations With Vacancies Across Europe* chapter; others are listed in the relevant country chapter. At the start of each country chapter there are some general notes on employment prospects and regulations on work permits, visas etc. The information in the individual entries has been supplied by the organisations/employers themselves, and is included at their request

The European Union, which allows inter-state mobility of workers who are nationals of EU member countries has 25 member states including eight former eastern bloc countries (the Czech Republic, Estonia, Hungary, Latvia, Lithuania, Poland, Slovakia and Slovenia) plus Malta and Southern Cyprus, making ten countries. These ten newer members are mostly countries where unemployment is high (18% in Poland) and earnings are an eighth of other EU countries' citizens. These means that their citizens have flooded into better off EU countries where wages are higher. Many students report that this has made competition for summer jobs in western Europe much keener. Some say the EU has faltered in its progress after the rejection of the EU Constitution by France and The Netherlands in 2005, but if all goes according to plan, Romania and Bulgaria will be the newest members in January 2007. If and when Turkey joins, it will not be for several years. For up-to-date information on regulations regarding taking up work in all EU member states consult the EURES website at www.europa.eu.int/eures or the individual countries' embassies in your own country.

While there are few opportunities for paid employment in eastern Europe and developing countries, we have given details of voluntary organisations willing to accept unskilled workers for short periods of time. Even in those countries where paid employment is available, voluntary work has a number of advantages. Hours of work are likely to be shorter, leaving more time available for recreational and cultural activities, which are generally regarded an integral part of workcamp life. In most cases, volunteers are drawn from a number of countries, so that contact is made not only with local residents, but also with young people from all over the world.

Only brief details have been given on opportunities in the USA. Opportunities there are so numerous that they are included in a separate volume entitled *Summer Jobs in the USA*.

We wish you the best of luck in landing a summer job that you have chosen from the selection within, please note however, that the publishers cannot undertake to contact individual employers or to offer any assistance in arranging specific jobs.

**Victoria Pybus & David Woodworth**
**October 2006**

# Opting for a Summer Job Abroad

The reasons why young people look for alternatives to the conventional summer job in their hometown are many and varied. Often it is just a case of itchy feet. Travelling abroad to do a holiday job is one of the best ways to shake off the boredom and routine of living at home and working locally. Whereas months of slogging at a local burger bar will allow you to save some money, time spent working abroad may alter your view of where you are heading in life.

Many students cite positive reasons for choosing to work abroad: to experience a foreign culture from the inside rather than as an onlooker, to fill a gap in their life's timetable in a productive way, **to improve their knowledge of foreign languages** and cultures, to **gain practical skills**. Usually there is an element of all these at work.

Working abroad is one of the means by which students and others can afford to stay overseas for an extended period, to have a chance to **absorb a foreign culture**, to meet foreign people on their own terms and to gain a better perspective on their own culture and habits. Sweeping generalisations about the valuable cultural insights afforded by working in a foreign land should be tempered with a careful consideration of the reality of doing a job abroad. In most cases, the expression 'working holiday' is an oxymoron like 'cruel kindness'. Jobs are jobs wherever you do them, and there is little scope for developing a social life and exploring museums if you are stranded in an obscure industrial town teaching English six days a week or manning reception in a damp caravan for a camping holiday operator. After perusing the jobs listed in this volume, it will be necessary to ask yourself whether you think you are sufficiently adaptable to work for a season in a Swiss hotel, Latvian summer camp, Danish strawberry farm or whatever catches your eye.

**Earning and saving** during the summer vacation have become crucially important to the vast majority of students since grants for higher education have been whittled away and students' tuition fees and debts on graduation have become astronomical. A secondary consideration for some is that a summer job might **enhance a future CV** and allow you to gain useful experience or new skills. Jobs abroad can fulfil both these requirements. Some areas of career interest can just as easily be served by a summer job abroad as at home in fields as diverse as archaeology and social services, teaching and agriculture.

**Employers normally favour candidates who have demonstrated initiative and spent their time productively** using a broad range of skills and working abroad will help you to fulfil these criteria. This does not necessarily mean finding an internship with a New York investment bank. Increasingly, employers are becoming open-minded to the fact that high-flying summer work is hard to come by and that transferable skills are what matter. For instance, those people who attain the position of barge manager on the French waterways will have demonstrated language and communication skills, leadership abilities, client service and a hardy stomach. Someone who works as a bar attendant may well have demonstrated these same skills plus a degree of numeracy and a faculty for working long hours under pressure.

Undoubtedly there are some drawbacks as well. It is more difficult to land a job when you are not available for interview and when you are not fluent in the dominant language of the region. Then there is the hassle of getting abroad and possible administrative formalities such as visas and insurance. You will have to sever yourself temporarily from your commitments at home (boyfriends/girlfriends, pets, teams and clubs). One of the main drawbacks of a summer job abroad is that if anything goes wrong, you are a long way from the safety net of home. This was terrifyingly illustrated in summer 2005 when working holidaymakers from Britain were caught up in the New Orleans hurricane disaster and found that they were almost completely responsible for ensuring their own survival. Job descriptions may sound more glamorous than the reality (as is true with jobs anywhere) so that a job serving cocktails in paradise may turn out to be clearing ashtrays in a seedy discotheque.

Certain obstacles in the mind of the irresolute must be overcome: What jobs can I get? Do I need specific skills? What if I only speak English? This introductory section sets out to allay anxieties and to encourage readers to peruse details of the thousands of summer jobs available. Those who have shed their unrealistic expectations are normally exhilarated by the novelty and challenge of finding and doing a summer job abroad.

Finding a summer job abroad may strike you as a daunting task. However this book leads you through the process in a systematic way and provides sufficient listings to help you find a job suited to your needs. Some jobs listed pay very well and come with room and board; others are voluntary and therefore unpaid. Some last for the whole season (June to September or longer); others are just for a couple of weeks. Working abroad for a short period will enable the dream to become a reality, of being immersed in a different culture, meeting new friends and earning money at the same time.

# Where to Go and What to Do

At the risk of oversimplifying the choices, the seeker of a summer job abroad must either fix up a definite job before leaving home or take a gamble on finding something on arrival. There is a lot to recommend prior planning, especially for people who have seldom travelled on their own and who feel some trepidation at the prospect of going abroad

If you have no predisposition to choose one country over another based on previous holidays, language studies at school or information from friends or relatives who live abroad, you are free to consider any job listed in this book. It will soon become apparent that there are far fewer listings in developing countries, simply because paid work in the developing world is rarely available to foreigners. Yet many students arrange to live for next to nothing doing something positive (see the section on Volunteering below).

Some organisations and employers listed in this directory accept a tiny handful of individuals who satisfy stringent requirements; others accept almost anyone who can pay the required fee, for example agencies that recruit paying volunteers for conservation work in exotic places or to teach English. Some work schemes and official exchanges require a lot of advance planning since it is not unusual for an application deadline to fall three to six months before departure.

The kind of job you find will determine the stratum of society in which you will mix and therefore the content of the experience. The traveller who spends a few weeks picking olives for a Cretan farmer will get a very different insight into Greece from the traveller who looks after the children of an Athenian shipping magnate. And both will probably have more culturally worthwhile experiences than the traveller who settles for working at a beach café frequented only by his or her partying compatriots.

The more unusual and interesting the job the more competition it will attract. For example it can be safely assumed that only a small percentage of applicants to the American Scandinavian Foundation are accepted as engineering trainees in Finland and only a few of the many drama students who would like to spend the summer

working in a travelling theatre in Italy, actually get to have that experience. On the other hand, less glamorous options can absorb an almost unlimited number of people, for example working as a counsellor on an American children's summer camp or fruit picking in Australia. All these possibilities are included in this book.

The question of work permits and visas must be tackled by British students who plan to work in a country outside Europe. The standard situation among all European Union countries (plus Iceland, Liechtenstein and Norway) is that nationals of any member state have the right to work (or look for work) for up to three months. Before the end of that period they should apply to the police or the local authority for a residence permit, showing their passport and job contract, a process that can be more bureaucratic and difficult than the legislation would indicate.

The most recent European Union member states: Poland, Hungary, Latvia, Lithuania, Estonia, The Czech Republic, Slovakia, Slovenia, Cyprus and Malta will require some years before their economies are comparable to those of most of Western Europe and some of the older members may impose restrictions on citizens of these new member countries receiving full EU working rights in their countries for several years. Unemployment in some of the new eastern European member countries is over 17%). The same applies to the anticipated new members Romania and Bulgaria (due to join in 2007).

Work permits and residence visas outside Europe or for North American jobseekers worldwide are not readily available in many countries and for many kinds of job. In most cases, the job-seeker from overseas must find an employer willing to apply to the immigration authorities on his or her behalf well in advance of the job's starting date, while they are still in their home country. A more accessible alternative is to join an organised exchange programme like the ones administered by IST Plus (www.istplus. com) part of Worldwide Council Exchanges and BUNAC, where the red tape is taken care of by a sponsoring organisation (see the introduction to the Worldwide chapter). Britons and other EU citizens who want to work outside Europe must investigate possibilities country-by-country (see sections on Red Tape in the country chapters).

# Seasonal Work Available

## The Tourist Industry

The tourist industry is a mainstay of summer job seekers. The seasonal nature of hotel and restaurant work discourages a stable working population, so that hotel proprietors often rely on foreign and student labour during the busy summer season. Also, many tourist destinations are in remote places; young people have ended up working in hotels in some of the most beautiful corners of the world from high in the Alps to national parks in the USA (and working some of the longest hours in them).

In a few cases, agencies can place eligible British students in continental hotels for the season but mostly it is a case of applying to individual hotels. Only in a few cases can agencies and leisure groups place people without any relevant experience (e.g. in a café or takeaway in your home town) or knowledge of the relevant language.

The earlier you decide to apply for seasonal hotel work the better are your chances. Hotels often recruit months before the summer season, and it is advisable to contact as many hotels as possible by March, preferably in their own language. Knowledge of more than one language is an immense asset for work in Europe. If you have an interest in working in a particular country and want to cast your net wider than the hotels listed in this directory, get a list of hotels from their tourist office in London or from a guide or the internet and contact the largest ones.

If you secure a hotel job without speaking the language of the country and lack relevant experience, you will probably be placed at the bottom of the pecking order, e.g. in the laundry or washing dishes. Reception and bar jobs are usually the most sought after and highly paid. However, the lowly jobs have their saving graces. The usual hours of chamber staff (7am-2pm) allow plenty of free time and of course you do not have to deal with guests. The same complaints crop up again and again among people who have worked in hotel kitchens: long and unsociable hours, low wages, dodgy accommodation and food, and hot working conditions.

But there are benefits as well. The vast majority of hotels provide their staff with accommodation and meals; a deduction may be made from wages for living expenses but in most cases this will not be unreasonable. Excellent camaraderie and team spirit, the opportunity to learn a foreign language, beautiful surroundings and the ease with which wages can be saved, including the possibility of an end-of-season bonus, are further incentives to consider a season in a foreign hotel.

## Resorts and Holiday Centres

Camping holiday operators employ a huge number of students and young people for the summer season. The Holidaybreak group alone (see entry in *Europewide* section), which includes Eurocamp and Keycamp, recruits up to 2,000 campsite couriers and children's couriers. The courier's job is to clean the tents and caravans between visitors, greet clients and deal with difficulties (particularly illness or car breakdowns) and introduce clients to the attractions of the area or even arrange and host social functions

and amuse the children. All of this will be rewarded with on average £90-£100 a week in addition to free tent accommodation. Many companies offer half-season contracts April to mid-July and mid-July to the end of September. Setting up and dismantling the campsites in March/April and September (known as *montage* and *démontage*) is often done by a separate team. The work is hard but the language requirements are nil. The majority of vacancies are in France, though the major companies employ people from Austria to Denmark.

Successful couriers make the job look easy, but it does demand a lot of hard work and patience. Occasionally it is very hard to keep up the happy, smiling, never-ruffled courier look, but most seem to end up enjoying the job since it provides accommodation, a guaranteed weekly wage and the chance to work with like-minded people.

The big companies interview hundreds of candidates and have filled most posts by the end of January. But there is a high dropout rate and vacancies are filled from a reserve list, so it is worth ringing around the companies later on for cancellations. Despite keen competition, anyone who has studied a European language and has an outgoing personality stands a good chance if he or she applies early and widely enough.

Many specialist tour companies employ leaders for their clients (children and/or adults) who want a walking, cycling, watersports holiday, etc. Any competent sailor, canoeist, diver, climber, horse rider, etc. should have no difficulty marketing their skills abroad. A list of special interest and activity tour operators (to whom people with specialist skills can apply) is available from AITO, the Association of Independent Tour Operators (133A St Margaret's Road, Twickenham TW1 1RG; www.aito.co.uk). In the US, consult the *Specialty Travel Index* (PO Box 458 San Anselmo, CA 94979; www.specialtytravel.com); the directory is issued twice a year at a cost of $10 (£57) in the US, $22 (£12.27) abroad.

For people who are pursuing a career in travel and tourism, it would be worth looking at another Vacation Work title *Working in Tourism* (£11.95).

# Agriculture

Farmers from Norway to Tasmania (with the notable exception of developing countries) are unable to bring in their harvests without assistance from outside their local community and often reward their itinerant labour force well. Finding out where harvesting jobs occur is a matter of doing some research (for example in the book *Work Your Way Around the World*) and asking around for instance at hostels and the pubs frequented by farmers. Small-scale farmers are less inclined to publicise vacancies in a directory like this one than hoteliers, though this book contains details of interesting farm work schemes in Switzerland and Norway, and some large Australian, Danish and Dutch farms are listed.

The organic farming movement is a very useful source of agricultural contacts. Organic growers everywhere take on volunteers to help them minimise or abolish the use of chemicals and heavy machinery. Various coordinating bodies go under the name of WWOOF - World Wide Opportunities on Organic Farms. National WWOOF coordinators compile a worklist of their member farmers willing to provide free room and board, which is part of membership to volunteers who help out and who are genuinely interested in furthering the aims of the organic movement. Each national group has its own aims, system, fees and rules but most expect applicants to have gained some experience on an organic farm in their own country first. WWOOF is an exchange: in return for your help on organic farms, gardens and homesteads, you receive meals, a place to sleep and a practical insight into organic growing. (If the topic arises at immigration present yourself as a volunteer student of organic farming organising an educational farm visit or a cultural exchange.)

WWOOF has a global website *www.wwoof.org* with links to the national offices in the countries that have a WWOOF coordinator. WWOOF organisations exist in many countries worldwide – developed and developing. Individual farm listings in other countries, i.e. those with no national organisation, are known as WWOOF Independents. It is necessary to join WWOOF before you can obtain addresses of these properties. If you are starting in Britain, send an s.a.e. to the UK branch of WWOOF (PO Box 2675, Lewes, Sussex BN7 1RB; www.wwoof.org.uk) who will send you a membership application form. Membership costs £15 per year or £20 for joint membership and includes a subscription to their bi-monthly newsletter which contains small adverts for opportunities both in Britain and abroad, UK website included application forms for residents and non-residents.

# Teaching English

There are areas of the world where the boom in English language learning seems to know no bounds, from Ecuador to Slovenia, Lithuania to Vietnam. In some private language institutes, being a native speaker and adopting a professional manner are sometimes sufficient qualifications to get a job. But for more stable teaching jobs in recognised language schools, you will have to sign a contract (minimum three months, usually nine) and have some kind of qualification which ranges from a university degree to a certificate in education with a specialisation in ELT (English Language Teaching is now the preferred label).

To fix up a job in advance, make use of the internet and check adverts in the Education section of the *Guardian* every Tuesday. In a few cases, a carefully crafted CV and enthusiastic personality are as important as EFL training and experience. There is also increasing scope for untrained but eager volunteers willing to pay an agency to place them in a language teaching situation abroad (for example, see the entry for i-to-i in the *Worldwide* chapter).

Native speaker teachers are nearly always employed to stimulate conversation rather than to teach grammar. Yet a basic knowledge of English grammar is a great asset when more advanced pupils ask awkward questions. The wages paid to English teachers are usually reasonable, and in developing countries are quite often well in excess of the average local wage. In return you may be asked to teach some fairly unsociable hours since most private English classes take place after working hours, and so schedules split between early morning and evening are commonplace.

Most language institutes operate throughout the academic year and close for the summer though some run summer courses or more commonly are affiliated with residential summer language camps where English and sports are taught to children and teenagers. These create jobs for monitors and counsellors as well as for EFL teachers. (See, for example, entries for ACLE in Italy chapter, Village Camps in the France and Switzerland chapters and APASS in the Poland chapter).

A good source of information about the whole topic of English teaching is *Teaching English Abroad* (560 pages) by Susan Griffith, available from www.vacationwork.co.uk.

## Au Pairs, Nannies & Mothers' Helps

These days, young British women are much less likely to consider au pairing as a summer job than was formerly the case. Being an au pair is seen as an unadventurous option compared with helping to conserve an Amazon rainforest or teaching English to Nepalese children, which is the type of alternative offered by the many, rather expensive, gap year companies. Nevertheless, au pairing remains an excellent way to acquire fluency in a foreign language. Girls (and sometimes young men) can arrange to live with a family, helping to look after the children in exchange for pocket money. The terms au pair, mother's help and nanny are often applied rather loosely, since all are primarily live-in jobs concerned with looking after children. Nannies may have some formal training and take full charge of the children. Mother's helps work full-time and undertake general housework and/or cooking as well as childcare. Au pairs are supposed to work fewer hours and are expected to learn a foreign language (except in the USA) while living with a family. The Council of Europe guidelines stipulate that au pairs should be aged 17-30 (though these limits are flexible), should be expected to work about five hours a day, plus a couple of evenings of babysitting, with one full day off per week; they must be given a private room and full board, health insurance, opportunities to learn the language and weekly pocket money of £55 (or between €50-75) in most cases, plus board and lodging.

A number of agencies both in the UK and in the destination countries are described in this book. A list of agencies can be found at *www.europa-pages.com/au-pair*. After satisfying an agency that you are a suitable candidate for a live-in childcare position, you will have to wait until an acceptable match can be made with a family abroad. Make enquiries as early as possible, since there is a shortage of summer-only positions. In the first instance contact several agencies to compare terms and conditions. If your requirements are very specific as regards location or family circumstances, ring around some agencies and ask them to be blunt about their chances of being able to fix you up with what you want. In the UK agencies are permitted to charge a fee of up to £40 plus VAT only after a placement has been verified.

The advantage of a summer placement is that the au pair will accompany the family to their holiday destination at the seaside or in the mountains; the disadvantage is that the children will be out of school and therefore potentially a full-time responsibility.

Anyone interested in finding out about all aspects of live-in childcare should consult *The Au Pair & Nanny's Guide to Working Abroad* (Vacation Work Publications, £12.95).

## Volunteering

Charities and aid organisations offer a range of structured and unstructured voluntary opportunities around the world. For example, enterprising summer workers have participated in interesting projects from helping a local native settlement to build a community centre in Arctic Canada, to working with hill tribes in the state of Haryana in northern India.

Every year the international workcamps movement mobilises thousands of volunteers from many countries to join a programme of conflict resolution and community development. As well as providing volunteers with the means to live cheaply for two to four weeks in a foreign country, workcamps enable unskilled volunteers to become involved in what can be useful work for the community (e.g. building footpaths, working with disabled people), to meet people from many different backgrounds and to increase their awareness of other lifestyles and social problems.

When starting your research for a longer stint abroad as a volunteer, it is important to maintain realistic expectations. Ideally, your research should begin well in advance of your intended departure so that applications can be lodged, sponsorship money raised, language courses and other preparatory courses attended, and so on. When you receive the literature or check the website of voluntary organisations, consider the tone as well as the content. For example, profit-making commercial companies that charge high fees for participating in their programmes are more likely to produce glossy brochures that read almost like a tour operator's, whereas underfunded charities or small grassroots organisations with no publicity budget will probably duplicate their information on an ancient photocopier. Most organisations, with big budgets or no budget have a website or at least an email address.

Many voluntary agencies require more than idle curiosity about a country; they require a strong wish to become involved in a specific project and in many cases an ideological commitment to a cause. Almost without exception, volunteers must be self-funding, which serves to deter all but the committed.

For anyone with a green conscience, numerous conservation organisations throughout the world welcome volunteers for short or long periods. Projects range from tree planting to gibbon counting. Unfortunately, the more glamorous projects such as helping to conserve a coral reef or accompanying scientific research expeditions into wild and woolly places charge volunteers a great deal of money for the privilege of helping.

For a specialist directory of opportunities, consult *Green Volunteers: The World Guide to Voluntary Work in Nature Conservation* ,and *World Volunteers,* a guide to opportunities in the developing world, both published in Italy and distributed by Vacation Work Publications in Europe (£10.99 each plus £1.75 postage). Related titles from the Vacation Work are *Working with the Environment* and *Working with Animals.* Also look at the website for the Ecovolunteer Programme of wildlife and conservation projects worldwide (*www.ecovolunteer.org.uk*). *The International Directory of Voluntary Work,* also published by Vacation Work, contains advice and listings of all types of voluntary work worldwide. The website World Wide Volunteering (www. wwv.org.uk) details over 1,000 organisations in over 200 countries. In schools, public libraries and universities access to the site is free; otherwise it costs £10 for three searches per year.

Several organisations assist scientific expeditions by supplying fee-paying volunteers. For details of scientific expedition organisations which use self-financing volunteers, see entries for Coral Cay Conservation, Earthwatch and Trekforce among others in the Worldwide chapter.

# Maximise Your Chances

## Plan of Attack

1. Remember that most employers prefer to take on a person to work for the whole of the season rather than several people to work for shorter periods. If you are able to

work for longer than the minimum period quoted, let the employer know at an early stage since this is often a deciding factor.

2. Most employers like to make their staff arrangements in good time so try to apply early, but not earlier than the date mentioned in the job details or later than the closing date for applications, if given. Some of the biggest employers may maintain reserve lists to cover late staff cancellations, so it might pay off to apply after the deadline, but don't be disappointed if you receive no reply.

3. Apply as widely as possible. If more than one job seems to be suitable or appeals to you, apply for all of them. Make sure that you are qualified for the position for which you are applying. Check minimum age and work period requirements and any special qualifications needed, particularly if a good knowledge of another language is called for. If there is any shortfall, emphasise other skills and qualifications that may be useful.

4. Compose a short formal letter, explaining which position interests you, when you are available and why you think you are suitable. If possible produce this letter on a computer; if not, take care to make it legible. Always mention that the job has been seen in this book as many of the employers in it have a long-standing and trusting relationship with Vacation Work and its publications.

5. Try to address the potential employer in his or her language. It is not only polite to do so, but there is a possibility that he or she is unable to speak English.

6. Enclose with your letter a standard *curriculum vitae* (cv or résumé) on a single A4 sheet covering the following points and any other details you consider relevant:

- Personal details (name, address, nationality, age, date of birth, marital status)
- Previous work experience, especially of similar type of work.
- Special qualifications, especially when they have some relevance to the job in question, e.g. canoe instructor's certificate, typing speeds or fluency in another language
- Education (brief details of type of education, examinations passed).

7. Enclose a small recent passport-sized photo of yourself. (This may not be necessary when applying to a voluntary organisation.)

8. Employers are more likely to reply promptly if you enclose an International Reply Coupon (available at the Post Office). This will not guarantee a reply, but it will make one more likely.

9. If there is no reply from the employer within a reasonable period of time (say two weeks), it may be advisable to follow up the written/e-mailed application with a telephone call or an e-mail. The employer may be impressed by your initiative and perseverance if it is matched by enthusiasm and politeness. Otherwise, s/he may feel hassled. In a few cases it is expected that applicants should make themselves available for an interview or visit the employer in person. Where this is the case, the applicant is likely to find more success if he can back up claims of suitability with a written CV and references.

10. When a job is offered to you, check details of wages, hours and other conditions of

work with the employer. Do not be afraid to negotiate; you are always entitled to ask whether or not different terms are possible.

11. Please note that wages are normally quoted in sterling but will usually be paid in foreign currency including euros: exchange rates may fluctuate. The details given in the Directory have been supplied by the employer and will normally be correct, but it is wise to obtain written confirmation of them before taking up the position. You should insist that you receive a contract of employment before you set off for your job if the journey involves any great expense, or if the employer seems at all vague about the details of the work you will do.

12. When you are offered a job, please confirm acceptance or otherwise as quickly as possible. Do not accept more than one job. If you need to juggle possible outcomes, keep the prospective employers informed of your intentions and the expected timescale. If plans change and you do not want to take up a job you have already accepted, it is only fair to let the employer know immediately.

13. If you are offered more than one job, decide quickly which one you prefer and inform both employers of your decision as promptly as possible.

14. Those who contact employers and apply for positions via e-mail should ensure that if a CV is attached, that it is written in a programme that is readable and receivable by the receiver and that it contains no viruses.

## The Internet

The majority of job vacancies (summer or permanent) are posted on the internet. Yet the plethora of resources can be bewildering and not infrequently disappointing - the number and range of jobs posted often fall short of the claims. No employer looking for two waitresses and a bellhop for the summer wants to publicise this fact through cyberspace since they are bound to be inundated with SPAM and applications from Merseyside to Mongolia. The internet as a job-finding tool works best for those with specific experience and skills, for example people looking for TEFL jobs abroad.

Still, internet surfers will find a host of potentially useful links on the web. Many websites promise to provide free on-line recruitment services for travellers. These include *www.seasonworkers.com*, *www.hotrecruit.co.uk*, *The Working Traveller* (*www. payaway.co.uk*), *www.coolworks.com* (recommended for seasonal work in the North American tourist industry), *www.anyworkanywhere.com*, *www.summerjobseeker. com* (travel, leisure, tourism), *www.jobmonkey.com*, and so on. Elsewhere on the web, committed individuals around the world manage non-commercial sites on everything from English-language teaching to bar-tending. The Vacation-Work website (*www. vacationwork.co.uk*) has a section listing job vacancies for travellers both in Britain and abroad and an excellent links page.

**Applying for jobs via the internet:** many employers and organisations now accept letters of application and CVs by e-mail. Many provide their own application forms which you can download from their website.

# BEFORE YOU GO:
# Essential Preparation

## Travel

Student travellers can take advantage of a comprehensive range of special discounts both at home and abroad which enable them to go almost anywhere in the world on the cheap. To qualify for a range of discounts on train, plane and bus fares, on selected accommodation, admission to museums, etc., you need an **International Student Identity Card (ISIC)** which is recognised all over the world. The card is obtainable for £7 or by post for £7.50 from ISIC Mail Order, DPS Hull Ltd, Unit 132, Louis Pearlman Centre, Goulden Street, Hull HU3 4DL; www.isiccard.com. The ISIC card is valid for 15 months from September 1st. All full-time students are eligible (though some flight carriers do not offer discounts to students over the age of 31). An alternative card is the International Student Exchange Identity Card (covers ages from 12 to 26) available from ISE Cards, 11043 North Saint Andrew's Way, Scottsdale AZ 85254, USA (☎1-800-255-8000; www.isecard.com) at a cost of $25 (£14).

Both cards are available from STA Travel (☎0870 60 6070; www.statravel.co.uk – to find your nearest outlet, use their websites or the telephone directory), Student Flights (Students Union, Keele University, Staffordshire ST5 5BJ; ☎752-715215; fax 01752-715915; www.studentflights.co.uk) and some other student travel outlets. The ISIC card and the ISE Card are available to persons of all nationalities; applications should include proof of student status, a passport photo, full name, date of birth, nationality, address and a cheque or postal order. The ISIC fee of $22 (approx £12.27) comes with a basic accident/sickness insurance package. Valuable discounts are also available for air travel. Student and youth discount flights are operated by the major student travel organisations under the umbrella of the Student Air Travel Association – these include STA travel and Student Flights, mentioned above. Most of the flights are open to ISIC card holders under 30 (some have different age restrictions) together with their spouses and dependent children travelling on the same flight or to young persons with a valid EURO<26 or Go 25 card.

Specialist youth and student travel agencies are an excellent source of information for just about every kind of discount. Staff are often themselves seasoned travellers and can be a mine of information on budget travel in foreign countries. But check out the no-frills airlines and cheap flights websites as well to compare prices before making a final decision.

The leading youth and budget travel specialist in the UK is STA Travel which can organise flexible deals, domestic flights, overland transport, accommodation and tours. It publishes brochures-cum-magazines which survey travel options for students; pick up STA's *The Guide*. STA (STA Travel, 6 Wrights Lane, London W8 6TA; ☎0870 1600599; www.statravel.co.uk) is a major international travel agency with 450 branches worldwide including 65 in the UK. As well as worldwide airfares, they sell discounted rail and coach tickets, budget accommodation and insurance and many other packaged products.

In America, in addition to the major student travel agencies such as STA Travel mentioned above in the context of student cards, discount tickets are available online on a standby basis from agencies like Air-Tech (☎212-219-7000; e-mail fly@airtech.com; www.airtech.com), Air Treks (442 Post St, Suite 400, San Francisco, CA 94102; ☎1-800-350-0612; e-mail travel@airtreks-inc.com; www.airtreks.com) and Air-

Hitch (e-mail info@airhitch.org; www.airhitch.org). The cheapest fares from the US are available to people who are flexible about departure dates and destinations; the passenger chooses a block of possible dates (up to a five-day 'window') and preferred destinations. The company then tries to match these requirements with empty airline seats being released at knock-down prices. The website www.studentuniverse.com is also worth a look for cheap flights.

From the UK to Europe it is usually cheaper to fly on one of the no-frills ticketless airlines shuttling between Stansted, Luton and most of the UK's regional airports and many European destinations, than it is by rail or bus. The list below is only a selection. There are new companies and new destinations happening all the time so it pays to keep an eye on the press and use the internet. You can also check the websites that check for the cheapest fares such as http://cheapflights.com and Skyscanner. Note that quoted prices may not include taxes that can add up to £30 to the fare and that you usually have to book by deadlines to get the cheapest fares. These airlines do not take bookings via travel agents so it is necessary to contact them directly on the internet: they fly to and from various European cities:

○ *BMI Baby* – ☎0870 264 2229; www.bmibaby.com
○ *EasyJet* – ☎0871 500 100; www.easyjet.com.
○ *First Choice* – ☎0870 850 3999; www.firstchoiceairways.com
○ *GB Airways* – ☎0870 8509850; www.gbairways.com
○ *Ryanair* – ☎ 0871 246 0000; www.ryanair.com.
○ *Thomsonfly* – ☎ 0870 1900 737; www.thomsonfly.com.

Cheap youth rail travel is open to everyone under the age of 26. Inter-Rail is available on a zonal basis - from £145 for a 16-day 1 zone pass, to £259 for a month long all-zones pass covering all 30 countries on the network as well as entitling you to discounts on *Eurostar* and cross-Channel travel. Inter-Rail passes are available from youth travel agencies and from Rail Europe (178 Piccadilly, London W1J 9AL; ☎08705 848848; www.raileurope.co.uk). Inter-rail passes are also available for the over-26s, but the cost is higher e.g. £405 for a month for all zones.

Eurolines, the UK's largest scheduled coach operator to Europe and Ireland with over 500 destinations, offers a discount to passengers under 26. Return prices to Paris, Amsterdam, Brussels and Dublin start from £57. To book or plan a journey visit www. eurolines.co.uk or call 08705 143 219. It pays to compare prices between coach and rail because the differences are sometimes more than you would expect. Book 7 days before the date of travel to get the lowest possible coach fares.

One of the most interesting revolutions in independent and youth travel has been the explosion of backpackers' bus services which are hop-on hop-off coach services following prescribed routes. These can be found in New Zealand, Australia, USA, Canada, South Africa and Russia as well as on the European continent and in Britain and Ireland. For example Busabout covers 41 cities in 11 European countries. A four-week long coach pass on *Busabout Europe* (258 Vauxhall Bridge Road, London SW1V 1BS; ☎020-7950 1661; www.busabout.com) costs £359 for those under 26. Alternatively you can buy a Flexi-pass; for example 8 days of travel up to 31 October costs £259. In North America trips run by *Green Tortoise* (494 Broadway, San Francisco, California 94133; 800-867-8647; www. greentortoise.com) use vehicles converted to sleep about 35 people and make interesting tours, detours and stopovers around the Americas and Mexico.

# What to Pack

Even if you are travelling directly to your place of work, don't load yourself down with excess baggage. Most people who go abroad for a summer job want to do at least some independent travelling when their job ends and will find themselves seriously hampered if they are carrying around a 30-kilo rucksack. When you're buying a backpack/rucksack in a shop try to place a significant weight in it so you can feel how comfortable it might be to carry on your back, otherwise you'll be misled by lifting something usually filled with foam.

While aiming to travel as lightly as possible you should consider the advantage of taking certain extra pieces of equipment. For example a Swiss army knife (make sure it is not packed in your airline hand luggage) is often invaluable (if only for its corkscrew) and a comfortable pair of shoes is essential since most summer jobs will involve long hours on your feet whether in a hotel dining room or in a farmer's field. Ideally, talk to someone who has done the job before who might recommend an obscure piece of equipment you'd never think of, for example a pair of fingerless gloves for cold-weather fruit-picking or a bin-liner to put inside your rucksack to keep your stuff dry, a basic sewing kit for mending backpacks or clothes, a couple of metres of light strong cord to make a washing line etc.

You might allow yourself the odd lightweight luxury, such as an mp3 player, a short-wave radio or a digital camera. You can always post some belongings on ahead, with the employer's permission. Try to leave at home anything of either great monetary or sentimental value as their temporary absence is nothing compared to their permanent loss.

Good maps and guides are usually considered essential tools for a trip. If you are in London or Bristol, the famous map shop Stanfords (12-14 Long Acre, Covent Garden, WC2E 9LP ☎020-7836 1321; in Bristol at 29 Corn Street, Bristol BS1 1HT ☎0117-929-9966; Manchester at 39 Spring Gardens Manchester M2 2BG ☎0161-8310251) can supply most needs. Other specialist travel material shops include Daunt Books for Travellers (83 Marylebone High Street, W1M 4DE; ☎ 020-7224 2295). The Map Shop (15 High St, Upton-on-Severn, Worcestershire WR8 0HJ; ☎01684 593146/ themapshop@btinternet.com; www.themapshop.co.uk) does an extensive mail order business and will send you the relevant catalogue. Another specialist is Maps Worldwide, Datum House, Lancaster Road, Melksham, Wilts. SN12 6XJ (☎01225 707004; www.mapsworldwide.com).

There are dozens of travel specialists throughout North America, including the *Complete Traveller Antiquarian Bookstore* (199 Madison Ave, New York, NY 10016; ☎212-685-9007; fax 212-481-3253; www.ctrarebooks.com; info@ctrarebooks.com) which also issues a free mail-order catalogue and, in Canada, *Wanderlust* (e-mail info@wanderlust.com; www.wanderlust.com).

## Visas and Red Tape

Up-to-date visa information is available from national consulates in London/ Washington or on the internet. For example the visa agency *Thames Consular Services* in London (Thames Consular Services Ltd, Unit 4, The Courtyard, Swan Centre, Fishers Lane, London W4 1RX; ☎020-89952492; www.thamesconsular.com) allows you to search visa requirements and costs for individual countries and specialise in providing UK residents with visas for most countries.

As mentioned earlier, the free reciprocity of labour within the European Union means that its citizens have the right to work anywhere within the EU although this does not mean that red tape has been done away with for European nationals wanting to work in Europe. Until 2004 the standard situation amongst EU countries (plus Norway and Iceland which belonged to the European Economic Area or EEA) was that nationals of any EU state had the right to work without a work permit and to look for work in another member state for up to three months. This basic precept of the EU became complicated in 2004 with the introduction of a batch of new member countries, as not all the original members permitted nationals of new members to enter to work there immediately.

Where working is permitted, before the end of that three months period workers should apply to the police or the local authority for a residence permit, showing their passport and job contract.

Outside Europe, obtaining permission to work is next to impossible for short periods unless you are participating in an approved exchange programme where the red tape is taken care of by a sponsoring organisation. The same applies to non-European students looking for seasonal jobs in Europe. Established organisations with work abroad programmes are invaluable for shouldering the red tape problems and for providing a soft landing for first time travellers.

For example BUNAC (16 Bowling Green Lane, London EC1R 0QH; ☎020-7251-3472; www.bunac.org.uk) is a student club that helps students and other young people to work abroad while BUNAC USA (PO Box 430, Southbury, CT06488; www.bunac.org) assists a large number of Americans to work in Britain for up six months and in other countries around the world. BUNAC in the UK has a choice of programmes to the United States, Canada, Costa Rica, Australia, New Zealand, Peru, South Africa, Ghana and Cambodia, and in all cases assists participants to obtain the appropriate short-term working visas. In some programmes, participants have jobs arranged for them, for instance as counsellors or domestic staff at American children's summer camps; in others, it is up to individuals to find their own jobs once they arrive at their destination.

IST Plus, Ltd, in London oversees work abroad programmes for Britons in the USA, Canada, Australia, New Zealand, Thailand, Japan and China (Rosedale House, Rosedale Road, Surrey, Richmond, TW9 2SZ; ☎020-8939 9057; www.istplus.com) The CIEE in the US does likewise for American students who want to work in Ireland, France, Canada, Australia, New Zealand, Japan, Thailand or China: see their entry under the heading *Other Employment Abroad* in the *Worldwide* chapter.

Many other youth exchange organisations and commercial agencies offer packages which help students to arrange work or volunteer positions abroad. For example *Camp America* and *Camp Counselors USA* are major recruitment organisations which arrange for thousands of young people to work in the US mostly on summer camps (see chapter on the USA). Other agencies specialise in placing young people (both women and men) in families as au pairs, as voluntary English teachers or in a range of other capacities – see the entries for individual countries.

**The Schengen Visa.** This is a visa for entry and in no way supportive or indicative of individual states' work permit regulations. Some member states of the European Union, namely Austria, Belgium, Denmark, Finland, France, Germany, Greece, Iceland, Italy, Luxembourg, the Netherlands, Norway, Portugal, Spain and Sweden, are signatories of The Schengen Convention and issue a new type of uniform Visa, called the Schengen visa.

The Schengen Visa issued by an Embassy or Consulate of the above mentioned countries allows the holder to move freely in all these countries within the validity of the visa. To obtain this type of visa you will be required to hold a passport or travel document that is recognised by all of the Schengen member states and valid at least three months beyond the validity of the visa. If your passport or travel document is valid only for certain Schengen states then the validity of your visa will be restricted to those states.

If you intend to visit only one schengen country, you must apply for a visa at the Embassy or Consulate of that country. If you intend to visit several Schengen countries, you must apply for a visa at the Embassy or Consulate of the country in which your main destination is situated. If you intend to visit several schengen countries without having a main destination, you should apply for a visa at the Embassy or Consulate of the first country of entry.

A Schengen Visa is not the appropriate visa if you wish to remain in a Schengen member state for longer than 3 months or take up employment or establish a business or trade or profession. The list of countries whose citizens do not require a visa to enter any schengen member state for a period of up to 90 days is as follows:

All member countries of the European Union, Plus Andorra, Argentina, Australia, Bolivia, Brazil, Brunei, Bulgaria, Canada, Chile, Costa Rica, Croatia, Ecuador, El Salvador, Guatemala, Holy See, Honduras, Hong Kong (Special Passport), Israel, Japan, Macao (Special Passport), Malaysia, Mexico, Monaco, New Zealand, Nicaragua, Panama, Paraguay, Romania, San Marino, Singapore, South Korea, Switzerland, United States Of America, Uruguay, Venezuela. If you are a citizen of a country which has not been included in the above lists you will need a Schengen Visa.

# Accommodation

Employers who regularly employ foreign young people will either provide accommodation or help their staff to arrange lodgings locally. The majority of jobs listed in this book come with accommodation; usually shared with other workers. Always find out ahead of time what the deal is: how much do you lose from your wages to cover accommodation? What facilities (especially for self-catering) are provided? How close to your place of work is it? Will there be extra costs for food, utilities, etc.? Are staff allowed to move out if they find more congenial or cheaper accommodation?

Much of the accommodation provided by employers for staff is very basic indeed and you should be prepared for something rather more insalubrious than you are used to at home or at university. The only job which might provide more luxurious accommodation is as an au pair or any live-in job where you live in the employer's own house which may come with its own drawbacks.

If accommodation is not provided with the job, try to arrange something in advance, and certainly for the first couple of nights. If necessary make the journey to your destination several days early to fix up a suitable room. In cities, if the backpackers' hostels are full, try universities, which might rent out student accommodation that has been vacated for the summer or whose notice boards may include details of housing. In holiday resorts, accommodation may be at a premium and you will have to use your ingenuity to find something you can afford.

Annual membership of the *Youth Hostels Association* costs £15.95 a year if you're over 26, £9.95 if you're not; you can join at any YHA hostel or shop or at their HQ (Membership Department, YHA (England and Wales), Trevelyan House, Matlock, Derbyshire DE4 3YH; ☎ 0870 7708868; www.yha.org.uk). Seasonal demand abroad can be high, so it is always preferable to book in advance if you know your itinerary. You can pre-book beds over the internet on www.hihostels.org or through individual hostels and national offices listed in the *Hostelling International Guide*, which contains details of 4,000 hostels worldwide. The Guide can be ordered from the YHA website, or telephone the above number. The guide is priced £9.99 or £7.50 for members including postage).

Hostels of Europe and Hostels of America offer membership to a network of more than 500 Hostels on the best-travelled routes. Members get discounts of 5%-15% on accommodation, internet access, tours, etc. Information and on-line bookings can be made through www.hostels.net which is a searchable database of independent hostels in Europe, America and Down Under.

Hostels worldwide employ young people for a variety of jobs during the summer. In exchange for their labour, staff normally receive free board and lodging and some pocket money. The wardens or managers of individual hostels normally recruit their own staff.

# Money

The average budget of a travelling student varies hugely depending on where they are travelling. Obviously, India and Vietnam are going to be much cheaper than Switzerland or anywhere in Scandinavia. Whatever the size of your travelling fund, you should give some thought to how and in what form to carry your money. Travellers' cheques are much safer than cash, though they cost an extra 1% and banks able to cash them are not always near to hand. The most universally recognised brands are American Express, Thomas Cook and Visa. It is advisable also to keep a small amount of cash. The easiest way to look up the exchange rate of any world currency is to check on the internet (e.g. www.xe.com/ucc or www.oanda.com) or to look at the Monday edition of the *Financial Times*.

Euro notes and coins are the currency in Austria, Belgium, Finland, France, Germany, Greece, Ireland, Italy, Luxembourg, the Netherlands, Portugal and Spain. Please note that most wages etc in this book are quoted in English pounds sterling: exchange rates can fluctuate, so you are always advised to convert wages quoted at the current rate before accepting a job.

Ask your bank for a list of cash machines in the countries you intend to visit. Otherwise you can find these listed at www.mastercard.com.

Theft takes many forms, from the highly trained gangs of gypsy children who artfully pick pockets in European railway stations to more violent attacks in South African or South American cities. Risks can be reduced by carrying your wealth in several places including a comfortable money belt worn inside your clothing, steering clear of seedy or crowded areas, remaining particularly alert in railway stations and moderating your intake of alcohol. If you are robbed, you must obtain a police report (often for a fee) to stand any chance of recouping part of your loss from your insurer (assuming the loss of cash is covered in your policy) or from your travellers' cheque company. Always keep a separate record of the cheque numbers you are carrying, so you can instantly identify the serial numbers of the ones lost or stolen.

If you do end up in dire financial straits and do not have a credit card, you should contact someone at home who is in a position to send money. You may contact your bank back home and ask them to wire money to you, often through the Swift service. This can only be done through a bank in the town you're in – something you have to arrange with your own bank, so you know where to pick the money up. Sample charges might be £15-£20 through high street banks.

Western Union offers an international money transfer service whereby cash deposited at one branch can be withdrawn by you from any other branch or agency, which your benefactor need not specify. Western Union agents – there are 90,000 of them in nearly 200 countries – come in all shapes and sizes (e.g. travel agencies, stationers, chemists). The person sending money to you simply turns up at a Western Union counter, hands over the desired sum plus the fee, which is £8 for up to £25 transferred, £21 for £100-£200, £37 for £500 and so on. For an extra £7 your benefactor can do this over the phone with a credit card. In the UK, ring 0800 833833 for further details, a list of outlets and a complete rate schedule.

Thomas Cook, American Express and the Post Office offer a similar service called Moneygram. Cash deposited at one of their foreign exchange counters is available within ten minutes at the named destination or can be collected up to 45 days later. The standard fee for sending £500 (for example) is £36. Ring 0800 897198 for details.

# Insurance and Health

The National Health Service ceases to cover British nationals once they leave the United Kingdom. If you are a national of the European Economic Area (the EU plus Liechtenstein, Norway and Iceland) and will be working in another EEA country, you will be covered by the European Community Social Security Regulations. Advice and the leaflet SA29 *Your Social Security Insurance, Benefits and Health Care Rights in the European Community* may be obtained free of charge from the Inland Revenue, National Insurance Contributions Office, International Services, Room TC114, Benton Park View, Longbenton, Newcastle-upon-Tyne NE98 1ZZ (☎ 0845-9154811). Those intending to work abroad can obtain further details from the leaflet SA29 or by contacting International Services (on the details shown above) with details of their intended employment abroad.

Leaflet T6 (Health Advice for Travellers) available from post offices contains an application form to obtain an EHIC (European Health Insurance Cardwhich entitles you to free emergency medical treatment while you are travelling in the EEA and with certain restrictions also in Switzerland. You can also apply for an EHIC over the phone (0845 6062030) or online (www.dh.gov.uk/travellers. An EHIC is not valid once you have a job abroad and is only for travellers who make their national insurance contributions to the UK. Form E128 is issued which gives entitlement to a full range of health care for those working in any EEA country. This form also applies to students staying temporarily in another EEA country as part of their studies. For information on your entitlement to a certificate E128, please contact International Services on the details above.

The EHIC will also gradually replace the E128 (see paragraph above) and will initially be valid for two years and is renewable on the proviso that the applicant still makes their national insurance contributions in the UK.

When British nationals begin work abroad they may be required to pay foreign social security contributions in order to be eligible for health cover. Leaflet T6 gives details of the special health agreements that the United Kingdom has with non-EU countries including Australia, the Channel Islands, New Zealand and several Eastern European countries which enable visitors to use their health services. In countries outside the EEA and not listed in leaflet T6, British citizens can use the public health service only if they are contributing to its Social Security scheme: for example, in Switzerland they must be paid-up members of a Swiss sickness insurance fund.

Foreign health services rarely offer as comprehensive a free service for emergency treatment as the NHS does; while some offer free treatment, others will only subsidise the cost and any part of the treatment not covered by the free health service is met by private health insurance top up schemes. In some countries the ambulance ride has to be paid for, but not the treatment. The cost of bringing a person back to the UK in the case of illness or death is never covered under the reciprocal arrangements so it is considered essential to purchase private insurance in addition to carrying an EHIC. Ordinary travel insurance policies cover only those risks that a holidaymaker can expect to face and will not cover work-related injuries such as treating backs damaged while grape-picking, or burns caused by an overboiling goulash in a restaurant kitchen.

The following companies should be able to arrange insurance cover for most people going to work abroad, as long as they are advised of the exact nature of the physical/manual job to be undertaken:

*Club Direct,* Dominican House, St. John's Street, Chichester, West Sussex EC2M 4SQ (☎0800 083 2455; www Club Direct.com). Work abroad is covered as long as it does not involve heavy machinery.
*Columbus Direct,* 17 Devonshire Square, London EC2M 4SQ (☎020-7375 0011;

fax 0845-761030; www.columbusdirect.com). Provides a Globetrotter policy for those working abroad for short or long periods (up to 12 months).

*The Travel Insurance Agency,* Suite 2, Percy Mews, 775B High Road, North Finchley, London N12 8JY (☎ 020-8446 5414; fax 020-8446 5417; www.travelinsurers. com). Policies only for travellers, including those working abroad.

*Worldwide Travel Insurance Services Ltd,* The Business Centre, 1-7 Commercial Road, Paddock Wood, Tonbridge, Kent TN12 6YT (☎01892-833338; fax 01892-837744; e-mail sales@worldwideinsure.com; www.worldwideinsure.com). Comprehensive policies for most work abroad from 5 days to 24 months. Manual labour cover can be purchased from overseas for an additional premium.

*Endsleigh Insurance,* Endsleigh Insurance Services Ltd, Endsleigh House, Cheltenham Glos GL50 3NR; www.endsleigh.co.uk). Offices in most university towns. Twelve months of cover from £202. Age limit 35.

If you are planning to include developing countries on your itinerary, you will want to take the necessary health precautions, though this won't be cheap unless you are able to have your injections at your local NHS surgery where most injections are free or given for a minimal charge. Malaria poses an increasing danger and expert advice should be sought about which medications to take for the specific parts of the world you intend to visit.

Tap water is unsafe to drink in the more remote parts of the world so it will be necessary to give some thought as to the method of water purification you will use (filtering, boiling or chemical additives). Remember that water used to wash vegetables, brush teeth or make ice cubes is also potentially risky. Tap water throughout Western Europe is safe to drink.

MASTA (Medical Advisory Service for Travellers Abroad) runs Travel Health Centres in London at Margaret Street; Canary Wharf; Wimpole Street; Basuto Road, Fulham and nationwide (for further information on this and other MASTA clubs nation-wide visit www.masta.org) and also maintains an up-to-date database on travellers' diseases and their prevention. You can ring their interactive Travellers' Health Line on 0906-5501402 with your destinations (up to six countries) and they will send you a basic health brief by return, for the price of the telephone call (£1 per minute).

Increasingly, people are seeking advice via the internet; check for example www. fitfortravel.scot.nhs.uk; www.tmb.ie and www.travelhealth.co.uk. The BBC's Health Travel Site www.bbc.co.uk/health/travel is a solid source of information about travel health ranging from tummy trouble to water quality and snake bites.

Many women are reluctant to travel alone yet thousands do so with great pleasure. Sensible precautions include behaving with decorum and making sure your dress sense does not clash with local sensibilities and most crucially, trusting your instincts about potentially suspect characters and situations. General advice on minimising the risks of independent travel is contained in the book *World Wise – Your Passport to Safer Travel* published by Thomas Cook in association with the Suzy Lamplugh Trust and the Foreign Office (www.suzylamplugh.org/worldwise; £7.99 plus postage). Arguably its advice is over-cautious, advising travellers never to hitch-hike, ride a motorbike or accept an invitation to a private house. Travellers will have to decide for themselves when to follow this advice and when to ignore it.

### The Euro
At the time of going to press the following rates applied:

£1 = €1.48      €1 = 67p      $1 = € 0.52      €1 = $1.27

Where wages have been quoted in euros by an employer we have put the sterling value in brackets afterwards converted at the above rates

# Organisations with Vacancies Worldwide

# Agricultural Work

**GLOBAL CHOICES:** Barkat House, 116-118 Finchley Road, London NW3 5HT (☎020-7433 2501; fax 0870 330 5955; e-mail info@globalchoices.co.uk; www.globalchoices.co.uk.
Global Choices offers **Voluntary Work Internships, Practical Training** and **Work Experience** Worldwide from 2 weeks to 18 months. Destinations include Argentina, Austria, Brazil, Chile, Costa Rica, Ecuador, France, Nepal, New Zealand, Portugal, Peru, Spain, Tanzania and Ukraine. Placements are offered in many fields, industrial, business, science, conservation, agriculture, travel and tourism, volunteering, teaching and more. Cost depends on programme.

**IAEA/AgriVenture:** Speedwell Farm Bungalow, Nettle Bank, Wisbech, Cambridgeshire, PE14 OSA (tel/fax 01945 450999; e-mail uk@agriventure.com; www. agriventure.com).
**Farming or Horticultural Working Programmes** to Australia, New Zealand, Canada, USA and Japan are arranged by AgriVenture. Applicants must be aged 18-30, have no dependants, be British citizens, have a full driving licence and have experience or an interest in agriculture or horticulture. Programmes depart all year round (applications required usually2 months minimum before departure).
Programme costs start at around £2100 and include: return flights (and transfer to host family), full travel and work insurance, work permits, job placement, departure information meeting, seminar in host country and full emergency back-up through offices in hosting country.
For a free brochure or more information *telephone* freephone 0800 783 2186 or e-mail with your name, address and postcode.
Some European citizens can participate in the following countries' programmes. *Further information* from the European AgriVenture Office (in Denmark) on +45 59 51 15 25 or e-mail europe@agriventure.com
Canadian and USA citizens can *call* AgriVenture in Calgary on + 1 403 255 7799 or e-mail canada@agriventure.com and can visit Japan, Australia, New Zealand, UK and various other European destinations.
New Zealand citizens can *call* AgriVenture in Cambridge, New Zealand on + 64 7 823 5700 or e-mail nz@agriventure.com and can visit Japan, USA, Canada, UK and various European destinations.
Australian citizens can *call* AgriVenture in Sydney on + 61 2 91 81 3122 or e-mail australia@agriventure.com and can visit Japan, USA, Canada, UK and various European destinations.

**WWOOF (World Wide Opportunities on Organic Farms)**
WWOOF exists to give people the opportunity of gaining first hand experience of organic farming and gardening in return for spending a weekend or longer helping on a farm. Since WWOOF began in England in 1971, similar schemes have developed in other

countries around the world. Each national group has its own aims, system, fees and rules, e.g. WWOOF Australia, WWOOF Italy. They are all similar in that they offer volunteers the chance to learn in a practical way the growing methods of their host. Each group will supply a booklet listing WWOOF hosts to members from which volunteers can choose a farm. Most national organisations expect applicants to have gained experience on an organic farm in their own country. Where countries do not have a national WWOOF organisation, individual hosts are listed with WWOOF Independents.

For further information applicants should *contact* WWOOF (UK) (PO Box 2675, Lewes, Sussex BN7 1RB; e-mail hello@wwoof.org.uk; www.wwoof.org.uk), or WWOOF Independents in countries currently including France, Spain, Portugal, Ireland, South America, South Africa and India (addresses from www.wwoof.org), for information and application forms.

# Hotel Work and Catering

**CRYSTAL**: 12-42 Wood Street, Kingston-Upon-Thames, Surrey, KT11SG (☎0845-0550258; e-mail crystal@responsibility.com; www.workinwinter.com)
Crystal holidays has a number of different programmes which incorporate Crystal the Lakes, Crystal the Active, Crystal International Academy, Crystal the Sports, Crystal the Schools and Crystal the Finest.

Crystal recruits for both winter and summer positions throughout the year in many exciting European and worldwide destinations. Positions include: **Resort Reps, Qualified Nannies** and **children's Reps, Chalet Hosts, Chefs, Hotel Staff, Maintenance Staff,** Qualified **Sailing** and **Windsurfing Instructors** and various other qualified **sports instructors**. Work available in a variety of destinations throughout the year. Positions are available for qualified and unqualified staff with a flexible and friendly attitude. Must have a good understanding of customer requirements and the ability to work within a busy team.

Please *apply* on-line at www.workinwinter.com .

# Industrial and Office Work

**GLOBAL CHOICES:** Barkat House, 116-118 Finchley Road, London NW3 5HT (☎020-7433 2501; fax 0870 330 5955; e-mail info@globalchoices.co.uk; www. globalchoices.co.uk.
Global Choices offers Voluntary Work **Internships, Practical Training and Work Experience Worldwide** from 2 weeks to 18 months. Destinations include Argentina, Austria, Brazil, Chile, Costa Rica, Ecuador, France, Nepal, New Zealand, Portugal, Peru, Spain, Tanzania and Ukraine. Placements are offered in many fields, industrial, business, science, conservation, agriculture, travel and tourism, volunteering, teaching and more. Cost depends on programme.

**INTERNATIONAL CO-OPERATIVE EDUCATION:** 15 Spiros Way, Menlo Park, California 94025 (☎650 323 4944; fax 650 323 1104; icemenlo@aol.com; www. icemenlo.com).
ICE arranges paid summer work for 2-3 months in Australia, Belgium, China, England, Germany, Japan, Singapore, South America, Switzerland. Jobs include **retail sales,**

**banking, computer technology, hotels and restaurants, offices** etc.; most require knowledge of the relevant language. Placement fee is $700 plus an application fee of $250.

*Applications* to the above address.

**INTERNATIONAL ASSOCIATION FOR THE EXCHANGE OF STUDENTS FOR TECHNICAL EXPERIENCE (IAESTE):** IAESTE UK, 10 Spring Gardens, London SW1A 2BN (☎020-7389 4114; www.iaeste.org.uk).
IAESTE operate an exchange scheme whereby students in undergraduate degree level scientific and technical studies are offered **course-related traineeships** in industrial, business, governmental and research organisations in over 80 countries. IAESTE selected trainees are employed on short term contracts, usually for up to 3 months, undertaking specific scientific, or professional tasks. Students are responsible for their own travel and insurance costs, but are paid a salary by the host employer to cover their cost of living.
More information and *applications* available from the above address.

# Sports, Couriers and Camping

**AIRTOURS, ASPRO, DIRECT HOLIDAYS, PANORAMA & MANOS HOLIDAYS:** Head Office: Airtours Holidays, Wavell House, Holcombe Road, Helmshore, Rossendale, Lancs. BB4 4PA (☎0870-241 2642; overseasjobs@mytravel. co.uk; www.mytravelcareers.co.uk). All companies are UK tour operators and part of the My Travel group.
**Customer Services Representatives** based overseas, to look after one or more properties, visit customers on a daily basis to ensure they have the best holiday ever. Also responsible for airport transfers, welcome events, maximising the sale of excursions and additional services offered in resort and handling any problems that may arise. Aged 20+. Must have minimum 12 months' experience working in a customer service or sales environment and be reliable, resilient, efficient and hard working.
**Customer Service Assistants** welcome customers at the companies' more popular resorts, care for them during the transfers and ensure that their holiday begins without a hitch. Also help to guide customers on excursions and assist the Customer Service Representatives with welcome events. Age 19+. Should have at least 6 months experience of working a customer service environment and be reliable, efficient, flexible and hard working. In addition needs bags of enthusiasm and stamina.
**Escapades Reps** are responsible for ensuring that 18-30 customers have the holiday of a lifetime. To organise and guide day and evening events such as beach parties, bar crawls and clubbing nights out and become the customers' best friend, inspiring them to live the Escapades holiday experience. Obligatory to work harder than you've ever worked before and provide a great service in a very highly pressured sales environment. Age 19+ with an affinity to the youth market, limitless energy, initiative and enthusiasm and bags of stamina.
**Children's Representative** responsible for the set up and day-to-day running of overseas children's clubs and the safety, welfare and enjoyment of younger customers, ensuring that the children you look after have a brilliant holiday. Age 18+ must possess experience of working with groups of children aged 3-10 along with at least three months' experience in a customer service environment.

**Nursery Nurse** to be responsible for the organisation and day-to-day running of nursery facilities, ensuring that the children are well-cared for so their parents can enjoy a well-earned break. Age 18+, must have experience of working with children aged 0-3 along with a CACHE/NNEB or equivalent qualification. In addition should have at least 3 months' experience of working in a customer service environment.

**Entertainers** to be responsible for providing a comprehensive day and evening entertainment programme in larger company hotels. Age 18+. Need not be professional entertainers but talent would be a distinct advantage. Should have at least 6 months experience in a customer service environment.

All the above posts can be *applied for on-line* at www.mytravel.careers.co.uk or call the recruitment line 0870 241642.

**CONTIKI HOLIDAYS:** Wells House, 15 Elmfield Road, Bromley BR1 1LS; ☎020-8290 6777; fax 020-8225 4246; e-mail travel@contiki.co.uk; www.contiki.com. A company that specialises in coach tours holidays for 18 to 35 year olds throughout. Europe, Australia, the USA, New Zealand, and the UK.

**Tour Managers and Drivers** are employed on a seasonal basis from March to October. All successful trainees receive thorough training in the form of a seven-week road trip in Europe. Recruitment starts in September for the following year's season. Applicants must hold an EU passport or be able to obtain a valid visa which gives them the legal right to work in the UK.

*Applications* to gary.willment@contiki.com or the above address.

**COSMOS:** Wren Court, 17 London Road, Bromley, Kent, BR1 1DE (☎0208-6954724; fax 020-8466 0699; e-mail overseasdept@cosmos.co.uk; www.cosmos. co.uk; www.somewhere2stay.com). Cosmos is an independent tour operator, providing holidays in the Mediterranean and further afield.

**Holiday Consultants** Customer service, sales, guiding excursions, airport duties. Starting salary £400.

**Children's/Crèche Representatives** to organise activities and provide activities for children aged 3-11. Starting salary £460.

**Operations Assistants** To provide administrative support to a busy resort and management team. Starting salary £650.

Summer season runs from March through to October. Flights and accommodation are provided.

*Applications* to the above address from September 2006 for summer 2007, or call 0208-6954724 for an application pack.

**DRAGOMAN OVERLAND:** Camp Green, Kenton Road, Debenham, Suffolk IP14 6LA (☎0870 499 4475; fax 01728 861127; e-mail info@dragoman.com; www. dragoman.co.uk). Overland adventure tours worldwide. Dragoman Overland employ overland crew to drive their expedition vehicles through developing countries, showing travellers the wonders of the world.

**Leaders** for trips to Africa, Asia and the Americas. Aged 25 or over. Good spoken English required.

*Applications* and requests for further information should be made to the above address or e-mail.

**EXODUS:** Grange Mills, Weir Rd, London SW12 0NE (☎ 0870 240 5550; fax 0208 675 5276; e-mail nnikolsky@exodus.co.uk; www.exodus.co.uk). Exodus is an adventure company that specialises in walking and trekking, discovery, overland, snow sports, biking and multi-activity holidays. Applicants will be working in Europe,

Africa, Asia, Central America and Cuba.

**Walking & Trekking Leaders** with high altitude walking experience and mountain qualifications such as SML and WML. Aged 25 and over. Must have a second language, interest in the outdoors, experience of independent travel and hill walking/ group leading. Work is available throughout the year.

**Leaders for Destinations Programme** to lead trips of one or two weeks' duration. Trips are based in Europe and are either sightseeing, gentle walking or a mixture of both. The ideal candidate should be flexible and available to work between May and November at short notice. A second language is also desirable. Suitable for older applicants.

**Tour Leaders** required to lead trips overseas. Must be 25+. Snow and mountaineering skills desirable. Must also bring an aspect of cultural knowledge. Wages from £22.50 to £42.50 per day. Whilst away tour leaders will be working 24/7, 7 days a week. Dates of work are from May to October plus Christmas and Easter. Minimum period of work is 6 to 7 months a year. Board and accommodation are provided. Knowledge of French, Spanish or Italian is required.

*Applications* invited throughout the year. Please download an application form from the website link: www.exodus.co.uk/vacancies.html.

**EXPLORE!:** 1 Frederick Street, Aldershot, Hants., GU11 1LQ (☎01252-760200; fax 01252-760207; e-mail ops@explore.co.uk; www.explore.co.uk). Explore! is Europe's largest adventure travel tour operator.

**Tour Leaders** to work 7 days per week for 3-6 months leading tour groups of 16-24 clients per group, to 100+ countries around the world. Applicants with language skills and previous travel experience essential. Fees start at £25 a day. Full training given.

Tour leaders are on duty 24/7 but the work is satisfying. You must be available to leave the UK for certain set periods of time. Work is available throughout the year, with the minimum period of work being 3 weeks, although the peak periods of Christmas, Summer holidays and Easter are the most popular times.

*Applications* to the above address are accepted all year round and must be on an application form, which can be downloaded from the website.

**FIRST CHOICE SUMMER SUN:** Jetset House, Church Road, Lowfield Heath, Crawley, West Sussex, RH11 OPQ (☎0870-750 1204; fax 01293-816-541 ; overseas. recruitment@firstchoice.co.uk; www.firstchoice4jobs.co.uk). First Choice Holidays are a large, award-winning tour operator with worldwide destinations.

First Choice embraces a number of brand name holidays including JWT, Falcon and Sunsail. They need the following staff to work abroad across these companies: **Resort Representative, Children's Representative, Transfer Representative, Finance and Administration Staff** are just a few of the positions available on the summer sun programme.

Applicants should have excellent customer service skills, be attentive to detail in order to provide a high level of service to customers, and for most of the positions a flair for sales is also required; previous experience beneficial. All applicants should be at least 18 years old and must be confident, able to speak publicly to groups of varying sizes, sociable, committed and self-motivated. A job with First Choice provides an opportunity to travel, meet and make new friends, improve language skills and gain experience. All of First Choice's overseas positions are 100% hard work but you'll have fun too! Applicants must have a National Insurance Number and either an EU/EEA passport or relevant EU/EEA work permit/visa. For all positions, the period of work is flexible between March and October. Accommodation is provided free of charge.

*Recruitment* takes place all year round: *EU/EEA applicants only.* Full details of all the above positions and how to apply can be found on the website www.firstchoice4jobs. co.uk.

**THE IMAGINATIVE TRAVELLER:** TL Jobs, The Imaginative Traveller, 1 Betts Avenue, Martlesham Heath, Nr Ipswich, Suffolk IP5 3RH, UK (www.imaginative-traveller.com). A leading adventure tour operator that employs 80-100 tour leaders to work in adventurous locations around the world. Operates small group, active journeys worldwide.

**Tour leaders.** Comprehensive training is provided for those willing to work at least 13 months overseas. Need to be responsible, self-reliant traveller with great people skills and a positive attitude. Good spoken English is required.

An *application form* and information pack is available from the above address: applicants should include a letter explaining why they would be suitable for the role.

**JOB-EXPRESS:** Postbus 1459, NL-1300 BL Almere-Holland, The Netherlands (☎+31-36 530 2000; fax +31-36 530 0300; www.expatcompany.nl). Dutch recruitment and international employment agency specialising in international positions in the Netherlands. This agency seeks staff for a number of temporary and permanent jobs around the Netherlands.

Jobs for Higher-Educated Professionals are frequently available for Dutch speakers as well as English speakers with knowledge of one other EU language: permanent positions available for English speakers with fluency in French, German, Italian or Spanish.

*Applications* are invited all year round for these positions; contact Job-Express at the above address for more details.

**KUMUKA WORLDWIDE:** 40 Earls Court Road, London W8 6EJ (☎020-7937 8855/0800 389 2328; e-mail humanresources@kumuka.com; www.kumuka.co.uk.). Leading specialists in worldwide Adventure Travel, Kumuka have been successfully operating exciting tours for the intrepid traveller for more than 23 years. Covering Africa, Latin America, Asia, Europe, the Middle East and Antarctica, Kumuka recruits outgoing people with a strong interest in travel.
**Tour Leaders** (age 23+) are chosen according to experience and personality.
**Drivers** ( must hold PCV or HGV licence or be willing to obtain one. Applicants must have sound mechanical knowledge and travel experience in Africa, the Middle East or South America. Training provided.
*Applications* via the above e-mail address.

**MARK WARNER:** 20 Kensington Church Street, London, W8 4EP (☎08700 330750 or 08700 330760 for children's places); e-mail recruitment@markwarner. co.uk; www.markwarner.co.uk/recruitment.
**Accountants, Receptionists, Watersports Instructors, Tennis and Aerobics Instructors, Chefs, Kitchen Porters, First Aid, Nannies, Handymen, Nightwatchmen** and more are required to work in hotels in Corsica, Sardinia, Greece and Turkey during the summer from April to October and Egypt, and Sri Lanka and Mauritius year round. Wages from £50 per week plus full board, medical insurance, travel expenses and free use of watersport and activity facilities. Some reserve staff also needed throughout the season. Requirements for languages, experience, qualifications etc. vary according to the job applied for.
For further details, please *contact* the Resorts Recruitment Department on the above number.

**POWDER BYRNE:** 250 Upper Richmond Road, London SW15 6TG (☎020-8246 5342; fax 020-246 5321; www.powderbyrne.com). Powder Byrne is an exclusive tour operator offering tailor-made holidays, working alongside 4 and 5 star luxury hotels, to provide a top of the range holiday package. They are looking for highly motivated customer-focused team players to work in their summer resorts programme in exotic holiday destinations, such as France, Cyprus, Italy, Portugal, Tunisia, Mauritius, Dubai and Mallorca.
**Resort Managers** required for managing a team of staff in resort, to provide a high calibre of services to Powder Byrne clients and to liaise with head office. Applicants should be 24+, have previous management experience, a clean driving licence, a professional approach and have the ability to think on their feet. Wages £440+ per month plus package.
**Resort Drivers** required for transporting guests in exclusive company minibuses and assist the Resort Manager in providing a high level of customer service to Powder Byrne clients. Applicants should be 21+, good time-keepers, reliable and have customer service experience. Full, clean driving licence essential. Wages £220+ per month plus package.
**Crèche Managers** required for managing resort crèches for children aged six months to three years. Applicants should have relevant experience and be NNEB qualified or equivalent. (Non-qualified assistants are also required). Wages £400+ per month plus package.
**Children's Club Coordinators** to organise and run the kids' clubs for nine to fourteen year olds. Applicants must have child care experience and lots of energy (would suit teachers during the school holidays). Sports orientated candidates preferred. Wages £320+ per month plus package.
Accommodation, food, transport, resort insurance and uniform provided. Duration

of contracts vary from six months to two weeks between April and October. Knowledge of French, Italian and Spanish are desirable but not essential.
*Applications* are taken on-line at www.powderbyrne.co.uk.

**PURE VACATIONS LTD**: (☎01227-264264; fax: 01227-281700; e-mail info@ purevacations.com; www.purevacations.com). Pure Vacations Ltd is a world leading specialist tour operator. Programmes include snowboarding, surfing, golfing, rafting, ranching and more.
**Surf Guide/Instructor** (10) Surf tuition and surf guiding plus representative duties. Must have lifesaving qualification and surf training qualification from a recognised body such a BSA or ESF. Must have good organisational skills.
**Resort Manager** (4) Surf tuition and surf guiding plus representative duties. Must have lifesaving qualification and surf training qualification from a recognised body such a BSA or ESF. Must have good organisational skills.
**Tour guide** to run guided tours to historical sites and activities such as rafting. Must have qualification relevant to field.
Positions are available worldwide throughout the year. Hours of work are variable, no wages are paid but accommodation is provided. Minimum period of work 12 weeks. Knowledge of languages is preferred, particularly Spanish, French or Portuguese.
For more information *contact* the above e-mail address. *Applications* invited from Sept 2006 onwards.

**SUNSAIL LTD:** The Port House, Port Solent, Portsmouth, Hampshire PO6 4TH (☎ 02392-334-600; www.sunsail.co.uk; e-mail recruitment@sunsail.com). Sunsail are the leaders in worldwide sailing holidays with 29 bases worldwide employing around 1000 staff. Most positions are seasonal, but as Sunsail is part of the First Choice Group there are opportunities for year round employment.
**Flotilla Skipper** Must be RYA Yachtmaster Commercially endorsed professional sailor with unlimited patience and a friendly personality. To be responsible for the organisation/safety of guests aboard up to 13 cruising yachts. Duties include navigational briefings/assistance in all sailing matters and excellent organisational skills. Considerable yacht skippering experience and people skills essential.
**Flotilla/Base Engineers** Experience maintaining diesel and petrol engines essential. Plumbing, electrical and fibreglassing skills are valuable. Previous knowledge of marine systems and sailing an advantage.
**Flotilla Hostess** to work as part of a team of three staff to look after flotilla guests. Duties include dealing with local suppliers, organising BBQs/events and customer care of up to 70 guests. Knowledge of German/French particularly useful.
**Customer Service Liaison** Responsible for briefings of Sunsail's French and German clients. Fluent English, French and German essential and knowledge of boat systems an advantage.
All the above positions require staff who are flexible and used to dealing with guests.
**Hotel Managers, Front of House/Food and Beverage Managers, Chefs, Barpersons, Receptionists, Waiting Staff, Childcare Assistants (NNEB/ BTECH, RGN), Activities Assistants also needed to work in Sunsail Beach Clubs.** All positions are in Greece and Turkey. In addition to the specific responsibilities of the role, staff also commit a great deal of time to socialising with and looking after guests.
**Watersports Managers, RYA Windsurf/Dinghy Instructors and BWSF Water-Ski Instructors** are required to instruct RYA courses and provide rigging assistance and rescue cover for beach operations.

All positions to work 6-day week. Benefits include shared accommodation, all meals in the club, paid holiday, return flights on successful completion of the contracted period, full uniform, discounted holidays, bar discount in the club and free use of all the equipment. To work from April-November, certain vacancies also available for summer holiday periods. Minimum age 18. Relevant qualifications essential.

To *apply* visit the website www.sunsail.co.uk/hr and fill in an online application form.

**THOMAS COOK TOUR OPERATIONS:** Thomas Cook Business Park, Units 13-14 Coningsby Road, Peterborough PE3 8SB; www.thomascookjobs.com. Thomas Cook Tour Operations is the country's oldest name in the travel business, and part of the worldwide Thomas Cook AG Group. The company is looking for enthusiastic, responsible people to work overseas and help provide exceptional holidays to all customers within their brands, Thomas Cook, JMC, Sunset. As the face of Thomas Cook Tour Operations in resort, you must be hard working and have a real passion for delivering excellent customer service.

**Overseas Representatives** to be responsible for ensuring that customer holiday expectations are exceeded. Customer facing experience, a genuine desire to help and stamina to work long hours are all essential. Minimum age 20 years old.

**KidsWORLD Representatives** to supervise and entertain groups of children aged 3-12 years. Experience of working with large groups of children is essential. Minimum age 18 years. Successful applicants have to undergo a police check.

**KidsWORLD Qualified Representatives** to look after and care for younger children aged between 6 months and 2 years, a qualification in childcare is essential. Minimum age 18 years. Successful applicants have to undergo a police check.

**Overseas Administrators** the overseas offices are the nerve centre of Thomas Cook Tour Operations overseas operation. Office experience and people used to working under pressure are required. A sound knowledge of MS word, Excel and Outlook is essential. Minimum age 19 years.

Contracts run from March to October with a possibility to continue throughout the winter. All applicants must have a valid EU or British passport and be a British resident.

*Apply* via the website www.thomascookjobs.com.

**TUCAN:** 316 Uxbridge Road, Acton, London W3 9QP, UK (☎0208-896 1600; sue@ tucantravel.com).
Tucan Travel is the world's leading adventure travel specialist for Latin America, operating tours throughout South and Central America, including Cuba, all year round.

**Tour Leaders** are always required to guide international groups on set itineraries within Latin America. Applicants should be age 24-45 and speak excellent English, and preferably intermediate Spanish as well. The standard period of commitment is one year and full training is provided in Latin America.

*Applications* should be made by e-mail with a completed application form found at www.tucantravel.com in the 'employment' section.

**TUI-UK Ltd:** Wigmore House, Wigmore Place, Wigmore Lane, Luton, LU2 9TN (☎0845-0550255; e-mail overseasrecruitment@s-h-g.co.uk; www.thomson.co.uk).
Thomson is part of The World of TUI, and incorporates Thomson, Summer Sun, Thomson Lakes and Mountains, Thomson Ski and Snowboarding and Thomson Faraway Shores. They recruit staff for both summer and winter throughout the year in many exciting European and worldwide destinations. **Holiday Reps, Qualified**

**Nannies and Children's Representatives** and **Entertainers** to work in a variety of destinations throughout the year are always required. Positions are available for qualified and unqualified staff with a flexible and friendly attitude. Must have a good understanding of customer requirements and the ability to work within a busy team. Please *apply* online at www.thomson.co.uk

**VENTURE CO:** The Ironyard, 64-66 The Market Place, Warwick (☎01926-411122; fax 01926-411133; mail@ventureco-worldwide.com; www.ventureco-worldwide.com).
VentureCo is a Gap Year and Career Gap provider operating in South America and the Galapagos, Central America, East Africa and Indochina.
**Expedition Leaders (8)** to lead groups for 4 months. £600 to £1,050 monthly, plus expenses, which includes all board and accommodation. Some overseas travel/work experience and be minimum age 25 and be prepared to work 24/24 7. Period of work is from January to May. Must be group-oriented and enjoy working with 18-25 year olds.
*Apply* immediately to the above address or e-mail.

**WORLD CHALLENGE EXPEDITIONS:** Black Arrow House, 2 Chandos Road, London NW10 6NF (☎08704 873173; e-mail leaderinfo@world-challenge.co.uk; www.world-challenge.co.uk). World Challenge run expeditions and adventure activities in the UK and overseas. All expeditions and activities are designed to enable education through exploration and to raise motivation in young people through developing skills in leadership, team building, decision-making and problem solving.
**Expedition Leaders (400)** World Challenge Expeditions requires male and female leaders for expeditions to Central and South America, Africa and Asia.
Fee negotiable and all expenses paid. Periods of work are four weeks between late June and late August.
*Apply* to Leader Recruitment Team on the above details.

# Voluntary Work

## Children

**MONDO CHALLENGE:** Malsor House, Gayton Road, Milton Malsor, Northampton NN7 3AB (☎01604-858225; fax 01604-859323; e-mail info@mondochallenge.org; www.mondochallenge.org.)
Mondo Challenge is a non-profit organisation which sends volunteers (post university, career break, early retired, etc) to help with teaching and business development programmes in Africa, Asia and South America. Programmes are community-based, providing volunteers with an insight into local cultures and a chance to experience a different way of life. Destinations include: Nepal, Sri Lanka, Tanzania, Kenya, The Gambia, Senegal, Chile and Ecuador.
    All Nationalities and ages accepted (average age 27). About half of all volunteers are non-UK based with a large number of volunteers from North America, Europe and Australia. For teaching projects, the minimum qualification is A level or equivalent in the subject to be taught. For business development, a minimum of 3 years' business experience is required. Must be able to cope with remote posting and to relate to people of other cultures. Enthusiasm, flexibility and good communication skills are

essential.

A normal stay lasts 2-4 months and start dates are flexible. The cost for 3 months is £1100. Board and lodging with a local family costs an extra £15 (approx) per week. *Further information* from the above address.

**SCRIPTURE UNION:** 207-209 Queensway, Bletchley, Milton Keynes, Bucks MK2 2EB (☎01908-856177; fax 01908-856012; e-mail holidays@scriptureunion.org.uk; www.scriptureunion.org.uk). Scripture Union activities include programmes for Bible reading, missions and **residential holidays for children and young people, work in schools, youth work and the publishing of Christian resources.**
**Activity Team (2,000):** to work about one week throughout the summer. Volunteers are expected to **help organise Christian activity holidays for young people.** Volunteers work on sites in Britain and overseas. Applicants must be in sympathy with the aims of Scripture Union, committed Christians and over 18 years old. There is always a need for those who have qualifications or interests in outdoor activities, sports, working with the disabled, first aid or life saving.

*Applications* from December onwards to the Holidays Administrator, at the above address.

# Conservation & Environment

**AFRICAN CONSERVATION EXPERIENCE:** PO Box 206, Faversham, Kent ME13 8RE (☎0870-241 5816; e-mail info@ConservationAfrica.net; www. conservationafrica.com).
ACE is a relatively small organisation that takes interest in each volunteer as an individual. It is the most experienced organisation for conservation projects in Southern Africa and has been arranging projects for over 5 years.

Voluntary Conservation Work Placements: lasting 4-12 weeks around the year for people on game reserves in Southern Africa, including South Africa, Botswana and Zimbabwe. Tasks may include darting rhino for relocation or elephants for fitting tracking collars. **Game capture, tagging, assisting with wildlife veterinary work, game counts and monitoring** may be part of the work programme. Marine projects involve **dolphin and whale research, seal and sea bird monitoring. Lion, Hyena and Leopard monitoring is often involved.** Applicants must have reasonable physical fitness and be able to cope with mental challenges. Enthusiasm for conservation is essential. The programme may be of special interest to students of environmental, zoological and biological sciences, veterinary science and animal care. No previous experience or qualifications necessary.

Applicants are invited to attend Open Days at various venues across the UK. Costs vary depending on reserve and time of year; support and advice are given on fund-raising.

*Applications* to the above address.

**CORAL CAY CONSERVATION LTD:** 40-41 Osnaburgh Street, London, NW13ND, (☎0870-7500668; fax 0870-7500667; e-mail recruitment@coralcay. org; www.coralcay.org). Coral Cay Conservation recruits paying volunteers to help alleviate poverty through research, education, training and alternative livelihood programmes worldwide. Volunteers are provided with full training; no previous experience required.
**Expedition Leaders** to oversee running of marine or forest expeditions. Management experience is desirable. Plus, for marine expeditions scuba diving qualifications and for forest expeditions a Mountain Leader qualification is preferable.

**Science Officers** to oversee coral reef and/or tropical forest scientific training and survey programmes. Minimum qualification: degree and proven field research experience.
**Scuba Instructors** to provide scuba training for expedition personnel and host country counterparts. PADI OWSI and EFRI as minimum.
**Medical Officers** to oversee all aspects of expedition medical health. Minimum qualification: paramedic, registered nurse or doctor with A & E experience.

The above are needed to work for Coral Cay Conservation (CCC), a non-profit organisation **established in 1986 to provide support for the conservation and sustainable use of tropical and marine resources.** CCC maintains full-time expedition projects in the Philippines, Trinidad, Fiji and Tobago. No wage is paid and expedition staff are required to cover the costs of their flights and insurance. CCC covers accommodation, food and other subsistence costs.

Either e-mail, or send *applications* to the above address.

**EARTHWATCH INSTITUTE (EUROPE):** 267 Banbury Road, Oxford, OX2 7HT (☎01865-318831; fax 01865-311383; www.earthwatch.org; e-mail projects@ earthwatch.org.uk for volunteer project enquiries; info@earthwatch.org.uk for general enquiries).
Volunteers to work with scientists as part of a team conducting research into a variety of environmental conservation and heritage projects in the UK, and all over the world. Project fees range from £150 to £2000, over a period of two days or up to three weeks. No formal qualifications or experience are required.

For further details *contact* the above address.

**ECOVOLUNTEER PROGRAM:** Meyersweg 29, 7553 AX Hengelo, Netherlands (☎+31-74 250 8250; fax +31-74 250 6572; e-mail info@ecovolunteer.org; www. ecovolunteer.org or for Britons www.ecovolunteer.org.uk). The Ecovolunteer Program organises wildlife conservation projects and wildlife research projects operated by local conservation organisations worldwide.

Volunteers: (500-600) work varies from **practical fieldwork** to **production and support jobs in wildlife rescue centres**, to **visitor education, maintenance work, and household duties,** dependent on each individual project.

Volunteers are recruited for projects lasting from 1 week to 6 months. The minimum age of volunteers is 18; participants must be in good physical health. Accommodation is provided.

A list of the national agencies can be found at www.ecovolunteer.org/contact.html or obtained from the above address as there are offices in Austria, Belgium, Brazil, France, Hungary, Italy, the Netherlands, Spain, Switzerland the UK. More than 30 projects; their latest projects include an animal sanctuary in Florida, a brown bear project in Russia, and a Toucan bird project in Brazil.

*Applications* should be made to the national Ecovolunteer agency of the country in which the applicant is resident.

**EXPLORATIONS IN TRAVEL:** 2458 River Road, Guilford, Vermont. 05301 USA (☎ 1-802-257-0152; fax: 1-802-257-2784; e-mail explore@volunteertravel.com; www. volunteertravel.com). Explorations in Travel arrange volunteer placements around the world, throughout the year, with placements arranged individually.
Volunteers to work with **wildlife and domestic animal rescue organisations, rainforest reserves, organic farms, environmental and conservation projects, sustainable tourism and schools.** Placements are in, Belize, Costa Rica, Ecuador, Guatemala and Puerto Rico. Periods of work etc. by arrangement; most placements are available throughout the year. Volunteers most often pay a local family for room

and board. Minimum age 18.
For further details *contact* the Program Director, at the above address.

**FRONTIER:** 50-52 Rivington Street, London EC2A 3QP (☎020-7613 2422; fax 020-7613 2992; e-mail info@frontier.ac.uk; www.frontier.ac.uk).
Frontier is a non-profit international conservation and development NGO operating since 1989.
Frontier offers the opportunity to work in coral reefs, African savannahs, forests and mangrove areas as part of conservation programmes in far-off destinations. Programmes are established in response to problems; surveys of damaged areas are carried out so that possible solutions can be identified. For example, dynamite fishing in Tanzania was destroying the delicate web of marine life so Frontier volunteers carried out more than 6000 dives in order to establish a marine park where marine life will be protected.
As Frontier is a professional agency, volunteers get the chance to work on real wildlife and habitat conservation programmes. Volunteers also work on capacity-building initiatives aimed at developing sustainable livelihoods for the world's most impoverished and marginalized communities.
Destinations include Tanzania, Madagascar, Cambodia, Fiji, Nicaragua, Peru, Nepal, Tibet, Costa Rica, Mexico, Guatemala, Thailand, and Vietnam. There are 250 placements per year. The minimum age is 17 and no specific qualifications are needed as training is given. Marine expeditions include free scuba diving training and TEFL training. Candidates can build UCAS points by studying in the field for a BTEC Advanced Diploma in Tropical Habitat Conservation or a BTEC Advanced Certificate in Expedition Management on select programmes. Placements are for 4 weeks or longer and take place throughout the year.
Depending on location and duration, costs are between £1,100 and £3,950. This covers all individual costs, including a UK training weekend, scientific and dive training, all internal travel and airport pick-ups, visas, food and accommodation, but excludes international flights and insurance.
*Contact* the above website for more details, a free information pack and application form.

**GLOBAL CHOICES:** Barkat House, 116-118 Finchley Road, London NW3 5HT (☎020-7433 2501; fax 0870 330 5955; e-mail info@globalchoices.co.uk; www. globalchoices.co.uk.
Global Choices offers **Voluntary Work Internships, Practical Training and Work Experience Worldwide** from 2 weeks to 18 months. Destinations include Argentina, Austria, Brazil, Chile, Costa Rica, Ecuador, France, Nepal, New Zealand, Portugal, Peru, Spain, Tanzania and Ukraine. Placements are offered in many fields, industrial, business, science, conservation, agriculture, travel and tourism, volunteering, teaching and more. Cost depends on programme.

**GREENFORCE:** 11-15 Betterton street, Covent Garden, London WC2H 9BP (☎020 7470 8888; e-mail info@greenforce.org; www.greenforce.org).
Volunteers required for work one of Greenforce's **wildlife research projects** in Ecuador, Tanzania, Fiji, Nepal/Tibet and the Bahamas. Working for a host country partner such as WWF or the Red Cross, volunteers receive all necessary training in country.
Training includes PADI dive qualifications on their marine projects in Fiji and the Bahamas, and language classes in all other locations. Working as field assistants,

volunteers carry out tasks such as tracking animal movements and studying coral reef species.

Adventure/ sport expeditions and internships are also available around the globe. For further details *contact* the above address or website and make an appointment at head office to discuss a suitable expedition.

**INKANATURA TRAVEL:** Manuel Bañón 461, San Isidro, Lima, Peru (☎014-402022; fax 014-229225; e-mail reservascus@inkanatura.com.pe; opcix@inkanatura.com.pe; www.inkanatura.com). Two conservation organisations, Selva Sur and Peru Verde have formed a non-profit travel agency to **promote ecotourism** and assist **conservation work** in order to save Peru's unique biodiversity. Volunteers are also needed for projects in Bolivia and Brazil.

**Resident Naturalists** required for four lodges in southeastern Peru to **guide tourists and take on small research projects. Possible wildlife studies include tapirs, spider monkeys (and 5 other small monkey species), peccaries, macaws, bats, deer, large macaws and the endangered Giant River Otter.** Duration is 90 days, with an option to extend. After training and depending on experience, the applicant may be able to get a contract for guiding tourists. Free food and lodging will be provided as well as transport from Cusco. A deposit of £166/$300 will be required to cover the first month, which will be forfeited if the volunteer leaves before the end of the 90 day period without good cause. If a volunteer should abandon the project without good cause he/she will also have to pay for his/her own transport home.

**Volunteers to assist research projects.** Duration of stay is 4 weeks. Food and lodging costs of £11/$20 per day must be met by the volunteer as must insurance and the cost of travel to the project. US residents can obtain a tax break on these costs.

Some of the projects that volunteers can work on occur throughout the year, while others run from late October-January. There are also opportunities for independent research, to teach English and help train local residents/indigenous people who are running ecotourism schemes near reserves in Manu, Tambopata, Lower Urubamba and Madidi.

Full details of these projects, costs and how to *apply* can be obtained from the above address or on the website.

**INTERNATIONAL CONSERVATION HOLIDAYS:** BTCV, Conservation Centre Booking Service, Balby Road, Doncaster DN4 ORH; (☎01302-572244; fax 01302-310167; e-mail information@btcv.org.uk; www.btcv.org).

BTCV is the UK's leading practical conservation charity. Founded in 1959, they help over 130,000 volunteers per year to take hands on action to improve urban and rural environments.

Volunteers to take part in **international conservation projects** in Bulgaria, Canada, France, Germany, Iceland, Japan, Portugal, and the USA. Board, accommodation and insurance provided for from £350 per week. Projects take place throughout the year and last from 1-3 weeks. Minimum age 18: knowledge of languages not essential. Volunteers must pay their own travel expenses.

For full details of BTCV's Conservation Holiday programme, *contact* BTCV for an up-to-date brochure; full project details are also available on the BTCV website.

**OVERSEAS DEVELOPMENT INSTITUTE:** 111, Westminster Bridge Road, London, SE1 7JD (☎020-7922 0300; fax 020-7922 0399; www.odi.org.uk)

ODI runs the Overseas Development Institute Fellowship Scheme which enables recent young economics graduates to work for two years in the public sectors of developing countries in Africa, the Caribbean and the Pacific. Candidates may be of any nationality but must have (or be studying for) a postgraduate qualification in economics or a related field. The Fellowship Scheme provides **practical work experience in developing countries and around the world.** 25 Fellowships are awarded annually.

*Application* forms and a booklet are available each November from the website at www.odi.org.uk/fellows.

**TREKFORCE EXPEDITIONS:** Naldred Farm Offices, Borde Hill Lane, Haywards Heath, West Sussex RH16 1XR (☎01444-474123; fax 01444-474101; e-mail info@ trekforce.org.uk; www.trekforce.org.uk).

Trekforce is a registered charity that offers a once in a lifetime opportunity to play your part in international conservation. Volunteers participate in **conservation expeditions** lasting from two to eight weeks in Central and South America and South East Asia. During this time you will be living in stunning but endangered rainforests, completing a vital conservation project.

Trekforce also offer extended programmes of three to five months incorporating a two-month project, up to one month learning a new language and two months teaching in a rural school.

Every expedition is unique and volunteers work to complete an entire project. All projects make a significant long-term difference and are carried out with the highest levels of safety and backup with permanently staffed field bases in each country. Volunteers get an in-depth knowledge of new cultures by living with local families whilst on language and teaching phases.

Each volunteer has to raise funds for Trekforce and friendly help and advice are given throughout. Training includes a briefing day in the UK prior to departure and then full training is given in safety, first aid and outdoor skills once on expedition.

Volunteers (aged 18+) must be enthusiastic, hard-working and have a sense of adventure – no two days will be the same.

To find out more you can attend an informal Trekforce Introduction Day, a chance to meet previous volunteers and find out more information about project work, jungle life and fundraising. Dates of Introduction Days and information on all aspects of the expeditions can be found on the website (see above).

*Apply* online for more information.

# Gap Year/Year Out

**AFRICA AND ASIA VENTURE:** 10 Market Place, Devizes, Wilts., SN10 1HT (☎01380-729009; fax 01380-720060; e-mail av@aventure.co.uk; www.aventure. co.uk). 'AV' has ten years of experience offering 18-23-year-old volunteers 4-5 month rewarding **projects in teaching, community and conservation** in Africa, the Indian Himalayas, Nepal and for those keen to improve their Spanish, Mexico. You can also take part in shorter vacation expeditions in Kenya that combine community work with travel and adventure.

Gap Year with AV will start with an in-country orientation course covering customs, country and TEFL, then experience of a rewarding project, followed by travel opportunities including a fantastic safari travelling in game reserves, deserts, or white water rafting. All this supported by excellent back-up enabling you to experience first hand countries away from the tourist trail.

*Apply* on the above number or online.

**GAP ACTIVITY PROJECTS LIMITED:** GAP House, 44 Queen's Road, Reading, Berkshire RG1 4BB, (☎0118-9594914; fax 0118-9576634; e-mail volunteer@

gap.org.uk; www.gap.org.uk). GAP is a registered charity based in Reading which organises voluntary work opportunities for 17-25 year-olds who wish to take a 'year out' between school and higher education, employment or training. Successful volunteers undertake full-time work for between three and twelve months in return for which they receive food, accommodation and (usually) a living allowance.

Currently opportunities exist in Argentina, Australia, Brazil, Canada, China, Ecuador, Fiji & the South Pacific, Germany, Ghana, India, Japan, Malawi, Malaysia, Mexico, New Zealand, Paraguay, Russia, South Africa, Thailand, the USA and Vietnam. A wide variety of projects is on offer including **teaching English as a foreign language, general duties in schools, assisting on community projects or caring for the sick and people with disabilities, outdoor activities and sports coaching, conservation work and scientific surveys.**

GAP has no closing date for applications, although you stand a better chance of being placed on your first choice project, if you apply early. GAP welcomes applications at any time from year 12 onwards. Every applicant is invited to interview with interviews taking place from the middle of October onwards in Reading, Leeds, Dublin, Belfast, Glasgow and other regional locations. Brochures are available each year from August onwards for placements starting a year later.

To receive a copy of the GAP brochure and application form students should *contact* careers staff at their school or college, or telephone, e-mail or write to the GAP office, stating clearly for which year they will be applying.

**GLOBAL CHOICES:** Barkat House, 116-118 Finchley Road, London NW3 5HT (☎020-7433 2501; fax 0870 330 5955; e-mail info@globalchoices.co.uk; www. globalchoices.co.uk.
Global Choices offers **Voluntary Work Internships, Practical Training** and **Work Experience Worldwide** from 2 weeks to 18 months. Destinations include Argentina, Austria, Brazil, Chile, Costa Rica, Ecuador, France, Nepal, New Zealand, Portugal, Peru, Spain, Tanzania and Ukraine. Placements are offered in many fields, industrial, business, science, conservation, agriculture, travel and tourism, volunteering, teaching and more. Cost depends on programme.

**GLOBAL VISION INTERNATIONAL:** 130 Amwell Farmhouse, Nomansland, Wheathampstead, St. Albans, Herts, AL4 8EJ (☎0870 608 8898; fax 0870 609 2319; e-mail info@gvi.co.uk; www.gvi.co.uk); in the US: GVI North America, PO Box 8124, Delray Beach, Florida 33482-8124; (☎888-653-6028; 561-282-6992 both toll-free numbers; info@gviusa.com; www.gviusa.com).
Volunteers for projects in Belize, Brazil, Costa Rica, East Africa, Ecuador, Guatemala, Mexico, Madagascar, Nepal, Namibia, Panama, Rwanda, The Seychelles, South Africa, Sri Lanka, Sumatra, Thailand, USA, Kenya, Tanzania, New Mexico, Arizona, Guatemala, Nepal and the USA. Projects are very varied **from volunteering with animal conservation projects to caring for orphans**. Length of projects varies from two, three, four or five weeks up to a year. Costs also vary. £1,000 for three weeks in Madagascar, flights not included. No special qualifications are required but volunteers should be aged at least 18.

For more information *contact* the Program Director in the UK or US as appropriate, at above addresses.

**GWENDALYNE :** c/o Twin Training and Travel Ltd, 2nd Floor, 67-71 Lewisham High St., Lewisham, London SE13 SJX (☎020 8297 3251; fax 020 8297 0984; e-mail info@gwendalyne.com; www.gwendalyne.com).
Gwendalyne is a newly launched Outbound department of Twin Training and Travel

offering a range of work experience and volunteer programmes around the world. Some programmes are in conjunction with Euro-Academy language courses. Countries include USA (career training) Brazil, Canada, Finland, France, Germany, Ireland and Spain. Work programmes in Australia, France, New Zealand, Norway, South Africa, USA and other countries. Placement fees range from £300-£400 excluding courses and accommodation.

Applicants must meet the age requirements of the relevant visa. In some cases a language course is compulsory before beginning the assignment. Placement lengths are various with a maximum on some of 12 months. Applications take one to three months to process. Volunteers for projects in Belize, Brazil, Costa Rica, East Africa, Ecuador, Guatemala, Mexico, Madagascar, Nepal, Namibia, Panama, Rwanda, The Seychelles, South Africa, Sri Lanka, Sumatra, Thailand, USA, Kenya, Tanzania, New Mexico, Arizona, Guatemala, Nepal and the USA. Projects are very varied from volunteering with animal conservation projects to caring for orphans. Length of projects varies from two, three, four or five weeks up to a year. Costs also vary. £1,000 for three weeks in Madagascar, flights not included. No special qualifications are required but volunteers should be aged at least 18.

For more information *contact* Piero Donat, Global Work Experience Manager at the above address.

**INVOLVEMENT VOLUNTEERS ASSOCIATION INC (IVI):** PO Box 218, Port Melbourne, Victoria 3207, Australia (☎+61 3 9646 9392; fax +61 3 9646 5504; e-mail ivworldwide@volunteering.org.au; www.volunteering.org.au).

Involvement Volunteers Association Inc. is a government registered, non-profit, non-governmental organisation which charges fees to cover administration cost for a programme of any number of Networked International Volunteering; placements with suggested travel arrangements in any number of the countries in a period of up to 12 months. IV associates and agents support the volunteers around the world. IVI was established in 1988 with the aim of making voluntary work available to people who wish to assist others and to learn from their volunteer experiences.

IV volunteers participate in Networked International Volunteering as individuals or groups of individual volunteers in their own Program of Placements, as unpaid participants – the real volunteers. The aim of Involvement Volunteering is to enable volunteers to **assist not-for-profit organisations in projects related to the natural environment** (at farms, national or zoological parks, animal reserves or historic places) or social service in the community (at homes, camps or schools for disadvantaged people, orphanages etc in towns and villages).

Placements of 2-12 weeks are currently available in Albania, Argentina, Australia, Austria, Bangladesh, Bolivia, Brazil, Cambodia, Cameroon, China, Columbia, Czech Republic, East Timor, Ecuador, Estonia, Egypt, Fiji, Finland, France, Germany, Ghana, Greece, Guatemala, Guinea-Bissau, Iceland, India, Italy, Israel, Japan, Jordan, Kenya, Korea, Kosovo, Latvia, Lebanon, Lithuania, Macedonia, Mexico, Mongolia, Namibia, Nepal, New Zealand, Palestine, Panama, Peru, Philippines, Poland, Sabah (Malaysia), Samoa, Serbia, South Africa, Spain, Tanzania, Thailand, Togo, Turkey, Uganda, UK, Ukraine, USA, Venezuela, Vietnam and Zambia. Single Placement Programs or Multiple Placement Programs (as many placements as can be fitted in a 12 month period travelling the world) can provide valuable practical experience related to potential tertiary education, completed degree courses or completed careers (for early retirees). Some placements have food and accommodation provided while some can cost up to about £35 per week for food and accommodation, depending on the economy of the country and the host organisation.

Where appropriate, IV volunteers are met on arrival at the airport and provided with

24-hour back-up if need be during their visit. Advice is given on banking, specially discounted internal travel, special trips, eco trips, discounted scuba diving courses, sea kayaking, snorkelling and sailing in suitable areas.

**European applicants** can *contact* Involvement Volunteers-Germany, Volksdorfer Strasse 32, 22081 Hamburg, Germany (☎+49 40 41269450; fax +49 40 5113229; e-mail ivgermany@volunteering.org.au or ivworldwide@volunteering.org.au).

**OUTREACH INTERNATIONAL:** Bartletts Farm, Hayes Road, Compton Dundon, Somerset TA11 6PF ( ☎/fax 01458 274957; e-mail gap@outreachinternational.co.uk; www.outreachinternational.co.uk. A small, specialist gap organisation with carefully selected projects in specific parts of Cambodia, Sri Lanka, Costa Rica, Ecuador, Galapagos Islands and on the Pacific Coast of Mexico. The projects have enough variety to ensure that the interests and skills of individual volunteers can be put to good use.

The placements include helping at orphanages, supporting a busy centre for street children, teaching disabled children, teaching English in coastal schools, helping at a medical centre and offering support at a busy children's hospital, humanitarian work, physiotherapy, carrying out conservation work in the Amazon rainforest, working at a centre for rescued wild animals and art and craft projects. No specific skills or qualifications are normally required although trained physiotherapists are needed for some projects. These are humble, grass root initiatives where you can make a significant difference to the lives of local people. The projects are well organised and have a clear and genuine need for volunteer support. Each one is regularly visited and assessed by the Outreach International director. In addition to providing a three-month experience a number of volunteers have used this as a stepping-stone towards a career in overseas work.

Participants travel to their destination in small groups but work on a project in pairs, which minimises the cultural impact of living in a foreign land and enables immersion in the host community. Placements can be tailor-made to fit in with summer holidays.

Applications would be welcome from confident, energetic people with a desire to travel, learn a language and offer their help to a worthwhile cause. All potential volunteers are interviewed informally to help them make an informed decision about whether the placement is right for them.

The cost of £2,650 includes full health, baggage and public liability insurance, a generous food allowance and comfortable accommodation, a comprehensive language course on arrival and a cd language course in the UK, full in-country support, visa, all project-related travel, a weekend trip, and training in the UK including a fund-raising

awareness day.
    Further details from www.outreachinternational.co.uk or from the UK Head Office
on 01458-274957.

**PROJECT TRUST:** The Hebridean Centre, Ballyhough, Isle of Coll, Argyll PA78
6TE (☎01879-230-444; fax 01879-230-357; e-mail info@projecttrust.org.uk).
Project Trust arranges for volunteers to spend a whole year in an exciting country,
becoming part of a community and learning another language.
Project Trust is an educational charity, which sends 200 school leavers overseas
every year to over twenty countries around the world. At present these are: Bolivia,
Botswana, Brazil, Chile, China, Dominican Republic, Guyana, Hong Kong, Honduras,
Japan, Malawi, Malaysia, Morocco, Namibia, Niger, Peru, South Africa, Sri Lanka,
Swaziland, Thailand, Uganda and Vietnam. There are a wide variety of projects on
offer, from **teaching** to **development work, outward bound activities, and child
and health care**. Placements are for twelve months.
    All volunteers attend a selection course on the Isle of Coll in the autumn before they go
overseas. Week-long training courses take place on the Isle of Coll after final exams in the
summer, and following a year overseas the volunteers assemble again on the Isle of Coll to
debrief on their experiences before dispersing to university or their future careers.
    The cost is £4,190 for the year which includes insurance and travel, full support
overseas, food and accommodation. Fundraising workshops are held throughout the
country to help volunteers raise the necessary finance.
    *Apply* as early as possible to avoid disappointment.

**QUEST OVERSEAS:** The North-West Stables, Borde Hill Estate, Balcombe Road,
Haywards Heath, West Sussex RH16 1XP (☎01444-474744; fax 01444-474 799 e-
mail info@questoverseas.com; www.questoverseas.com).
Quest Overseas are Project and Expedition specialists in South America and Africa.
They offer trips for gap year students, university students and people taking career
sabbaticals.
**Gap year students** can apply to join a 3-month Combined Expedition. The specialist
3-month Quests in South America consist of a 3-week one-to-one Spanish course, 4
weeks on a conservation or community project, and a six week expedition trekking,
mountain-biking and white-water rafting through Peru, Bolivia and Chile.
**Combined expeditions to Africa** need volunteers to work for 6 weeks either on game
reserves in Swaziland (ecological surveys, trail building) or in villages in Tanzania,
Malawi or Kenya (building schools, water tanks and playgrounds as well as teaching and
working in the communities). All Africa projects are followed by an adventurous six-week
Expedition including scuba-diving in the beautiful Mozambique and safari in Botswana.
    Quest Overseas also organises Team Expeditions, Work placements and Specialist
Expeditions for all ages and backgrounds to Africa or South America all year round.
    Shorter Expeditions start from two weeks, exploring some of the best and most
adventurous parts of South America and Africa or carrying out worthwhile work
across the continents – a real assault on the senses!
    Expedition costs range between £850 and £4920 – which includes board and
accommodation as well as on-going support for the project. Flights and insurance are
not included.
    Quest Overseas regularly recruits project and expedition leaders to lead teams
in Africa and South America. Check the 'About You' section of the website for
application criteria.
    *Applications* should be made through the website as early as possible in order to
allow you to get your first choice of project.

**RALEIGH INTERNATIONAL:** Raleigh House, 27 Parsons Green Lane London SW6 4HZ (☎020-7371 8585; e-mail info@raleigh.org.uk; www.raleighinternational. org). Raleigh International is a leading international youth development charity. It inspires people from all backgrounds and nationalities to discover their full potential by working together on **sustainable environmental,and community projects** and **challenging adventure programmes** around the world. For the last 21 years, the charity has enabled over 30,000 people to volunteer on 1,800 different development projects overseas.

Raleigh International's 10-week programmes give young people between 17 and 24 years old and volunteer staff over 25 years old the chance to live and work with a diverse group of people. Raleigh International's current countries include, Costa Rica, Namibia, Nicaragua and Malaysian Borneo.

During each programme all of the volunteers work on three projects - one community, one environment and one adventure project. Examples include building a primary school in Malaysia or trekking through the mountain ranges of Namibia.

More information on the website: www.raleighinternational.org.

If you are interested, please *attend an information event* to find out more.

**TEACHING & PROJECTS ABROAD:** Aldsworth Parade, Goring, Sussex BN12 4TX (☎01903 708300; fax 01903 501026; e-mail info@projects-abroad.co.uk; www. projects-abroad.co.uk
Sends around 3000 people abroad annually on a variety of projects in developing countries. Countries include: Argentina, Bolivia, Chile, Costa Rica, Mexico, Peru, Cambodia, China, India, Mongolia, Nepal, Sri Lanka and Thailand, Ghana, Senegal, South Africa, Swaziland, Moldova and Romania.

**TRAVELLERS WORLDWIDE:** 7 Mulberry Close, Ferring, West Sussex BN12 5HY (☎01903-502595; fax 01903 500364; e-mail info@travellersworldwide.com; www.travellersworldwide.com). A Founder Member of the Year Out Group.
Structured voluntary placements costing from £745, involving **teaching conversational English (also music, sports, drama and other subjects), conservation (with urangutans, elephants, lions, dolphins, etc.), language courses, structured work experience (journalism, law, medicine, etc.) and cultural courses (photography, tango, etc)** in Argentina, Australia, Bolivia,Brazil, Brunei, China, Cuba, Ghana, Guatemala, India, Kenya, Malaysia, Peru, Russia, South Africa, Sri Lanka, Zambia and Zimbabwe. Placements last from 2 weeks to a year, with flexible start dates all year round. Hundreds of projects are available worldwide and are described in detail on their website. If you have something not currently provided in mind, Travellers Worldwide will attempt to arrange it for you, so don't hesitate to ask.

No formal qualifications required. Sample charges for 3 months in Sri Lanka are £1,495 and £1,095 in China. Prices include food and accommodation, meeting at the nearest airport, plus support and back-up from local staff in destination countries, but exclude flights, visa costs and insurance. (Travellers can arrange the latter but many volunteers prefer the flexibility of organising their own.)

*Applications* should be made to the above address.

**VENTURE CO WORLDWIDE:** The Ironyard, 64-66 The Market Place, Warwick (☎01926-411122;    fax01926-411133;    mail@ventureco-worldwide.com;    www. ventureco-worldwide.com). VentureCo is a Gap Year and Career Gap provider with programmes in South and Central America, Asia, East Africa and Indo-China and China. About 275 gap year students per year, aged from 17 ½ to 19 years, and those on a career gap (minimum age 20) participate in **projects which combine language**

schools, local aid projects and expeditions.
**Programmes** last for 4 months and depart year round. There are also shorter VentureGo programmes (1-3 months), in Peru, the Galapagos or East Africa, departing in July; these trips can be fitted in to the long summer vacation. Cost is approximately £4,500 including flights and insurance; 4-week VentureGo trips from £2,826.

Applicants attend a 'Workshop' as part of the selection process. Preparation weekends held in the UK, and expedition skills training in country.

*Apply* immediately to the above address or e-mail.

# Social & Community Schemes

**AFS INTERCULTURAL PROGRAMMES UK:** Leeming House, Vicar Lane, Leeds LS2 7JF (☎0113-242 6136; fax 0113-243 0631; e-mail info-unitedkingdom@ afs.org; www.afsuk.org).
AFS is an international non-profit association of 54 national organisations and is one of the world's largest voluntary organisations providing over 11,000 participants with an intercultural learning experience each year.
**Volunteer Programme** 6 month placements with AFS International Volunteer Programmes in Latin America or Africa on voluntary projects dedicated to **healthcare, education, social welfare, environmental protection and other pressing human issues such as homelessness among urban poor, (with a special emphasis on meeting the needs of children).** Participants live with a local volunteer host family and are provided with an excellent support structure. Applicants must be aged 18-29 and no language skills or qualifications are required. Departures from the UK are in January and July. Cost is £3,300.
**School Programme** A unique opportunity for young people aged 16-18 to spend an academic year studying in one of over 20 countries. Participants live with a local host family and enrol in the local school/college system. Departures from the UK are between July and September. Must be able to fundraise for both programmes.
*Applications* to the above address.

**CONCORDIA:** 19 North Street, Portslade, Brighton, BN41 1DH (☎01273-422218; fax 01273 421182; e-mail info@concordia-iye.org.uk; www.concordia-iye.org.uk). Concordia is a small not-for-profit charity committed to international youth exchange. Their International Volunteer Programme offers volunteers aged 16+ the opportunity to join international teams of volunteers working on **community-based projects** in over 60 countries worldwide. Projects are diverse ranging from **nature conservation, restoration, archaeology, construction, art and culture** to projects that are socially based including

**work with adults or children with special needs, children's play-schemes and teaching**. Projects last for 2-4 weeks with the main season from June to September and smaller winter/spring programme. Generally the work doesn't require specific skills or experience, though real motivation and commitment to the project are a must.

Volunteers pay a registration fee of £110 (£70 for projects in the UK) and fund their own travel. Board and accommodation is free of charge. Concordia also recruits volunteers (20+) to act as Group Coordinators on UK based projects, for which training is provided and all expenses are paid. Details of projects will be published in April. Early application is advised.

Concordia can only place volunteers who are resident in the UK. Volunteers applying from abroad should contact a volunteer organisation in their own country or country in which they are based.

For further information on volunteering or coordinating please check the website or contact the International Volunteer Coordinator at the above address.

**CROSS-CULTURAL SOLUTIONS:** UK Office: Tower Point 44 North Road, Brighton, BN1 1YR (☎0845 458 2781/2782; e-mail infouk@ crossculturalsolutions.org; www.crossculturalsolutions.org.) See website for further postal addresses.

Established in 1995, Cross-Cultural Solutions is a registered charity and a recognised leader in the field of international volunteering, sending thousands of volunteers overseas every year. Volunteer programmes operate year-round in Africa, Asia, Latin America and Russia and range from 1 to 12 weeks. Volunteers **work side-by-side with local people on locally designed and driven projects,** enabling them to participate in meaningful community development and see a country from a whole new perspective.

The CCS experience also includes cultural and learning activities so that volunteers learn about the local culture. These include an in-depth orientation, language training, guest speakers and more. There is also plenty of free time to relax, reflect, or explore the community. CCS provide a Home-Base for all volunteers. Here, all daily needs are taken care of, including lodging, meals and transportation. Through each of these elements volunteers are able to immerse themselves into the culture of the country and fully realise their experience. Programme fees cover the costs of accommodation in the CCS home base, meals and ground transportation, plus individual attention and guidance from an experienced and knowledgeable programme manager, coordination of the Volunteer Placement, perspectives programming activities, a 24-hour emergency hotline in the USA, and medical insurance. Prices start at £1389 for a two-week programme.

For more information please *contact* Cross-Cultural Solutions using the above contact information.

**GLOBAL CHOICES:** Barkat House, 116-118 Finchley Road, London NW3 5HT (☎020-7433 2501; fax 0870 330 5955; e-mail info@globalchoices.co.uk; www. globalchoices.co.uk.

Global Choices offers Voluntary Work Internships, Practical Training and Work Experience Worldwide from 2 weeks to 18 months. Destinations include Argentina, Austria, Brazil, Chile, Costa Rica, Ecuador, France, Nepal, New Zealand, Portugal, Peru, Spain, Tanzania and Ukraine. Placements are offered in many fields, industrial, business, science, conservation, agriculture, travel and tourism, volunteering, teaching and more. Cost depends on programme.

**GLOBAL CITIZENS NETWORK:** 130 N. Howell Street, St Paul, Minnesota 55104, USA (☎651-644-0960; e-mail info@globalcitizens.org; www.globalcitizens.org).

Volunteers for projects in Kenya, Tanzania, Guatemala, Nepal, Thailand, Ecuador, Peru, USA and Mexico. Build, plant, grow, learn. Connect with indigenous peoples and contribute to peace throughout the world with Global Citizens Network, an organisation offering short-term volunteer trips that last a lifetime. Volunteer trips last 1, 2, or 3 weeks and are ongoing throughout the year. Programmes involve volunteers include **building a health centre, teaching in a school and renovating a youth centre.** Volunteers pay a programme fee of $750-$2050 (£400-£1100), which includes most in-country costs (food, lodging, transportation etc.); the airfare is extra. No special qualifications are required but volunteers should be aged at least 18. Volunteers under 18 years must be accompanied by parent or guardian.

For more information *contact* the Program Director at the above address.

**HABITAT FOR HUMANITY GREAT BRITAIN:** 11 Parsons Street, Banbury, Oxon OX16 5LW (☎01295-220188; fax 01295-264230; e-mail info@hfhgb.org; www.habitatforhumanity.org.uk). Habitat for Humanity is an international house-building charity. Each year teams of 10-15 volunteers travel overseas to **help build simple, decent houses alongside local people**, who are in desperate need of shelter.

Each trip lasts about 2 weeks and is ideal for those interested in travel and a Habitat For Humanity volunteer experience. Trips are designed to promote cross-cultural understanding and raise awareness of the urgent issue of substandard housing. Applicants should be over 18; no experience or building skill is necessary.

Each applicant pays for their direct costs and raises money to build more houses. Costs include food, insurance and sight-seeing activities during rest days.

*For further information* on trips for individuals or groups, please visit the website or *contact* the Global village department (see above).

**SKILLSHARE INTERNATIONAL:** 126 New Walk Street, Leicester LE1 7JA (☎0116 254 1862; fax 0116 254 2614; e-mail recruitment@skillshare.org' www. skillshare.org)
Skillshare recruits professionals to share their skills and experience with local communities for further economic and social development in Botswana, Kenya, Lesotho, Mozambique, Namibia, South Africa, Swaziland, Tanzania, Uganda, India and Nepal. Its vision is a world without poverty, injustice and inequality where people, regardless of cultural, social, and political divides come together for mutual benefit living in peaceful co-existence.

Projects cover a wide-range of activities and **general management, agricultural, technical, educational and medical** skills are all required. Applicants should be aged 21, have relevant qualifications and experience, particularly in training others.

Placements are usually for two years. Skillshare offers a modest living allowance, flights/travel to the placement and return, medical cover, and pre and post placement grants to assist with relocation. The living allowance is adequate to cover your living costs whilst in the country of placement but not adequate for savings or meeting other costs you may have in your country of residence.

An information pack is available from the above address.

**TEARFUND TRANSFORM INTERNATIONAL PROGRAMME:** 100 Church Road, Teddington, Middlesex TW11 8QE (☎0208 943 7777; e-mail transform@ tearfund.org; www.youth.tearfund.org/transform). Tearfund is an evangelical Christian development charity working with local partners to **bring help and hope to communities in need**. In 2006 Tearfund supported hundreds of projects in over 90 countries.

Volunteers to work for 4-6 weeks from early July to the end of August, to join teams of 8-12 people. Assignments are in a number of countries and include **practical work, renovation and work with children**.

A contribution of approx £1,800 which includes orientation, travel, food and accommodation is required.

Applicants should be over 18 and committed Christians. Details are available from the Enquiry Unit at the above address and *applications* should be received by mid-February.

# Workcamps

**INTERNATIONAL VOLUNTARY SERVICE (BRITISH BRANCH OF SERVICE CIVIL INTERNATIONAL):** IVS Field Office, Old Hall, East Bergholt, Colchester C07 6TQ (☎01206-298215; e-mail ivssouth@ivs-gb.org.uk; www.ivs-gb.org.uk).

International Voluntary Service sends volunteers to international workcamps and short-term projects across a choice of 50 countries in eastern and western Europe including the former Soviet Union, as well as Japan, North Africa, Turkey, the US and Australia. Volunteers work for two to four weeks in an international team of 10-20 people, sharing domestic and social life as well as the work. The projects include **work with children, work with people with physical or mental disabilities, solidarity work with people of other countries, and manual work, often connected with ecology or conservation.** The projects are not holidays. The work can be hard and demands commitment.

Most workcamps are between June and September and last one to three weeks. Volunteers must pay for membership of IVS, a registration fee of £40-£120 and their own travel costs. Free board and accommodation are provided on the project. For certain countries previous experience of voluntary work is required or preferred. English is the language of most projects, but other languages are an advantage. IVS is working towards equal opportunities, and welcomes applications from women, black people, people with disabilities, people from ethnic minorities, gay men and lesbians. IVS can only accept applications from people with an address in Britain. The address of the American branch of Service Civil International for volunteers living in the USA, or US nationals is 5474 Walnut Level Road, Crozet, VA 22932, USA; e-mail scitalk@sci-ivs.org; www.sci-ivs.org

*Applications* should posted to the address above after downloading an application form from the website. Applications can also be sent to IVS North, Oxford Place Centre, Oxford Place, Leeds LS1 3AX (☎0113 246 9900; fax 0113 246 9910; ivsnorth@ivs-gb.org.uk). Camp Listings for each summer are compiled by April of each year and available on the website. It is also worth checking the website from time-to-time as updates arrive continuously. If you want to receive the April list of workcamps by post, it is available free; just telephone the offices to ask for a copy to be sent to you.

**SERVICE CIVIL INTERNATIONAL/SCI-INTERNATIONAL:** see the entry for International Voluntary Service above.

**UNA EXCHANGE:** Temple of Peace, Cathays Park, Cardiff CF10 3AP (☎029-20-223088; e-mail info@unaexchange.org; www.unaexchange.org).

Organises projects in Wales for international volunteers and sends volunteers to projects abroad. Most projects last 2-4 weeks between the months of April and September but there are also ones at other times of year and longer-term opportunities. Projects include a huge variety of social, environmental and renovation work from helping to set up a festival in France to working with children in the Ukraine. UNA Exchange also operates a 'North-South' programme of projects in Africa, Latin America and South East Asia. To participate in this programme, volunteers need to attend a training weekend in Cardiff. There is an administration fee of £110 for projects abroad, which covers all food and accommodation .

There are longer-term (6-12 month) projects available, mainly in Europe, through the European Voluntary Service (EVS) and Medium Term Volunteer (MTV) programmes.

*Further details* available on the constantly updated website (www.unaexchnage org).

**VOLUNTEERS FOR PEACE (VFP):** 1034, Tiffany Road, Belmont, Vermont 05730, USA (☎802-259-2759; fax 802-259-2922; e-mail vfp@vfp.org; www.vfp.org).
Coordinates **International Workcamps** lasting 2-3 weeks in 100 countries in Western and Eastern Europe, North and West Africa and North, South and Central America. Work includes **construction, environmental, agricultural and social work**. A full listing of VFP's programmes can be found in VFP's *International Workcamp Directory* ($20 post-paid in the USA or online at www.vfp.org).

*For further details* phone, write or e-mail for a free Newsletter.

**YOUTH ACTION FOR PEACE:** Yap UK, POB 43670, London SE22 OXX (☎08701 657 927; e-mail action@yap-uk.org; www.yap-uk.org).
**Volunteers** needed to take part in voluntary work projects (workcamps) organised by YAP in the UK and its sister organisations in 80 countries in Europe, the Americas, Africa and Asia. The work undertaken may consist of tasks such as restoration, entertaining children in need or environmental, social or artistic work. Projects generally last for two to three weeks each, and take place all year round, but mainly in the summer. There are possibilities of longer-term projects (3-12 months)

Participants will usually be working for around 30-35 hours per week with volunteers from different countries and local people; food, accommodation and leisure activities are provided. No particular qualifications are necessary, but applicants must normally be aged at least 18. There is an extra fee (on average US$200) payable on arrival for projects taking place in Africa, Asia and Latin America. Volunteers must organise their own travel.

For further details *check* the above address.

# Work at Sea

**GLOBAL CREW NETWORK:** 23 Old Mill Gardens, Berkhamsted, Hertfordshire, HP4 2NZ (☎ 07773-361959; e-mail info@globalcrewnetwork. com; www.globalcrewnetwork.com).
**Yacht Crew** wanted for tall ships, traditional boats and luxury yachts worldwide. Discounts on membership available for students.

For details see www.globalcrewnetwork or *contact* the above address.

**GOLDEN STAR CRUISES** 85, Akti Miaouli Piraeus 185 38 Greece. (☎(00 30210) 4290650-5; fax (00 30210) 4290660; fax (Vera Devourou) (00 3010) 4290658 e-mail gscruz@goldenstarcruises.com; www.goldenstarcruises.com).
**Wine Stewardesses** to serve in restaurants and lounges (in cruise ships): 10 hours per day, 7 days a week. Wage approximately €400/£280 (plus commission) per month, plus insurance. Free accommodation on board. Requested period: from March to

November for at least 5 months. Pleasant personality and knowledge of one (at least) European language.

**Hostesses** for passengers entertainment (office work, reception etc) Wage €700-€1000 (£490-£700) per month. 10 hours per day, 7 days per week. Requested period from March-November. Excellent knowledge of at least 2 European languages. Pleasant personality and energetic. Knowledge of the Japanese language will be an advantage.

*Applications* from December to the above address, attn. Mrs Devourou,

**P&O CRUISES:** Richmond House, Terminus Terrace, Southampton, SO14 3PN, UK (☎023-8065 7030).

**Port Presenters** are required to promote shore excursions in the Caribbean and Americas. Work periods spent on board will be extensive.

*Applications* should be made by CV and covering letter to Martin Young at the above address.

**OPENWIDE INTERNATIONAL LTD:** 24/26 Arcadia Avenue, Finchley Central, London N3 2JU; (☎020-8349 7194; e-mail contact@openwideinternational.com; www.r1solutions.co.uk). Europe's largest entertainment consultancy and the leaders on providing innovative entertainment to the leisure and tourism industry. Working with Openwide is an excellent way to develop professional and creative skills as an entertainer; over 150 people are recruited annually to work on cruise ships.

**Cruise Staff Entertainers and Performers** to work on ships in the Mediterranean and Caribbean.

**Dancers, Vocalists, Presenters, DJs and Children's Entertainers** required to deliver daytime and evening entertainment programmes.

Excellent PR skills essential; knowledge of a Scandinavian language desirable. Salaries from £200+ per week plus meals, accommodation and flight. Full training given. Positions are available all year round. Contracts approx. 6 months.

All *applicants* are invited to send a CV and photographs to the Recruitment Department at Openwide International and also to visit their website: auditions held all year round.

# Au Pairs, Nannies, Family Helps & Exchanges

**A-ONE AU-PAIRS and NANNIES:** Court Lodge House, 9 Rookes Lane, Lymington, Hants., SO41 8FP (☎01264-332500; fax 01264-362050; e-mail info@aupairsetc. co.uk; www.aupairsetc.co.uk).

**Au Pairs/Au Pairs Plus** required for light housework and childcare 5 days per week. Wages, board and accommodation vary according to hours worked. Places available throughout Europe and America. Applicants should be 18-27 years old.

Contact Karen Hopwood, Proprietor, for details.

**ACADEMY AU PAIR & NANNY AGENCY:** 42 Milsted Road, Rainham, Kent ME8 6SU; (tel/fax 01634-310808; e-mail enquiries@aupair-select.com; www.aupair-select.com).

**Au Pairs** to work 30 hours a week. Salary £45 per week.

**Mother's Helps** Salary £120+ per week.
**Nannies** salary £200+ per week.

Applicants are placed in the following countries: England, France, Germany, Spain, Italy, The Netherlands, Belgium, Austria, Switzerland, Canada and Australia and occasionally other countries. Period of work varies from country to country but is usually 6 months and 2-3 months during the summer. Applicants must have childcare experience and be aged between 18 and 28.

For more information about agency fees and details contact the above address.

**CHILDCARE INTERNATIONAL:** Childcare International Ltd., Trafalgar House, Grenville Place, London NW7 3SA (☎020-8906 3116; fax 020-8906 3461; e-mail office@childint.co.uk; www.childint.co.uk).

Childcare Europe, Childcare Canada, Childcare South Africa, and Childcare Australia offer **au pair/au pair plus, mother's help** and **nanny positions** with associate agencies overseas: provides the opportunity to live abroad in a secure family environment caring for children and helping in the home. Opportunities to learn a language and experience different cultures through both study and everyday life. Salary provided according to age and experience. Full support available from a local representative to assist with language course and meeting friends. Placements in Canada require a one year minimum stay; applicants must have a nanny qualification and/or good childcare experience.

*Applications* to the above address.

**CLUB AVENTURE – AVENTURES JEUNESSE:** 757 Mont-Royal Est, Montreal, Quebec, H2J 1W8, Canada (☎+1-877 527 0999 or 514-527 0999; fax +1 514-527 3999; e-mail info@aventuresjeunesse.com; www.aventuresjeunesse.com)

In business since 1976, Club Aventure arranges International Work and Travel abroad programmes including au pair placements in Denmark, Iceland, the Netherlands and France. Minimum stay is 2-3 months and minimum age is 18. Applicants must be Canadian citizens, have completed secondary education, have a basic knowledge of English or the language of the country and have recent childcare references.

Applications to the above address.

**INTER-SEJOURS:** 179 Rue de Courcelles, F-75017 Paris, France (☎33 1-47 63 06 81; e-mail aideinfo.intersejours@wanadoo.fr; http://asso.intersejours.free.fr). Inter-Sejours is a non-profit making organisation with 37 years of experience. An immediate start is possible.

**Au Pairs** placed in Australia, Austria, Canada, Denmark, France, Germany, Ireland, Italy, the Netherlands, New Zealand, Spain, Sweden the USA and the UK. Working hours 15 to 30 hours a week depending on country. Pocket money minimum €300 per month. Some summer stays of 2-3 months available, but normal minimum stay 6-9 months; applicants who can stay for the whole school year preferred. Applicants should be aged 18-30; previous childcare experience an advantage.

**Paying Guest** stays also arranged with lessons and activities, around the year. Inter-Sejours also organise work placements in hotels and restaurants throughout England, Spain and internships in Ireland, and also strawberry picking in Denmark, and language and humanitarian work programmes in the USA, India, Sri Lanka, South Africa, Nepal and Tibet with linguistic stays in Costa Rica, Guatemala Peru, Bolivia, and Ecuador.

For *further details* contact the above address

**NEILSON:** Locksview, Brighton Marina, Brighton, East Sussex BN2 5HA (☎0870-2412901 fax 0870-9099089; www.neilson.com/recruitment; e-mail recruitment@

neilson.com). Neilson is a holiday company committed to providing excellent quality activity holidays. They pride themselves on having a high staff/client ratio and the exceptional calibre of their overseas staff.

**Child Minders** (30) (NNEB, BTEC or equivalent preferred) to care for 0-5 year olds in the resorts. Summer and winter (ski) work is available. Working 6 days a week. Pay from £95 per week. Flights paid to and from resort, accommodation, insurance and uniform provided. Applicants should be at least 18 years old with experience of working with children, a sense of fun, and be creative team players.

*Contact* The Overseas Recruitment Team, at the above address or on recruitment@ neilson.com.

**SOLIHULL AU PAIR & NANNY AGENCY:** 5 Parklands, Blossomfield Road, Solihull B91 1NG (☎07973 886979; fax 0121-2339731; e-mail aupairs1@btconnect. com; www.au-pairs4u.com.

Based in Birmingham, Lorraine regularly travels to London and can arrange interviews all over the UK and in Ireland. Established some 40 years, Lorraine uses her vast experience to place au pairs.

**Au Pairs**. Pocket money £180-£240 per month placed in major European countries:- France, Italy, Spain are the most popular countries and pocket money is paid in Euros. Mainly working with overseas contacts to locate excellent host families.

**AuPairCare**. Round-trip airfare from your home country to the USA. 5 day/4 night training session in a Central New York Hotel. Medical insurance provided plus private room and full board with carefully screened host family. A weekly stipend of $139-$200 per week is paid; the higher amount is for those who have a recognised childcare qualification. A local Area Director lives nearby and regular social and cultural activities are arranged with other au pairs. You will receive $500 (£278) towards your education as you are required to study in the USA. You will also receive two weeks paid vacation. There is a 24-hour telephone helpline. Opportunity to travel in the 13th month. Comprehensive training and support.

The agency will deal with all visa requirements, tickets and arrange the interview and paperwork. For this American programme, you must be aged 18 - 26 and be able to drive, have a good knowledge of English and be able to commit to a 12-month stay.

Contact www.aupairs2usa.com and fill in the online pre-application form.

**THE CHILDCARE COMPANY:** Emberton House, 26 Shakespeare Road, Bedford MK40 2ED (☎0845 458 1550/1; www.thechildcarecompany.co.uk).

The Childcare Company is a leading childcare recruitment agency, which was established in 1980.

**Ski/Summer Resort Nannies** Destinations include France, Corsica, Spain, the Balearics, Turkey, Italy, Sardinia, Greece, Austria and Switzerland. Winter season perks include free skiing lessons, lift pass, and tuition. Summer season perks include free water sports and tuition. All applicants must hold a childcare qualification or one year of full-time experience with children.

**Au Pair and Nanny Programme to the USA** Must be aged 18-26 with a full driving licence. Placements for qualified NNEB, BTEC National Diploma and NVQ level III in childcare to work with young babies. Also placements for unqualified applicants to work with school-age children; good babysitting experience essential.

**Au Pair Programme in Europe** Ideal for UK applicants who would like to improve their language skills and would like to spend time in France, Spain, Italy or Germany; an excellent way to learn something about another culture and become fluent in another language. Good support is available from partner agencies.

All applicants should be aged 18+ with childcare training and qualifications in

childcare and must be available for the whole summer season (or whole winter season if applying for a ski resort job).
*Applications* to the above address.

**TRAVEL ACTIVE:** PO Box 107, N5800 AC Venray, The Netherlands (☎+31 478 551900; fax +31 470 551911; e-mail info@travelactive.nl).
Travel Active is Holland's largest youth exchange organisation, offering **work exchange, au pair** and **high school programmes** on a global scale.
Travel Active also receives students from all over the world on its incoming high school, au pair and work exchange programmes. For these programmes Travel Active also offers its own tailor-made insurance. Youngsters may choose from a variety of work programmes, with or without job placement. Internships are also available. Several programmes combine a language course with a job placement. Travel Active is a member of FIYTO, ALTO, IAEWEP and a founding member of IAPA.
For further details *contact* the above address.

**UK AND OVERSEAS AGENCY LTD:** Vigilant House, 120 Wilton Road, London SW1V 1JZ (☎020-7808 7898; fax 020-7808 7899; e-mail london@nannys.co.uk; www.nannys.co.uk).
Established over thirty-five years ago, the UK and Overseas Agency places live-in, live-out nannies, au pairs, housekeepers and maternity nurses in locations worldwide.
**Nannies, Au Pairs, Mothers' Helps, House Keepers:** offers jobs throughout the UK, Europe and in the Middle East, Australia, Japan, Singapore, as well as many other countries.
All applicants must speak English. The agency employs both experienced and inexperienced staff. The only stipulated requirements are good references and police clearance. Conditions vary, as do hours of work. The minimum period for summer work is three months. The usual period of stay is one year. All positions provide board and lodging free of charge.
Recruitment is ongoing. It will normally take between two and ten weeks to find a suitable overseas placement.
*Apply* through the website: completed applications with photos and references must be sent by post.

# Other Employment Abroad

**ALLIANCE ABROAD GROUP:** 1221 South Mopac Expressway, Suite 250, Austin, TX 78746, USA (☎512-457-8062/1-866-6-ABROAD; fax (413) 460-3502; vnoel@allianceabroad.com; www.allianceabroad.com). Founded in 1992, Alliance Abroad Group, L.P. offers customized internship, work, teach and volunteer programs for students and graduates in and outside of the USA. Opportunities include working in Australia and New Zealand, teaching in China, Argentina and Spain, interning in the USA and volunteering in South America and South Africa. Placements include North, Central and South America, Europe, Asia and Oceania. All programs included guaranteed placement, visa assistance, orientation materials, health and travel insurance, 24/7 emergency support, personal in-country coordinators. For most programs airport pickup, salary/stipend, meals and accommodation are provided.
*Contact* the above address or e-mails for details.

**ANYWORK ANYWHERE**: www.anyworkanywhere.com. This organisation provides a free source of information to people looking for work throughout the UK and worldwide via their web site.

**Tour Guides, Overland Drivers, Ski / Board Instructors & Guides, Chalet Chefs & Hosts, All levels of Hotel & Pub Staff, Nannies, Barge & Yacht Crew, Care Workers, Teachers, Nurses, Holiday & Theme Park, Campsite and Summer Resort Staff** are amongst the jobs listed as well as a wide and changing variety of many others. Interested candidates can simply contact their chosen advertiser and apply direct, with no registration necessary. The site also provides a broad range of other resources for work and travel worldwide.

For further information *consult* www.anyworkanywhere.com.

**BUNAC:** 16 Bowling Green Lane, London EC1R OQH (☎020-7251 3472; fax 020-7251 0215; e-mail enquiries@bunac.org.uk; www.bunac.org).
BUNAC, a non-profit organisation, has enabled over 250,000 Gap Year, full-time students and other young people to work overseas since 1962. BUNAC is a national club and helps members to obtain jobs, work permits and affordable flight packages. There are a great variety of programmes on offer including summer camp counselling in the USA and work and travel programmes to the USA, Canada, China, Australia, New Zealand, Peru, South Africa, Ghana, Costa Rica, Peru and Cambodia.

BUNAC provides help and advice on jobs, accommodation and travel as well as providing back-up services while working and travelling.

For *further information* contact the above address.

**CIEE:** (Council on International Educational Exchange), 3 Copley Place, Third Floor, Boston MA 02116 (1-617-247-0350); fax 1-212-247-2911; e-mail wat@ciee.org; www.ciee.org).
CIEE is a non-profit organisation that, in affiliation with co-operative organisations in North and West Africa, Europe, North America and Japan (30 countries in all), sponsors numerous international exchange opportunities for young people to live, study, train, work and travel in the United States. CIEE's Work and Travel USA Program is designed so that students can become more than tourists, experiencing life in the US firsthand by working alongside US citizens in temporary employment. Students typically work in summer employment that includes jobs in the hospitality industry, food service, theme parks, national parks and numerous other service-oriented businesses. Through the visa arranged by CIEE, a student's work experience can last for up to four months and they can travel around the US for a further month. CIEE's Trainee Program is structured so as to make it

possible for students to find training in their field of study and explore life in the USA with the maximum freedom and at minimum cost. The training enhances professional skills in one's field of endeavour, and allows valuable experience to be gained. Trainees are exposed to American techniques and methodologies, and can improve their expertise to help them achieve their individual career objectives. Cost of participation varies depending on the type and length of program. CIEE's local partner organisations provide a variety of additional services which may included discounted airfares and other options to help make the student's CIEE program fun and affordable.

For more information please contact CIEE at the above address.

**INTEREXCHANGE:** 161 Sixth Avenue, New York, NY 10013, USA (☎212-924-0446; fax 212-924-0575; e-mail info@interexchange.org; www.interexchange.org). Inter-Exchange is a non-profit organisation dedicated to promoting cultural awareness through a wide range of work and travel, language school, volunteer, professional training, internship and au pair programmes within the United States and around the world. In the USA they offer J-1 Visa programs and H-2B Visa programs for Au Pair, Seasonal Work, Internship, Camp Counselor and Staff positions. InterExchange also offers Working Abroad placements for US residents to travel to Australia, Costa Rica, France, Germany, England, India, Italy, Kenya, Mexico, Namibia, the Netherlands, Norway, Peru, South Africa, Spain and Zimbabwe as Au Pairs, Interns, Volunteers, Seasonal Workers, Farm Workers and Language Students. Most InterExchange programmes include placements.

For further details *contact* Inter-Exchange at the above address.

**i-to-i:** 261 Low Lane, Leeds LS18 5NY (☎0870-333 2332, quoting SJ1006; fax 0113-2054619; e-mail info@i-to-i.com; www.i-to-i.com). i-to-i is an award-winning organisation providing worthwhile work and travel opportunities throughout the world.

i-to-i offers around volunteer 500 projects across 23 countries worldwide along with self development programmes and paid work programmes. It also provides onsite and online TEFL (Teaching English as a Foreign Language) training for those who want to combine teaching as part of their travel experience or find work overseas. More than 5,000 volunteers are placed each year. All projects are thoroughly researched and volunteers are met and supported whilst away by in-country coordinators. All prices include pre-departure training (TEFL for teaching placements), comprehensive insurance and 24-hour support from the UK. Food and accommodation are included on most projects and some also offer local language courses on arrival. i-to-i projects are suitable for all ages with special projects available for school students and corporate groups.

**Volunteer projects:** from 1-24 weeks in duration; project types include; **voluntary teaching, conservation, community development, building, sports and media as well as humanitarian tours.** Current projects include a panda conservation project in China, surfing programmes in South Africa, reporting for an English newspaper in Sri Lanka, and teaching English to orphans in India. Accommodation varies from homestays with local families to guesthouses, and apartments. Projects are available all year round from one week to a complete year out.

**Paid work overseas:** i-to-i also provides paid teaching placements across the globe and working holiday programmes in Australia.

**TEFL Training:** i-to-i offers a range of TEFL courses including intensive weekend

TEFL courses in the UK, the US, Ireland and Australia. Fees start from £195. An online TEFL course is also available at www.onlineTEFL.com allowing study from any location worldwide. Further courses add practical training with teaching practice sessions overseas. All courses are designed for travellers and include a module on finding work abroad. i-to-i also offers a database of more than 8,000 job contacts for TEFL tutees.

For further details contact the above address quoting SJ1006.

**OVERSEAS WORKING HOLIDAYS:** Level 1, Fife Road, Kingston, Surrey, KT1 1SF (0845 344 0366; fax 0870 460 4578; e-mail info@owh.co.uk; www.owh.co.uk) Working holidays in various countries. **Summer resort work** in Canada and France and paid **English teaching placements** in Thailand, China, Poland and Korea.

Placements are for gap years or shorter placements. All jobs, visas and accommodation are arranged. Programme fees are from £299 to £599. Also available: **African Experience Volunteer** placements. Job interviews for all programmes are carried out pre-departure.

*Applications* through the website above or telephone 0845-344 0366.

**SEASONWORKERS.COM:** Houdini Media Ltd, PO BOX 29132, Dunfermline, KY11 4YU; (☎/fax 01383-723344; e-mail info@seasonworkers.com; www. seasonworkers.com). Season Workers is a website that lists hundreds of **rep, ski, outdoor, education, TEFL and childcare jobs** and **gap year opportunities.** Season Workers has won various awards including Best Recruitment website at the 2004 Travel and Tourism Web Awards in London.

You can use Season Workers to thoroughly research every avenue and apply online for information packs on hundreds of different summer jobs. Whatever your age, experience or aspirations there will be a summer job on SeasonWorkers for you. The site also includes a vibrant messageboard for help and chat about summer jobs, and when you return, and have lost contact with all the people you met, the 'Season Workers Reunion' service helps get you reunited.

Go to www.seasonworkers.com and get started.

**TRAVEL ACTIVE:** PO Box 107, N-5800 AC Venray, The Netherlands (☎+31-478 551900; fax +31-478 551911; e-mail info@travelactive.nl; www.travelactive. nl). Travel Active is Holland's largest youth exchange organisation, offering work exchange, au pair and high school programmes on a global scale.

Travel Active also receives students from all over the world on its incoming high school, au pair and work exchange programmes. For these programmes Travel Active also offers its own, tailor-made insurance. Dutch and Belgian youngsters may choose from a variety of work programmes, with or without job placement. Internships are also available. Several programmes combine a language course with a job placement. Travel Active is member of FIYTO, ALTO, IAEWEP and a founding member of IAPA.

For *further details* contact the above address.

**WWW.VOOVS.COM:** 26 Vine Close, Welwyn Garden City, Hertfordshire AL8 7PS (☎01707-396511; e-mail info@voovs.com). A seasonal recruitment website offering the following positions.
**Summer jobs:** beach resort/camping/activity/lakes and mountains/barges/flotilla jobs from April to October. Vacancies for instructors, nannies, couriers, chefs, bar and hotel staff etc. Wages start at £50 per week, with accommodation and transport provided. To work a 6-day week usually.
**Cruise ships and yachts:** cruise ship/yachting jobs available around the year. Varied

contracts. Wages from £500 a month.

**Ski resort & winter jobs:** ski resort jobs including work in chalets, hotels and bars, ski and snowboard hire retail shops, ski technicians ski instructors as reps, ski guides, nannies, resort admin, accounts, sales, resort and area managers. Wages start at £50 per week; ski pass, transport to resort and accommodation/food provided. To work a six-day week.

**Gap year:** gap year job ideas for around the globe. Voluntary to TEFL, ski and snowboard instructor courses and useful information and links on gap year activities.

**Hospitality and leisure:** other jobs on offer include: hotel, restaurant and bar work, theme park jobs, TEFL and fruit picking.

Most positions applicants must be aged over 18. Positions available in UK & Ireland, across Europe and around the globe.

*For further details* see www.voovs.com.

**WORK & TRAVEL COMPANY:** 45 High Street, Tunbridge Wells, Kent, TN11XL; (☎01892-516164 fax 0189231-523172; e-mail info@worktravelcompany.co.uk; www.realgap.co.uk). Work and Travel Company offers opportunities for people taking time out of working and studying to travel and work around the world. They provide visas, information before you leave, services such as meet and greet, and accommodation on arrival, help with finding a job, or a training placement, health, accident and baggage insurance, discounts, and many other services on the ground at your destination. Areas covered are Australia, United States of America, New Zealand, Southern Africa and Central and South America.

Costs of programmes vary e.g. £99 for a working holiday visa in Australia and £1319 for a month working at an animal rescue centre in Costa Rica.

Further details and *application* on the website above.

# Organisations with Vacancies Across Europe

## General

**JOBCENTRE PLUS:** International Jobsearch Advice, Jobcentre Plus Regional Office, 6<sup>th</sup> Floor, Whitehall II, Whitehall Quay, Leeds LS1 4HR; (☎0113 307 8090; fax 0113 3078213; e-mail international-jobsearch-advice@jobcentreplus.gsi.gov.uk; www.jobcentreplus.gov.uk).
Jobcentre Plus handles vacancies for work in the UK and overseas, which can be accessed through the job search facility on the Jobcentre Plus website or via touchpoint screens called Jobpoints, available in all Jobcentre Plus offices and Jobcentres, or by calling Jobseeker Direct on 0845 6060234. Jobcentre Plus also publishes a series of fact sheets for each of the EEA countries (see Useful Publications).

*EURES Website (www.eures-jobs.com):* as part of the European Employment Services (EURES) network, Jobcentre Plus receives new jobs from Europe on a daily basis. To find out more about the EURES network and to get information about living and working in EEA countries visit the EURES job mobility portal www.europa.eu.int/eures. This site has a job bank of vacancies based in Europe and a facility to post CVs so that employers throughout Europe may view them.

## Boats

**EUROPEAN WATERWAYS:** 35 Wharf Road, Wraysbury, Staines, Middlesex TW19 5JQ (fax 01784-483072; e-mail accounts@GoBarging.com; www.GoBarging.com). Owners and operators of luxury hotel barges cruising rivers and canals in England, Scotland and France.
**Cordon Bleu Chefs** Wages £1,000-£1,200 per month. Must have training to Cordon Bleu standard, hold a driving licence and be at least 25 years old.
**Deckhand Mechanics** £750 per month. Must have a driving licence, some mechanical experience and be at least 25 years old.
**Tour Guides** £750 per month. Full clean, driving licence required, an interest in culture and history and some experience in hospitality also necessary.
**Stewards/Stewardesses** £650 per month. Duties include cleaning, ironing, waitressing. Must be hard working and have some experience in hospitality.
A knowledge of French is essential for all positions in France. Period of work is from April to October. All positions include on-board accommodation, meals and uniform.
Apply sending a CV and photo to the above address or e-mail.

# Hotel Work and Catering

**CHOICE HOTELS EUROPE:** 112 Station Road, Edgware, HA8 7BJ (☎020-8233 2001; fax 020-8233 2080; e-mail careers@choicehotelseurope.com). Owns, manages and franchises over 500 hotels in 13 European countries. Positions are primarily for the UK and Ireland, but guidance and advice can be given for other countries. **Receptionists, Chefs, Waiter/Waitresses, Bar Persons.** Minimum period of work 6 months, 1 year in front office. 39 hours per week spread over 5 days. Salary in accordance with minimum wages regulations. Applications are considered all year round. Applicants should have a smart appearance, pleasant customer oriented personality and be over 18 years old. Priority given to those with hotel qualifications and/or experience and good English (fluent for front office) additional language skills an advantage.

*Applications* via the above website.

**OPENWIDE INTERNATIONAL LTD.:** 4/26 Arcadia Avenue, Finchley Central, London N3 2JU; (☎020-8349 7194; e-mail contact@openwideinternational.com; www.r1solutions.co.uk). Openwide International is Europe's largest independent supplier of entertainers and all-round personalities to the mainstream leisure and tourism industry. Working with Openwide is an excellent way to develop professional skills and over 100 people are recruited annually to work in hotels. **Entertainers** with bright, enthusiastic personalities and excellent PR and communication skills to work in hotels in Spain, Cyprus, Greece, Balearics, Turkey and the Canaries. A knowledge of Spanish, German or French would be an advantage but not essential. All successful applicants will be given full training on the running of daytime and evening entertainment programmes.

Positions are available all year round; minimum period of work 6 months with salaries between £130 and £225 per week plus meals, accommodation and flight. Main season is May to November.

All applicants are invited to send CVs and *applications* to the Overseas Recruitment Department at Openwide International and also visit their website.

**SCOTT DUNN:** Fovant Mews, 12 Noyna Rd, London, SW17 7PH (☎020-8682 5005; fax 020-8682 5090; e-mail recruitment@scottdunn.com). A small, very professional company, which provides beautiful villas and chalets in stunning locations all over Europe. From their teams Scott Dunn expect an attitude of, 'nothing is too much trouble'. Doing a season for Scott Dunn is definitely hard work but also incredibly good fun, and they offer a competitive package to the right applicants. **Resort Managers** (12): required to run all aspects of the resort operations. Applicants must have previous management and hospitality experience, as well as fluency in the local language (Spanish and Portuguese for summer positions, French and German for winter positions). **Chalet and Villa Chefs/Cooks** (33) required to plan the menu and cook to a very high standard for the clients in their exclusive villas and chalets. Applicants must have completed a six month cooking course, or have extensive experience and flair. Must be organised and outgoing. **Chalet and Villa Hosts** (35) required to assist the chef, look after the guests and maintain a high level of service. No formal qualifications necessary, although hospitality experience is essential. Applicants must be outgoing, organised and have excellent customer service skills.

**CAMPING LIFE**

France
Spain
Italy
Austria
Germany
Switzerland
Luxembourg
Holland
Croatia

# Come and join our team!

Do you have customer service experience? We are looking for hardworking, enthusiastic, flexible, level-headed individuals to join our team this summer..

- positions at over 100 campsites across Europe
- supervisory, childcare, courier jobs and jobs for couples available
- opportunities available from March – October (2 months minimum term contract)
- competitive salary + travel to site + accommodation provided

To apply, complete an on-line application form at

## www.gvnrecruitment.com

Alternatively, call the Overseas Recruitment Department

☏ 01383 629012

**Nannies** (20) Required to care for the younger guests. Must have a recognised childcare qualification, at least one year's childcare experience and be organised, confident and outgoing.

**Beauty Therapists** (5): required to provide mobile beauty services to guests. Applicants must have a recognised qualification, at least one year's experience and be organised, flexible and be pro-active.

**Drivers / Maintenance People** (15): available in winter only. Required to transport people and goods within resort, to manage and maintain all Scott Dunn properties and equipment, and to carry out any repairs or maintenance as and when necessary. Applicants must be flexible and have a practical mind. Previous hospitality experience is desirable.

Board and accommodation are provided free of charge. Package and hours to be discussed at interview. Work is available during the winter and summer season. Knowledge of French, Spanish, Italian or Portuguese useful, but not mandatory.

For summer positions *apply* in January, or for winter positions apply from June.

# Industrial and Office Work

**THE AMERICAN SCANDINAVIAN FOUNDATION (ASF):** Scandinavia House, 58 Park Avenue, New York, NY 10016, USA (☎212-879-9779; fax 212-249-3444; e-mail trainscan@amscan.org; www.amscan.org). A non-profit organisation set up in 1910 to promote educational and cultural exchange between the USA and Denmark, Finland, Iceland, Norway and Sweden. Through the ASF reciprocal training programme young Americans aged over 21 are able to live and work in Scandinavia on a temporary basis.

ASF offers short-term training placements to American students and recent graduates. Recent fields for placement have been: hospital management, chemical engineering, forestry ecology, wildlife fieldwork, construction engineering, and marketing. An income is provided. Knowledge of a Scandinavian language is not required. Trainees are expected to cover the cost of a round-trip airfare and have medical insurance. There are also positions Teaching English in Finland during the Academic Year. If an American is able to arrange a job outside the ASF scheme, ASF offers help with arranging work permits. All that is required is written confirmation from the training firm specifying the dates of training, the income, type of work and the name of the training supervisor. A non-returnable application fee of $50 (£33 approx.) is charged but this includes a one-year membership of the foundation.

Those interested should *contact* ASF at the above address.

**CELTIC WELCOMES LTD**: Eglinton Chambers,21 Wellington Square, Ayr, Scotland, KA7 1HD (☎ 01292-885656; fax: 01292-885757; e-mail diana@ celticwelcomes.com; www.celticwelcomes.com). Celtic Welcomes is a tour wholesaler and incoming tours agency specialising in tours throughout Great Britain and Ireland, also running outbound Tours to Europe. Clients are located all over the world.

**Marketing Trainees**: required for marketing tours to clients worldwide. Must have good English, both spoken and written. Must have university or college degree with language and/or tourism content. Wages on application.

**Admin Trainees**: required for tour reservations and general administration. Must have good English, both spoken and written. Must have university or college degree with language and/or tourism content. Wages on application.

**Sales Trainees**: required for the sales of tours to clients worldwide. Must have good English, both spoken and written. Must have university or college degree with language and/or tourism content. Wages on application.

**Reservations Trainees**: required for administering to clients worldwide. Must have good English, both spoken and written. Must have university or college degree with language and/or tourism content. Wages on application.

Working hours are flexible up to a maximum of 37.5 hours, 5 days per week. Minimum period of work is 3 months. Board and accommodation are provided as part of package. Knowledge of English plus another EU language is essential.

*Apply* at any time.

# Sports, Couriers and Camping

**ACORN ADVENTURE:** Acorn House, Prospect Road, Halesowen. Birmingham B62 8DU. (☎0121-504 2066; fax 0121-504 2059; e-mail chris.lloyd@acornadventure. co.uk; www.jobs-acorn.co.uk). Adventure Activity Holiday company offering groups multi-activity camping holidays in North Wales, the Lake District, Spain and Italy as well as France.

**Instructors, Village Managers, Catering Supervisor, Catering Assistant.** 300 seasonal staff needed mid-April to September (some shorter contracts). Activities include sailing, canoeing, kayaking, climbing, abseiling and caving. Excellent rates of pay, plus supplement/bonus subject to centre and position. All positions are available in the UK, France and Italy. Instructor and village representative positions also available in Spain.

*Applications* by post should be marked for the attention of Recruitment and a full information pack will be sent to you, or *apply* online.

**ALAN ROGERS GUIDES LTD**: Spelmonden Old Oast, Spelmonden Road, Goudhurst, Kent TN17 1HE (☎01580-214000; e-mail contact@alanrogers.com). Alan Rogers Guides are the UK's leading guides to campsites throughout the UK and Europe.

**Campsite Inspectors** required for periods during May to September. Must have a thorough knowledge and experience of camping and or caravanning in Europe. Must have own caravan or motorhome. An inspection fee and expenses are paid.

*Applications* should be made to the Campsites Director at the above address.

**AMERICAN COUNCIL FOR INTERNATIONAL STUDIES (ACIS):** AIFS (UK), 38 Queen's Gate, London SW7 5HR (☎020-7590 7474; fax 020-7590 7475; e-mail tm_dept@acis.com; www.acis.com). ACIS has been offering quality educational travel for over 20 years. Tour managers are vital to the success of the company, and are given unequalled training and support.

**Tour Managers (100)** to lead American high school teachers and students on educational trips through Europe. The length of trips varies from 9-15 days and may visit one or several countries. All trip details and itineraries are pre-arranged. Busiest periods are March/April and June/July. Tour Managers for both short and long periods are needed; minimum is 10 days. Tour Managers meet groups on arrival, travel with them, act as commentators and guides, keep accounts, direct bus drivers, troubleshoot etc. Fluency in French, Italian, German or Spanish is essential for trips outside the UK and Ireland. Applicants must be over 21, and either have or be studying for a

university degree. Daily salary, accommodation provided with the groups in 3/4-star hotels, generous tips, insurance and back-up provided.
*Apply online* via the website where there is an application form.

**BOMBARD BALLOON ADVENTURES:** Château de Laborde, Laborde Au Château 21200 Beaune, France. (www.bombardsociety.org/jobs). Since 1977, Bombard Balloon Adventures has provided complete luxury travel programmes built around hot-air ballooning. During the summer season (May-Oct), the team travels to France, Tuscany, Switzerland, Austria, and the Czech Republic; and to the Swiss Alps in winter (Jan-Feb).
**Ground Crew (15)** to assist in preparation and packing of ballooning equipment, driving, and general household chores. Complete job description is on www.bombardsociety.org/jobs. Requires a clean driving licence, excellent physical fitness, a cheerful personality, responsible driving skills, the ability to live with others, and a neat, clean-cut appearance. Language skills are a plus but not a requirement. Period of work by arrangement.
*Applicants* should send a CV including height, weight, and nationality; a scanned ID photo and copy of driving licence; and dates of availability to Michael Lincicome by e-mail (preferred) at jobs2007@bombardsociety.org or to the address above.

**CAMPING LIFE:** GVN Camping Recruitment, East Port House, Dunfermline, KY12 7JG (☎01383-629012; fax 01383-629071; e-mail campingrecruitment@gvnrecruitment.com; www.gvnrecruitment.com). Camping Life provide good value mobile home and tent holidays at large family campsites in France, Spain and Italy.
**Campsite Courier.** Involves cleaning accommodation, welcoming families to the site and showing them to their accommodation. Visiting customers, providing local information and basic maintenance are very important parts of the job. Campsite Courier opportunities are also available for couples to work on site together. Senior courier positions available. For more details see website.
**Children's Courier.** Camping Life has its own full-time Children's Club which is open from May to the beginning of September. Couriers plan and deliver an exciting and fun-packed programme of varied activities for children aged 4 to 12. Must be enthusiastic, energetic, and have good communication skills. A tent is provided as a Club venue and for equipment storage. Children's couriers also help out with campsite duties as needed.
Package includes competitive salary, tent accommodation, medical insurance, uniform and return travel from a UK port of entry. Full season positions start in March, April or May and end in September/October. High season staff needed to work at least two months during the peak season.
*Please call* the Recruitment Department for more information and an application form, or *apply online* at www.gvnrecruitment.com.

**CANVAS HOLIDAYS:** GVN Camping Recruitment, East Port House, Dunfermline, KY12 7JG (☎01383-629012; fax 01383-629071; e-mail campingrecruitment@gvnrecruitment.com; www.gvnrecruitment.com). Canvas Holidays provide luxury mobile home and tent holidays at over 100 campsites.throughout Europe.
**Campsite Courier.** Involves cleaning accommodation, welcoming families to the site and showing them to their accommodation. Visiting customers, providing local information and basic maintenance are very important parts of the job. Campsite Courier Opportunities are also available for couples to work on site together. For details of management positions, see website.
**Children's Courier.** Needed to work at Hoopi's Club. Applicants must have formal

experience of working with children. Children's couriers should be energetic, enthusiastic and have good communication skills. A tent is provided as a Club venue and for equipment storage; this has to be kept safe, clean and tidy. Visiting new arrivals on site is an important and fun part of the job. Children's couriers also help with other campsite duties as needed. Visit recruitment website for information about working with teenagers (Buzz Courier) and wildlife and the environment (Wild & Active Courier).

Package includes competitive salary, tent accommodation, medical insurance, uniform and return travel from a UK port of entry. Full season positions start in March, April or May and end in September/October. High season staff needed to work at least two months during the peak season.

*Please call* the Recruitment Department for more information and an application form, or *apply online* at www.gvnrecruitment.com.

**CASTERBRIDGE TOURS LTD:** Salcombe House, Long Street, Sherborne, Dorset DT9 3BU (☎01935-810810; fax 01935-815815; e-mail sales@casterbridge-tours. co.uk). Casterbridge operate customised Group Tours throughout Britain and Europe. They have three specialist divisions: Student Educational Study Tours; Concert Tours for Performing Choirs, Orchestras and Bands; Adult Special Interest Tours.
**Tour Managers/Guides** to escort groups in Europe. Wages from £280 per week, with board and lodging provided. To work all hours necessary, seven days per week. Period of work by arrangement between March and June. Applicants are expected to attend a training course; knowledge of languages useful.

*Applications* to the above address.

**CLUB CANTABRICA HOLIDAYS LTD:** 146/148 London Road, St. Albans, Herts AL1 1PQ (☎01727-866-177; fax 01727-843766; recruitment@cantabrica.co.uk; www.cantabrica.co.uk). Club Cantabrica is an independent tour operator with 30 years of experience. Offering luxury coach, air and self-drive holidays on excellent sites in France (including the French Alps). Italy and Spain. Opportunities also available for their ski programme in the Austrian Tyrol and the French Alps.
**Resort Manager (12)** to manage sites varying in size from 25-100 units. Must have previous campsite rep. experience and French, Italian or Spanish language skills. Wages between £200 and £220 per week, including bonus and commission.
**Campsite Couriers (30)** to work on camp sites in France, Italy, and Spain. Work involves looking after clients, setting up and closing down site, tent and mobile home cleaning and maintenance, paperwork and excursion sales. Wages £100 per week plus commission, including bonus.
**Peak Season Courier (15)** to cover same tasks as couriers but for June-September only. Minimum period of work 3 months. Wages £100 per week. Including bonus.
**Children's' Courier (11)** to run Kids' Club on campsites, must have experience of working with children and relevant qualification. Wages £100 per week plus commission and bonus.
**Maintenance Staff (11)** to carry out maintenance and upkeep work on tents and mobile homes. Applicants should have excellent practical skills. Wages £95-£125 per week.
**Hotel Staff (8)** including **General Duties Rep.** and **Chef** to help run the Club Hotel in Chamonix Valley - fluent French required.

Free accommodation provided. To work approximately 40 hours per 6 day week, from April to October, except Peak Season staff. Couriers should be enthusiastic and have plenty of stamina, with knowledge of languages an advantage. Applicants should be over 18 years old (over 21 for managers). Experience preferable.

*Applications* with curriculum vitae to the above address (please specify winter or summer); applicants can also e-mail recruitment@cantabrica.co.uk. Or visit www. cantabrica.co.uk

**CLUB EUROPE HOLIDAYS LTD**: Fairway House, 53 Dartmouth Road, London SE23 3HN (☎020-8699 7788; fax 020-8699 7770; e-mail kim.s@club-europe.co.uk; www.club-europe.co.uk).

Club Europe Holidays employs Concert Tour Managers on a freelance basis, to accompany school and youth ensembles on tour in Europe. The nature of their business means that most of the work is on offer during the spring and summer school holidays, making the positions ideal for students and teachers.

**Concert Tour Manager** Duties include reconfirming booked excursions and concerts; and introducing the group at the venues; iinterpreting and communicating the client's needs with the accommodation and local agents; coordinating any minor alterations to the itinerary with the coach drivers and accompanying the group at all times including all concerts and excursions. We are looking for friendly confident staff with excellent organisational and communication skills. Applicants should be fluent in English and at least one other European language. Tours are to France, Germany, Italy, Austria, Spain, Holland and Belgium.

Tour length varies from 3-8 days; pay increases with experience but starts at £55 per day. Tour Managers are provided with the same board and accommodation as the client.

*Applications* invited from 1ˢᵗ January.

**CONCEPT HOLIDAYS**: 56 Landsdowne Place, Hove East Sussex BN3 1FG (☎0870 241 0427; fax: 0870 036 0500; e-mail info@conceptholidays.co.uk www. conceptholidays.co.uk). Concept Holidays specialise in small, friendly and affordable active beach club holidays in Greece, Spain and Croatia.

**Windsurfing/Sailing Instructor** (up to 20 at a time) required for Concept's water sports centres in Greece and Croatia. The ideal candidate should be RYA sailing qualified and/or windsurf instructor qualified and be able to use initiative as well as being a good team player. Sound knowledge of boat and engine maintenance is an advantage. Wages from £100 per week depending on experience.

Staff get return flights, transfers to and from resort, shared, self-catering accommodation, (half-board in Croatia), full use of watersports centre equipment, uniform, competitive salary and the opportunity to be involved in all aspects of running a centre and resort representative activities. Hours of work are variable; staff work 6 days a week for a minimum period of 6 weeks between May and October.

*Applications* to the above e-mail address.

**CRYSTAL FINEST**: King's Place, 12-42 Wood Street, Kingston-Upon-Thames, Surrey, KT1 1JY (0845-0550251; e-mail ski.jobs@crystalfinest.co.uk; www. crystalfinest.co.uk). Crystal Finest is part of TUI UK, one of the top specialist tour operators in the UK. They offer a selection of luxury catered chalet and hotel holidays on their winter ski programme in the World's Premier Ski Resorts.

**Resort Representatives**: November-April. All employees must have at least 10 weeks of snow experience, hold a clean driving licence and ideally speak a second EU language. Crystal Finest Representatives need to be independent and have a thorough understanding of customer requirements. Previous management experience is desirable. Crystal Finest recruits Resort Representatives, Chalet Chefs, Cooking Chalet Hosts, Chalet Assistants, Nannies, Drivers and Massage Therapists for the winter ski season.

Applications to Crystal Finest on the above e-mail address.

**EQUITY TRAVEL:** 1 Jubilee Street, Brighton, East Sussex, BN1 1AL (☎+44 (0)1273-886911; fax +44 (0)1273-203212; e-mail recruitment@equity.co.uk; www. equityski.co.uk/employment). Equity Travel is a direct sell tour operator, organising educational tours, sports tours, ski holidays and weekend breaks with the emphasis on customer service, quality and value for money. Equity Travel require staff of all levels to work overseas including hotel managers, chefs, ski reps and tour reps. Please visit website for more information.

**Representatives** to work with school groups on cookery, language or sports tours in France, Germany, Italy and Spain. Reps have a briefing at the Brighton office before travelling and a day in resort to set up prior to the group's arrival. Duties include liaising between the group, hotelier and coach driver; organisation of pre-booked, course-related excursions and interviews; translating during demonstrations and helping pupils with course-related work. Wages of £30 per day, plus full board, accommodation, travel expenses, insurance and uniform. Positions are available for periods varying from two days to one week between February and October. Minimum age 21. Applicants must be fluent in French, German, Italian or Spanish, well organised and able to work on their own initiative. They must be able to relate to children and will ideally have some experience of working with school groups or in a public service industry. A driving licence is required for most tours.

Equity Ski also require reps for peak season Ski weeks throughout the winter.

*Apply* with a CV and a covering letter to Carrie Husband at the above address.

**ESPRIT HOLIDAYS LTD:** 185 Fleet Road, Fleet, Hants GU51 3BL (☎01252-618318; fax 01252-618328; e-mail recruitment@esprit-holidays.co.uk; www.esprit-holidays.co.uk)   Esprit Alpine Sun run Alpine holidays (France, Italy and Austria) for families in catered chalets and hotels and provide childcare in nurseries and Alpine adventure clubs for children aged 4 months to 15 years old. Staff need friendly and out-going personalities and previous experience to run Chalet Hotels and Chalets. Dedicated, fun-loving and enthusiastic nannies also needed to run Esprit Nurseries and Alpies Club.

**Hotel/Resort Manager:**. Age 25+, with good command of spoken French or German., hospitality and customer service experience. Management and supervisory skills. Full clean driving licence.

**Nannies:** aged 18+, DCE NNEB, NVQ3, BTEC or NVQ level 3. Required to take care of babies and toddlers in Esprit's nurseries.

**Alpies Rangers:** age 21+ with experience as play scheme leaders, children's sports coaches or as a trained teacher. Required to run adventure activity clubs. Should have a mature, fun loving personality.

All staff must be EU passport holders available from mid-June to mid-September. Ideal for anyone who has an interest in alpine activities, i.e. mountain walking and biking, white water rafting etc.

All staff assist with chalet cleaning, babysitting and hosting guests. Weekly wage, with food and accommodation, uniform, swimming pool pass and transport provided.

Further *information* can be obtained regarding vacancies on their website: www. esprit-holidays.co.uk.

**EUROCAMP:** Overseas Recruitment Department (Ref SJ/07) (☎01606-787525; www.holidaybreakjobs.com. Eurocamp is a leading tour operator in quality self-drive camping and mobile home holidays in Europe. Each year the company seeks to recruit up to 1,500 enthusiastic people for the following positions:

**Campsite Courier:** job involves cleaning and preparing customer accommodation, providing assistance, acting as an information service and performing some administrative duties. Couriers need to be flexible to meet the needs of the customer to provide them with excellent service. Minimum age 18 years. Applicants should be independent with plenty of initiative and relish a challenging and rewarding position. They should also possess a friendly and helpful personality. Previous customer service experience would be an advantage. Applicants should be available to work from April/May to September.

**Children's Courier:** work involves organising a wide range of exciting activities for children aged 4-13. Applicants should possess initiative, imagination and enthusiasm along with good safety awareness. Previous childcare experience is essential. Minimum age is 18 years and applicants should be available from April/May to September. Languages are not a requirement but would be an advantage (in particular German). Successful candidates will be asked to apply for an Enhanced Disclosure.

**Senior Couriers:** required to work alongside a team of Campsite Couriers and organise their daily workload, as well as carrying out the normal day-to-day duties of a Campsite Courier. Applicants should have experience of leading a team.

**Site Managers:** required to lead a large team of Campsite Couriers, organising their daily workloads and ensuring they provide the very best customer service. Applicants should be 21 or over, have proven managerial experience, excellent communication skills and language ability.

**Montage/Demontage:** for a period of approximately 6-8 weeks at the beginning/end of season to erect/dismantle equipment.

Comprehensive training is provided together with a competitive salary, insurance, return travel and accommodation. Applications are accepted from September/October and *can only be accepted from UK/EU passport holders*. Interviews will be conducted in Hartford, Cheshire between October and April.

Applicants should *apply* on-line at **www.holidaybreakjobs.com** or telephone 01606 787525 for an Application Pack.

**FREEWHEEL HOLIDAYS**: Minster Chambers, Church Street, Southwell, Notts., NG22 0HD (☎+44 01636 815636; fax: +44 01636 813110; e-mail info@ freewheelholidays.com; www.freewheelholidays.com).
Freewheel Holidays is a successful independent tour operator whose guests enjoy cycling through wonderful landscapes in Austria, Belgium, Denmark, France, Spain and Switzerland, experiencing sights, sounds and cultures of different regions (little or no traffic, hills going down not up!) – while their hosts manage the luggage and logistics. Freewheel are looking for mature, outgoing, resourceful people with full driving licence and knowledge of bicycle maintenance to be **Freewheel Hosts**. Hosts provide information and support to guests, meet them at airports and stations, transfer luggage and liaise with hotels. Applicants should be mature, speak proficient German, French or Spanish, possess a full driver's licence and First Aid qualification and have knowledge of bicycle maintenance. Couples welcome to apply; one wage but free accommodation and possibilities for partner to earn additional monies on pro rata basis. Accommodation and training provided. Wages £170 per week.

Work available early July to the end of August, minimum period of work is 4 weeks. Hosts work approximately 30-35 hours per week, approximately 6 days a week (depending on guest numbers). All applicants must speak either native or fluent English as well as another appropriate language.

*Applications* from 1st March.

**HALSBURY TRAVEL:** 35 Churchill Park, Colwick Business Estate, Nottingham NG4 2HF (☎0115-9404 303; fax 0115-9404 304; e-mail rachel@halsbury.com;

www.halsbury.com). Halsbury Travel is an ABTA/ATOL Bonded Tour Operator, specialising in School Group, European and Worldwide Tours. Established in 1986 they are one of the leading UK student group tour operators.

**Group Leaders** (100) Required to work with touring groups in France, Germany or Spain. Wage £165 per week plus accommodation and meals.

**Language Tutors** (20) required to work with touring groups in France, Germany and Spain. £25 per week plus accommodation and meals. (3-4 hours work a day).

**Couriers** (50) required to accompany History, Geography, Art and Business Studies, Sports and Travel, Leisure/Tourism Groups. Wages of £30 per day, plus accommodation and meals.

**Ski Reps** (10). Required to accompany ski groups to French Resorts, liaise with local partners, organise evening activities or assist the groups as required. £165 per week plus accommodation, meals and ski equipment. Discount offered on your ski-pass (please note that it is not a skiing holiday! Applicants should be customer focused).

All applicants should be fluent in the language/or a native of the country they wish to work in. Most positions involve 8-hour days 6 days per week, working for a minimum period of 1 week. Board and accommodation is provided.

*Applications* are invited to the above address in May/June for the winter season, (skiing jobs), and in January or February for jobs in the summer season.

**HOLIDAYBREAK:** Ref SJ/07, Hartford Manor, Greenbank Lane, Northwich, Cheshire, CW8 1HW (☎01606-787525; fax 0870-3667640; www.holidaybreakjobs.com).

**Couriers** to welcome customers, clean customer accommodation, provide local information and deal with any problems. There is also some basic accounting and administration.

**Children's Couriers** to organise a wide range of exciting activities for children aged 4-13. Applicants must have experience of working with groups of children and possess initiative, imagination and enthusiasm along with safety awareness. Successful candidates will be asked to apply for an Enhanced Disclosure from the CRB. (See www.disclosure.gov.uk) for further details.

**Montage/Demontage Assistants** to assist with preparing the campsites and erecting tents at the beginning of the season and also to dismantle tents and store equipment at the end of the season. Must be prepared to work in all weathers. Successful candidates will be asked to apply for an Enhanced Disclosure from the CRB as above.

**Area Assistant** to assist and support the Overseas Manager in both administrative and on site duties. Duties include basic accounts, marketing reports, Health and Safety audits and travel organisation. Other duties would include collecting couriers from the local stations/airports, taking couriers shopping, gathering local information and other Courier duties. Must be aged 21+ with a full clean driving licence.

**Team Leaders:** incorporating the role of campsite courier with the additional responsibility for organising and managing the team and ensuring the smooth running of the site team.

All staff will be provided with accommodation, return travel, training, competitive salary, uniform and subsidised insurance. Must be aged 18+ and an EU passport holder. Interviews are held in Cheshire in the UK.

Applicants should *apply* on-line at **www.holidaybreakjobs.com** or telephone 01606 787525 for an Application Pack.

**INGHAMS TRAVEL:** 10-18 Putney Hill, London SW15 6AX (☎020-8780 4400; fax 020-8780 8805; e-mail travel@inghams.com; www.inghams.co.uk). Inghams Travel is the largest independent operator of lakes and mountains holidays in the UK with an excellent reputation built up over the last 70 years; they offer quality lakes and

mountains holidays to Europe and aim to attract the best staff in the industry and the offered salaries and conditions of employment reflect this policy.
**Representatives** (approx.160) for client service, administration, sales, guiding of excursions and general problem solving. Salary £800-£1,200 per month including commission. Knowledge of French, German, Italian or Spanish is required. Minimum age 23.

All staff to work 6 days a week in one of the following countries: Andorra, Austria, France, Italy and Switzerland. Minimum period of work 3-4 months from May to September. Free board and accommodation is provided. Applicants must be friendly, outgoing flexible team players with enthusiasm and a good sense of humour and must be customer care orientated and have a liking for the country and culture.

*Applications* all year round to the above address.

**SIBLU HOLIDAYS:** Recruitment Team, Bryanston Court, Selden Hill, Hemel Hempstead, HP2 4TN (☎ 01442-293231; recruitment@siblu.com; www.siblu.com). Siblu Holidays exclusively own holiday parks in France, and also operate on 16 fantastic parks in France, Spain and Italy. The following roles are offered in these countries for seasonal work:
**Park Representatives:** duties include cleaning and maintaining accommodation, welcoming new arrivals, reception duties, paperwork and administration.
**Children's Club Representatives:** duties include creating and running a daytime entertainment programme for children between the ages of 5 and 12 years old, associated paperwork and assisting Park Representatives. Experience of working with children is desirable.
**Assistant Park Representatives:** duties include cleaning and preparation of accommodation, welcoming new arrivals and reception duties.
**Lifeguards:** NPLQ qualified, duties include poolside supervision, cleaning of pool area and supervision of slides and flumes.
**Reception Team Members:** applicants must be fluent in French, duties include the welcome and check-in of guests, providing park and local information, cash handling (*bureau de change*) and problem solving.
**Accommodation Team Members:** duties include cleaning and preparing guest accommodation, bed making and customer visits.
**Bar Team Members:** applicants must be conversational in French, duties include bar service, cash handling, cleaning & washing of glasses, terrace service and re-stocking of bar.
**Entertainers:** dancers, vocalists and children's entertainers, working as part of a team to provide daytime and evening entertainment programme for guests of all ages.

Team members will receive a competitive salary, accommodation on park, uniform, medical cover and travel costs to park. The season runs between March and October, with varying contract dates. Limited high season positions are available.

Please telephone the above number for a recruitment pack or visit the website to *apply* online.

**SPECIALISED TRAVEL LTD:** 12-15 Hanger Green, London, W5 3EL (☎020-8799 8360; fax 020-8998 7965; e-mail admin@stlon.com) Established in 1955, a tour operator specialising in concert tours of mainland Europe and the UK for both amateur and professional musical groups (choirs, bands and orchestras).
**Couriers/Tour Leaders**(1-2 per tour) to escort choirs, bands and orchestras from the USA on concert tours throughout the UK and Europe. To be responsible for all daily events, confirming accommodation, transportation, concert arrangements and leading sight-seeing excursions. Knowledge of touring and musical background is an advantage. Excellent organisational skills, leadership qualities and initiative required.

Work is available for a minimum of one tour in spring and summer. Work will be full-time for the duration of each tour (usually 10-20 days). Board and accommodation is included for the duration of each tour. Wage level depends on the particular tour. Confidence in the native language of the country being toured is required.

*Applications from EU nationals only* are invited throughout the year to the above address.

**SPORT & EDUCATIONAL TRAVEL LTD**: 3 Dukes Head Street, Lowestoft, Suffolk, NR32 1JY (☎01502-567914; fax 01502-500993; e-mail info@set-uk.com). Sport & Educational Travel Ltd has been established since 1991 and organises group travel for school parties, with students aged between 11-17 years old. All durations of visits are organised – from day trips to weeklong stays – to France, Belgium, Germany and Spain. The trips range from an introduction to Northern France and visits to Paris (including Disneyland) to World War I &II tours. For all of these visits couriers are needed to accompany the groups, to provide factual information during the trip in both English and the local language, as well as managing checking-in procedures, visits and general timings throughout the visit.

**Couriers**: must speak fluently one or more languages relevant to the destination. Knowledge of area would be an advantage but not essential as full training is given. For overnight visits or longer, accommodation and meals are provided on the same basis as the groups accompanied. Wages are from £100 for a day trip; on longer trips it is £100 for first day and £60 for every subsequent day.

Applications for this post to Mr G Bishop, Managing Director at the above address.

**TALL STORIES:** Brassey House, New Zealand Avenue, Walton on Thames, Surrey KT12 1QD (☎01932-252002; fax 01932-252970; e-mail info@tallstories.co.uk; www.tallstories.co.uk). Tall Stories offer adventure sports holidays in France, Spain, Austria, Mallorca and Corsica for people with no previous experience. Activities include rafting, mountain biking, trekking, kayaking, paragliding, snowboarding and many many more.

**Representatives** to work as sports reps for an adventure sports holiday company, acting as hosts to small groups of 8-16 clients in Austria, Corsica, France, Mallorca and Spain. Duties include airport transfers, organising hotels and sports as well as organising evening entertainment, and generally making the holidays of guests as good as possible. Reps are needed from mid-May to mid-September. Applicants should have outdoor sporting interests and should preferably speak French, Spanish or German, hold a clean driving licence (PSV licence an advantage) and get on with people. Must have experience of working with people: those with previous experience of rep work preferred. Must be aged 23 or over.

**Chalet Person** to cater for groups of 10-16 people in France and Austria; work includes cooking breakfast and evening meals, budgeting, cleaning, and looking after the running of a chalet. Period of work from end of May to mid-September.

Wages for above positions from £120 per week, plus food, accommodation and travel.

*Applications* should be sent to the Personnel Manager at the above address.

**TIME OUT TOURIST SERVICE**: Prinzenalle 7, 40549 Dusseldorf, Germany. (☎+49 21152 391 149; fax: +49 21152 391 200; e-mail deutschland@timeoutourism. com; www.timeoutourism.com). An international company operating in Egypt, Greece, Spain and Tunisia with international staff in a 4 and 5 star club working with animators from Austria, Germany, Holland, Britain and Italy.

**Chief Animator (10)** to do all general organising, must be well organised. Wages €950 (approx £625) per month minimum. Must be able to stay for long period of time and work with people from other countries.

**Sport Animator (80)** required to organise events and play in sports tournaments in a holiday village. Must be a good organiser. Wages €550 (approx £362) per month.

**Miniclub (80)** needed to organise a programme for young children and babies, must be patient and love children. Wages €550 (approx £362) per month.

**Decorator** (30) required to paint scenery for a stage, must be a very good painter. Wages €550 (approx £362) to €600 (approx £395) per month minimum.

**Aerobics Instructor (80)** to organise a programme of aerobics, stretching and water aerobics. Must have good aerobics skills. Wages €550 (approx £362) per month.

**DJ (30)** to DJ in the evenings and partake in sports in daytime. Must have plenty of DJ-ing experience. Wages €550 (approx £362) per month.

Employees work long hours from 10 am until night-time with meal breaks, 6 or 7 days a week. Staff are needed for both summer and winter seasons from 1st April to 30th October and 1st October to 30th March, minimum period of work 3 months. Board and lodging is provided free of charge as is a return flight.

Applicants must speak English and German, other languages are also helpful. *Applications* invited as soon as possible.

**TRACKS TRAVEL LTD:** The Flots, Brookland, Romney Marsh, Kent TN29 9TG (☎01797-344164; fax 01797-344135; e-mail info@tracks-travel.com; www.tracks-travel. com). Tracks Travel is a coach tour operator operating throughout the UK and Europe.

**Drivers** with a valid UK PCV licence required.

**Tour Managers** must be good with a microphone, and confident in dealing with large groups.

**Cooks** Must be able to cook for large groups. Relevant experience preferred.

Wage for all positions to be confirmed. Board and accommodation are available. Work is available throughout the year, but all applicants should be prepared to work for a minimum of 2 full seasons. Hours of work vary, depending on the nature of the tour. Knowledge of languages other than English is not required.

*Applications* should be made to the above address at any time of year.

**VENUE HOLIDAYS:** 1 Norwood St, Ashford, Kent TN23 1QU (☎01233-629950; fax 01233-634494; e-mail info@venueholidays.co.uk; www.venueholidays.co.uk). Venue Holidays is a medium sized family run business supplying package camping and mobile home holidays. They offer the opportunity to live in a new environment, meet interesting people, travel and perhaps catch a tan.

**Supervisors** required March to October. Must possess a clean driver's licence. Age 20+. Should have experience of working in the holiday industry or a similar role. Wages from £700 per month. Good knowledge of Italian and/or German is advantageous.

**Campsite Representatives (30)** for work in Italy, France and Spain. Duties to include cleaning and maintaining holiday units, welcoming clients and looking after them during their stay, sorting out any problems, and liaising between the campsite's management and the UK office. Wage of £450 per month with accommodation provided. To work hours as required. Minimum period of work is two months; the complete season runs from April to October. Applicants need to be fit, cheerful and to be able to work under pressure. Knowledge of French, German, Italian or Spanish would be advantageous but are not essential.

**Montage/Demontage Assistants** required March to May and September/October. Jobs include setting up tents, preparing the campsite units for occupation and cleaning accommodation prior to the season. In September/October the process must be done in reverse. Experience of driving commercial vans useful. Should be physically fit, unaffected by adverse weather conditions and willing to visit a large number of campsites in France, Italy and Spain.

*Applications* should be sent to the above address from November.

# Voluntary Work and Archaeology

**ATD FOURTH WORLD:** 48 Addington Square, London SE5 7LB (tel; 020-7703 3231; fax 020-7252 4276; e-mail atd@atd-uk.org; www.atd-uk.org).
ATD Fourth World is an international organisation which adopts a human rights approach to tackling extreme poverty, supporting the efforts of very disadvantaged and excluded families in fighting poverty and taking an active role in the community. As part of their work ATD organises workcamps, street workshops and family stays all over the European Union.

The workcamps are a **combination of manual work** in and around ATD's buildings, **conversation and reflection on poverty**. The street workshops take a festival atmosphere, involving artists, craftsmen, sportsmen and volunteers to underprivileged areas. The family stays allow families split by poverty with children in care and/or adults in homes to come together for a break.

The camps, street workcamps and family stays take place from July to September, and most last two weeks: participants must pay for their own travel costs, plus a contribution towards food and accommodation.

For further information *write*, enclosing a stamped addressed envelope or and International Reply Coupon.to the above address or ATD Quart Monde, Summer Activities Team, 107 avenue du General Leclerc, 95480 Pierrelaye, France or e-mail engage.ete@atd-quartmonde.org.

**BRIDGES FOR EDUCATION INC:** 94 Lamarck Drive, Buffalo, New York 14226, USA (☎+1 716 839-0180; fax +1 716 939-9493; e-mail jbc@bridges4edu.org; www.bridges4edu.org).
Volunteer English Teachers. The purpose of Bridges for Education (BFE) is to promote tolerance and understanding using English as a bridge. BFE sends Canadian and American volunteer teachers, educated adults and college students to **teach conversational English in the summer in Eastern and Central Europe.** Since 1994, BFE has organised 84 camps in nine countries serving 11,000 students from 38 countries. High School students whose parents or teachers are participants may also join a BFE team.

About 130 volunteers are placed each year. BFE is not a religious or ethnic organisation. Those skilled in teaching English as a Second Language are preferred but teachers who are certified in any area are welcome. The team is prepared in basic ESL prior to departure. Applicants must be in good health. Programmes are posted in December and January.

Volunteers teach for three weeks together as a team in the summer. They receive free room and board while they teach and an additional week of travel within the host country (the board and lodging and a modest stipend are provided by the host country).

*Applications from US or Canadian citizens only* should be sent to the above address or made online.

**THE DISAWAY TRUST:** 51 Sunningdale Road, Worthing, West Sussex, BN13 2NQ

(☎01903-830796; www.disaway.co.uk).
The Disaway Trust relies on helpers to enable them to provide holidays for adults who would be otherwise unable to have a holiday.

About 60 volunteers are required for 8-14 day periods during the year to **help disabled people on holiday**. The organisation usually arranges two or three holidays a year which take place between May and October. A 50% contribution is required toward cost of travel, accommodation, board and entertainment.

No special qualifications or experience are required. The holiday venues are in the British Isles and in the Mediterranean.

Apply to Nicki Green for further details including information on dates and locations. The information pack for 2007 will be available mid-January 2007.

**EMMAUS INTERNATIONAL:** 183, bis rue Vaillant Couturier, Boite Postale 91, F-94143 Alfortville, France (+33-148 93 29 50; fax +33-143 53 19 26; e-mail contact@ emmaus-international.org; www.emmaus-international.org).
**Volunteers** to take part in summer camps in several European countries. The work consists of **rag-picking and recycling materials to raise money for the poor.** Applicants must pay their own travelling costs but receive free food and accommodation.

For further details *contact* the above address.

**EUROPEAN VOLUNTARY SERVICE:** EVS Unit, EIL Cultural and Educational Travel, 287 Worcester Road, Malvern, WR14 1AB (☎Freephone 0800 018 4015 or 01684-562577; fax 016845-562212; e-mail k.morris@eiluk.org).
EIL is an approved sending and hosting organisation for the European Commission's European Voluntary Service scheme.
EVS is for 18-25 year old EU citizens who want to work for 6-12 months in a **community-based project** in another European country. Travel, food, accommodation, medical insurance and an allowance are provided.

For more details *contact* the above address.

**GEC:** 25 boulevard Paul Pors, 84800 L'Isle sur la Sorgue, France; (☎+33 4 90 27 21 20; fax: +33 4 90 86 82 19; www.apare-gec.org).
L'APARE GEC is an NGO which promotes transnational co-operation by bringing together professionals, local participants and young volunteers from around Europe and the Mediterranean region. Its objective is to carry out projects that contribute to the protection and enhancement of the environment and local heritage. The GEC develops voluntary efforts in favour of the environment and heritage preservation across Europe and the Mediterranean regions.
**Euro-Mediterranean Campuses**: The campuses are intended for students from Europe and Mediterranean countries. They take the form of workshops with about fifteen participants working in multi-disciplinary international groups for three to five weeks, during the students' summer holidays. They include **field studies and surveys that use professional skills in the areas of heritage preservation and the environment (in the widest possible sense):** architecture, history of art, regional development, sociology, law etc.)

**RIVE: The International Network of Volunteers for the Environment, Heritage and Sustainable Development:** RIVE programmes (carried out in the context of the European Voluntary Service) allow participants to invest their skills in voluntary projects abroad, to the benefit of local communities. This programme is designed for young people from 18 to 25 years old, of whatever nationality or professional training, as long as they reside in a participating country of Europe. The projects last from six to twelve months. They can be held in urban or rural settings. The teams are made up of one to three young volunteers, preferably from different disciplines and cultural backgrounds. *Applications* to the above address.

**INTERNATIONALE BOUWORDE (INTERNATIONAL BUILDING COMPANIONS):** for addresses see below.
Recruits volunteers for **construction work** camps **on behalf of the socially, physically and mentally underprivileged**. The camps take place in Austria, Belgium, the Czech Republic, France, Germany, Hungary, Italy, Lithuania, the Netherlands, Poland, Romania, Slovakia, Switzerland and the Ukraine.
Volunteers work for 8 hours per day, 5 days per week. Free board, accommodation and liability and accident insurance are provided: travel costs and insurance (approx. £60) are the responsibility of the volunteer. Camps last for 2-3 weeks and take place between June and September; Bouworde in Belgium and Italy operates workcamps around the year. Individual country branches are as below:

O *Belgium*: (Flemish speaking): Bouworde, Tiensesteenweg 157, B-3010 Leuven (☎016 25 91 44; fax 016 25 91 60). Represents IBO as a whole.
O *Austria*: Gentzgasse 117/47, 1180 Wien; (☎+43 774 95 12; fax +43 774 95 12; e-mail bauorden@oebo.at; www.bauorden.at).
O *Czech Republic*: Sokolska 517, 46 822 Zelezny Brod (☎ +420 483 38 95 72; fax +420 383 38 95 72; e-mail arch.tomesek.zb@iol.cz).
O *France:* Compagnons Batisseurs, Secrétariat International, Ferme de la Capelanie, 39, Chemin de Verdun, 81100, Castres, France (☎33 5-63 72 59 64; fax 33-5-63 72 59 81).
O *Germany:* Internationaler Bauorden, Liebigstrasse 23, D-67551 Worms-Horchheim (☎06241-37900; fax 06241-37902; e-mail bauorden@t-online. de; www.home.t-online.de/home/ibo-d/).
O *Italy:* IBO Associazione Italian Soci Costruttori, Via Montebello, 46/A 44100 Ferrara (☎0532-243279; fax 0532-245-689; e-mail info@iboitalia. org; www.iboitalia.org).
O *Netherlands*: Internationale Bouworde, St Annastrat 172, NL-6524 GT Nijmegen (☎31-24-3226074; fax 31-24-3226076; e-mail info@bouworde. nl www.bouworde.nl).
O *Switzerland:* Internationaler Bauorden, Sekretariat Schweiz, Bahnhofstr. 8, CH-9450 Altstätten (☎+41-71-755 1671; e-mail info@bauorden.ch; www. baurden.ch).

*Applications*, mentioning the country preferred, should be sent to the relevant address listed above.

**TEJO (TUTMONDA ESPERANTISTA JUNULARA ORGANIZO):** Nieuwe Binnenweg 176, 3015 BJ Rotterdam, the Netherlands (☎+31 10 436 1044; fax 31 10 436 1751).
Volunteers to join **work camps** in various European countries arranged by TEJO, the World Organisation of Young Esperantists. Work to be done may be on **reconstruction projects**. Accommodation provided. Period of work normally from 1 to 2 weeks.
Applicants should be aged between 16 and 30. No previous experience necessary: all camps include Esperanto lessons for beginners, and a few are limited to Esperanto speakers.
For details *contact* the above address including an International Reply Coupon.

# Au Pairs, Nannies, Family Helps & Exchanges

**THE AU PAIR AGENCY:** 231 Hale Lane, Edgware, Middlesex HA8 9QF (☎020-8958 1750; fax 020-8958 5261; e-mail elaine@aupairagency.com; www.aupairagency.com). Established 1986.
**Au Pairs** from Britain mainly placed in France, Spain, Majorca, Italy and Germany.
**Mothers' Helps** placed in France.
Applicants should be aged between 18 and 25. Non-smokers preferred; drivers always welcomed. Summer stays of 12 weeks possible – early applicants receive priority. At all other times, a minimum commitment of 9-12 months is required. A reasonable knowledge of the language of the chosen country is needed. The Au Pair agency does not place au pairs in the USA. Although the agency works with all the British government approved participating countries, it cannot place applicants from one country, via London, into another country. e.g. it cannot place au-pairs from Spain with families in Turkey.
The Au Pair Agency also places hundreds of au pairs from permitted, participating countries in Britain each year.
All applicants receive pocket money plus full board and lodging. For *further details* contact Mrs Newman on the above number at least 12 weeks before preferred starting date.

**AU PAIR AGENCY BOURNEMOUTH:** 45 Strouden Road, Bournemouth, BH9 1QL (☎01202-532600; fax: 01202-532600; e-mail andrea.rose@virgin.net).
The Au Pair Agency Bournemouth offers placements for British applicants throughout Western and Eastern Europe.
**Au Pair (20)** summer placements, **(70)** long-term placements lasting one academic year. Au Pairs are expected to work 25 hours per week, 5 days a week. Wages are minimum £55 per week (overtime is paid extra). Applicants must love children and have experience in childcare (e.g. babysitting) and a basic knowledge of cleaning. Applicants must speak English.
British applicants are charged £40 on departure. There is a 24-hour emergency mobile number is provided for au pairs during the placement.
*Applications* to Andrea Rose see above for contact details.

**AU PAIR CONNECTIONS:** 39 Tamarisk Road, Wildern Gate, Hedge End, Hants SO30 4TN (☎01489-780438; fax 01489-692656; e-mail apconnectenthworld.com; www.aupairconnections.co.uk).
**Au Pairs, Mothers' Helps** placed mainly in France, Spain including the Balearic Islands, and also in Italy, Austria and sometimes elsewhere in Europe; applicants from overseas also placed in the UK. Pocket money approx. £50 per week. Minimum stays normally 6 months, but some summer stays of 10 weeks. Applicants must have experience of childcare, babysitting etc; a good knowledge of English is also useful as some families want their children tutored in English. For further details
*Applications* to Denise Blighe at the above address or e-mail.

**COUNTY NANNIES:** Cherry Gardens, Nouds Lane, Lynsted, Kent ME9 0ES (☎01795-522544; fax 01795-522878; e-mail info@au-pairinternational.com; www. countynannies.com).

**Au Pairs** recruited throughout the year for the UK and Europe. Live-in, £55 per week minimum pocket money or equivalent. 25 hours work per week, 2 days off. Unlimited number of posts available for 6-24 months stay, also 8-12-week summer placements. The families in the UK are mostly in London, London suburbs and the southern counties and South Coast. Vacancies in Europe are mainly in cities and coastal towns.

**Other services:** Au Pair International's sister company County Nannies provides fully qualified **Nannies, Maternity Nurses and Mother's Helps.** County Nannies cover Kent, London, South East England and the Home Counties.

*Applications* to the above address in writing, by fax or e-mail.

**BLOOMSBURY BUREAU:** 14 Tottenham Court Road, PO Box 625, London W1T 1JY; (☎020-3122 0025; fax 020-7430 2325; e-mail bloomsburo@aol.com; www. bloomsburyaupairs.co.uk).

This agency has been operating for over thirty years, and every placement is personally supervised by the principal.

**Au Pairs** hundreds of EU nationals needed for placements London, Jersey and Ireland as well as Austria, France, Germany, Italy and Spain. Applicants also welcomed from English-speaking countries (USA, Australia, New Zealand and South Africa). Placements throughout the year. Pocket money €90 per week, in return for 30 hours help with childcare and light housework and helping with English.

*Applications* at the above address or online at www.bloomsburyaupairs.co.uk.

**EDGWARE AND SOLIHULL AU PAIR & NANNY AGENCY:** PO Box 147, Radlett WD7 8WX (☎01923-289737; fax 01923-289739; e-mail info@the-aupair-shop.com; www.the-aupair-shop.com).

**Au Pairs** for families all over Europe and the UK placed in all the main and capital cities, e.g. London, Paris, Rome, Barcelona. Good childcare experience and character references are essential.

*Applications:* for details of how to obtain application forms visit the website above.

**EN FAMILLE OVERSEAS**: La Maison Jaune, Avenue du Stade, 34210 Siran, France (☎+33 468914990; UK 01206 546 741; fax +33 468914990; e-mail marylou. toms@wanadoo.fr, www.enfamilleoverseas.co.uk).

Paying Guest Stays Arranged in France, Germany, Italy and Spain. Homestays with attendance at small private schools also arranged. Families in England for non-English speakers too.

*Applications* to the above address.

**JOLAINE AU PAIR & DOMESTIC AGENCY:** 18 Escot Way, Barnet, Hertfordshire EN5 3AN (☎020-8449 1334; fax 020-8449 9183; e-mail aupair@jolaine.prestel. co.uk; www.jolaineagency.com).

**Au Pair/Mother's Help** stays: Jolaine Agency can arrange for applicants to be placed with families in Europe. Families in the UK prefer applicants who can stay for 9 months plus; summer stays limited in the UK. Accommodation with British Families also available as a Paying Guest. Reduced charges for Paying Guest Stays given to groups/extended stays.

For further information please *contact* Jolaine Agency via telephone/fax/email.

**M KELLY AU PAIR AGENCY**: 17 Ingram Way, Greenford, Middlesex UB6 8Q9 (tel/fax 020-8575 3336; fax: 020-8575 3336; e-mail info@mkellyaupair.co.uk; www. mkellyaupair.co.uk).

**Summer Placement (20)** expected to work 25 hours a week minimum. Pocket money £55 per week minimum. Applicants must be between 18 and 27 years old.
**Long Term Placement (95 – 100)**. Same working conditions as above.
   Placements are available in all countries offering the Au Pair Programme. Minimum stay is 6 weeks; maximum stay is 2 years. Depending on placement help with travel and languages can be arranged.
   Apply to Marian Kelly see above for details.

**UK NANNIES AND AU PAIRS**: 19 The Severals, Newmarket CB8 7YW (☎01638-560812; e-mail help@uknanniesandaupairs.com or jobs@theuknannyagency.com; www.theuknannyagency.co.uk; www.theukaupairagency.co.uk.
Hundreds of placements available in Europe, wages can vary from £50 per week to £400 per week, hours vary from 25 to 60 hours a week with overtime paid. Placements can last between 1 month and 2 years. Applicants must be 18+.
   *Apply* via e-mail see above for address.

**WORLDNETUK**, Work and Travel Specialists, Emberton House, 26 Shakespeare Road, Bedford MK40 2ED (☎0845 458 1550/1; www.worldnetuk.com).
WorldNetUk is affiliated to The Childcare Solution, which is a leading childcare recruitment agency established for over 20 years. There are four offices in the UK and partner agencies throughout the world.
**Ski/Summer Resort Nannies**. Destinations include France, Corsica, Spain, Balearics, Turkey, Italy, Sardinia, Greece, Austria and Switzerland. Winter season includes free ski lessons, lift pass and tuition. Summer season includes free water sports and tuition. All applicants must hold a childcare qualification or one years full-time experience with children.
**Au Pair programme to the UK.** Carefully selected families in the United Kingdom. Placements for candidates from all EU countries and Andorra, Bosnia-Herzegovina, Croatia, the Faroes, Greenland, Liechtenstein, Macedonia, Monaco, San Marino, Slovak Republic, Switzerland, Turkey, Bulgaria, and Romania.
**Hospitality placements in the UK.** Career opportunities in leading hotels throughout the UK for chefs (all grades), housekeeping and reception staff.
**Camp USA.** Counsellors and support staff for camps throughout the US; 8-10 week placements. All departures in June, with the opportunity to travel at end of stay. Applicants must be 18 upwards.
**Au Pair and Nanny programme to the USA** for 18-26 year olds with full driving licence. Placements for qualified NNEB, Btec National Diploma and NVQ level III in childcare to work with young babies. Also placements for unqualified applicants to work with school age children but good babysitting experience would be essential. Applications can be processed from the UK, France, Czech Republic and Turkey.
**Au Pair programme to Europe.** UK applicants who would like to improve their language skills needed to spend time in France, Spain, Italy or Germany; an excellent way to learn something of another culture and become fluent in another language. Good support always from partner agencies.
   For further information *visit* the website www.worldnetuk.com.

# Western Europe

## Andorra

Only limited opportunities for finding temporary employment exist in Andorra, because of its small size. Opportunities are best in the tourist industry – particularly in the winter ski season: there is a chapter on Andorra in *Working in Ski Resorts – Europe & North America* (Vacation Work: www.vacationwork.co.uk). You might be able to get leads on hotel work in the summer through the Andorra Hoteliers Association (ADHA), Av. De les Escoles, 9 2n 2a, Escaldes-Engordany –CP AD700; e-mail adha@Andorra.ad. Once governed jointly by France and Spain, Andorra has been a sovereign country in its own right since 1993, and while it straddles the borders of France and Spain, Andorra is not itself a member of the European Union. This means that all foreigners, including nationals of EEA countries, need work permits before they can take up employment. Applicants from neighbouring countries and then EU and EEA countries are usually given precedence over other nationalities. Permits for temporary and seasonal work have to be obtained by the employer and are non-renewable.

### Hotel Work and Catering

**HOTEL ROC BLANC:** Plaça Coprinceps, 5, Escaldes-Engordany, Andorra (☎+376-871400; fax +376-860 244; e-mail hotelrocblanc@gruprocblanc.com).
**Receptionist/Restaurant Assistant** (1) to work 6 days a week. Required all year. Applicants must have a knowledge of French, English and Spanish. Board and lodging provided.
*Applications* from April to the above address.

### Teaching and Language Schools

**CENTRE ANDORRÀ DE LLENGÜES:** 15 Av del Fener, Andorra la Vella, Andorra (☎+376-804030; fax +376-822472; e-mail centrandorra.lang@andorra.ad; www. call.ad). A small family-run language school established in 1976 in the very centre of Andorra La Vella. Students range from six year old children to professional adult employees. All levels.
**Teachers** (2/3) of English as a foreign language. €1,400 per month. To work 27 hours per 5 day week. Board and lodging available from €300-€500 per month. Minimum period of work 9 months between September/October and June.
A university degree, plus TEFL qualification, plus at least three years of experience is requested. Applicants should be between 30 and 65 and willing to work between 8am and 10pm. Non-smokers preferred. A good knowledge of French or Spanish is an asset. The posts would be ideal for a teaching couple.
*Applications* in the first instance can be made by e-mail.

## Austria

There is an English language magazine for Austria on the internet - *Austria Today* (www.austriatoday.at). It and the Austrian Embassy's website – www.bmaa.gv.at

are excellent sources of information on jobs the social, cultural and economic conditions of Austria; in particular, look at *Living and Working in Austria* on the website which contains details of immigration, work and residence permits and social security procedures as well as information for the job seeker about Austrian Employment offices.

For many years Austria has offered seasonal work in its summer and winter tourist industries. However, unemployment is currently around 5.1% and is continuing to rise. Eastern Europeans, especially from the countries newly acceded to the EU take an estimated 25% of jobs in the tourist industry. Some knowledge of German will normally be necessary unless you are working for a foreign tour operator with English-speaking clients.

During the summer, fruit is grown along the banks of the Danube, and in the early Autumn chances of finding a job grape-picking are best in the Wachau area around Durnstein west of Vienna, or Burgenland on the Hungarian border around the Neusiedler See.

The public employment service of Austria, the *Arbeitsmarktservice (AMS)*, publishes its vacancies on its website – www.ams.or.at – (or at Arbeitsmarktservice, Vienna, Weihburggasse 30, A-1011 Vienna ☎0043-1-515 25-0). For hotel and catering vacancies in the South Tyrol try the season work bureaux called BerufsInfoZentren (BIZ) such as the AMS Euro Biz/JobCenter International, Schöpfstrasse 5, 6020 Innsbruck (512-58 63 00/fax 512-58 63 00-20; eurobiz. Innsbruck@702.ams.or.at). Private employment agencies operate in Austria, but most of these specialise in executive positions or seasonal positions in the tourist industry for German speakers. It may be possible to find employment by placing an advertisement in daily newspapers: try *Salzburger Nachrichten* (Karolingerstrasse 40, 5021 Salzburg; ☎+43-662-83730; www.salzburg.com), *Kurier* (Seidengasse 11, A-1070 Vienna; ☎+43-(0)1-52100; fax 01-5210 02263; www.kurier.at) and *Die Presse* (Parkring 12a. 1015 Vienna; ☎0043-(0)1-51414; fax 01-5141 4400; www. diepresse.at). *Die Presse* also organises an annual initiative to get leading Austrian companies to take on students for summer traineeships. These papers advertise job vacancies as well on Fridays, Saturdays and Sundays. See also *Der Standard*, (www. DerStandard.at) one of the biggest newspapers concerning job vacancies.

There are opportunities for voluntary work in Austria arranged by UNA Exchange.

# RED TAPE

**Visa Requirements:** visa requirements depend upon the nationality of the visitor. Certain nationals do not require a visa providing their stay in Austria does not exceed 3 months. EU/EEA citizens have the right to live and work in Austria without a work permit or residence permit.

**Residence Permits:** *EWR Lichtbildausweis* is an ID card which EU/EEA nationals can apply for within 3 months of arrival, though it is not compulsory. For Non-EU/EEA nationals wishing to work or live in Austria must apply for a residence permit *(Aufenthaltsgesetz)*. Once a work permit is granted, it must be presented together with an application for residence permit. The form can be obtained from the Embassy. As a rule, first application for a residence permit must be submitted from abroad either directly to the relevant authority or by means of the Austrian Diplomatic Mission (not Honorary Consulates). A residence permit is also required if you intend to take up seasonal work in Austria. It will normally be valid for 6 months.

**Work Permits:** British and Irish citizens and nationals of other EU/EEA countries (and Liechtenstein) do not need work permits. Owing to its proximity to many of the new (2004) Eastern European members of the EU, a potentially seven-year transition phase has been set up between Austria and these countries to prevent a flooding of the national labour market and new EU members are subject to the same regulations as non-EU countries. Non-EU/EEA nationals require work (*Sicherungs bescheinigung*) and residence permits for all types of employment, including au-pair positions. Work permits have to be applied for by the future employer in Austria and must be obtained prior to departure from the country of residence. Work permits are not granted while on a visit to Austria. The website www.help. gv.at gives useful details of all aspects of working in Austria.

**Au Pair:** au pairs from outside the EU/EEA must obtain work and residence permits as above with the assistance of the mediating agency and/or the au-pair family in Austria who must inform the local employment office *(Arbeitsmarktservice)*. A couple of useful organisations in this respect are Au Pair 4You (Hasnerstr. 31/32, 1160 Vienna; ☎+43 1 990 1574; fax +43 1 990 1574 2; e-mail office@au-pair4you.at; www.au-pair4you.at) and Au Pair-Vermittlung (Johannesgasse 16/1 1010 Vienna; ☎+43 1 512 7941; fax +43 1 5139460; e-mail aupair-asd@kath-jugend.at).

**Voluntary Work:** work permits are also required by non-EEA nationals for work with recognised voluntary organisations.

# Agricultural Work

**WWOOF AUSTRIA:** Einoedhofweg 48, A-8042 Graz, (fax 43-(0)316-464951; mobile +43-(0)676505-1639 e-mail wwoof.welcome@utanet.at; www.wwoof. welcome.at.tf). WWOOF Austria received the Ford Conservation and Environmental Award 2001.

**Volunteers** required to take part in a form of cultural exchange where you live with and help a farming family, learning about organic farming methods in the process (see WWOOF entry in *Worldwide*). Work is available on more than 160 farms. Movement between farms is possible. Board and accommodation will be provided, however a separate wage will not. Applicants from outside the European Union must secure their own travel insurance and all wwoofers pay for their own travel. In Austria they are covered by an insurance against accidents. A year's membership for WWOOF Austria costs approx. €20 + €2 for postage (approx £15). Membership includes a list of Austrian organic farmers looking for work-for-keep volunteer helpers.

For more information *contact* Hildegard Gottlieb at the above address.

# Hotel Work and Catering

**HOTEL BRISTOL:** Markatplatz 4, A-5020 Salzburg, Austria. (☎+43(0) 662-873 557; fax +43 (0) 6628-735 576; e-mail hotelbristol@salzburg.co.at).
**Housemaid:** around £450 per month.
**Waiting Staff:** around £400 per month.
To work 8 hours per day, 6 days per week. Minimum period of work 8 weeks. Please note that no accommodation is available at the hotel. Applicants must speak German.
*Applications* to the above address.

**HOTEL HOCHFIRST:** A-6456 Obergurgl Nr 37, Austria (☎05256-163250; fax +43 5256-163030; e-mail info@hochfirst.com; www.hochfirst.com).
**Housemaids (2), Waiters/Waitresses (2), Kitchen Assistants (2).** £125-£157 per month. Knowledge of German and experience in the hotel and catering industry

required. 10-11 hour days, 6-7 day week. Working shifts between 7am and 10pm. Board and lodging provided free. Minimum work period 2 months.
*Applications* in January/February to Franz Gstrein at the above address.

**HOTEL MARIAHILF:** A-8020 Graz, Mariahilfstrasse 9, Austria. (☎+43 316-713163; fax +43 316-7131360; e-mail office@mariahilf.at; www.mariahilf.at).
**Kitchen Assistants, Bar Staff.** Wage by arrangement. Hours 7-10am, 6 days per week. Free board and accommodation. Must have previous experience or some knowledge of German. Period of work May to October.
*Applications* to Irmgard Kossar.

**PENSION BERGKRISTALL:** A-9844 Heiligenblut, Austria. (☎+43 4824-2005; fax +43 4824-2995-33; e-mail bergkristall@heiligenblut.net; www.heiligenblut.net)
**Assistant** to wait at table and clean rooms. £255, approximately per month. To work around 4 hours per day, 7 days per week. In winter it is possible to ski daily from 1pm. Free board and lodging provided. Periods of work from July to September or December to March: minimum period of work two months. Applicants should be able to speak English and German.
*Applications* to Herr H. Fleissner at the above address in April in the summer season or October for the winter season.

**HOTEL POST KG:** Fam Hofer, A-5672 Fusch/Glstr, Land Salzburg, Austria.
**Waiting Assistant (1) and Receptionist (1).** Wages approximately £400 per month. To work 8-10 hours per day, 6 days per week. Minimum period of work is 2 months. Free board and lodging are provided. Knowledge of German and French are required.
*Applications* to the above address between April and June.

**SPORTHOTEL GUNTER SINGER:** A-6622 Berwang, Tirol, Austria (tel+43-5674-8181; fax +43-5674-818183). The hotel is a member of Relais & Châteaux hotels and is situated in a small village in the mountains. It caters for international guests.
**Assistants (2)** to serve and clean in a restaurant.
**Housemaid** to clean the rooms of guests, the lounge, reception, etc.
Wages from £400 to £500 per month. Around 8 hours per day, 5½ days per week. Free board and accommodation provided. Minimum period of work from 1 July to 10 September. Knowledge of some German required, plus some French if possible. *Applicants must be EU nationals.*
*Applications* to the above address from January-March.

**TRAUM-HOTEL CLUB MONTANARA:** Seestrasse 5, A-6673 Haldensee/Gran, Austria (☎+43-5675-6431; fax +43-5675-6436).
**Lifeguards, Open Air Swimming Pool Attendants, Buffet Assistants,** Wages and period of work by arrangement. To work 9½ hours per day, 47½ hours per week. Board and accommodation provided. Applicants must speak German.
*Applications* to Frau Sonja Huber at the above address at any time.

# Sports, Couriers and Camping
**BENTS BICYCLE & WALKING TOURS:** The Blue Cross, Orleton, Ludlow, Shropshire SY8 4HN (☎01568-780800; fax 01568-780801; e-mail info@bentstours. com; www.bentstours.com).
**Company Representatives (4-5)** for a tour operator offering cycling and walking holidays in France, Germany and Austria. Duties to include meeting clients at the

airport, maintaining bicycles, transporting luggage between hotels and generally taking care of the needs of clients. Wages of around £600 per month with board and accommodation provided. To work varied hours as needs of work dictate, but generally around 40 hours per up to 7-day week.

Minimum period of work 8 weeks between the end of May and end of September. Applicants should have a reasonable grasp of either spoken German or French and, fluent English. They must also possess a full valid driving licence.

*Applications* should be sent, with a photograph, to Stephen Bent at the above address from January.

**CANVAS HOLIDAYS:** GVN Camping Recruitment, East Port House, Dunfermline, KY12 7JG (☎01383-629012; fax 01383-629071; e-mail campingrecruitment@ gvnrecruitment.com; www.gvnrecruitment.com). Canvas Holidays provide luxury mobile home and tent holidays at over 100 campsites.throughout Europe.
**Campsite Courier.** Involves cleaning accommodation, welcoming families to the site and showing them to their accommodation. Visiting customers, providing local information and basic maintenance are very important parts of the job. Campsite Courier Opportunities are also available for couples to work on site together. For details of management positions, see website.

Package includes competitive salary, tent accommodation, medical insurance, uniform and return travel from a UK port of entry. Full season positions start in March, April or May and end in September/October. High season staff needed to work at least two months during the peak season.

*Please call* the Recruitment Department for more information and an application form, or *apply online* at www.gvnrecruitment.com.

**EUROCAMP:** Overseas Recruitment Department (Ref SJ/07) (☎01606-787525). Eurocamp is a leading tour operator in quality self-drive camping and mobile home holidays in Europe. Each year the company seeks to recruit up to 1,500 enthusiastic people for the following positions:
**Campsite Courier:** job involves cleaning and preparing customer accommodation, providing assistance, acting as an information service and performing some administrative duties. Couriers need to be flexible to meet the needs of the customer to provide them with excellent service. Minimum age 18 years. Applicants should be independent with plenty of initiative and relish a challenging and rewarding position. They should also possess a friendly and helpful personality. Previous customer service experience would be an advantage. Applicants should be available to work from April/May to September.
**Children's Courier:** work involves organising a wide range of exciting activities for children aged 4-13. Applicants should possess initiative, imagination and enthusiasm along with good safety awareness. Previous childcare experience is essential. Minimum age is 18 years and applicants should be available from April/May to September. Languages are not a requirement but would be an advantage (in particular German). Successful candidates will be asked to apply for an Enhanced Disclosure.
**Senior Couriers:** required to work alongside a team of Campsite Couriers and organise their daily workload, as well as carrying out the normal day-to-day duties of a Campsite Courier. Applicants should have good language skills and experience of leading a team.
**Site Managers:** required to lead a large team of Campsite Couriers, organising their daily workloads and ensuring they provide the very best customer service. Applicants should be 21 or over, have proven managerial experience, excellent communication skills and language ability.

**Montage/Demontage:** for a period of approximately 6-8 weeks at the beginning/end of season to erect/dismantle equipment.

Comprehensive training is provided together with a competitive salary, insurance, return travel and accommodation. Applications are accepted from September/October and _can only be accepted from UK/EU passport holders_. Interviews will be conducted in Hartford, Cheshire between October and April.

_Applicants should apply on-line_ at **www.holidaybreakjobs.com** or telephone 01606-787525 for an Application Pack.

## Teaching and Language Schools

**AUSTRO-BRITISH SOCIETY:** Wickenburggasse 19, 1080 Vienna. tel/fax: +43 (0)1 406 11 41.

**English teachers (8-10)** qualified English teachers required to teach a minimum of 2 semesters. Wages are from €19 (approx £12.80) per hour net, depending on course. British teachers are preferred.

Assistance given with accommodation if possible. All candidates must be interviewed

_Applications_ to Mrs. Brigitta Serenyi-Ringhoffer, Secretary.

**ENGLISH FOR KIDS:** A. Postgasse 11/19, 1010 Vienna, Austria (☎+43-(0)1-667 45 79; fax 01-667 51 63; e-mail magik@e4kids.co.at; www.e4kids.co.at). The teaching venue is a beautifully renovated, 17th century, four-square building around a large central yard and it is situated in 40 hectares of meadows and woods.

**TEFL Teachers:** (8-10) with CELTA or Trinity Certificate (minimum grade B) and some formal teaching experience required for (a) residential summer camps in Upper Austria. Period of work 3 weeks in August. Pupils' age range is 10-15; (b) day camps in Vienna. Period of work 4 weeks in July and August. Pupils age range is from 5-10 and 10-15.

Salary varies depending on qualifications, ranging from €560 (approx £378) for two weeks plus full board and accommodation and travel expenses within Austria. The teaching style is full immersion with in-house methods following carefully planned syllabus and teachers' manual, supplemented with CD-Roms etc.

_Apply_ to Irena Köstenbauer, Principal, at the above address.

## Work with Children

**AU PAIR AUSTRIA:** Mariahilferstrasse 99/2/37, 1060 Vienna Austria (tel/fax+43 1-920 3843 or +43 1-595 5745; e-mail office@aupairaustria.com; www.aupairaustria. com). In business since 2001 and a member of IAPA.

All nationalities placed. Minimum stay of 8 weeks for summer au pairs, and between 6-12 months for the academic year. There are places for 200 incoming au pairs and 30 outgoing au pairs. Candidates submit a written application and must undergo an interview.

_Contact_ Gabriela Kummer, Chief Executive Officer.

**ENGLISH FOR CHILDREN - SUMMER CAMP:** Weichselweg 4, 1220 Vienna, Austria (☎+43 1958 19 72-0; fax +43 19581972-14; e-mail office@englishforchildren. com; www.englishforchildren.com).

**Camp Counsellors:** to instruct in sports, arts & crafts, music, Drama/and or English. To work in a total immersion summer camp, motivating children to speak English through different activities: sports, English language classes, arts & crafts, music, and to acquaint children with the different cultures of the English speaking world through games and songs etc.

Applicants must have experience of working with children aged 6-13, and of camps, be versatile, conscientious, oriented towards children and safety and have an outgoing personality. Experience in more than one subject area preferable.

To work during July, 8am-4pm over a 4-week period Monday to Friday. Help with finding accommodation is available and lunch is included in the working day.

*Applications* from English speakers invited from January to English Language Day Camp, at the above address.

**YOUNG AUSTRIA GmbH**, Alpenstrasse 108a, A-5020 Salzburg, AUSTRIA (tel. +43/662 62 57 58-0, fax: +43/662 62 57 58-2, e-mail office@youngaustria.at or gudrun. doringer@youngaustria.at). 'English In Action!' is Young Austria!'s international Summer English language camp for young people, age 9 - 17, in beautiful Alpine settings near Salzburg.

**Staff** to work in *English In Action!* Summer English language camps. The English camps are held in two and one-week sessions, throughout the summer (July and August).

**Resident Supervisor, English Teaching Positions** (Academic Supervisor and Project Coordinators) and in the sports and free-time activities area (**Sports & Activities Supervisor and Coordinators**). Tutors can work on projects of their choice, including drama, grammar and a variety of recreational activities.

*More information*, including downloading application forms, can be found at www.camps.at, and/or www.youngaustria.at.

# Belgium

Unemployment in Belgium is fairly high compared with other Western European countries and is currently reaching 8.1%, but the economy is stable and there are work opportunities.

Although small in area Belgium is densely populated and can seem complicated to the outsider, as three languages are spoken within the country's federal states. These languages are Dutch or Flemish, French and German. In broad terms Dutch is spoken in the north (Flanders) and French in the south (Wallonia), with both being spoken in Brussels in the centre of the country; German is spoken mainly in the Eastern Cantons. With its coastal resorts Belgium has an active hotel and tourism industry in the north which makes seasonal work in Belgium a viable prospect. The recruitment office for hotel and catering staff is Hospitality Solutions (part of the Adecco group of temporary jobs agencies). They have offices in Brussels (rue du Fossé-aux-Loups, Molvengracht 33, 1000 Brussels; (☎+32 (0)2/218 81 20; www. horeca-jobs.com) and Antwerp and the website is in English.

EU nationals looking for work can get help from the Belgian employment services, which are organised on a regional basis. They cover three main areas: in the Flemish region the services are known as the *Vlaamse Dienst voor Arbeidsbemiddeling en Beroepsopleiding (VDAB)* - headquarters at Keizerslaan 11, B-1000 Brussels (e-mail info@vdab.be; www.vdab.be); in the French region they are *Office Wallon de la Formation Professionnelle et de l'Emploi (FOREM)* at Boulevard Zoe Drion 25, 6000 Charleroi (☎+32-71-20-50 40; e-mail communic@forem.be; www.hotjob.be/ forem.be); and in the Brussels Region they are known as *Office Régional Bruxellois de l'Emploi (ORBEM)/Brusselse Gewestelijke Dienst voor Arbeidsbemiddeling*

*(BGDA)* based at Boulevard Anspach 65, B-1000 Brussels (☎+32-2-505-14-11; e-mail info@orbem.be or info@bgda.be; www.orbem.be or www.bgda.be). There are local employment offices in most towns.

There are also some employment offices specialising in temporary work, known as the T-Interim, which are operated as Dutch and French speaking offices under the aegis of VDAB and FOREM; as may be expected the VDAB T-Interim offices are in Flanders and the French T-Interim offices are found in Wallonia, with ORBEM/ BGDA running the T-Interim offices for Brussels. These offices can only help people who visit them in person, and the staff are multi-lingual in most cases. They can assist in finding secretarial work, especially in Brussels where there are a large number of multinational companies needing bilingual staff. Other opportunities they may have available consist of manual work in supermarkets and warehouses or engineering and computing. They are most likely to be able to help you during the summer, when companies need to replace their permanent staff who are away on holiday. T-Interims can be found on the internet at www.vdab/be/t-interim and www.forem.be/tinterim. Below are addresses of these offices in some of the larger towns:

○ *T-Interim:* Sint Jacobsmarkt 66 A1, B-2000 Antwerp (☎03-232-98-60; fax 03-231-27-33).
○ *T-Service :* Rue des Faubourg 37, B-6700, Arlon (☎063-22-66-45; fax 063-212-96-48).
○ *T-Interim:* 24 Rue Général Molitz, B-6700 Arlon (☎063-22-66-45; fax 063-21-96-48; e-mail mh.pivetta@tinterim.com).
○ *T-Interim:* Smedenstraat 4, B-8000 Brugge.
○ *T-Interim:* H.Lippensplein 22, B-8000, Brugge (☎050-269-89-50; fax 050-269-89-59).
○ *T-Interim:* Keizerslaan 11, B-1000 Brussels (☎02-514-57-00 ; fax 020-511-49-20; e-mail info@vdab.be; www.vdab.be).
○ *T-Service Interim:* Anspachlaan 69, 1000 Brussels (☎02 511.23.85).
○ *T-Interim:* Boulevard Zoe Drion 25, B-6000, Charleroi (☎071-20-50-40; fax 071-30-93-66).
○ *T-Interim:* Neuestrasse 3, B-4700 Eupen (☎087-74-34-75; fax 087/55 22 64; e-mail n.lancel@tinterim.com).
○ *T-Interim:* Burgstraat 49, B-9000, Ghent (tel. 09.224.09.20).
○ *T-Interim:* Thonissenlaan 18 bi, B-3500 Hasselt (☎011-26-49-90; fax 011-26-49-99).
○ *T-Interim:* Reepkaai 3 bus 19, B-8500 Kortrijk (☎056-25-36-90; fax 056-20-29-56).
○ *T-Interim:* Boulevard de la Sauveniere 60, B-4000 Liege (☎04-230-30-80; fax 04-232 03 71; e-mail l.dechany@tinterim.com).
○ *T-Interim:* Schuttersvest 75, B-2800 Mechelen (☎015-71-94-10; fax 015-71-94-09).
○ *T-Interim:* Witherenstraat 19, B-1800 Vilvoorde (☎02-253-98-63; fax 02-252-23-99).
○ *T-Interim* can also be found on the internet at www.tinterim.com.

You could also try advertising yourself as being available for work. One of the main newspapers published in Belgium is Le Soir (French) at Rue Royale 120, B-1000 Brussels (☎02-225-55-00/54-32; e-mail journal@lesoir.be; www.lesoir. be). The daily newspaper De Standaard is published by VUM, Gossetlaan 30a, B-1702 Groot-Bijgaarden (Brussels) (☎032-2-467-22-11; www.standaard.be). There is a weekly English language magazine called *The Bulletin;* it comes out on

Thursdays and is available from newsstands. *The Bulletin* can be contacted at 1038, Chaussée de Waterloo, B-1180 Brussels (☎02-373-99-09; e-mail info@ackroyd. be; www.belgiumpost.com) and offers of work are listed on their website www. xPATS.com. Twice a year they publish a very useful magazine-type supplement called *Newcomer* aimed at new arrivals in Belgium.

Americans can apply through Interexchange in New York (see entry in Worldwide chapter) to be placed in a summer job, internship or teaching position in Belgium. Applicants over 18 with a working knowledge of French (or Dutch) can be placed in companies or organisations for between one and three months. The programme fee is $700 (£390) and the application deadline is late April; full details on the website (www.interexchange.org).

Voluntary work in Belgium can be arranged for UK nationals by Concordia, International Voluntary Service, Youth Action For Peace or UNA Exchange. CIEE in New York helps to place Americans in short term voluntary positions in this country, as does Service Civil International (see the International Voluntary Service entry). Entries for these organisations can be found in the *Worldwide* chapter at the beginning of the book.

Those looking for work on Belgian farms should be warned that most conventional Belgian farms are highly mechanised and thus offer little scope for casual work.

The *Fédération Infor Jeunes Wallonie-Bruxelles* is a non-profit organisation which coordinates 11 youth information offices plus 28 local points of contacts in French-speaking Belgium. These can give advice on work as well as leisure, youth rights, accommodation, etc. A leaflet listing the addresses is available from the *Fédération Infor Jeunes* at Henri Lemaitre 25, B-5000 Namur (☎081/71 15 90; e-mail federation@inforjeunes.be) or can be found on their website: www. inforjeunes.be). Among Infor Jeune's services, they operate holiday job placement offices (*Service Job Vacances*) between March and September.

For yet further information consult the free booklet *Working in Belgium* published by the Employment Service (see the *Useful Publications* section towards the end of this book) or for jobs abroad you can contact the European Employment Service (EURES; http://europa.eu.int/jobs/eures): EURES VDAB (☎070-345000), EURES BGDA/ORBEM (☎02-505-14-20), or EURES FOREM (☎087-30-71-10). The following three temporary work offices in Brussels are part of the BGDA/ORBEM:

**Office Régional :** Boulevard Anspach 65, 1000 Brussels; ☎02 505 14 11; fax 02 511 30 52; info@serviceinterim.be.
**Schaerbeek**: Grand Rue au Bois 156, 1030 Schaerbeek; ☎02/733 10 61; 02/733 17 06; info@orbem.be; www.orbem.be.
**Uccle:** Chaussée d'Alsemberg 764, 1180 Uccle; ☎02/333 26 00; fax 02 376 80 77.

# RED TAPE

**Visa Requirements***:* Visas are not required by EU/EEA citizens, or those of many other countries (including the USA, Canada, Japan, Australia and New Zealand and listed at www.diplobel.org.\uk) provided they have a valid passport and that the visit is for less than three months. Other nationalities will have to obtain an entry permit, which should be applied for at a Belgian Embassy or Consulate in advance of travel in the applicant's country of residence.
**Residence Permits***:* All non-Belgians must register at the local Town Hall within eight days of arrival to obtain a residence permit. EU nationals should take documents proving that they have sufficient funds and a valid passport.

**Work Permits:** These are not required by EU/EEA nationals; others must first arrange a job, then the prospective employer should apply for a work permit at the regional ministry of employment. There are some exceptions to work permit requirements according to the employment to be taken up; consult embassies and consulates for details.

**Au Pair:** permitted subject to strict regulation including minimum pay and compulsory language course attendance – contact the embassy.

**Voluntary Work:** it is not normally necessary to obtain permits for short-term voluntary work with recognised organisations.

# Hotel Work and Catering

**ANTIGONE HOTEL:** Jordaenskaai 11-12, 2000 Antwerpen, Belgium (☎+32 (3) 231 66 77; fax: +32 3231 37 74; e-mail info@antigonehotel.be; www.antigonehotel. be). A small family run hotel with 3 locations including a sandwich bar.

**Housekeeping** required for general cleaning. Wages are €750 (approx £500 per month).

**Receptionist** required to work on front desk of the hotel. Wages are €900 (approx £600).

Employees work 8 hours a day, 5 days a week. Period of work available May to September minimum stay 4 weeks. Board and lodging are available free of charge. Knowledge of English plus one other European language required.

*Applications* are invited from May 2007.

**ASTRID PARK PLAZA:** Koninigin Astridplein 7, 2018 Antwerpen, Belgium (☎+ 32 3 203 12 34; fax: +32 3 203 12 51; e-mail appres@parkplazahotels.be; www. parkplaza.com (go to Astrid Park Plaza)) Astrid Park Plaza Hotel is situated in the heart of Antwerp, opposite the Central Station and Antwerp Zoo. It is next to Aquatopia and within walking distance of the main shopping streets.

**Kitchen staff (3):** required to help in the kitchens preparing recipes and ingredients. Must be willing to work flexible hours. Knowledge of HACCP (Hazard Analysis and Critical Point Control) is a must. Wages €8.66 (approx £5.70) per hour. Applicants required to work 38 hours a week, 5 days a week. Dates of work are July to September, minimum period of work 8-10 weeks. Applicants must speak English and Dutch if possible.

*Applications* from end of May 2007.

**HOTEL LIDO:** Zwaluwenlaan, 18 Albert Plage, B-8300 Knokke-Heist, Belgium (☎050-60 19 25; fax 050-61 04 57; e-mail info@lido-hotel.be or lido.hotel.knokke@ vt4.net)

**Waiting Staff** (2), Basic French required.

**Kitchen Assistants** (1) to work from 9-12am, 1-3pm and 6-9.30pm. Wages £650 net per month with board and lodging provided free. Minimum period of work one or two months between June and September.

*Applications* with a CV and recent photograph to A. Simoens at the above address.

**HOSTELLERIE 'LE RY D'AVE':** Sourd d'Ave 5, B-5580 Ave-ee-Auffe, Rochefort, Belgium (☎+32-(0)84-388220; fax 084-389388; e-mail ry.d.ave@skynet.be; www. rydave.be). A small family run rustic style hotel-restaurant, owned by M & Mme Marot-Champion. M. Marot-Champion runs the kitchen while Mme Marot-Champion is in charge of the restaurant.

**Receptionist, Waiter/Waitress** required to work a 40 hour week, of 8 hours per day over 5 days. Wages around £650 per month. Outgoing friendly personality, with a hotel diploma or relevant experience necessary and preferably knowledge of English, Dutch, French or German. Board and lodging are free. Period of work between mid-May and mid-September.

*Applications* should be sent between February and May to M. & Mme Marot-Champion.

**RADISSON SAS BRUSSELS**: Human Resources Dept, Rue du Fossé aux Loups, 47, 1000 Brussels (☎ +32 2 227 30 47; fax: +32 2 219 92 10; e-mail sales.Brussels@ radissonSAS.com; www.radisson.com/careers/htm). Radisson SAS Brussels is a 5 star hotel in the centre of Brussels. It comprises 281 bedrooms, a gastronomique restaurant, 'The Sea Grill,' a traditional restaurant, 'L'Atrium and 'Bar Dessiné and 18 conference rooms.

**Waiter/Waitress (200+)** required for waiting tables. Must be amiable, flexible and must smile! Wages are €1700 (approx £1137) per month.

**Chambermaid (300+)** required to clean rooms and to do the linen. Must be physically fit. Wages are €1400 (approx £937) per month.

Staff work 38 hours per week, 5 days a week. Dates of work are from July to August, minimum period of work is one month. No board and lodging is available, knowledge of English, French and some Dutch is required.

*Applications* invited from May, please supply nationality and date of birth on application.

**HOTEL ROYAL:** Zeelaan 180 Avenue de la Mer, B-8470 Le Panne, Belgium (☎+32 5841-1116; fax +32 5841-1016; e-mail info@hotel-royal.be; www.hotel-royal.be)

**Assistant Cook**. £150 per month. Must be catering student or qualified.

**Waitresses (2)**. £150. per month.

10 hours per day. 6-day week. Free board and accommodation. Knowledge of Dutch and French required. Minimum period of work 2 months between 1st June and 30th September.

*Applications* in January to the above address.

# Teaching and Language Schools

**SKI TEN INTERNATIONAL:** Château d'Émines B-5080 Émines, Belgium (☎+32-81-21 30 51; fax 81-20 02 63; e-mail martine@ski-ten.be; www.skiten.com)

Ski Ten offers a marvellous experience of working a month in an international team at the Château d'Émines which has 14-hectares of grounds with lakes, swimming pool etc.

**English Teacher, Tennis Teacher** and **Sports Teacher** required to work and live in a summer camp in July and August. The successful candidate will work for six hours a day; duties will include looking after, eating with and arranging games for the children in their care. In return for this, a salary of approximately £600 and accommodation will be provided. Some knowledge of French and previous experience working with children would be useful.

*Applications* should be sent in writing, with a photograph, to the above address

**VENTURE ABROAD:** Rayburn House, Parcel Terrace, Derby, DE1 1LY (☎01332-342050; 01332-224960; e-mail tours@ventureabroad.co.uk; www.ventureabroad.co.uk). Venture Abroad organise package holidays for scout and guide groups to the continent. They arrange travel and accommodation and provide representatives in the resort.

**Resort Representatives (2-3)** to work in Belgium and Switzerland; checking in groups, dealing with accommodation enquiries, organising and accompanying local excursions etc.

Applicants should be practical, resourceful and calm under pressure. Speaking German an advantage. To work six days a week, flexible hours. Five weeks minimum work from June to August.

*Applications* to the above address.

# Denmark

Denmark's low level of unemployment (currently around 4.5%), and very high standard of living, would appear to provide a big incentive for jobseekers to look for work there. However, until recent times foreigners have had a hard time of it, especially if they didn't have some notion of the Danish language. However, according to the Ministry of Science, Technology and Innovation 'English-speaking jobs in Denmark are becoming more and more common', as Denmark's large companies such as Carlsberg, Novo and Nordea, and increasingly smaller companies too, adopt English as their corporate language. Non-EU/EEA citizens will find it hard to obtain a job in Denmark, as work permits are only issued where an employer can prove that there is no EU citizen who can do that job. Citizens of the newer EU members from Eastern Europe also have restricted access to Danish jobs in the transitional phase of their membership.

Anyone serious about wanting to work in Denmark should obtain a copy of the free booklet *Working in Denmark* published by the Employment Service in Britain (see the *Useful Publications* chapter towards the end of this book). The useful leaflet called *Working in Denmark* is available from Use It Tourist Information, part of the Youth Information, at Radhusstraede 13, 1466 Copenhagen K, Denmark (☎+45-33-730620; fax +45 33 73 06 49; e-mail useit@kff.kk.dk; www.useit.dk). Please note that *Use It* is not an employment agency but an information centre for low budget travellers. The Ministry of Science, Technology and Innovation website www.workindenmark.dk, is also very informative.

Despite the increasing mechanisation of farming there is still a need for fruit pickers during the summer; up to 1,000 people are needed each year for the strawberry harvest. Be warned, however, that the hours can be very long when you are paid by the kilo with picking taking place between 6am and noon. The main harvests are strawberries in June/July, cherries in July/August, apples in September/October and tomatoes throughout the summer. Fruit producing areas are scattered around the country: some of the most important are to be found to the north of Copenhagen, around Arhus, and to the east and west of Odense.

You may be able to obtain a job on a farm or other work by contacting the pan-European agency EURES through your local job centre; vacancies for the fruit harvest and other seasonal work are announced in the spring on the Danish EURES website www.eures.dk where an online application can be made.

Another method is to advertise in the farming magazine LandbrugsAvisen (Vester Farimagsgade 6, 2 sal, DK-1606 Copenhagen V; ☎+45-33-39-4700; fax +45-33-39-4729; www.landbrugsAvisen.dk).

It is also possible to arrange unpaid work on an organic farm. Another possibility is to contact VHH (the Danish WWOOF) to obtain a list of their 25-30 member farmers, most of whom speak English. In return for three or four hours of work per day, you get free food and lodging. Always phone or write before arriving. The list can be obtained only after sending £5/US$10 to Inga Nielsen, Asenvej 35, 9881 Bindslev (☎+45 9893 8607; e-mail info@wwoof.dk; www.wwoof.dk).

The Danish state employment service is obliged to help Britons and other EU nationals who call at their offices to find a job. The administrative headquarters of the employment service – the National Labour Market Authority (*Arbejdsmarkedsstyrelsen*) – is at Blegdamsvej 56, Postbox 2722, DK-2100 Copenhagen (☎+45-3528-8100; e-mail ams@ams.dk; www.ams.dk). When you are actually in Denmark, you can find the address of your nearest employment office under *Arbejdsformidlingen* in the local telephone directory.

There are also opportunities for voluntary work in Denmark, arranged by International Voluntary Service, UNA Exchange, Youth Action for Peace and Concordia for British applicants and CIEE and Service Civil International for Americans. See the *Worldwide* chapter for details. It is also possible to work as a volunteer as the mid-June Roskilde Festival (see www.roskilde-festival.dk or e-mail your profile to david@sonordica.org or go to www.gimle.dk or telephone ☎45 46 37 1982). Volunteers are expected to be self-funding. A camping ground is provided and shifts last 8 hours.

There are a number of private employment agencies in Denmark, but most are looking for trained secretarial staff who speak fluent Danish.

An advertisement in a Danish paper may bring an offer of employment. Crane Media Partners Ltd, 20-28 Dalling Road, Hammersmith, W6 OJB (☎020-8237 8601; fax 020-8735 9941) are advertising agents for *Berlingske Tidende*. *Morgenavisen-Jyllands-Posten*, one of the more important papers for job advertisements, is published at Grondalsvej 3, DK-8260 Viby J, Denmark (☎+45-87-38-38-38).

# RED TAPE

**Visa Requirements:** visas are not required by citizens of EU countries.
**Residence Permits:** A residence permit (*Opholdsbevis*) should be applied for through Kobenhavns Overpraesidium at Hammerensgade 1, 1267 Copenhagen K, Denmark, (☎33 12 23 80). EU nationals wishing to stay in Denmark for longer than 3 months and all visitors from non-EU countries must gain a residence permit.
**Work Permits:** The Royal Danish Embassy has indicated that nationals of countries not in the EU or Scandinavia will not be granted work permits except where the employer can prove that the applicant has a unique skill. The exceptions are Australian and New Zealand nationals aged 18-30, who are entitled to apply for a Working Holiday Visa which entitles them to work in Denmark for up to six months. Further details can be obtained from the Danish Immigration Service website (www.udlst.dk). EU, Australian and New Zealand nationals who wish to take up employment in Denmark may stay there for a period not exceeding 3 months from the date of arrival in order to seek employment provided they have sufficient funds to support themselves.
**Au Pair:** allowed, but subject to the regulations outlined above. Prospective au pairs will need an au pair contract.
**Voluntary Work:** all work, paid and unpaid, is subject to the above regulations.

# Agricultural Work

**BIRKHOLM FRUGT & BAER:** V/Bjarne Knutsen, Hornelandevej 2 D, DK-5600 Faaborg, Denmark (tel/fax +45 6260-2262; e-mail birkholm@strawberrypicking.dk; www.strawberrypicking.dk).
**Strawberry Pickers:** for the season which lasts for around six weeks from 1st June, approximately. Payment at piecework rates of around £0.50 per kilo. Workers are given space to put up their own tents and have the use of a bathroom and basic cooking facilities. Minimum period of work two weeks. *Applicants must be EEA nationals.*
*Contact* the above address or check the website for further information.

# Voluntary Work and Archaeology

**MELLEMFOLKELIGT SAMVIRKE (MS):** Borgergade 14, 1300 Copenhagen K (☎+ 45 7731 0022; +45 7731 0121; globalcontact@ms.dk; www.globalcontact.dk). Volunteers to work in international work camps in Denmark and Greenland. The camps normally involve community projects such as **conservation of playgrounds, renovation, conservation, archaeological work, nature protection, reconditioning of used tools to be later sent to Africa,** etc. Board and accommodation are provided but the participants must provide their own travelling expenses.
The camps last from 2 to 3 weeks between July and August. Applicants should be aged over 18. British applicants should apply through Concordia (2nd Floor, 19 North Street, Portslade, BN41 1DH www.concordia-iye.org.uk) and the UNA Exchange (Temple of Peace, Cathays Park, Cardiff CF10 3AP; www.unaexchange.org).
*Applications* to the above address.

# Finland

Finland offers short-term paid training opportunities. The Center for International Mobility CIMO (PO Box 343, 00531 Helsinki, Finland; 09-7747 7033/fax 09-7747 7064; cimoinfo@cimo.fi/ www.cimo.fi or http://finland.cimo.fi), coordinates IAESTE (the International Association for the Exchange of Students for Technical Experience) exchange in Finland. IAESTE trainees obtain technical experience abroad relative to their studies. Participation in the IAESTE exchange is normally open to students of universities, institutes of technology and similar institutions of higher education in the fields of engineering, technology and science. British students who are interested in an IAESTE placement in Finland should apply through IAESTE in their home country (www.iaeste.org.uk). The website is in English.
Voluntary work in Finland can be arranged for British applicants by International Voluntary Service, Concordia and UNA Exchange as well as Service Civil International (see the IVS entry) and CIEE for Americans; see the *Worldwide* chapter for details. You may be able to find a job by advertising in a Finnish newspaper. *Helsingin Sanomat* is the largest circulation paper in Finland as well as *Turun Sanomat* and *Aamulehti.*

# RED TAPE

**Visa Requirements:** citizens of most countries, including the United Kingdom, the

United States of America, Australia and New Zealand and all Western European countries do not normally require a visa for a visit of less than three months unless they are taking up employment.
**Residence Permits:** EU nationals are allowed to enter and work in Finland for up to three months, if they wish to stay longer then a residence permit must be obtained from the local police station. Non-EU/EEA nationals must obtain work and residence permits prior to entering the country.
**Work Permits:** British and Irish citizens and nationals of other EEA countries do not need work permits in order to work in Finland. If you are from a non-EEA country your application for such permits may be made at a Finnish Embassy and for this you will need a letter and permission to work (obtained by the employer from their local employment office) from your prospective employer in Finland. The application is then taken to your nearest embassy where work and residence permits must be obtained. Anyone intending to work in Finland should not enter the country before all formalities have been completed.
**Working Holidays:** Australian and New Zealand citizens can now apply to the Finnish Embassy for a working holiday of up to one year. Full details can be found at www.virtual.finland.fi or www.suomi.fi.
**Au Pair:** in Finland this type of arrangement is popular and can be made for male as well as female students.

## Hotel Work and Catering

**HOTEL RUOTSINSALMI:** Kirkkokatu 14, Kotka 10, Finland (358 40575-3358)
**Waiter** and **Waitress:** wages by arrangement. Preferably with experience.
**Kitchen Assistants/Dish Washers (2).** Wages on application.

An 8 hour day, 5 day week is worked. Board and accommodation available at approximately £35 per month. Must have some knowledge of Swedish, and if possible Finnish. Minimum period of work 2/3 months between 1 May and 31 August.

*Applications* until the end of March to the above address.

# France

France has long been one of the most popular destinations for British and Irish people looking for summer work. This is due to its physical proximity: the fact that French is the first (and often only) foreign language learned; and, possibly most important of all, because during the summer France still needs many extra temporary workers for both its vibrant tourist trade and farm work, even though there is currently fairly high unemployment of about 9.7% mainly amongst young people. Theme parks like Disneyland Paris or Parc Asterix need extra staff through peak times such as the summer holidays. Disneyland Paris alone employs many thousands of seasonal workers.

This chapter contains details of many jobs in the tourist industry: you can find others in the *Worldwide* chapter at the beginning of the book and in the weekly hotel trade magazine *L'Hotellerie* published at 5, rue Antoine Bourdelle, 75015 Paris, (☎45 48 64 64; fax 45 48 04 23; www.lhotellerie.fr) where you can check out the classified jobs section (arranged by region) at any time online.

British and Irish citizens, along with other EU nationals, are allowed to use the French national employment service (*Agence Nationale pour l'Emploi*), the headquarters of which is at Le Galilee, 4 rue Galilee, 93198 Noisy-le-Grand

(☎149-31-74-00), although the offices in towns throughout France will know more about vacancies in their region. There is also a comprehensive website detailing the services provided by ANPE in both French and English: www.anpe. fr. British citizens can apply for work through the service by visiting any of almost 600 *Agences Nationales pour l'Emploi* (ANPE) around the country. The ANPE for Narbonne (ANPE, BP 802, 29 rue Mazzini, 11008 Narbonne Cedex) has seasonal hotel vacancies from May to September, and others can provide details of when agricultural work is available.

There are also a number of private employment agencies such as *Manpower*, *Kelly*, *Bis*, *Select France*, and *Ecco* in large cities which can help people who speak reasonable French to find temporary jobs in offices, private houses, warehouses, etc. They can be found in the Yellow Pages (*Les Pages Jaunes*) under *Agences de Travail Temporaire*. These can normally only find jobs for people who visit in person.

For further information relevant to British citizens consult the free booklet *Working in France* published by the UK's national Jobcentre Plus (see the *Useful Publications* chapter towards the end of this book).

There is a *Work in France Programme* for American citizens with the CEI (see *Work Abroad Schemes for US Citizens* below) and there are similar schemes for Australians and New Zealanders.

Seasonal farm work can be difficult to obtain from outside France. If you cannot arrange a job in advance using the information in this chapter it is best to be on the spot and approach farmers in person, or ask at the local employment offices, town halls (*mairies*) or youth hostels. A word of warning: if you arrange to go grape picking with an organisation not mentioned in this chapter read the small print carefully: you may be buying just a journey out to France, with no guarantee of a job at the end.

For help in finding temporary work during the grape-picking season, you could contact ANPE. ANPE have offices in most large towns in France's main agricultural regions. Each office can offer around 1000 jobs to those who wish to work on farms up to 50km from the town, apple-picking and grape-picking being the most prevalent jobs available and within a the prior month or so, they will be able to inform you of the approximate date of the beginning of the harvest.

The addresses and dates for the ANPE below are provided only as a guide: there is no guarantee either that they will have definite vacancies to offer, and the exact dates of harvests can vary considerably from year to year and from region to region. The work period also varies. The ANPE office in Castelnaudry asked to be removed from this edition as the maize-topping work in their region only lasts 4 days.

*For temporary agricultural work (July-September):*
○   ANPE, 33 avenue Henri Farbos, F-40000 Mont de Marsan (☎5-58-85-43-40).
*For grape picking (by region):*
**Alsace** – 15th October
○   ANPE, 54, Avenue de la République, BP 50868021, Colmar (☎3-89-20-80-70; fax 0389-20-80-78).
**Beaujolais** – 10th September
○   ANPE, 8 Rue du 14 Juillet, 69220 Belleville (☎0-4-74-66-14-10).
**Bordeaux** – 25th September
○   ANPE, 34, avenue du General Leclerc, F-33210 Langon (☎05-57-98-02-60).
○   ANPE, Chemin du Casse, F-33500 Libourne (☎5-57-55-32-20).
○   ANPE, 19, rue Adrien Chauvet, BP 108, 33250 Pauillac (☎5-56-73-20-

# Keycamp
## HOLIDAYS

Keycamp is Europe's leading Tour Operator and the leader in self-drive, self-catering holidays on campsites in Europe. Operating in 8 countries throughout Europe on over 100 campsites, we sell family holidays to customers from the UK, Ireland, Holland, and Denmark.

We employ around 1,200 campsite staff every year from many of these countries and can offer a large range of positions to suit all our overseas employees.

We are looking for people for various positions that involve **customer service, cleaning accommodation, working with children, leading a team and administration.** We also employ teams of people at the beginning and end of the season to help us erect and dismantle tents. Successful applicants will be asked to apply for a Standard or Enhanced Disclosure.*

**We will provide:**
- Competitive Salary
- Accommodation
- Uniform
- Subsidised Insurance
- Training
- Travel To Resort

**You will need to be:**
- 18+
- An EU passport holder (or have a work permit for any of the countries that we operate in)
- Available to start work between April and July

If you think you have the qualities to provide our customers with the 'perfect family holiday' please apply online at **www.holidaybreakjobs.com** or phone **01606 787525** for an application pack. Please quote **SJ/07**.

* Further information about Disclosures can be found at www.disclosure.gov.uk or by phoning 0870 90 90 811.

50; fax 5-56-59-62-49).
**Burgundy** – 10th September
   O   ANPE, 6 boulevard St. Jacques, B.P. 115, F-21203 Beaune (☎3-80-25-07-06).
   O   ANPE, 71 rue Jean-Macé, F-71031 Mâcon Cedex (☎3-85-21-93-20; fax 03-85-38-46-88).
**Languedoc-Roussilon** – 15th September
   O   ANPE, BP 65, 29 av. Léon Blum, 30205 Bagnols sur Ceze.
   O   ANPE, BP 4236, 13 Alphonse Mas, 34544 Beziers Cedex.
   O   ANPE, 90 Avenue Pierre Sémard, BP 586 Iéna,11009 Carcassonne Iéna Cedex.
   O   ANPE, BP 3054, 60 rue Siegfried, 30002 Nimes Cedex.
**Indre et Loire** – early September to Mid-October (Apple-picking also available).
   O   ANPE Joue Les Tours, Champ Girault, 57 rue Chantepie, B.P. 304, 37303 Joue Les Tours CEDEX (☎2-47-60-58-58).

Workers are also needed to help harvest the following fruits, especially in the valleys of the Loire and the Rhône and the south east and south west of the country. The dates given are only approximate: bear in mind that harvests tend to begin first in the south of the country.

   O   *Strawberries:* May to mid-June
   O   *Cherries:* mid-May to early July
   O   *Peaches:* June to September
   O   *Pears:* mid-July to mid-November
   O   *Apples:* mid-August (but chiefly from mid-September) to mid-October.

French farmers employ over 100,000 foreigners for seasonal work during the summer. Many of these are skilled 'professional' seasonal workers from Spain, Poland, Portugal and Morocco who return to the same regions every year: if there is a choice of applicants for a job, a farmer will prefer an experienced worker to a total beginner. In recent years there has also been an influx of people from Eastern Europe who are desperate for work and prepared to work for less than the minimum wage (*le SMIC*), of €8.27/£5.50 (July 2006) for any farmer who will employ them illegally. Anyone going to France to look for farm work should be prepared to move from area to area in the search for a job: it would also be wise to take enough money to cover the cost of returning home in case of failure. Also be warned that payment is generally by piecework, so there are no wages if picking is suspended because of bad weather.

   The publishers Mitchell Beazley produce a series of useful guides to wine regions (Alsace, Bordeaux, Provence, Rhone and Loire) under the title *Touring in Wine Country* which cost £12.99 each. You can remove some of the uncertainty of the job hunt by visiting farmers to arrange a job before their harvests start: by doing so you should also be given an informed estimate of when the harvest will start. Note that although vineyard owners normally provide accommodation for grape pickers, workers on other harvests will normally need camping equipment.

   The increasing sophistication of the ANPE means that grape-picking and fruit picking jobs are advertised on their website (www.anpe.fr) in English.

   France is rich in opportunities for voluntary work, as the entries at the end of this chapter will testify. The CEI in Paris and Service Civil International (see the IVS entry) can assist Americans. International Voluntary Service (IVS), UNA Exchange, Youth Action for Peace and Concordia can help can UK residents to find short-term voluntary work; their entries can be found in the *Worldwide* chapter at the beginning of the book.

A great many archaeological digs and building restoration projects are carried out each year. The French Ministry of Culture has two departments dealing with antiquities, one focuses on archaeology and the other on the restoration of monuments (Ministère de la Culture, *Direction de l'Architecture et du Patrimoine, Sous-Direction de l'Archeologie*, 4 rue d'Aboukir, 75002 Paris (☎1-40-15-77-81) and Ministère de la Culture, *Direction du Patrimoine, Sous-Direction des Monuments Historiques* at the same address (☎1-40-15-76-81). Each year the ministry publishes in a brochure and on the internet (www.culture. gouv.fr/fouilles) a list of these archaeological fieldwork projects throughout France requiring up to 5,000 volunteers. Another brochure, *Chantiers de benevoles* published by Rempart (see entry under Voluntary Work), lists projects relating to building restoration. It has pages in English or can be found at www.rempart.com.

Advertising for a job in France can be arranged in the Paris edition of the *International Herald Tribune* contact the London office, 40, Marsh Wall, London E14 9TP (☎020-7836 4802; e-mail ukadv@iht.com), or New York Office, 850 Third Avenue, New York, NY 10022 (☎212-752 3890; e-mail usadv@iht.com), or on the internet www.iht.com.

# RED TAPE

**Visa Requirements:** visas are not required for visits to France by EU, American, Canadian, Australian or New Zealand nationals. Others should check with their nearest French Consulate.

**Residence Permits:** in November 2003, France abolished the need for EU citizens to have a *carte de séjour* (residence permit) for stays of any length. You can apply for one voluntarily as it can be a useful proof of ID for long-term foreign residents, but as the paperwork involved is so cumbersome, it is likely that most long-stayers will not bother. If you decide you want one, application for this permit should be made on a special form available from the *Prefecture de Police* in Paris, or the local *Prefecture* or *Mairie* (town hall) elsewhere. The following documents are required: passport, birth certificate, proof of accommodation, proof of payment of contributions to the French Social Security, 3 passport photos, a contract of employment, pension receipts or student status documents. Non-EU nationals need to possess a long stay visa before applying for a *carte de séjour*, and a work permit before obtaining either. Application for a long stay visa should be lodged with a French consulate in the applicant's country of residence.

**Work Permits:** Members of the EU/EEA do not need work permits to work in France. The standard procedure for non-EEA nationals is that the prospective employer in France must apply to the *Office des Migrations Internationales* in Paris (44 Rue Bargue, 75015 Paris; ☎0153-695370; www.omi.social.fr) only after receiving permission from the DDTEFP which oversees the employment of foreign professionals.

**Work Abroad Schemes for US Citizens:** there is a special scheme allowing American students to work in France run by the CEI (Centre d'Echanges Internationaux). To participate applicants must be in full-time higher education and have at least intermediate French skills (tests are available on request). Three types of scheme are available through the 'Work in France' department, the Job Placement, the Internship Placement and the Self-Service placement.

**Self-Service Placement:** allows students a 3-month temporary work permit during their school holidays. Participants receive help finding jobs via a network of

employers willing to employ foreign students and help finding housing.
**Internship Placement**: offers an internship covered by a written work placement agreement, which must be signed by the student, the employer and the university. The work placement may not last longer than a year. The placement assigned to a student should have a direct link to the subject they are studying.
**Job Placement**: after interviews with students and thanks to a large network of employers, the CEI organises job appointments between students and employers in order for the participants to begin work very soon after their arrival in France. As an association recognised by the Ministry of Employment the CEI is capable of validating a work placement found by the students themselves.
For more information please visit www.cei4vents.com or contact the CEI French Centre, 1 rue Gozlin, 75006 Paris (☎ +33 (0)1 40 51 11 86; wif@cei4vents.com).
**Au Pair**: the family with which you are to stay should apply to the Direction Departmentale de Travail for the necessary Accord de Placement au pair d'un stagiaire aide-familial.
**Voluntary Work**: a work permit is necessary for non-EEA nationals.

# Agricultural Work

**APPELLATION CONTROLLEE**: Ulgersmaweg 26, 9731 BT Groningen, The Netherlands (☎0+31 (0)50 5492434; fax +31 (0)50 5492428; e-mail info@apcon. nl; www.apcon.nl). An organisation that organises working holidays in France and England.
**France Fruit Picking Programme** taking place in the Maine et Loire department of Western France. The job involves picking various fruits beginning with strawberries in May and followed by raspberries, bilberries and melons later on. Wages at either piece work rate (average earnings £25-£40 per day) or at an hourly rate (approx. £30 per day). Normal minimum stay on a farm is three weeks but can be up to six months. Accommodation will be either camping or the farmer may provided clean, basic accommodation. Hours of work may vary from 5 to 8 per day depending on weather and amount of fruit ready to pick.
   **Grape picking** takes place in the Beaujolais, Maconais and Bourgogne regions in September. Wages around £30 per day plus board and lodging. To work 8 hours per day, 7 days per week; period of work is one to four weeks.
   Minimum age for all work is 18 years. of Western France. The job involves picking various fruits beginning with strawberries in May and followed by raspberries, bilberries and melons later on. Wages at either piece work rate (average earnings £25-£40 per day) or at an hourly rate (approx. £30 per day). Normal minimum stay on a farm is three weeks. Accommodation will be either camping or the farmer may provided clean, basic accommodation.
   *Applications* to the above address.

**BERNARD LACOMBE**: Les Crouzets, F-12160 Baraqueuille, France (☎05-65-69-01-46).
**Farm Helper** to milk cows and feed animals on a farm in the South of France. To work 4 hours a day, 6 days a week. Pocket money and board and lodging provided. Some knowledge of French required. Minimum period of work 1 month at any time of the year. Applicants must be hard-working and like nature and animals. There is also the possibility of some supplementary Bed & Breakfast related work.
   *Applications* to M. Lacombe at the above address.

**G. ESPINASSE:** Sevignac, Druelle F-12510, Olemps, France (☎ +33 (0)5 65 69 36 81; e-mail
**Farm Helper** to carry out all types of work in the field and assist with breeding (mainly sheep), also to study and practise bio-organic farming. No salary but about £30 per month pocket money and the opportunity to learn about herbal medicines and the occult sciences. Board and lodging provided. Some knowledge of French useful. Minimum period of work 1-2 months all year round.
    *Applications*, in French, as soon as possible to the above address.

**S.C.A. SOLDIVE:** BP 72 - Brie, F-79102 THOUARS Cedex, FRANCE (☎05-49-67-41-61; fax 05-49-67-43-56; e-mail SOLDIVE@wanadoo.fr).
**Farm Labourers (1,500)** to harvest melons.
**Workers (30)** to pack the fruit in factories.
**Mechanics (30)** to repair and maintain farm machinery, must speak French.
    Wages are at French SMIC rates. To work 6 days per week and 8 hours per day. Minimum period of work 2 months between July and September. EU nationals, must be in possession of a temporary residence permit, student card.
    *Applications* to the above address.

# Boats

**CONTINENTAL WATERWAYS:** P.O. Box 31, Godalming, Surrey GU8 6JH; French Office: Continentale de Croisières SA, 1 Promenade du Rhin, BP 41748, F-21017, Dijon, France, (☎ 01252-703577; fax 01252-702860; France ☎ +33 380 53 1530; fax +33 380 41 6773; e-mail crew@continentalwaterways.co.uk or gbryant@gct.com; www.continentalwaterways.co.uk (recruitment); www.continentalwaterways.com (Marketing). Continental Waterways have operated a fleet of luxury floating hotel barges on the waterways of France for the last 30 years.
**Crew Members** required to work from March to November in a fleet of 9 luxury hotel barges, including 2 large river boats, crewed by French, British and other EU nationalities. The company require high standards and are looking for highly committed team players to provide excellent service to American passengers. This is an ideal job for those who wish to improve their language skills, appreciate gourmet food, wine and cheese and who wish to immerse themselves in French culture for 7 months. Benefits include 4 week on, 2 week off rotation, holiday pay at the season end, medical insurance, uniform and training. *Applicants must have a valid permanent National Insurance number and hold a British or EU passport.*
    Download an *application form* and send it to Gail Byrant, Crew Recruitment at the above UK address.

**CROISIERES TOURISTIQUES FRANCAISES,** 2 Route de Semur, F-21150 Venarey-les-Laumes, France (☎3-80-96-17-10; fax 3-80-96-19-18; e-mail ctf.boat@club-internet.fr). Croisieres Touristiques Francaises owns and operates five ultra-deluxe hotel barges, offering six-night cruises in five regions of central France The clientele is principally North American.
**Chefs.** Gross salary from £1.300 per month. Required to plan menus and prepare gourmet cuisine. Professional training and experience in haute cuisine establishments essential. Some knowledge of French useful.
**Drivers/Guides.** Gross salary from £1,100 per month. Applicants must have a P.S.V. licence, should speak fluent French and have a full knowledge of French heritage and culture.
**Pilots.** Gross salary from £1,300 per month. Must have French Inland Waterways

Permit to drive 38m Hotel Barge and have mechanical experience. Some knowledge of French useful.
**Stewardesses.** Gross salary from £900 per month. Work involves cleaning cabins, general housekeeping, food/bar service and care of passengers. Knowledge of French useful, but not essential.
**Deckhands.** Gross salary from £900 per month. To assist the pilot during navigation and mooring and to carry out exterior maintenance of the barge. Some knowledge of French useful.

Crew Members must be EU nationals, or possess appropriate visas permitting work in France and be available for work from April to early November. Salaries quoted are for inexperienced crew members and include accommodation, full board and uniform. Social Security coverage is taken care of by the Company. Gratuities are divided equally amongst crew members. Minimum age 21. For all positions the hours of work are long, over a five to six day week. Applicants must be energetic, personable, and able to provide a consistently high standard of service.

*Apply* with cv, contact telephone number and recent photo to Mr. Thierry Bresson at the above address.

# Holiday Centres

**DISNEYLAND PARIS:** Casting, BP110, F-77777 Marne La Vallée cedex 4, France (www.Disneylandparis.com/uk/employment).
**Permanent or Seasonal Staff** to work in the restaurants, on counter service or reception, in sales, for the attractions, sports and leisure attractions of the Disneyland Paris Resort situated 30 km east of Paris. Both temporary contracts lasting 2-8 months from March (minimum availability July-August) or permanent contracts starting at any time. 35 hour working week; monthly gross wage of £775 less social security contributions. Assistance is given in finding accommodation and a contribution towards travel expenses is given to those who complete their contract.

Applicants should be at least 18, have a good working knowledge of French and be customer-service orientated. Experience not essential.

*Applications* in writing to the above address.

# Hotel Work and Catering

**ALP ACTIVE:** Unit 10, Chesterton Mill, French's Road, Cambridge, CB4 3NP; (☎0845 1209 872; fax 0845 6449385; info@alpactive.com; www.alpactive.com). Alp Active provides activity sports holidays in the French Alps. It is aimed at anyone from keen mountain-bikers to families.
**Mountain Bike Guides (3)** to work six-day week guiding clients around the Portes du Soleil Area. Must be Mountain Leader 2 qualified. Wages approx. £450 plus benefits.
**Resort Assistants (2)** to work a six-day week same hours as guides. General resort back-up and support. Wages approximately £400 plus benefits.

All staff get free board and lodging.

*Apply* immediately to the above address or e-mail.

**ALPINE ELEMENTS:** 1 Risborough Street, London, SE1 OHF (08700 111360; info:alpineelements.co.uk; www.alpineelements.co.uk)
Alpine Elements arrange chalet and self-catering holidays in Chamonix, Morzine, Les Gets, Meriel, Alpe d'Huez, Val d'Isere, Les Arcs Courchevel and Tignes in France. The Summer Alpine Programme runs from May to September. Staff are employed

as **chalet hosts, resort managers, hotel chefs and reps.** Staff should be 18+ and be British passport-holders. Reps must hold a clean driving licence. Staff get two weeks of training in France and the UK.

Applicants should send their CV and a covering letter to the above address or e-mail for the attention of Mr G. Niedermann.

**ALPINE TRACKS:** 40 High Street, Menai Bridge, Anglesey LL59 5EF (☎01248-717440; fax 01248-717441; e-mail info@alpinetracks.com or sales@alpinetracks.com; www.alpinetracks.com). Alpine Tracks are a friendly and informal small professional holiday company operating chalets with a high level of personal service in the French Alps for skiers and mountain bikers.

**Chef, Cleaners (3), Minibus Driver, Bar Person, Mountain Bike and Ski Guides** to earn between £350-£500 for dining and bar work, catering for up to 30 people. Applicants should be friendly, outgoing, preferably French speakers and hold relevant qualifications. Hours of work are 7am to 10am and 5pm to 9pm 7 days per week, between 1 July and 30 September; minimum period of work 2 months. Board and lodging are provided at no cost.

*Applications* to the above address.

**L'ALAMBIC ROCK CAFÉ**: 48 Avenue de la Mer, F-85160 St Jean de Monts, France (☎00 33 25158 06 83). A lively and very busy Tex Mex restaurant and Rock Café situated in the main tourist area of St Jean. The friendly French owner employs a staff of 10 for the season.

**Barman/Woman, Waiter/Waitress:** Dynamic, fun loving and fit young people sought to work in June, July and August. Must speak good French and have previous experience in fast-moving bar/restaurant. Wage £170 per week and free accommodation.

To *apply* send a CV and photo to Paul Babu at the above address.

**HOTEL RESTAURANT ALTAIR:** 18 Boulevard Féart, F-35800 Dinard, France (☎02-99 46 13 58; fax 02-99 88 20 49). Pleasant two-star hotel-restaurant with terrace, near St Malo.

**Chef, Waiter/Waitress, Chambermaid** required to work hours as required by the job over a 5½ day week, minimum of 4 hours work per day. Waiting staff will be serving meals in the restaurant and on the terrace. Wages and period of work by arrangement. Applicants should speak French and English or German, and have some previous experience of hotel work.

Places are available all year round and *applications* should be sent to the above address.

**HOTEL AMIGO**: 1-3 Rue de l'Amigo, 1000 Bruxelles (☎+32 2 547 47 47; fax: +32 2 513 52 77; e-mail hotelamigo@hotelamigo.com; www.roccofortehotels.com).

**Telephonist** responsible for answering calls to the switchboard, answering telephones internal and external, taking messages, faxes and passing them on, providing information as requested by callers, keeping accounts of calls for billing guests, organising morning alarm calls etc. Some office work involved. Must be 18 or over and speak French, English and Dutch.

**Shop Administrator** responsible for ordering and restocking, stock checking, receiving deliveries and cleaning. Must be 18 years or above and speak French. Wages €1511.66 (approx £1015) per month.

Dates of work from 1ˢᵗ July to 31ˢᵗ August minimum period of work 2 weeks. Staff are expected to work 38 hours per week, 5 days a week. Food but not lodging is available for the cost of €1.09 (approx 73p) a day. Knowledge of French and English required.

*Applications* are invited from April to May.

**HOTEL DES BAINS ET ARVERNE:** Ave de la Promenade, 15800 Vic sur Cere, France (☎+33(0)471-47-50-16; fax 04 71 49 63 82; www.arvernehotel.com). **Waitresses and Chambermaids:** Wages approx. €500 (approx £350) per month plus tips, food, accommodation. To work 5 days per week during the summer from April to October. Must have catering experience.

*Applications* should be sent to Mr Michel at the above address with a curriculum vitae in French and a recent photo, stating when available to work.

**L'AUBERGE DU CHOUCAS:** F-05220 Monetier le Bains, Serre-Chevalier 1500, Hautes-Alpes, France (☎492-24-42-73; fax 492-24-51-60). The hotel is a converted old farm, and prides itself on its attentive service and its gastronomic food. It is located in a charming and lively village in one of the most important ski resorts in France. The area is a popular tourist destination throughout the year.
**Hotel Staff (2)**; wages and duties by arrangement. To work 5 days per week. Board and accommodation provided. Minimum period of work 12 weeks in the summer or winter, or any other longer period.

There is a family atmosphere, but diligent work is demanded. Applicants should be discreet and well-educated, have a pleasant disposition, speak a minimum of basic French and preferably have previous hotel or restaurant work. The manageress attaches great importance to language ability and sensitivity to the culture. Some knowledge of German would also be an advantage.

*Applications* should be sent to Nicole Sanchez-Ventura at the above address.

**L'AUBERGE SUR LA MONTAGNE:** La Thuile, F-73640 Sainte Foy Tarentaise, France (☎4-79 06 95 83; fax 4-79 06 95 96; e-mail mail@auberge-montagne.co.uk; www.auberge-montagne.co.uk). This private 8-bed hotel is situated in the French alps between Val D'Isère and Bourg Saint Maurice. There are great opportunities for, walking, cycling, watersports and paragliding, as well as glacier skiing in summer.
**1 or 2 Chalet Hosts** required to clean rooms, public areas (bar, lounge and restaurant), wash up and serve breakfasts and dinner. Hours of work 2/4 hours per morning and 4/6 hours per evening 6-8 hours per day) 6 days per week. Minimum period of work is four weeks. Wages are €500 (£345) per month with free board and lodging. Applicants should have some previous experience and speak English and French.

To *apply* contact Sue & Andy MacInnes from May onwards.

**AUDE HOTEL:** aire de Narbonne, Vinasson, Autoroute A9, 11110 Vinasson, France (☎468-45-25-00; fax 468-45-25-20).
**Hotel Staff** to work in reception, serve in the restaurant, clean, take messages, various other duties as necessary. Wages at the usual national rate. To work 8 hours per day, with one day off per 48 hour week. Period of work by arrangement. Accommodation can be provided at the usual national rate. Applicants should have a good sense of service and a desire to work well; they should also, if possible, speak French, English, German and Italian.

*Applications* should be sent to the Manager at the above address between March and April.

**THE AVIATIC HOTEL:** 105 rue de Vaugirard, 75006 Paris, France (☎: +33 153 63 25 50; fax: +33 153 63 25 55; e-mail welcome@aviatic.fr; www.aviatic.fr. The Aviatic Hotel is an excellent, 3-star, family run establishment that takes pride in the

impeccable service offered to clients and respects its employees.
**Waiter/Waitress**: required to prepare, serve and tidy away after breakfast. Involves a lot of client interaction. Experience is a plus but not necessary, must be a team player and not mind early mornings.
**Chamber Maid**: required for thorough cleaning of the rooms and bathrooms, bed making, stock taking and replacing. This can be a very physical job. Must have enthusiasm and professionalism. Experience is a plus but not necessary.

Staff to work 39 hours per week, 5 days a week. Dates of work are between June and September, minimum period of work is 2 months. No board and lodging is available. Knowledge of English and French is essential and some Spanish is a plus.

*Applications* invited from March and April.

**HOSTELLERIE LE BEFFROI:** BP 85, F-84110 Vaison la Romaine, Provence, France (☎490-36-04-71; fax 490-36-24-78; info@le-beffroi.com; www.le-beffroi.com).
**Reception Assistant, Bar, Kitchen and Restaurant Staff**. Duties by arrangement. To work 8 hours per day, 5 days per week. Wages of around €1050 (£750) per month, board and accommodation provided. Minimum period of work 3 months between April and the end of September. Applicants should speak French (and German if possible) and must have experience of hotel or restaurant work.

*Applications* to Yann Christiansen at the above address.

**HOTEL BELLE ISLE SUR RISLE:** 112 Route de Rouen, F-27500 Pont-Audemer, France (☎232-56 96 22; fax 232-42 88 96; e-mail hotelbelle-isle@wanadoo.fr; www.bellile.com).
**Waiter (1), Receptionist (1)** to work at reception and switchboard. Salary according to qualifications and competence. 169 hours work a month. Minimum period of work 1-2 months during the summer vacation: July and August. Accommodation available in the local town at a maximum of £99 per month. Applicants must have excellent presentation. English and/or German languages required.

*Applications* at any time at the above address.

**HOTEL BELLEVUE:** F-63790 Chambon-sur-Lac, France (☎473-88 61 06; fax 473-88 63 53; lachotelbellevue@aol.com).
**General Assistant**. Wages by arrangement. Period of work July-1 September. Applicants must be keen workers, well-educated, and speak French. Knowledge of German and English an advantage.

*Applications* to Madame Amélie Dabert at the above address from April enclosing a photograph and an International Reply Coupon, or apply by e-mail.

**RELAIS DU BOIS SAINT GEORGES:** Parc Atlantique, Cours Genet, F-17100 Saintes, France (☎5-46-93 50 99; fax 5-46-93 34 93; e-mail info@relaisdubois.com; www.relaisdubois.com). This charming establishment is featured in *The Good Hotel Guide*.
**Kitchen Assistants** to help in the kitchens and assist the chambermaids each morning.

Applicants for both positions should be well-presented, motivated and good team workers. The period of work is from July to September; minimum period of work one month, working eight hours per day, five days a week. Board and accommodation is available if needed and is provided free of charge. Applicants should speak English and French.

*Applications* invited from January.

**CAMPING CLUB MAR ESTANG:** Mer Méditerranée, 66140 Canet en Roussillon, France (☎+33 (0)468 80 35 53; fax +33 (0)468 7332 94; e-mail contact@marestang. com; www.marestang.com).
**Disc Jockey (1), Ice Cream Attendants (2) Swimming Pool Attendants (4)** with or without qualification), **Receptionists (2), Bar Staff (6), Restaurant Staff (2), Beach Boy (1), Ground Staff (3), Night Security Staff (2), Sailing Instructor (1), Restaurant chef (1), Maids (3).** Wages €900 (£630) to €1400 (£980), depending on schedule and abilities.
   All contracts are seasonal from 2 to 5 months. Qualifications are needed only for restaurant chef, two of the pool attendants and sailing instructor. French must be spoken for receptionist, bar staff, ice cream, pool and sailing instruction.
   *Applications:* please send I.D. with photo with your application to Mr Laurent Raspaud at the above address.

**HOTEL CHATEAURENARD:** F-05350 Saint Veran, France (☎492-45-85-43; fax 492-45-84-20; e-mail info@hotel-chateaurenard.com; www.chateaurenard-stveran. com). This 20-room chalet-style hotel, run by a French speaking Australian with her French chef husband is located at the foot of the ski slopes (2080m). It has spectacular views overlooking the 18th Century village of Saint Veran, the Hautes Alpes, and the border with the Italian Piedmont.
**General Assistants (4)** to clean rooms, work in the restaurant and the laundry. To work 43 hours a week, 5 days a week. Wages at the usual national rate for hotel work. Board and accommodation provided. To work minimum period of 1 week over Christmas/New Year, 4 weeks in February/March or 4-6 weeks during July to August/ September. No special qualifications required except a happy nature and the ability to work with people and to work hard. Knowledge of French is essential.
   *Applications* to the Director at the above address.

**HOTEL-RESTAURANT CHEVAL-BLANC:** F-67510 Niedersteinbach, France (☎388-09-55-31; fax 388-09-50-24; e-mail contact@hotel-cheval-blanc.fr; www. hotel-cheval-blanc.fr). A 25 room hotel combined with a 120 place restaurant located in a small village in a natural park. Facilities include a tennis court and a swimming pool
**Assistant Waitress:** €800 (£560) per month plus tips.
**Kitchen Assistant:** €800 (£560) per month.
   5½ day week. Board and lodging provided free. Must have previous experience and knowledge of French and German. Period of work 3 months minimum from July to November.
   *Applications* to February to M Michel Zinck at the above address.

**CLUB CANTABRICA HOLIDAYS LTD:** 146/148 London Road, St. Albans, Herts AL1 1PQ (☎01727-866-177; fax 01727-843766; recruitment@cantabrica.co.uk; www.cantabrica.co.uk). Club Cantabrica is an independent tour operator with 30 years of experience. Offering luxury coach, air and self-drive holidays on excellent sites in France (including the French Alps). Italy and Spain. Opportunities also available for our ski programme in the Austrian Tyrol and the French Alps.
**Resort Manager (12)** to manage sites varying in size from 25-100 units. Must have previous campsite rep. experience and French, Italian or Spanish language skills. Wages between £200 and £220 per week, including bonus and commission.
**Campsite Couriers (30)** to work on camp sites in France, Italy, and Spain. Work involves looking after clients, setting up and closing down site, tent and mobile home cleaning and maintenance, paperwork and excursion sales. Wages £100 per week plus

commission, including bonus.

**Peak Season Courier (15)** to cover same tasks as couriers but for June-September only. Minimum period of work 3 months. Wages £100 per week. Including bonus.

**Children's' Courier (11)** to run Kids' Club on campsites, must have experience of working with children and relevant qualification. Wages £100 per week plus commission and bonus.

**Maintenance Staff (11)** to carry out maintenance and upkeep work on tents and mobile homes. Applicants should have excellent practical skills. Wages £95-£125 per week.

**Hotel Staff (8)** including **General Duties Rep.** and **Chef** to help run the Club Hotel in Chamonix Valley - fluent French required.

Free accommodation provided. To work approximately 40 hours per 6 day week, from April to October, except Peak Season staff. Couriers should be enthusiastic and have plenty of stamina, with knowledge of languages an advantage. Applicants should be over 18 years old (over 21 for managers). Experience preferable.

*Applications* with curriculum vitae to the above address (please specify winter or summer); applicants can also e-mail recruitment@cantabrica.co.uk. Or visit www. cantabrica.co.uk

**CLUB TELI:** 2 Chemin de Golemme, 74600 Seynod, France (☎0033-4-5052-2658; fax 4-5052-1016; e-mail clubteli@wanadoo.fr; www.teli.asso.fr). The Club TELI offers an interesting alternative for any person wishing to go abroad whether for a training course, a summer job or a career job. Club TELI is a non-profit organisation.
**Secretary:** Club TELI seeks interns (2 months minimum) who have a good knowledge of French. Age 20-30, good telephone manner. Wages: €150 per month (approx. £105) Seynod is a small town near Annecy (90 km to Chamonix-Mont Blanc, 45 km to Geneva).

*Apply* by e-mail to Dominique Girerd, Director.

**HOTEL-RESTAURANT LA CROIX BLANCHE DE SOLOGNE:** Place de l'Eglise R. Mothu, 41600 Chaumont-sur-Tharonne, France; (☎02 54 88 55 12; fax 02 54 88 60 40; e-mail lacroixblanchesologne@wanadoo.fr; www.hotel-sologne.com). Has been an inn since the 15th century (and before that a convent) with a tradition of women chef-owners dating back over 220 years.
**Waiting person** to work in the dining room. Experience or at least knowledge of how a restaurant dining-room works.
**Cooking person** with knowledge of *commis, aide cuisine* and *plongeur* (dishwasher).

Salary is €900 (£630) including free board and lodging. Hours of work 9am-2pm and 6pm-10pm (35 hours) five and a half days a week. Must speak French. Period of work is 1 July to 31 August.

Applications to Michel-Pierre Goacolou, at the above address any time from 1 January to 31 May.

**RESTAURANT CRUAUD:** 30 avenue Joffre, 84300, Cavaillon, France (☎/fax 06 80 26 69 98). François Cruaud is also a Conseiller Culinaire and Officier du Mérite Agricole and offers cookery courses and *Formation* for hotel and restaurant trainees. In 2005, he created the Association des Conseilles Alimentaires Français et Européens.
**Summer Staff** to work in a hotel and restaurant; wages and details of work by arrangement. To work 186 hours per month, 5 days per week. Board and lodging provided. To work from April to October. Applicants must speak French and English.

*Applications* should be sent to Mr and Mrs Cruaud at the above address from January.

**HOTEL DES DEUX ROCS:** 1 Place Font d'Amont, 83440 Seillans, France (☎04 94 76 87 32; fax 04 94 76 88 68).
**Commis de Cuisine, Waiting Assistants (2), Housekeeper.** Wages €1000/€1,200 (£700-£840). To work 41 hours per week, five to seven days a week. Minimum two months between June and September. Board and lodging provided.
*Apply* from March to the above address.

**DOMAINE SAINT CLAIR LE DONJON:** Chemin de Saint Clair, 76790 Etretat, France (☎+33 (0)143-30 77 79; fax +33 (0)170-60 11 30; e-mail direction@ hoteletretat.com or donjon@hotelspreference.com). Hotel and Restaurant with 21 rooms all with ensuite including jacuzzi. The restaurant is of gastronomic standard.
**Various dining room and kitchen positions, Receptionist** for a two-part organisation (hotel and restaurant) to work 8 hours per day 5/6 days per week in reception and room cleaning and in the restaurant (service, bar and kitchen). Wages from €850/£595 (waiter) to €1500/£1050 (for pastry chef), and €1300 (£910) for receptionist per month. Board and lodging provided at no extra cost. Period of work is April to September. Dining room staff should speak French and English, kitchen positions require experience and the receptionist must be fluent in French and English and have experience.
*Apply* to the Director at the above address.

**LE DOMAINE DE LA TORTINIERE:** F-37250 Montbazon-en-Touraine, France (☎247-34-35-00; fax 247-65-95-70; e-mail domaine.tortiniere@wanadoo.fr). A graceful second-empire turreted chateau converted into a hotel in 1954 and managed by the same family since then; guests are from France and the rest of the world.
**Barman/Bellboy (1/2)** to serve drinks from 3pm to midnight and to help staff at front desk, carry suitcases and show guests to their rooms. No wage, but free board and lodging. Minimum period of work 2 months between 1 March and 25 December. Applicants should be well presented and speak French and English.
*Applications* to Monsieur X. Olivereau at the above address.

**DOMAINE VALLEE HEUREUSE:** Route de Genève, F-39800 Poligny, France (☎+33 384-37 12 13; valleeheureuse@wanadoo.com; www.hotelvalleeheureuse)
**Waiter.** Hours: 9am-3pm and 7-10.30pm. Cleanliness, cheerfulness and good appearance essential. Waiting experience preferred. £300 plus tips per month.
**Chambermaid.** Hours: 8am-noon and 1-5pm. Must be of good appearance. Wages: £300 per month.
Free board provided. Some knowledge of French is required for both positions. Minimum age 18 years. Minimum period of work 1st April to 30th September.
*Applications* during April to the above address.

**HOTEL EDOUARD VII**: 39 Avenue de l'Opéra, 75002 Paris, France (☎ +33 142 61 56 90; fax: +33 142 61 47 73; e-mail marie@edouard7hotel.com; www.edouard7hotel. com) The Edouard VII Hotel is a well-known, stylish, 4-star, family-run establishment that takes pride in the impeccable service offered to clients.
**Waiter/Waitress**: required to prepare, serve and tidy away after breakfast. Involves a lot of client interaction. Experience is a plus but not necessary, must be a team player and not mind- early mornings.
**Luggage Porter**: required to welcome clients and transport their baggage, to run

occasional errands and supervise the lobby. This can be very physical work. Must be friendly, have a professional outlook and excellent people skills. Needs to be physically fit. Experience is a plus but not necessary.

**Chamber Maid**: required for thorough cleaning of the rooms and bathrooms, bed making, stock taking and replacing. This can be a very physical job. Must have enthusiasm and professionalism. Experience is a plus but not necessary.

Staff to work 39 hours per week, 5 days a week. Dates of work are between June and September, minimum period of work is 2 months. No board and lodging is available. Knowledge of English and French is essential and some Spanish is a plus.

*Applications* invited from March and April.

**EXODUS TRAVELS:** Grange Mills, Weir Road, London, SW12 ONE (☎020-8675 5550; fax 020-8673 0779; www.exodus.co.uk).

**Chalet Staff (2)** required for work in the French Pyrenees. Work is available throughout the year. Job involves cooking, cleaning, shopping, running the bar. 6 days/around 40 hrs work a week. A driving licence, some French and cooking experience are all useful, but not essential. Board, lodging and transport are paid for, and on top of this there is a wage of £180 per week from May-October. From Christmas to April one person is needed and pay is also £180.

*Applications* throughout the year should be sent to the above address.

**HOTEL-RESTAURANT LE FLEURAY:** F-37530 Cangey, Amboise, France (☎02-47-56-09-25; fax 02-47-56-93-97; e-mail lefleurayhotel@wanadoo.fr; www. lefleurayhotel.com). A small but expanding, friendly company, great opportunity for a language or hospitality student. Close to famous towns Amboise, Tours and Blois and surrounded by chateaux and vineyards.This highly acclaimed English-run, country house hotel is situated in a peaceful location in the Loire valley, only 55 minutes from Paris by TGV. It is listed in many *Best Hotel* guidebooks worldwide and has appeared in *The Times*, the *Telegraph* and *San Francisco Chronicle* newspapers.

**Hotel Staff** required for all aspects of work in the hotel (including restaurant service, housekeeping, kitchen work and gardening). Male and female staff required. Candidates must be outgoing, friendly, keen to work closely with a sophisticated international clientele and not be afraid of hard work. Knowledge of French is useful but not essential. Applicants will ideally be students, although those taking time off or who have graduated will be considered. To work ten hours per day (split shift – mornings and evenings, with afternoons off) six days per week. Minimum period of work, four months, between March and October. Attractive weekly wage, travel ticket and full board and accommodation provided.

*Applications* to the Newington Family at the above address.

**FOOTSIE BAR RESTAURANT:** 10-12 Rue Dannou, 75002 Paris, France (☎6-8645 4327).

**Waiting Staff** required to work in a fashionable bar and restaurant; wages, hours, period of work etc. by arrangement.

*Applications* to the above address.

**HOTEL LES FRENES:** 645 Avenue Vertes Rives, 84140 Montfavet, France; ☎+33 490 311793; +33 490 239503; contact@lesfrenes.com; www.lesfrenes.com). A Relais Chateaux luxury hotel and restaurant with very high standards.

**Waiter (2)** to carry plates and trays and other daily tasks. Must have experience of working in high standard restaurants.

**Room Staff (2)** to clean rooms and other daily tasks.

**Chef de Partie (2)** daily kitchen duties. Must have experience in a high standard restaurant.

All staff get board and lodging included in the negotiable salary. Minimum 3 months between 10 April and 15 November. Must speak fluent French and English and a third language is an asset.

*Apply* from January to Hervé Blancone at the above address/e-mail.

**GARDEN BEACH HOTEL:** 15-17 Bd. Baudoin, F-06160 Juan les Pins, France (☎492 93 57 57).
**Chamber Staff (2-4).** Wage by arrangement. To work 8 hours per day, 5½ days per week. Period of work from May to October.

*Applications* should be sent to the Personnel Manager at the above address.

**HOTEL IMPERIAL GAROUPE:** 770 Chemin de la Garoupe, 06600 Le Cap d'Antibes (☎04 92 93 31 61; fax 04 92 93 31 62; e-mail hotel-imp@webstore.fr; www.imperial-garoupe.com).
**Chef de Rang (3), Commis Chef (1)** to prepare food in the restaurant.
**Chambermaids (3)** required to clean and prepare bedrooms for guests.

All staff will work 8 hours a day, 5 days a week for at least 4 months between April and October. Board and accommodation are provided free, along with a wage of approx. £750. Applicants should be able to speak both French and English confidently.

*Applications* should be sent to Mr Gilbert Irondelle at the above address from January.

**RESTAURANT LE JEROBOAM:** Hotel Hermitage, Place Gambetta, 62170 Montreuil-sur-Mer, (☎+33 (0)321 06 7474; e-mail contact@hermitage-montreuil. com; www.hermitage-montreuil.com). A modern restaurant in a charming little French town with quality cooking and smiling service.
**Waitress** (1/2) to clean and wait tables. Most important qualification is good humour and a smile! Wages €500 (approx £337) per month. Expected to work 45 hours a week, 5 days a week with free board and lodgings. Minimum stay is two months between 1st June and 1st September. Applicants must speak English.

*Applications* and enquiries to Olivier Germain, at the above address at any time.

**JOBS IN THE ALPS (EMPLOYMENT AGENCY):** 17 High Street, Gretton, Northants NN17 3DE (e-mail info@jobs-in-the-alps.co.uk; www.jobs-in-the-alps. co.uk).
**Waiting Staff, Porters, Kitchen Porters and Housekeepers** (150 in the winter, 50 in summer) for Swiss and French hotels, cafes and restaurants at mountain resorts. Wages of circa £500 per month for a 5-day week with free board and accommodation. Good French and/or German required for most positions. Experience is not essential, but a good attitude to work and sense of fun are definite requirements. Periods of work: June to mid-September (minimum period three months including July and August), or December to April.

*Applications* should be sent by 30th April for Summer and 30th September for Winter to the above address.

**L'AUBERGE LIMOUSINE:** F-19320 La Roche-Canillac, France (☎05-55-29-12-06).
**Waiter, Barman, Chambermaid, Dishwasher** required for small hotel. Wages approx. £150 net per month for working a 45 hour week over 5½ days. Period of work April to end of September. Knowledge of English and French essential.

*Applications* should be made between February and March; contact Michele Coudert at the above address.

**LE RELAIS DU LYON D'OR:** 4 Rue d'Enfer, 86260 Angles sur L'Anglin, France (☎05494-83253; fax 054984-0228; e-mail contact@lyondor.com; www.lyondor.com). The Lyon D'or is situated in one of France's most beautiful villages. As the restaurant is only open in the evenings, opportunity to discover the wild, deserted riverbanks, on foot, by bike or by canoe. The Lyon D'Or is a three star hotel and restaurant in Angles sur l'Anglin, near Poitiers. The hotel is listed in all leading guides and is run by Anglo-French owners.
**Cleaners/Waiting Staff (3)** for general help in the hotel and restaurant. Applicants should have a positive attitude, a sense of humour. English and at least conversational French are essential. To work 9 hours a day, 5 days per week. Positions available between April and end of October; minimum period two months. The village is very isolated, so own transport is an advantage. Wages of £470 per month, plus bonus, and board and lodging. Applicants must be EU nationals or have the correct permits to work in France.
*Applications* to Heather Thoreau from December onwards at the above address.

**LE LOGIS DU FRESNE:** F-16130 Juillac-le-Coq, France (☎+ 33 (0)545 32 28 74; fax +33 (0)5 45 32 29 53; e-mail logisdufresne@wanadoo.fr). A three-star hotel run by Norwegian-French owners and situated 10km from Cognac in southwest France.
**Cleaners/Waiting Staff** to provide general help in the hotel. Wages of approx. £600 per month plus board, lodging and bonus. Minimum period of work one month between May and the end of September. Applicants should have a kindly attitude and speak English and conversational French; they must also either be EU nationals or have the correct permits to work in France.
*Applications* to Tone Butler at the above address with a photo if possible.

**HOTEL MANOIR DE BELLERIVE:** F-24480 Le Buisson de Cadouin, France (☎0553-221616; fax 0553-220905; e-mail manoir.Bellerive@wanadoo.fr; www.bellerivehotel.com). A typical French château, this hotel is situated near the River Dordogne in the heart of superb and serene grounds.
**Dining/Breakfast Assistant, Kitchen Pastry Helper, General Assistant.** Wages of approx. £720 per month net (Pastry chef: £750 net per month).
**Receptionist:** for reception and administrative work. Wages of £720 net per month. Must speak two European languages.
Employees will work split shifts five days per week. Minimum period of work eight weeks between April and October. Board and accommodation provided. Applicants should speak French, and possess the relevant qualifications for hotel work.
*Applications* from April onwards to the above address.

**HOSTELLERIE DE LA MARONNE:** Le Theil, F-15140 St Martin-Valmeroux, France (☎+33-(0)4-71-69-20-33; fax 04-71-69-28-22; e-mail maronne@maronne.com; www.maronne.com). A hotel-restaurant in the countryside near Clermont-Ferrand with 21 rooms, heated pool, tennis courts and sauna, attracting customers from all over the world.
**Waiting Staff/Receptionists (2)** to serve breakfast and supper. Experience preferred. €1200/£840 per month.
**Second Chef.** Wage of €1400/£980. Serving supper. Must provide a reference. Experience essential.
Experience of working in 3 or 4 star hotels necessary; knowledge of French is

preferred but not essential. To work 8 hours a day, 5 days a week, for a minimum of two months between 1 May and 15 September. Board and lodging provided free.
*Apply* from February to Alain Decock at the above address.

**HOTEL MIREILLE:** 2 Place St. Pierre, F-13200 Arles en Provence, France (☎+33-(0)4-90-70-74; fax 04-90-93-87-28; e-mail contact@hotel-mireille.com; www.hotel-mireille.com). This hotel is a hideaway nestled in the countryside of the Camargue, not far from the old town of Arles.
**Hotel trainee:** wages of €300 per month. Higher rate and board and lodging if staying for several months. To help with waiting tables, kitchen assistant. Also reception if fluent in French. Preferred length of stay is 5 months between March and early October.
*Applications* to Mireille Jacquemin the above address.

**HOTEL MOULIN DES POMMERATS:** F-89210 Venisy-St-Lorentin, France (☎86-35-08-04).
**Hotel Staff:** Wages and duties by arrangement. Board and lodging provided. Minimum period of work 1 month between July and September. Knowledge of languages not required.
*Applications* to the above address.

**HOTEL-RESTAURANT L'OCEAN:** 172, rue de St Martin, F-17580 Bois - Plage en Ré (☎05-46-09-23-07; fax 05-46-09-05-40; e-mail info@re-hotel-ocean.com; www.re-hotel-ocean.com). This hotel and restaurant are in a peaceful location with a unique and pleasant ambience, by a small and picturesque port.
**Waiting Staff (2)** to work between June and September, and possibly longer. Wages £690 approx in July and August; £660 approx during other months. To work split shifts, with two days free per week. Accommodation costs approx. £200 per month; Board is provided free of charge. Applicants should speak English and French.
*Applications* to the above address.

**HOTEL DE LA POSTE:** F-29950 Benodet, France.
**Barmaid, Waiting Assistants, Chambermaid, Receptionist.** Wages by arrangement. To work around 8 hours per day, 5½ days per week. No accommodation available. Minimum period of work 2 months between April and September. Applicants must speak French and English.
*Applications*, with photographs, to the above address from March.

**RESTAURANT DE LA POSTE & HOTEL LA RECONCE:** Le Bourg, 71600 Poisson, France (☎+33 (0)3 85 81 10 72; fax +33 (0)3 85 81 64 34).
**Waiter/Waitress/ Kitchen Staff:** Pay of €800 (approx £536) per month plus bed and board. Preparing tables and serving meals in a gastronomic restaurant. Must be well turned out, have good manners, be honest and speak French. 15 June to 15 September. To work 43 hours per week. Restaurant is based in a small village in southern Burgundy in the Charolais district and is attached to a small (six-bedroom) hotel.
*Applications* to Monsieur or Madame Jean Noel Dauvergne at the above address.

**HOTEL DU PONT NEUF:** F-00320 Le Veurdre, France (☎+33-470-66-40-12; fax 0033-470-66-44-15; e-mail hotel.le.pontneuf@wanadoo.fr; www.hotel-lepontneuf.com). This pleasant family-run hotel is situated in central France.
**Waiter/Waitress** and **Kitchen Staff** throughout the period of May to October. Applicants must be able to work for a minimum of three months. Five-day week of

approximately 39 hours per week. Job includes breakfast, lunch and dinner service with a break in the afternoons. Previous experience helpful but not necessary. Pay at national minimum wage (SMIC) plus full room and board. Placement would suit language students or those studying catering and hospitality. French language an advantage but not essential. Applicants should be confident, friendly and hardworking.

*Applications* from EU residents only, to the above address from January.

**HOTEL LE RIVET:** F-06450 Lantosque, France.
**Chambermaids** to serve breakfasts, make beds and do the laundry.
**Kitchen Assistants, Waitresses, Handyman, Washer Up**.
To work in a small three star hotel. Wages by arrangement: board and lodging provided. To work 8 hours per day, 6 days per week. Minimum period of work 8 weeks between 1 April and 15 October. Applicants should be serious, well behaved and dress in a suitable manner for exclusive hotel work.

*Applications* to M Henrik Winther at the above address from 1st March.

**CHATEAU DE ROCHECOTTE:** 37130 St Patrice, France (☎0247-961616; fax 0247-96 90 59; e-mail chateau.rochecotte@wanadoo.fr; www.chateau-de-rochecotte. fr). A chateau hotel in the Val de Loire with 34 rooms and gastronomic cuisine.
**Maitre d'Hotel.** In charge of the hotel. €1550 (£1030) per month. Minimum of 10 years of experience. Speaks English and French.
**Chef de Rang.** To run the restaurant/dining room. €1100 (£730) per month. Minimum of 5 years of experience. Speaks English and French.
**Receptionist.** €1100 per month. Good presentation. Must speak English and French.
**Commis de Salle.** €1020.
To work 5 days and 39 hours per week. Minimum period of work 7 months. Positions available from May to October. Accommodation available for €100 a month.

*Applications* should be made to Mme Brosset at the above address from 1 December 2006.

**HOSTELLERIE SAINT CLEMENT:** Curebourse, F-15800 Vic-Sur-Cere, France (☎471-47-51-71; fax 471-49-63-02).
**Waiter, Bar Person, Chamber Person:** Wage £150 per month approximately. 45 hours per week, 5½ days per week. Board and accommodation provided free of charge. Minimum period of work 2 months from July to August. Season runs from 1 June to 15 September. A knowledge of French and English is required.

*Applications* should be sent to the above address from February/March onwards.

**SIMON BUTLER SKIING:** Portsmouth Rd, Ripley, Surrey GU23 6EY (☎01483-212726; fax: 01483- 212725; e-mail info@simonbutlerskiing.co.uk; www. simonbutlerskiing.co.uk). Simon Butler Skiing is a small independent company operating in Megève for the last 22 years and has many returning staff each year. The company also runs a summer activities programme with hotel accommodation.
**Chalet People (4)** required to clean, and make breakfast. Must be confident and hard working.
**Handy Men (2)** must be able to fix broken bed legs, toilets etc. Should be confident and hard working.
All jobs are in Megève, French Alps. Speaking French makes life easier but is not essential. Staff work 6-7 hours per days, 6 days per week, minimum period of stay 3 months between June and September. Wages to be agreed on application, accommodation included.

*Applications* invited from March 2007.

**SIMPLY MORZINE**: 118 Redwood Avenue, Melton Mowbray, Leicester LE13 1HT (☎01664-568902; fax: 01664-568902; info@simply-morzine.co.uk; www.simply-morzine.co.uk). Simply Morzine is a professional company that is also family-run and offers specialist Alpine holidays. Posts with Simply Morzine are an excellent summer opportunity! The company's main clientele in June to September are artists, golfers and walkers while from July to August it is more likely to be families on activity/adventure holidays.

**Chalet Hosts (2)** required to clean chalets, to wait tables, help in kitchen and have contact with guests. Must have experience of working in restaurants, and/or hotels, general customer service and cleaning. Must be hardworking with great attention to detail! Chalet hosts work from 7.30am-11.30pm and 6pm-10pm, 5 to 6 days a week (approximately). Wages are £400 per month (approx) plus excellent package (see below).

**Chalet Chef** required to cater for approx 20 people to a very high dinner party standard. Responsible for breakfast, afternoon tea and 3 or 4 course evening meal. Needs to plan menus, budget, shop alone and maintain good impeccable hygiene standards. Must have minimum 1 year of experience with catering qualifications or 3 years of experience without. Chefs work similar hours and days as chalet hosts (see above). Wages are £550 per month (approx) plus excellent package (see below).

**Guide/ Driver/ Representative (2)** required to drive guests in resort minibuses for airport transfers and excursions/ activities. To lead mountain walks and mountain biking. General repping, welcoming guests, acting as a source of information, booking activities and solving problems. Must be an experienced driver with working knowledge of French. Must have a keen interest and experience of Alpine sports and outdoor pursuits. Guide/drivers work 8.30am-6pm, 5 to 6 days a week. Wages are £480 per month (approx) plus excellent package (see below).

Alongside wages employees are also offered a generous package including; activities insurance, accommodation, board, free/discounted alpine activities, return UK - Resort flights, good tips and a lift pass.

Dates of work are early June until mid September. Knowledge of French is useful but not imperative.

*Applications* are invited from March 2007 to the above contact details.

**HOTEL DE LA TONNELLERIE**: 12 rue des Eau Bleue, F-45190 Tavers, France (☎+33-2-38 44 68 15; fax +33-2-38 44 10 01; e-mail tonelri@club-internet.fr or reservation@tonelri.com; www.tonelni.com). A four star, family-run hotel-restaurant with a young staff team, catering to discerning clients; located in a small village between Orleans and Blois.

**Room Attendant (1-2)** to clean rooms.

**Dishwasher (1/2)** to clean dishes, pots and pans.

**General Help (1-2)** to carry luggage, warden duty and pool duty. No experience necessary, healthy, motivated and good-natured.

**Breakfast Attendant/Bar worker** to serve breakfast and clean the dishes. Some experience of waiting tables useful.

Hours of work are 41 per 5-day week. Period of work May to September, with a minimum period of work of two months. Wages €950 (£665) per month. Some free board and lodging is available. Ideally candidates should speak French and English.

*Applications* from 1 March to Marie-Christine Pouey at the above address.

**TRAVELBOUND**: Travelbound Recruitment Team, Sunsail, The Port House, Port Solent, Hants PO6 4TH; (☎02392-222329; e-mail hr@sunsail.com; www. firstchoice4jobs.co.uk). During the summer months TravelBound (Activity/ Educational Tour Operator) recruit for operational and hotel positions for their programmes located in France and Austria. Travelbound is a First Choice company. **Hotel Manager/Assistant Manager, Chefs, General Assistants.** A job with First Choice provides an opportunity to travel, meet and make new friends, improve language skills and gain experience. All of the overseas positions are 100% hard work but you'll have fun too! Full season in Austrian and French Alps lasts May-September and in Normandy February-October. Flexible contract lengths available. Applications are processed in January through to September. An attractive package including travel to and from resort, emergency medical insurance, food and accommodation. Applicants must be 18 or over, have a national insurance number and either an EU passport or relevant EU visa/permit. Please visit the website www.firstchoice4jobs. co.uk

*For more information* consult the website above from which an application form can be downloaded.

**HOTEL-RESTAURANT LES TROIS COLOMBES:** 148 avenue des Garrigues, 84210 Saint-Didier-les-Bains, Provence, France (☎04-90-66-07-01; fax 04-90-66-11-54).
A three-star hotel restaurant in the heart of scenic Provence.
**Restaurant Staff (2)** for waiting service, place-setting, taking orders and washing up, preferably with 2/3 years of experience in restaurant work. Hours of work are based around mealtimes over a 5-day week with board and lodging provided for approx. £45 per month. Applicants must be smartly dressed, well-groomed non-smokers, and preferably English speakers.
*Applications* are invited between April and May, with the working period being between 1 May and 30 September.

**UK OVERSEAS HANDLING (UKOH) INTERNATIONAL RECRUITMENT:** Third Floor, Link Line House, 65 Church Road, Hove, East Sussex BN3 2BD (☎0870-220 2148; fax 0870-752 2644; e-mail ukoh@ukoh.co.uk). UKOH recruit all kinds of resort/hotel staff for clients in France, but also offers a number of management trainee and student placement roles involved in all aspects of the resort and hotel management. **Management Trainee, Restaurant, Night Audit, Reception, Housekeeping, Pool Cleaners, Gardeners** and **Maintenance/Handy Staff**: Successful candidates should be over 21 years of age and EU passport holders with a permanent British National Insurance number. Must be bright, flexible, keen and prepared for hard work. Experience and an excellent standard of French essential for reception and restaurant positions. Some knowledge of French is useful for other posts. Package includes full board and shared accommodation.
Staff required between May and October (winter season also available) to work in hotels and tourist residences in the South and South-west coasts of France, and also in the Alps and cities of Paris and Montpellier.
*Applications* to the above address.

**HOTEL RESTAURANT LE VEYMONT:** F-26420 St Agnan-en-Vercore, France (☎475-48-20-19; fax 475-48-10-34).
**Chambermaid, Waitress:** Wage of £300 per month with accommodation provided. Period of work by arrangement; staff needed around the year. Applicants should speak some French.
*Applications* should be sent to the Manager at the above address.

# Industrial and Office Work

**THE AUTOMOBILE ASSOCIATION:** European Operations, 15th Floor, Fanum House, Basing View, Basingstoke RG21 4EA (☎01256-492398; e-mail elaine. badham@theaa.com).
**Call Handlers (up to 50)** to work in the AA's multilingual European Call Centre in Limonest, north of Lyon: the Centre provides 24-hour assistance to AA customers who have broken down or become involved in a road traffic accident in Europe. Salary approx €1,185 per month, overtime available. To work 35 hours per week on shifts between March and September. Minimum period of work 8 weeks (July and August essential). Local accommodation can be arranged. Applicants must speak English (mother-tongue), be fluent in French and preferably have one other European language; you will need to be efficient, responsible, compassionate and able to work under pressure.
_Applications_ with CV and passport-style photo to Elaine Badham by e-mail or to the above address.

**EUROGROUP:** 472 rue du Leysse, BP 429, 73004 Chambery, France (☎ +33 47 96 50 765; fax +33 47 96 50 808; e-mail candidatures@eurogroup-vacances.com; www.eurogroup-vacances.com). A group managing 34 hotels and holiday residences in France.
**Internships** involving work in the head office in Chambery in areas such as marketing, reservations, purchasing, planning etc. giving the opportunity to gain professional experience while improving language skills. $180-$380 per month plus food and accommodation. Period of work by arrangement. Applicants must speak good French and be enrolled in an EU university or school.
_Applications_ to Mme Catherine Oldfield at the above address.

**HORIZON HPL:** 22-26 rue du Sergent Bauchat, 75012 Paris, France (☎+33 (0)1 40 01 07 07; fax +33 (0)1 40 01 07 28; e-mail horizonl@club-internet.fr; http://horizon1. club.fr/english). Horizon HPL is a training centre established in 1991 which organises paid work placements in hotels, shops and companies in France for EU citizens. This includes French tuition and preparation to sit French examinations.
**Hotel Work/Company and Shop Staff:** placements are available all year round (in a variety of fields) from three months up to one year. Staff receive a trainee wage and free accommodation if working in a hotel. Applicants accepted between 17-50 years old. Prices from £660.
Other contacts: Aix-en-Provence (☎+33-4-42-26-50-85; e-mail hplaix@club-internet.fr) and Bilbao Interaupair (☎+34 94 475 47 46).
_Applicants_ should contact the agency two months in advance of intended work date, as an interview is necessary.

**SOLTOURS:** 46 rue de Rivoli, F-75004 Paris, France ( +33 (0)14-27 12 43 4; fax +33 (0)14-27 11 63 0; e-mail soltours@soltours.com).
**Sales Assistant** to work for a travel agent. Wages of approximately £700 per month. To work 8 hours per day, 5 days per week. No board or accommodation available. Minimum period of work 3 months between March and June. Applicants should be efficient, responsible and speak English.
_Applications_ to the above address from February.

# Sports, Couriers and Camping

**BALLOON FLIGHTS – FRANCE MONTGOLFIERES:** 24 rue Nationale, 414 Montrichard (☎0254 32 20 48; fax 02-54 32 20 07; jane@franceballoons.com; www. franceballoons.com).

One of only 10 balloon companies in France registered to carry passengers, has over 20 years of experience.

**Balloon Crew** required April-November to work for passenger-carrying operation with bases in the Burgundy and Loire Valley regions. Duties include maintaining and cleaning of vehicles and balloon equipment, driving and navigation of balloon chase vans, helping out in a balloon repair workshop, passenger liaison and secretarial work, etc. Farm work is also available. Knowledge of French preferred. *Applicants should be EU nationals or possess correct working papers.* Minimum age 21, with clean driving licence (preferably class E). No fixed days off; hours can be very long. Wages £500-£600 per month.

Please *send* a cv, a photo, and a copy of your driving licence.

**BELLE FRANCE:** Spelmonden Old Oast, Goudhurst, Kent, TN17 1HE (☎0870 4054056; fax 01580 214011; e-mail enquiries@bellefrance.co.uk).

Belle France is part of the Mark Hammerton Group Ltd., specialist in tour operating and publishing (Alan Rogers Camping Guides). A small, dynamic and friendly organisation.

**Bike Representatives (2)** to work for a tour operator offering cycling and walking holidays in France. The job includes maintaining bikes, transporting luggage, collecting customers from station, etc. Wage of approximately £150 per week. To work approximately 35 hours per week. Period of work from April to October. Applicants should be well organised, capable of working on their own, speak some French and hold a full clean driving license.

*Applications* to the above address by end of 2006.

**BENTS BICYCLE & WALKING TOURS:** The Blue Cross, Orleton, Ludlow, Shropshire SY8 4HN (☎01568-780800; fax 01568-780801; e-mail info@bentstours. com; www.bentstours.com).

**Company Representatives (4-5)** for a tour operator offering cycling and walking holidays in France, Germany and Austria. Duties to include meeting clients at the airport, maintaining bicycles, transporting luggage between hotels and generally taking care of the needs of clients. Wages of around £600 per month with board and accommodation provided. To work varied hours as needs of work dictate, but generally around 40 hours per up to 7-day week.

Minimum period of work 8 weeks between the end of May and end of September. Applicants should have a reasonable grasp of either spoken German or French and, fluent English. They must also possess a full valid driving licence.

*Applications* should be sent, with a photograph, to Stephen Bent at the above address from January.

**BOOTS & BIKES:** Hunter Kingston Holidays Ltd, 15 Husseywell Crescent, Bromley BR2 7LN (☎020-8462-6522; e-mail julia-kingston@bootsandbikes.co.uk; www. bootsandbikes.co.uk). Boots & Bikes organises independent walking and cycling holidays in France. They offer tours lasting 6-10 days, between small hotels and guest houses in rural France.

**Holiday Representatives (5)** to meet clients on arrival, give tour briefings, move bags between hotels, carry out cycle maintenance, deal with hoteliers, keep accounts and carry out other duties as necessary. Representatives should be fit and active, with an interest in outdoor activities, especially cycling and walking.

Boots & Bikes require adaptable, resourceful people who can think on their feet in a variety of situations. Minimum age 21 years. English and French language skills and a full, clean driving licence a must. Hours/days of work are flexible but the minimum period of work is two months between April and October. Wages £500 per month. Accommodation is provided.

*Applications* from February 2007, interviews will be held in London in early 2007.

**CAMPING CLUB MAR ESTANG:** Mer Méditerranée, 66140 Canet en Roussillon, France (☎+33 (0)468 80 35 53; fax +33 (0)468 7332 94; e-mail contact@marestang. com; www.marestang.com).
**Disc Jockey (1), Ice Cream Vendors (2) Swimming Pool Attendants** (4 with or without qualification), **Receptionists (2), Bar Staff (6), Restaurant Staff (2), Beach Boy (1), Ground Staff (3), Night Security Staff (2), Sailing Instructor (1), Restaurant chef (1), Maids (3).** Wages €900 (£630) to €1400 (£980), depending on schedule and abilities.

All contracts are seasonal from 2 to 5 months. Qualifications are needed only for restaurant chef, two of the pool attendants and sailing instructor. French must be spoken for receptionist, bar staff, ice cream, pool and sailing instruction.

*Applications:* please send I.D. with photo with your application to Mr Laurent Raspaud at the above address.

**CAMPING LIFE:** GVN Camping Recruitment, East Port House, Dunfermline, KY12 7JG (☎01383-629012; fax 01383-629071; e-mail campingrecruitment@ gvnrecruitment.com; www.gvnrecruitment.com). Camping Life provide good value mobile home and tent holidays at large family campsites in France, Spain and Italy.
**Campsite Courier.** Involves cleaning accommodation, welcoming families to the site and showing them to their accommodation. Visiting customers, providing local information and basic maintenance are very important parts of the job. Campsite Courier opportunities are also available for couples to work on site together. Senior courier positions available. For more details see website.
**Children's Courier.** Camping Life has its own full-time Children's Club which is open from May to the beginning of September. Couriers plan and deliver an exciting and fun-packed programme of varied activities for children aged 4 to 12. Must be enthusiastic, energetic, and have good communication skills. A tent is provided as a Club venue and for equipment storage. Children's couriers also help out with campsite duties as needed.

Package includes competitive salary, tent accommodation, medical insurance, uniform and return travel from a UK port of entry. Full season positions start in March, April or May and end in September/October. High season staff needed to work at least two months during the peak season.

*Please call* the Recruitment Department for more information and an application form, or *apply online* at www.gvnrecruitment.com.

**CANVAS HOLIDAYS:** GVN Camping Recruitment, East Port House, Dunfermline, KY12 7JG (☎01383-629012; fax 01383-629071; e-mail campingrecruitment@ gvnrecruitment.com; www.gvnrecruitment.com). Canvas Holidays provide luxury mobile home and tent holidays at over 100 campsites throughout Europe.
**Campsite Courier.** Involves cleaning accommodation, welcoming families to the

site and showing them to their accommodation. Visiting customers, providing local information and basic maintenance are very important parts of the job. Campsite Courier Opportunities are also available for couples to work on site together. For details of management positions, see website.

**Children's Courier.** Needed to work at Hoopi's Club. Applicants must have formal experience of working with children. Children's couriers should be energetic, enthusiastic and have good communication skills. A tent is provided as a Club venue and for equipment storage; this has to be kept safe, clean and tidy. Visiting new arrivals on site is an important and fun part of the job. Children's couriers also help with other campsite duties as needed. Visit recruitment website for information about working with teenagers (Buzz Courier) and wildlife and the environment (Wild & Active Courier).

Package includes competitive salary, tent accommodation, medical insurance, uniform and return travel from a UK port of entry. Full season positions start in March, April or May and end in September/October. High season staff needed to work at least two months during the peak season.

*Please call* the Recruitment Department for more information and an application form, or *apply online* at www.gvnrecruitment.com.

**CARISMA HOLIDAYS:** Bethel House, Heronsgate Road, Chorleywood WD3 5BB (☎01923-287339; e-mail info@carisma.co.uk). Carisma specialises in self-drive, family holidays in mobile homes on private sandy beaches in the sunny south-west of France. All Carisma's campsites are family-run and located on beaches.

**Site Managers.** £100 per week plus tips and accommodation. To work from 1 May to 24 September. French speakers preferred.

**Full Season Couriers:** £95 per week plus tips and accommodation. To work from May 12th to September 24th. French speakers preferred.
**High Season Couriers:** £90 per week plus tips and accommodation. To work from 1 July to 13 September. French speakers preferred.

To work on beach sites in France. To be responsible for client families, with duties involving welcoming families, providing information and advice, cleaning and maintaining mobile homes and babysitting. Self-catering accommodation is provided in tents.

Applicants should have a helpful and friendly disposition and experience of dealing with people. Travel costs are paid and full training is given on site. *Applicants should be EU nationals.*

Applications to C. Simpson at the above address.

**CENTRE D'ECHANGES INTERNATIONAUX:** 1 rue Gozlin, F-75006 Paris, France (☎+33 14 32 91 73 4; fax +33 14 23 90 62 1; e-mail jlponti@cei4vents.com; www.cei4vents.com).
**Youth Leaders** to teach one of the following activities; sports, dancing, music, crafts. Around £200 per month. To work in international holiday centres. Hours can be long; one day off per week. Free board and lodging provided.

Period of work covers July and August. Applicants must speak French: some knowledge of German an advantage. Applicants must have previous experience as an instructor in holiday camps.

Apply to the Director at the above address between March and May.

**CENTRE DE VOILE L'ABER-WRAC'H:** 4, Port de l'Aber-Wrach, F-29870 Landeda, France (☎298-09 064; fax 298-04 97 22).
**Sailing Instructors (2), Sailing Camp Leaders (2)** to work in Brittany. Period of work is July and August. Pay is around £110 weekly plus free board and lodging. Instructors work six and a half hours a day, six days a week and leaders six days a week all day and evenings. The minimum age is 18 and sailing instructors should be qualified.

*Applications* to the address above.

**CHATEAU DE L'EPERVIERE:** F-71240 Gigny sur Saone, Bourgogne Sud, France (☎0033-385-941-690; fax 0033-385-94-1697; e-mail info@domaine-eperviere.com; www.domaine-eperviere.com). A four star castle/campsite situated in the heart of Burgundy with indoor and outdoor pool, a jacuzzi and sauna. The campsite's key-words are conviviality and family atmosphere.
**Staff,** ideally students, to work on a campsite. Wages by arrangement. Minimum period of work two months between April and September; those available from early in April or until late September would be at an advantage. Applicants should have some qualifications or experience in waitressing, bartending or reception work.

Applicants must speak French, be aged 20-30, hard working, and be flexible, prepared to work long hours and friendly with clients; to *apply* send a CV and picture to Gert-Jan Engel at the above address.

**EUROCAMP:** Overseas Recruitment Department (Ref SJ/07) (☎01606-787525). Eurocamp is a leading tour operator in quality self-drive camping and mobile home holidays in Europe. Each year the company seeks to recruit up to 1,500 enthusiastic people for the following positions:
**Campsite Courier:** job involves cleaning and preparing customer accommodation, providing assistance, acting as an information service and performing some administrative duties. Couriers need to be flexible to meet the needs of the customer

# Eurocamp

Eurocamp is Europe's leading Tour Operator and the leader in self-drive, self-catering holidays on holiday parcs and campsites. Operating in 9 countries throughout Europe on over 200 parcs and sites, we sell family holidays to customers from the UK, Ireland, Holland, Germany, Switzerland, Austria, Denmark, Sweden and Poland.

We employ 2,000 campsite staff every year from many of these countries and can offer a large range of positions to suit all our overseas employees.

We are looking for people for various positions that involve **customer service, cleaning accommodation, working with children, leading a team and administration.** We also employ teams of people at the beginning and end of the season to help us erect and dismantle tents. Successful applicants will be asked to apply for a Standard or Enhanced Disclosure.*

**We will provide:**
- Competitive Salary
- Accommodation
- Uniform
- Subsidised Insurance
- Training
- Travel To Resort

**You will need to be:**
- 18+
- An EU passport holder (or have a work permit for any of the countries that we operate in)
- Available to *start* work between April and July

If you think you have the qualities to provide our customers with the 'perfect family holiday' please apply online at **www.holidaybreakjobs.com** or phone **01606 787525** for an application pack. Please quote **SJ/07.**

* Further information about Disclosures can be found at www.disclosure.gov.uk or by phoning 0870 90 90 811.

to provide them with excellent service. Minimum age 18. Applicants should be independent with plenty of initiative and relish a challenging and rewarding position. They should also possess a friendly and helpful personality. Previous customer service experience would be an advantage. Applicants should be available to work from April/May to September.

**Children's Courier:** work involves organising a wide range of exciting activities for children aged 4-13. Applicants should possess initiative, imagination and enthusiasm along with good safety awareness. Previous childcare experience is essential. Minimum age is 18 years and applicants should be available from April/May to September. Languages are not a requirement but would be an advantage (in particular German). Successful candidates will be asked to apply for an Enhanced Disclosure.

**Senior Couriers:** required to work alongside a team of Campsite Couriers and organise their daily workload, as well as carrying out the normal day-to-day duties of a Campsite Courier. Applicants should have good language skills and experience of leading a team.

**Site Managers:** required to lead a large team of Campsite Couriers, organising their daily workloads and ensuring they provide the very best customer service. Applicants should be 21 or over, have proven managerial experience, excellent communication skills and language ability.

**Montage/Demontage:** for a period of approximately 6-8 weeks at the beginning/end of season to erect/dismantle equipment.

Comprehensive training is provided together with a competitive salary, insurance, return travel and accommodation. Applications are accepted from September/October and *can only be accepted from UK/EU passport holders*. Interviews will be conducted in Hartford, Cheshire between October and April.

Applicants should *apply on-line* at **www.holidaybreakjobs.com** or *telephone* 01606-787525 for an Application Pack.

**FLEUR HOLIDAYS:** 4 All Hallows Road, Bispham, Blackpool, Lancs FY2 0AS (☎01253-593333; fax 01253-595151; e-mail reps@fleur-holidays.com; www.fleur-holidays.com). A company that offers mobile home and tent, holidays on quality sites in France, chosen for ambience.

**Area Controllers** required to cover groups of campsites to ensure couriers are performing to the required standards. Previous courier experience is essential. Wages in the region of £630 per month, plus £14 per week bonus paid on completion of contract; dependent on service. Vehicle provided or mileage allowance given. Accommodation provided. Period of employment may cover: start season – Easter to July, and/or High season – July to September. Basic French required.

**Representatives/Couriers** required meeting clients at reception, preparing mobile homes and tents, organising social events and children's clubs. Wages in the region of £430 per month plus £14 per week bonus paid on completion of contract. Each vacancy is an all round position with responsibility for the clients together with Fleur's representation at the campsite. Period of employment may cover any or all of: Start season – Easter to July; Mid season – May to July; High season – July to September. Basic French an advantage.

**Montage/Demontage**: required to assist in the preparation of mobile homes and the erecting of tents at the start of the season and /or the closing of mobile homes and taking down of tents at the end of the season. Period of employment: 6 to 8 weeks from March to May and/or 6-8 weeks in September and October.

Applicants should be 18+, and be physically fit and motivated. For Area Controllers and Couriers experience of working within the service industry would be an advantage.

For all positions, please *send* a full CV and covering letter with head and shoulders photograph, stating the exact dates that you are available to the above address: alternatively, request an application form from the Personnel Manager.

**HEADWATER HOLIDAYS:** The Old School House, Chester Road, Castle, Northwich, Cheshire, CW8 1LE (☎01606-720033; fax 01606-720001; e-mail info@ headwater.com; www.headwater.com). Headwater offers relaxed discovery and adventure holidays; their hallmarks are personal service, warm friendly hotels and good regional cuisine. Headwater guides and information packs help clients make their own discoveries off the beaten track.

**Overseas Representatives** to work in France, Italy, Spain and Austria. Duties include meeting clients at airports and stations, supervising local transportation for them and their luggage, hotel and client liaison, bike maintenance and on the spot problem solving. Good, working knowledge of the language and full, clean driving licence required. Organisational skills, resourcefulness and cheerfulness essential. Minimum age 21 years.

**Canoeing Instructors:** duties etc. as for Overseas Representatives but also include giving canoe instruction.

Wages from £140 per week; accommodation provided. To work hours as required. Staff required for full season from April to October.

Further information and an on-line *application* form can be found on the website, or an application form can be requested from the above address.

**IAN MEARNS HOLIDAYS:** Tannery Yard, Witney Street, Burford, Oxon OX18 4DP (☎01993-822655; fax 01993 822650; e-mail enquiries@ianmearnsholidays.co.uk; www.ianmearnsholidays.co.uk). Ian Mearns has many years' experience of operating family self-drive camping holidays in France.

**Campsite Courier** to be responsible for the day-to-day running of campsite, ensuring that clients get the highest level of customer service. Duties include preparing customers' accommodation for their arrival, welcoming them to the campsite and being on hand to help during their stay. Must be fit and hardworking. Minimum age 18.

**Area Supervisors** to be responsible for overseeing operations on up to nine campsites. Duties include montage/demontage team leader, visiting campsites to offer couriers support and supervision. Applicant should be over 21. Must have proven managerial experience, language skills and knowledge of the camping industry.

**Montage/demontage Assistants** to work with a small team of people setting up or closing down the company campsite operations in France for 6-8 weeks before and after the season. Minimum age 21.

All staff get competitive wages, accommodation, insurance, uniform, training and transport provided. Season dates are Easter/May-September, although some half-season positions are available.

*Application forms* and job descriptions can be requested from Millie at the above address.

**KEYCAMP HOLIDAYS:** Overseas Recruitment Department (Ref: SJ/07), Hartford Manor, Greenbank Lane, Northwich CW8 1H (☎01606-787525; www. holidaybreakjobs.com).

**Campsite Couriers:** to look after British, Dutch and Scandinavian customers on campsites in France. Duties include welcoming customers, providing local information, organising social activities on site and ensuring that all accommodation is prepared prior to arrival.

**Children's Courier:** to organise and provide up to 24 hours of activities per week for children aged 4-13 years, to advertise the club activities and visit families on arrival.

**Senior Courier:** incorporating the role of campsite courier with the additional responsibility of organising and managing the team and ensuring the smooth running of the Keycamp operation on site.

**Montage/Demontage:** for a period of approximately 6-8 weeks at the beginning/end of season to erect/dismantle equipment.

Minimum age 18 years. Accommodation, uniform, competitive salary and return travel and training provided. A working knowledge of French would be an advantage. Period of employment between March and July/October.

*Applicants* should apply on-line at **www.holidaybreakjobs.com** or telephone 01606-787525 for an Application Pack.

**MARK WARNER:** 20 Kensington Church Street, London, W8 4EP (☎08700 330750 or 08700 330760 for children's places); e-mail recruitment@markwarner. co.uk; www.markwarner.co.uk/recruitment.
**Accountants, Receptionists, Watersports Instructors, Tennis and Aerobics Instructors, Chefs, Kitchen Porters, First Aid, Nannies, Handymen, Nightwatchmen** and more are required to work in hotels in Corsica, Sardinia, Greece and Turkey during the summer from April to October and Egypt, and Sri Lanka and Mauritius year round. Wages from £50 per week plus full board, medical insurance, travel expenses and free use of watersport and activity facilities. Some reserve staff also needed throughout the season. Requirements for languages, experience, qualifications etc. vary according to the job applied for.

For further details, please *contact* the Resorts Recruitment Department on the above number.

**MATTHEWS HOLIDAYS:** 8 Bishopsmead Parade, East Horsley, Surrey KT24 6RP (☎01483-284044; information@matthewsfrance.co.uk; www.matthewsholidays.co.uk).
**Couriers/Campsite Representatives** to receive clients and maintain and clean mobile homes in western France (Brittany, the Vendée and South of France. £170 per week. 35 hour, 6 day week. Accommodation and board provided at the rate of £50 per week deducted from wages. Knowledge of French essential. Applicants should be at least 20 years of age and available to commence work during April or May and work until mid/late September. A few vacancies available for the period July-September.

*Applications* to the above e-mail or postal address. If applying by post enclose an s.a.e. Please give details of age, present occupation and other relevant experience, and date available to commence work.

**MASTERSUN HOLIDAYS:** Thames House, 63-67 Kingston Road, New Malden, Surrey, KT3 3PB (☎020-8942 9442; fax 020-8949 4396; e-mail resorts@mastersun. co. uk; www.mastersun.co.uk). Mastersun is a Christian holiday company that organises holidays in Greek and French resorts. Holidays are hotel-based and the complete package includes lots of water sports and activities.
**Resort & Programme Managers, Assistant Managers, Administration, Bookkeepers, Receptionists, Children's and Teens' Organisers, Chefs and Assistant Chefs, Kitchen Assistants, Bar and Restaurant Managers, Bar and Restaurant Staff, Waterfront Managers, Waterfront Instructors**; about 100 staff needed over the summer season. There are winter ski jobs as well.

*Applications:* ask for a job pack from the above address or e-mail, or download both pack and an application form from the website. Applications welcome at any time.

**NSS RIVIERA HOLIDAYS:** 288, Chemin du Caladou, F-06560 Valbonne, France. (☎/fax +33-4 93 12 95 81; e-mail nss@wanadoo.fr). NSS has a number of agents working in several European countries. Customers come from the UK, Holland, Belgium, Germany, Switzerland and Denmark. Working language is English.

**Active Couples** aged 45 or older needed to offer short-term help to a small British, privately-owned holiday operation in the South of France; to work in a complex of 27 chalets, cottages and mobile homes on a 4 star holiday village complex at Frejus, between St. Tropez and Cannes. Maintenance duties require people with some of the following DIY skills to a good standard: joinery, plumbing, electrics, building, painting & decorating, gardening and cleaning. In exchange for 3 days' work per week couples will receive free self-contained, furnished accommodation with own patio and private parking plus free electricity, gas, water, local rates, local taxes and site fees.

**Maintenance Helpers** are needed for periods ranging from 3-6 weeks in the Spring and Autumn. In addition the company have one couple working full-time as the company's **Representatives** on site from March to October. Applicants should be enthusiastic, self-motivated, self-taught and disciplined adults, preferably non-smokers, who own a reliable car.

*Applications* should be sent to Don Nimmo at the above address and provide information on each person, a recent photograph, a summary of the relevant skills for each person and stating preferred dates.

**NST TRAVEL GROUP:** Recruitment, 65 London Road, Stapleford, Cambridge, CB2 5DG (☎01253-503011; fax 01253-356955; e-mail info@nstgroupjobs.co.uk; www. nstgroupjobs.co.uk). NST Travel has two residential centres in France. Le Chateau d'Ebblingham, offering educational and French language courses for secondary school groups and Lou Valagran which offers adventurous activity holidays for secondary school groups.

**Group Co-coordinators (7)** for Le Château to accompany guests on excursions around the French countryside. Excellent working knowledge of French required.

**Activity Instructors (20)** for Lou Valagran to instruct a range of outdoor activities and to assist with the evening entertainment programme. Qualifications in canoeing, kayaking, caving, or climbing advantageous.

**Catering Assistants (5)** for Lou Valagran to assist the Catering Manager and be involved in all aspects of kitchen work. No previous experience required.

**Support Staff (6, for both centres),** including positions for drivers, boat loaders, bar, shop, support, cleaning and maintenance staff. No experience required though a full driving licence is needed for driving positions.

Staff required from January through to November. All positions are residential. Minimum period of work 2 months: average working week 42 hours over 6 days.

For more information and an application form please *contact* the above address.

**ORANGERIE DE LANNIRON**: Château de Lanniron, F-29336 Quimper, Cedex (☎+33 (0)2 98 90 62 02; fax: +33 (0)2 98 52 15 56; e-mail camping@lanniron.com; http://www.lanniron.com). A 10-acre campsite set in amongst 42 acres of woodland. Orangerie de Lanniron has holiday cottages, static caravans and space for touring caravans. It is 10 minutes drive away from Benodet and Quimper.

**Bar Person**. Required to run the bar, restock the bar and deal with money. Responsible for bar terrace and lounge.

**Shop Attendant/Cook** responsible for tending and restocking the grocery shop and preparation of takeaway food.

**Host/Hostess** to care for the camping guests, register arrivals and departures, making telephone calls, handling money and showing the guests their pitches.

**Animateur** responsible for entertaining both the young and older clients and organising garden parties and theme parties. Required to give information to guests about the entertainment programme.

**House Keeper** must be female. To clean guest accommodation and to wash linen. Applicants for all the posts must speak English and French and a third language such a Dutch or German would be useful. All staff work 35 hours a week. Wages are based on the national minimum wage and experience. Minimum period of work is 2 months in July and August. Accommodation is provided in a cottage (shared by three people) in May, June and September but in peak season (July and August) accommodation will be in tents.

Applicants should be well educated, honest, punctual and be able to endure stress. Applicants must also have previous experience in hotel or restaurant work and good references.

*Applications* to the above address.

**PGL TRAVEL:** Alton Court, Penyard Lane, Ross-on-Wye, Herefordshire HR9 5GL (☎0870 401 4411; recruitment@pgl.co.uk; www.pgl.co.uk/recruitment). With 27 activity centres located in the UK, France and Spain, PGL Travel provides adventure holidays and courses for children. Each year 2,500 people are needed to help run these adventure centres.

**Children's Group Leaders** required to take responsibility for groups, helping them to get the most out of their holiday. Minimum age 18. Previous experience of working with children is essential.

**General positions available** in catering, administration, driving (car or D1 towing), stores, site cleaning.

**Children's Activity Instructors** qualified or personally competent in canoeing, sailing, windsurfing, or multi-activities.

From £65-£100 per week plus full B & L. Vacancies available for the full season (February-October) or shorter periods between April and September. Overseas applicants eligible to work in the UK welcome.

*Applications* can be made online or a form obtained from the above address.

**ROCKLEY WATERSPORTS:** Poole, Dorset BH15 4RW (☎0870-777 0541; e-mail info@rockleywatersports.com; www.rockleywatersports.com). Based in beautiful Poole harbour and South-West France, Rockley teach water sports to all abilities and ages; and are one of Europe's most highly regarded water sports centres. About 150 seasonal staff are employed at any one time. These include:

**Watersports Instructors (over 100)**; experienced RYA sailing, windsurfing, BCU kayaking instructors are required to work in South West France at three of the largest RYA recognised water sports centres in Europe.

**Couriers/ Entertainments Team (45)** for duties including evening entertainments, aiding water based sessions and general site duties. The jobs offer the opportunity to gain water sports experience and use all the facilities of the centres.

The above are needed to work for flexible periods during the summer season, which runs from March until October.

For more information check the website or telephone for details of current vacancies.

**SANDPIPER HOLIDAYS LTD:** Walnut Cottage, Kenley, Shrewsbury, SY5 6NS (☎01746-785123; fax 01746-785100; e-mail sandpiperhols@bigfoot.com). Small friendly holiday tour operator specialising in self-drive camping holidays to France. Reps are chosen for their enthusiasm; they work hard, have a lot of fun and definitely improve their French.

**Representatives (8)** to look after clients, clean and maintain tents, mobile homes

# Not your usual commute!

siblu holidays exclusively own holiday parks in France,
and also operate on selected parks in
France, Italy and Spain.

As well as providing our guests with a memorable holiday, we want
to offer our team the work experience of a lifetime. We are looking
for enthusiastic and hard working individuals with an independent
streak who thrive on providing an outstanding experience for our guests.

We offer the following positions for 2007:
Park Representatives • Assistant Park Representatives
Children's Club Representatives • Lifeguards (with current NPLQ)
Reception Team (fluent in French) • Accommodation Team
Bar Team (conversational in French) • Entertainers

Included in your package is a competitive salary, accommodation on
park, travel costs, medical insurance, uniform and a discount on
holidays for family and friends.

If you are available between March and October and would like a **siblu**
summer to remember, please telephone **01442 293231**,
e-mail **recruitment@siblu.com** or apply online at **www.siblu.com.**

and organise children's activities on camp sites in France. Wages by arrangement (c.£400 per month plus end of season bonus). Period of work from mid-May to mid-September: applicants must be prepared to work for at least half the season.

Applicants must be over 19, prepared to work hard, and have a sense of humour. Accommodation is provided in tents.

*Telephone* the above number for an application form before the end of January.

**SELECT FRANCE:** Murcott, Kidlington, Oxford OX5 2RP (☎01865-331350; e-mail jobs@selectfrance.co.uk; www.selectfrance.com). Select France is a family company with a reputation for personal service. They use campsites in Brittany, the Vendée, Charente and the S. of France.

**Campsite Representative:** Successful applicants will be responsible for ensuring that the accommodation provided for clients is kept clean and well maintained. They will also be expected to keep up to date with a small amount of paperwork and organise some activities for children and adults. Some sites require couples.

Applicants, preferably over 21, must be cheerful, practical, responsible, self-reliant and above all, honest. Knowledge of French and a clean driving licence are desirable. Free accommodation and casual uniform provided. Period of work is from mid-May to end of September. Wages of around £400 per month, with the opportunity to earn more.

*Applications* to the above address.

**SIBLU HOLIDAYS:** Recruitment Team, Bryanston Court, Selden Hill, Hemel Hempstead, HP2 4TN (☎ 01442-293231; recruitment@siblu.com; www.siblu.com). Siblu Holidays exclusively own holiday parks in France, and also operate on 16 fantastic parks in France, Spain and Italy. The following roles are offered in France for seasonal work:

**Park Representatives:** duties include cleaning and maintaining accommodation, welcoming new arrivals, reception duties, paperwork and administration.

**Children's Club Representatives:** duties include creating and running a daytime entertainment programme for children between the ages of 5 and 12 years old, associated paperwork and assisting Park Representatives. Experience of working with children is desirable.

**Assistant Park Representatives:** duties include cleaning and preparation of accommodation, welcoming new arrivals and reception duties.

**Lifeguards:** NPLQ qualified, duties include poolside supervision, cleaning of pool area and supervision of slides and flumes.

**Reception Team Members:** applicants must be fluent in French, duties include the welcome and check-in of guests, providing park and local information, cash handling (*bureau de change*) and problem solving.

**Accommodation Team Members:** duties include cleaning and preparing guest accommodation, bed making and customer visits.

**Bar Team Members:** applicants must be conversational in French, duties include bar service, cash handling, cleaning & washing of glasses, terrace service and re-stocking of bar.

**Entertainers:** dancers, vocalists and children's entertainers, working as part of a team to provide daytime and evening entertainment programme for guests of all ages.

Team members will receive a competitive salary, accommodation on park, uniform, medical cover and travel costs to park. The season runs between March and October,

with varying contract dates. Limited high season positions are available.
Please telephone the above number for a recruitment pack or visit the website to *apply* online.

**SODISTOUR:** Mme Roussel, 126 Rue de la Fayette, 75010 Paris (☎+33 (0)144 83 43 74; fax+33 (0)144 83 43 74).
Operates three family entertainment centres.
**General Assistants and Tour Guides** needed: details on application.
*Applications* to the above address.

**SOLAIRE HOLIDAYS:** 43 Milcote Road, Solihull, B91 1JN (☎0121-778 5061 or 08700-540201; fax 0121-778 5065; e-mail holidays@solaire.co.uk; www.solaire. co.uk).
Solaire Holidays provides self-drive self-catering holidays to France and Spain. They also have their own holiday park in Southern Brittany.
**Site Couriers** (20) to look after clients and prepare accommodation. Knowledge of French/Spanish desirable. Wage £280-£400 per month.
Applicants can apply to work between April and October, May and September or July and August. Hours of work vary according to demand, but applicants can expect to work for six days a week, on a rota system. Accommodation is provided as part of contract. Food is not provided.
*Applications* are invited from December 2006 for 2007. Please send a CV when applying to the above address or e-mail.

**SUSI MADRON'S CYCLING FOR SOFTIES:** 2-4 Birch Polygon, Rusholme, Manchester M14 5HX (☎0161-248 8282; e-mail info@cycling-for-softies.co.uk.)
**Company Assistants** to work for a company offering cycling holidays in France. Fixed wage plus bonus. Minimum period of work 2 months between May and September. Full training in bicycle maintenance is given. Must be a keen cyclist, non-smoker, aged over 25 and speak French.
*Application* forms can be obtained by telephoning the above number.

**TJM TRAVEL:** 40 Lemon Street, Truro, Cornwall TR1 2NS (☎01872-272767; fax 01872-272110; e-mail jobs@tjm.co.uk; www.tjm.co.uk). TJM run hotels and activity centres in France, Spain and the UK in the summer months, and they operate ski holidays from French Alpine hotels in the winter.
**Hotel Managers (3)** required to run hotels in France and Spain, must have experience in the field. Wages from £600 per month.
**Water Sports Instructors (20):** to teach watersports to children, must hold instructor qualification. Wages from £300 per month. Required are qualified **Sailing (RYA), Canoe (BCU), Windsurfing** and **Snorkelling Instructors**, as well as **Beach Lifeguards**.
**Support Staff (10)** to help run hotels; no previous experience necessary. Wages from £260 per month.
**Hotel Staff; Manager, Chef, 2nd Chef, Reps, Waiting, Chamber & Kitchen Staff, Handypersons.** All required for hotel or activity centre work in France, Spain or the UK, all staff must have appropriate qualifications, experience and skills. Wages vary between £300 and £800 per month according to job and experience. Board and lodging provided. Staff work 7 hours a day; 6-day week. Working periods are (summer) May to August and (winter) December to April.
*Applications* must include passport photos, current CV and copies of any relevant certificates (including driving licence); apply by post or e-mail.

**VENDEE LOISIRS VACANCES:** 30 Parc des Demoiselles F-85160 St Jean de Monts, France (☎+33 251-58-04-02; e-mail vlv@wanadoo.fr; www.vlv.fr). Linda and Mark run a small friendly business offering mobile home holidays on 2 campsites in St Jean de Monts. They live locally and are on hand for help and advice.

**Representative/Children's Entertainment (2).** The job of the rep is to welcome, check out, and provide information for the client and to clean the mobiles. There is also a children's club to run 4 times a week in the morning and occasional evenings, plus afternoon activities such as boules, canoeing, horse riding etc.

Period of work mid-May to beginning of September. Wages £100 a week plus free on site accommodation, one day off per week, and most afternoons free. Ideal candidates would be French-speaking, experienced with children and would enjoy meeting people. Ideal for 2 friends.

*Write* to Linda Aplin at the above address enclosing a cv and photo.

**VILLAGE CAMPS:** Personnel Office, Department 808, Rue de la Morache 14, 1260 Nyon, Switzerland (+41 22-990 9405; fax +41 22-990 9494; e-mail personnel@villagecamps.ch; www.villagecamps.com/personnel). Exciting opportunity to work with children in an international environment.

**Activity Instructors** needed from May to October for summer and outdoor education programes across Europe in the summer and spring/autumn respectively.

**Nurses, Receptionists, Drivers, Specialists, TEFL/French/German Teachers, Domestic/Kitchen and Facilities Assistants** also required depending on programme and location. Agreement periods vary from 3 weeks to 8 weeks. Applicants must be a minimum of 21 years old (18+ for domestic/kitchen and facilities assistants) and have relevant experience and/or qualifications. A second language is desirable. A valid first aid and CPR certificate is required whilst at camp. Room and board, accident and liability insurance and a weekly allowance provided.

Recruitment starts in December. There is no deadline to submit applications but positions are limited. Interviews are by telephone. Please specify department 808 on application.

For *information* on dates, locations, positions available and to download an application form, visit www.villagecamps.com

# Teaching and Language Schools

**MRS JULIE LEGREE:** Syndicat Mixte Montaigu-Rocheserviere, 23 avenue Villebois Mareuil, F-85607 Montaigu cedex, France (☎02-51 46 45 45; fax 02-51 46 45 40; e-mail julie_legree@yahoo.co.uk or eef@montaigu@wanadoo.fr; www. explomr.com/english). This is a local government scheme which has been running for fifteen years. They are looking for Francophiles who wish to develop their social and professional skills.

**TEFL Teachers (4)** to teach English to 9-11 year old pupils in 19 different primary schools in the Vendée. Applicants should be outgoing, independent, organised and mature enough to act on their own initiative, as well as having a love of France and children.

**TEFL Teacher** to teach 14-21 year olds in a college and lycée as an *assistante*. Candidates will need the maturity and self-confidence to deal with teenagers, and be able to relate to a large teaching staff.

All posts require 20 hours a week teaching, per 4-day week, with no work on Wednesdays, weekends or school holidays. Full training is given and contracts run from October until May. Included in the remuneration package is free board and

lodging with local families and an allowance of approx. €177 (£119) per month, after national insurance contributions.
*Applications* by post to Mrs Julie Legree at the above address.

# Voluntary Work

## Archaeology

**CONSERVATEUR DU PATRIMOINE:** 3 rue Gregoire de Tours, F-63000 Clermont-Ferrand, France (☎473-91-61-97/473-41-27-23; fax 473-41-27-69).
Volunteers **(5)** for archaeological **field work in the volcanic Cantal Massif**, France. To **assist a dig of a mesolithic hunters settlement dated 10,000** years BC. To work 7 hours a day, 5 days a week. Volunteers required from July to August; minimum period of work 2 weeks. Accommodation provided at a cost of £120. Experience not essential but would be an advantage. Knowledge of French not necessary but useful.
*Applications* from March to Frédéric Surmely at the above address.

**INSTITUT D'HISTOIRE:** Universite du Mans, Avenue O. Messiaen, Le Mans, F-72017 France (☎243-83-31-64; fax 243-83-31-44).
Volunteers **(20)** to assist on archaeological digs. 8 hour day, 5½ day week. Board and lodging provided free. Applicants should be in good health and enjoy working as a team. Knowledge of French or English required. Minimum period of work 3 weeks in July.
*Applications* from April to Annie Renoux at the above address.

**MUSEUM NATIONAL D'HISTOIRE NATURELLE:** Institut de Paléontologie Humaine, 1 rue René Panhard, F-75013 Paris, France; e-mail iph@mnhn.fr .
Volunteers to take part in archaeological digs in France. To work 8½ hours per day, 6 days per week. Minimum period of work 15 days between April and June or 30 days between July and August. Minimum age 16. Applicants should be students or researchers in prehistory, archaeology or the natural sciences. Digs include excavations in the Caune de l'Arago Cave at Tautavel and at Lazaret Cave.
*Applications* to Professor de Lumley at the above address.

**SERVICE ARCHEOLOGIQUE DE DOUAI:** 191 rue St. Albin, F-59500 Douai, France (+33 (0)327 71 38 90; e-mail archeologie.douai@wanadoo.fr). This is a local association for archaeology and the preservation of local cultural heritage.
**Supervisors (2) to manage part of an archaeological excavation**. 7-hour day, 5 day week. £500 per month. Board and lodging provided free. Period of work 2 months from July 12 to beginning of September. Applicants should have experience in field archaeology and, if possible, a knowledge of French.
Volunteers also required to assist with the **excavation and drawing of maps**. About 70 adults are engaged annually.
Applicants must have tetanus vaccination and valid passport. Volunteers should bring a sleeping bag and high boots. Minimum stay 2 weeks. Accommodation is provided Monday to Friday. Application fee of €22,87 (approx £15.50).
*Applications* to P. Demolon at the above address from April.

**SERVICE REGIONAL DE L'ARCHEOLOGIE:** 6, rue de la Manufacture, F-45000 Orleans, France (☎ 238-78-85-41).
**Diggers and Draughtsmen (50).** To work on an archaeological dig in Orleans or in one of the other digs in Central France. Should have relevant experience: some knowledge of French is desirable. 8-hour day, 5-day week. No salary, but board and lodging are provided free. Minimum period of work 2 weeks between June and September.
*Applications* in April to the above address.

**SERVICE REGIONAL DE L'ARCHEOLOGIE DE BRETAGNE:** Hotel de Blossac, 6 rue du Chapitre, F-35044 Rennes Cedex, France (☎299-84-59-00; fax 02-99-84-59-19); www.culture.gouv.fr/bretagne/.
Volunteers **(10-30 per site)** to take part in **various archaeological digs in Brittany** between April and September. To work 7 hours per day, 5-5½ days per week. Board and accommodation, usually on a campsite, is in most cases provided free of charge, but on some sites there is a charge of £5 to cover insurance etc. Minimum period of work 2 weeks. No previous experience is necessary, but a basic knowledge of French is required. Applicants must be at least 18 years old.
The new programme will be available in April; *applications* should be sent to the above address from March.

# Heritage

**LES AMIS DE CHEVREAUX – CHATEL:** Rue du Château, F-39190 Chevreaux, France (Tel/fax +33 3 84 85 95 77; e-mail accjura@free.fr; http://accjura.free.fr).
The château of Chevreaux is situated in a hilltop village above the Bresse Plains.
Les Amis de Chevreaux is a place where young people of different nationalities can meet and spend time together. The work site in the Jura requires willing volunteers to help with the **restoration of the 12th century castle of Chevreaux.** Volunteers are needed for the last three weeks in July and the first three weeks in August and will be lodged on site (at the castle) in tents with camp beds; all sanitary and kitchen facilities are provided. Duties involve **cleaning, reconstruction of the ruins, stone working, carpentry, masonry, archaeology** or **topography.**
The work lasts 6 hours per day, 5 days a week. After work activities include swimming, horse riding and volleyball. At the weekends there is the opportunity to discover the rich patrimony and landscapes of the Jura. Age limits: 16-25. No special qualifications needed apart from good motivation, enthusiasm and willingness to play your part in keeping the camp running smoothly.
*Applications* to the above address.

**BARDOU:** Klaus & Jeane Erhardt, Bardou, par Mons-La-Trivalle, F-34390 Olargues, France (☎+33 4 67 97 72 43).
Bardou is a beautifully restored 16th century Hamlet owned by Klaus and Jean Erhardt. A couple of volunteer helpers are made welcome yearly during the months of April, May and June to help with spring cleaning, gardening and maintenance such as painting and to help keep the stone houses clean. The Hamlet attracts many visitors during the year, especially musicians, orchestras, actors and so on that are performing in the region. 20 hours weekly is asked with tasks. The minimum stay is one month. Volunteers are able to go to any of the cultural events locally. Shorter stays or those outside the project months cost from €8 (approx £5.39) per person/night in individual houses.
*Enquiries* should be sent to Klaus and Jean Erhardt enclosing an International Reply Coupon.

**CLUB DU VIEUX MANOIR:** Abbaye du Moncel à Pontpoint, F-60700 Pont Ste Maxence, France (e-mail secretariat@clubduvieuxmanoir.asso.fr or clubduvieuxmanoir@free.fr).

Founded in 1953, this is a volunteer association for young people who wish to spend some of their spare time doing rescue and restoration work on historic monuments and ancient sites. The volunteers share in the day-to-day organisation of the camp and site. The centres are at the Château Fort de Guise (Aisne), the Abbey Royale du Moncel à Pontpoint (Oise) and the Château d'Argy (Indre).

Volunteers required for work on the **restoration of ancient monuments and similar tasks**. Minimum age for volunteers is 15 years. There are no set hours to work but everyone is expected to lend a hand when the group decides to work on a project. Work is, of course, unpaid and volunteers are expected to contribute around £8 per day towards the cost of their keep. Accommodation is usually in tents. Training organised for participants of 16 years and over.

Long-term stays are a possibility for volunteers at the Château Fort de Guise. After a trial period of 15 days board and lodging will be offered by the association, minimum stay two months.

*Applications* to the address shown above.

**LA SABRANENQUE:** Centre International, rue de la Tour de L'Oume, F-30290 Saint Victor la Coste, France (☎466-50-05-05; e-mail info@sabranenque.com).

La Sabranenque is a non-profit organisation that has been working for 30 years for the preservation of rural habitat and traditional architecture.

**Volunteers (10 per session)** to help with the **restoration of villages, sites and simple monuments in France, using traditional building methods.** Work includes restoration of roofs, terraces, walls, paths or the reconstruction of small houses. Minimum period of work 2 weeks between 1st June and 30th August; at least one day each 2-week period is spent visiting the region. Board and accommodation are provided at a cost of £160 approx. per 2-week period. Applicants must be at least 18 years old and in good health.

*Applications* to the above address at any time.

**REMPART:** 1 rue des Guillemites, F-75004 Paris, France (☎1-42-71-96-55; fax 1-42-71-73-00; e-mail contact@rempart.com; www.rempart.com pages available in English).

Volunteer restorers and preservers for various **castles, fortresses, churches, chapels, abbeys, monasteries, farms, ancient villages, Gallo-Roman sites**, etc. on the 170 sites organised by REMPART every year, during holidays. 35 hours per week and one or two days are devoted to recreational and cultural activities. Board and accommodation are provided at a cost of £4-£5 per day. Volunteers help prepare the meals communally. Most stays are for two weeks. Volunteers pay their own travel expenses and should bring their own sleeping bags and working clothes. Work includes **masonry, woodwork, carpentry, coating, restoration and clearance work**. Opportunities for swimming, tennis, riding, water sports, cycling, exploring the region, and taking part in local festivities. Minimum age is 13, but preferably 18 for non-French residents, with no upper age limit. Some knowledge of French is needed. Previous experience is not necessary.

*Contact* the above address for this year's programme.

# Physically & Mentally Disabled

**ASSOCIATIONS DES PARALYSES DE FRANCE:** 17 Boulevard Auguste-Blanqui, F-75013 Paris, France (+33 (0)140 78 69 00; fax +33(0)145 89 40 57; www. apf.asso.fr).
Assistants required for **work in holiday centres for physically handicapped adults**. Board and accommodation and expenses provided. Minimum age 18 years. Period of work 15-21 days during the summer vacation. Applicants should be able to speak a little French.
*Applications* to APF Evasion at the above address.

# Workcamps

**LES AMIS DE CHEVREAUX – CHATEL:** Rue du Château, F-39190 Chevreaux, France (Tel/fax +33 3 84 85 95 77; e-mail accjura@free.fr; http://accjura.free.fr).
The chateau of Chevreaux is situated in a hilltop village above the Bresse Plains. Les Amis de Chevreaux is a place where young people of different nationalities can meet and spend time together. The work site in the Jura requires willing volunteers to help with the **restoration of the 12th century castle of Chevreaux**. Volunteers are needed for the last three weeks in July and the first three weeks in August and will be lodged on site (at the castle) in tents with a camp bed; all sanitary and kitchen facilities are provided. Duties involve **cleaning, reconstruction of the ruins, stone working, carpentry, masonry, archaeology or topography.**
The work lasts 6 hours per day, 5 days a week. After work activities include swimming, horse riding and volleyball. At the weekends there is the opportunity to discover the rich patrimony and landscapes of the Jura. Age limits: 16-25. No special qualifications needed apart from good motivation, enthusiasm and willingness to play your part in keeping the camp running smoothly.
*Applications* to the above address.

**APARE:** 25 Boulevard Paul Pors, 84800 L'Isle sur la Sorgue (☎33 (0)4-90-85-51-15; fax +33 (0)4-90-86-82-19; e-mail apare@apare-gec.org or mireillepons.apare@ yahoo.fr; www.apare-gec.org).
APARE is a voluntary organisation which aims to promote participation (especially among young people) through **volunteering in local development projects**. APARE, was set up in 1979, by a group of people who shared a passion for Provençal dry stone architecture. It has organised more than 300 voluntary workcamps in over 100 communes.
International Voluntary Work Camps in Provence and the Mediterranean Region, see also GEC/APARE entry in *Europe-Wide* section.
*Applications* to the above address.

**ASSOCIATIONCHANTIERSHISTOIRE&ARCHITECTUREMÉDIÉVALES:** 5 et 7 rue Guilleminot, 75014 Paris, France (☎+33-1 43 35 15 51; fax +33-1 43 20 46 82; www.cham.asso.fr).
Volunteers required for **conservation workcamps** at various locations in France. The work includes **restoration and repair of historic monuments, châteaux and churches**. Volunteers must be at least 16 years old and in good health. Tent accommodation and cooking facilities are provided, but volunteers need to bring their own bedding and work clothes. Placements are available from April, July and August and sometimes at other times of the year, with a minimum recommended stay of two

weeks. Volunteers receive on the job training under qualified supervisors and work about 6 hours per day.

For full details of the workcamps *write* to C.H.A.M. at the above address.

**CHANTIERS DE JEUNES PROVENCE COTE D'AZUR:** 7 Avenue Pierre de Coubertin F-06150 Cannes, La Bocca, France (☎0493-47-89-69; fax 0493-48-12-01; e-mail cjpca@club.internet.fr; stefvi@yahoo.com; www.club.internet.fr/perso/cjpca/).

Volunteers aged 13-17 to take part in the **restoration of historic monuments and in environmental protection projects:** projects consist of 5 hours work in the morning and organised activities such as sailing, climbing and diving in the afternoons/evenings. Accommodation provided. Camps take place in the country near Cannes or the island of Sainte Marguerite, and run for one or two weeks during the summer, Christmas or Easter holidays. Applicants must be sociable and speak French.

For further details *send* two International Reply Coupons to the above address with a letter written in French

**CONCORDIA:** 19 North Street, Portslade, Brighton, BN41 1DH (☎01273-422218; fax 01273 421182; e-mail info@concordia-iye.org.uk; www.concordia-iye.org.uk).

Concordia offers volunteers aged 16+ the opportunity to take part in international short-term volunteer projects in over 60 countries worldwide. The work is community based and ranges from **nature conservation, renovation, construction and social work including children's play schemes and teaching.** Volunteers pay a registration fee of £110 and fund their own travel. Board and accommodation are free of charge.

For further information on volunteering or coordinating please check the website or *contact* the International Volunteer Coordinator at the above address.

**ETUDES ET CHANTIERS (UNAREC):** Délégation Internationale, 3 rue des Petits-Gras, F-63000 Clermont-Ferrand, France (☎473-31-98-04; fax 473-31 98 09; e-mail unarec@wanadoo.fr or ecec.voluntariat@wanadoo.fr).

Organise voluntary workcamps for the upkeep, development and preservation of the environment. Work camps lasting for two or three weeks are held over the summer. Tasks vary and include such activities as **river cleaning, the preservation of old buildings and districts in small towns, organising local cultural festivals, etc.** Minimum age 18 years; camps are also held for younger teenagers aged 14-17. Application fees approx. £65 (including membership and insurance). British volunteers must apply through Concordia (see *Worldwide* chapter) or another UK organisation. An annual programme is produced in March.

For further details by e-mail *contact* unarec@wanadoo.fr.

**JEUNESSE ET RECONSTRUCTION:** 8-10 rue de Trévise, Paris 75009, France; www.volontariat.org.

The national and international volunteer organisation Jeunesse et Reconstruction organises workcamps in France in the Auvergne, Basse Normandie, Pays de La Loire, Midi-Pyrénées, Rhône Alpes, Languedoc-Rouissillon and PACA. Volunteers needed for workcamps throughout France. Type of work varies from camp to camp. **Examples in include sharing the daily lives and activities of disabled adults, laying out an orientation course and helping to organise a festival of music.** Work is unpaid, but free board and accommodation are provided. About 7 hours work per day, 5 days per week. Volunteers are likely to come from all over the world.

Applicants should normally be at least 18 years old, though there are some vacancies for 17-year-olds. Most camps last for 3 weeks. There are also possibilities for voluntary work lasting for three months, which provides pocket money. *Applications* to the above address.

**LES DEUX MOULINS:** Gontard, Dauphin, F-04300 Forcalquier, France; www. lesdeuxmoulins.asso.fr; e-mail gontard@les deuxmoulins.asso.fr.
**Volunteers to construct new buildings and improve existing amenities** at this holiday centre in the Luberon, Haute Provence built by and for young people of all nationalities. Minimum age of entry is 18 years and the centre is open throughout the summer. Volunteers pay part of the cost of board and accommodation. The organisation would like to stress that volunteers are unpaid but the work is by no means rigid or exacting.
　　For further details *contact* the address above.

**NEIGE ET MERVEILLES:** F-06430 St. Dalamas de Tende, France (☎493-04-62-40; fax 493-04-88-58; e-mail doc@neige-merveilles.com; www.neige-merveilles. com).
Volunteers **(4)** to take part in **international workcamps,** which take place between April and October. Food and accommodation provided. To work 6 hours per day, 5 days per week. Volunteers must pay their own insurance costs of approximately £50. Minimum age 18. This organisation also organises international workcamps for young people aged 15-17.
　　For *further details* contact the Recruitment Department at the above address.

# Other Volunteer Work in France

**CENTRE INTERNATIONAL D'ANTIBES/INSTITUT PREVERT:** 38 Bd d'Aguillon 06600 Antibes (☎4-92 90 71 70/92 90 71 71). The Centre is situated on the French Riviera, and teaches French to more than 5,000 foreign students a year.
**Assistants** for numerous work exchange places available including help with administration, helping in kitchens, chambermaid duties or general maintenance duties in a French language school for foreigners. No wages are paid but French courses and/or accommodation are provided. Places are available all year round for varying periods of one to six months.
　　For more information on their various work exchange programmes, or *to apply*, contact 'Work Exchange' at the above address, or e-mail wep@cia-france.com.

**MADAME DE MONTESQUIEU:** La Bassie, Bloux, 03320 Lurcy-Levis .(☎04 70 67 96 13; fax 04 70 67 84 52).
**Voluntary Assistants (1 or 2) to offer general help in and around a very pretty house with a garden, swimming pool and tennis court.** No wages are paid, but board and lodging is provided. Period of work (minimum one and a half months) by arrangement, with work available *all year*. Applicants must love cats and dogs (four and two of them respectively), French cuisine and nature. Madame de Montesquieu is the author of the cookery book, *Cuisinez la nature*. The positions would be ideal for those who wish to perfect their French, French cooking and renovate old potteries. La Bassie is in a remote area with the next town 8km away so applicants must also love the country.
　　For more details *contact* Mme Marie Laure de Montesquieu at the above address.

**MEINRAD BETSCHART:** Rue du Presbytére, F-21140 Montigny sur Armançon, France (☎33-(0)3-80-97-18-85).
**Helpers (4)** to assist with the renovation of an old house belonging to a sculptor and his German speaking family. Work includes tasks from wall-building to laying carpets, and

working in the garden and in the kitchen. To work 6 hours a day, 6 days a week. Pocket money of £82 per month plus board and accommodation. Minimum period of work 2 weeks. Applicants must be willing to perform practical work and have an interest in art.

*Applications* to the above address one month before date on which you wish to start work.

**SOURIRE ET NATURE:** chez André Risetti, rue de la Fontaine St. Marc, F-21140 Montigny sur Armançon, France (☎03-80-97-32-46; e-mail jean-pierre@ sourireetnature.com).

Volunteers required for the renovation of a hostel 70km west of Dijon, including **construction of stone walls, painting, gardening, and domestic work.** Instruction offered in methods and use of tools. Work can be tailored to applicants' particular skills. Work is available for volunteers aged 18-40 not only during the summer months but also throughout the year to work 5 days per week. Board and lodging are included. Knowledge of French (preferably), or English required.

Option 1: 30 hours work per week with approx. £30 pocket money provided.

Option 2: 15 hours work per week, with the applicant paying approx. with free lodging for a contribution of £10 towards food costs.

*Applications*, in writing, all year round to the above address enclosing a CV and references.

# Au Pairs, Nannies, Family Helps and Exchanges

**L'ACCUEIL FAMILIAL DES JEUNES ETRANGERS:** 23 rue du Cherche-Midi, F-75006 Paris, France (☎1-42-22-50-34; fax 1-45-44-60-48; e-mail accueil@afje-paris.org).

**Au Pairs:** (boys and girls) to assist families with housework and look after children for about 30 hours a week. Summer placements from 1 to 3 months possible all over France; applications for these must be received by 15 May. Also placements for the school year, preferably from the beginning of September or January to the end of June.

**Paying Guest:** stays for a usual minimum of 2 weeks in Paris and the suburbs (but in the provinces only during the holidays) also arranged for boys or girls aged over 18.

For further details *contact* the above address.

**ANGELS INTERNATIONAL AU PAIR AGENCY:** 3 The Hollies, Fifth Cross Road, Twickenham, Middx. TW2 5LJ (e-mail admin@angelsint.demon.co.uk; www. aupair1.com). Agency offering placements all over Europe and further afield. The agency offers full support for both families and Au Pairs, including language classes, trouble shooting and help with accommodation if required.

**Au Pair:** must have childcare experience. Expected to work 25-40 per day, wages vary from £55-£120.

*Applications* to Kathryn Wigg at the above e-mail address.

**'BUTTERFLY ET PAPILLON' SCHOOL OF INTERNATIONAL LANGUAGES & AU PAIR AGENCY:** 8, Av de Genève, F-74000 Annecy, France (☎+3 450-67-01-33; fax +33 450-67-03-51; e-mail pascale.butterfly@wanadoo.fr; www.butterfly-papillon.com).

**Au Pair:** Butterfly et Papillon welcome foreign 18-26 year old students for summer and year long au-pair placements and French courses in the French Alps (Annecy is close to the Swiss border and Geneva). Pocket money at least £170 per month. Board and French lessons available. 30 hours a week plus two evenings babysitting. Age limits: 18-26. Basic French required. Driving licence and experience with children preferred.

Butterfly et Papillon also run a **work exchange programme**. Under the auspices of the EU's Leonardo scheme, this programme offers foreign students the unique opportunity to live and work in France for up to 13 weeks. Families in the Au Pair programme are obliged to pay €900 (approx £607.50) towards French lessons if the student stays over 9 months.

*Applications* to Fleur Martin, Main Secretary, at the above address.

**INTERNATIONAL CATHOLIC SOCIETY FOR GIRLS (ACISJF) ADVISORY SERVICE:** 55 Nightingale Road, Rickmansworth, Herts., WD3 7BU (☎01923-778449 Office Hours Mon-Fri 10.30am-12.30pm; e-mail secretariat@acisjf-int.org; www.acisjf-int.org).

Advice on **au pair placements** abroad, mainly in France, for English applicants. Minimum age 18 years: minimum stay 3 months approx.

Any *enquiries* should be made enclosing a stamped addressed envelope, to the above address.

**INSTITUT EURO PROVENCE:** 69 rue de Rome, F-13001 Marseille, France (☎+33-4-91 33 90 60; fax 4-91 33 77 36; e-mail euro.provence@wanadoo.fr; www. perso.wanadoo.fr/euro.provence).

Institut Euro 'Provence' is recognised by both the ministries of Education and Youth and Sport. The French course offers free cultural activities which aim to promote harmony between students.

**Au Pairs** needed to look after children and carry out light housework required to work 30 hours per week plus two evenings baby-sitting. Au Pairs are required all year round, with the minimum period of work being two months in the summer and six months the rest of the year. Board and lodging are provided free and au pairs are paid by the family. Applicants will need basic French, but the institute provides low cost French classes.

For more details *contact* Mrs Patricia Guedj-Gandolfo.

**SOAMES INTERNATIONAL SERVICES/PARIS NANNIES:** 64 rue Anatole France, 92300 Levallois Perrec, France (☎01-47 30 44 04; soames.parisnannies@ wanadoo.fr; www.soamesparisnannies.com).

**Au Pairs:** wage approximately £45 per week.

**Nannies:** wage min. £160 per week.

**Mothers' Helps:** wage around £120 per week.

Minimum period of work 2 months; minimum age 18. Previous childcare experience desirable.

For further details *contact* the above address.

# Other Employment in France

**CENTRE D'INFORMATION ET DE DOCUMENTATION JEUNESSE:** 101 quai Branly, F-75740 Paris Cedex 15, France (☎01-44 49 12 00; 0825 090 630 (information line); www.cidj.com).

Advertises temporary jobs on a daily basis, mainly in Paris and the surrounding area, available to young people. It also gives information on cheap places to stay, on French university courses for foreigners and practical advice on the regulations as part of its general information serviced for young people. CIDJ also publishes booklets on a range of subjects for young people.

Please note: to get details of the jobs you must *visit* the centre personally; the CIDJ does not send out information on this subject; opening hours are 10am-6pm, Monday

, Tuesday, Wednesday and Friday, and from 1pm-6pm on Thursdays and 9.30 to 1pm, Saturday. (Nearest metro: Bir-Hakeim).

**SEJOURS INTERNATIONAUX LINGUISTIQUES ET CULTURELS:** 32 Rempart de l'Est, F-16022 Angoulême Cedex, France (☎+33-5-45 97 41 90; fax 5-45 94 20 63; e-mail webmaster@silc.fr or france@silc.fr; www.silc-france.com). **Work Experience** placements throughout France, as well as a variety of language **Study Courses, International Summer Centres, Individual Homestays and Private Tuition.** For details *contact* the above address.

# Germany

The bad news is that Germany is no longer such a good prospect for seasonal work as recent additions to the membership of the EU have flooded the market. Over the last couple of years German hotels have turned to Eastern Europe for their seasonal staff who now arrive by the busload delivered straight to the employers' doors. The other bad news is that unemployment is very high (10.3% 2006). In the five federal states of eastern Germany, unemployment is as high as 17%. However, though it requires great perseverance, it is not impossible for the truly determined with a grasp of German to get a job. The main opportunities are in the western and southern regions.

Many of the seasonal jobs available are in hotels, especially in tourist areas such as the Bavarian Alps, the Black Forest and resorts on the North Sea Coast. People going to work in a German hotel should note that managers may demand extra hours of work from their employees, and some will not always give extra time off or pay overtime as compensation. They may also ask workers to do jobs that are not specified in their contract by asking them to fill in for other members of staff. Anyone who feels that their contract is being breached and who cannot come to any agreement with their employer should appeal to the local *Arbeitsamt* (see below) for arbitration. Jobs in other sectors in the tourist industry can be found in this chapter and in the *Worldwide* chapter at the beginning of this book.

There are also fruit-picking jobs available, although not nearly as many as in France. During the summer the best region to try is the *Altes Land* which stretches between Stade and Hamburg in north Germany and includes the towns of Steinkirchen, Jork and Horneburg. The work there consists of picking cherries in July and August, and apples in September. Try also the Bergstrasse south of Frankfurt where apples and many other fruits are grown. Germany's vineyards also provide a source of work, particularly because in recent years, German winemakers have found it increasingly difficult to find workers to help with the grape harvest. The harvest begins in October and continues into November: the vineyards are concentrated in the south west of the country, especially along the valleys of the Rhine to the south of Bonn and Moselle.

The Happy Hands programme (Anne von Gleichen, Roemerberg 8, 60311, Frankfurt/Main, ☎ 069-293733 Fax: 069-295564 E-mail Anne.Gleichen@t-online.de; www.workingholidays.de) arranges working holidays on farms or in family-run country hotels for British and European students who know some German. Participants are given monthly pocket money and full board and lodging with families on farms or in country hotels. In return they help in the kitchen, serving German guests, look after children and/or horses, farm animals for 3-6 months though a six-week commitment is also allowed; some vacancies for female students in the autumn available. There is usually a higher proportion of female than male participants recruited. There is a registration fee. Contact first with an e-mail before booking. Early requests are appreciated.

It may also be possible to arrange voluntary work on an organic farm: see the entry on WWOOF in the *Worldwide* chapter for details. Volunteers would receive free board, lodging and training in return for their work. For more details contact WWOOF-Deutschland, Postfach 210259, 01263 Dresden, Germany (e-mail info@ wwoof.de; www.wwoof.de). Membership of the German branch of WWOOF costs €18 (about £12), and gives access to about 160 farm addresses.

On arrival in Germany, EU nationals may go the *Arbeitsamt* (employment office) in the area in which they wish to work and obtain information on job opportunities: its address will be in the local telephone directory. The system is computerised nationally and is reckoned highly efficient so it is not necessary to arrange a job in advance. However, if you prefer to have a job already arranged you can try to arrange a job through the EURES contact in your local employment office or through the Zentralstelle fur Arbeitsvermittlung (212.12 Internationale Nachwuchsförderung Studentenvermittlung, Postfach, 53107 Bonn; +49 228-713-1330; fax 0228-713 270 1037;Bonn-ZAV@.info-auslaendische-studenten@arbeitsagentur.de; www. arbeitsamt.de) which is the official government office dealing with job applications from abroad. The Zentralstelle may be able to help find work in hotels, on farms, or in factories: it has a special department to help students of any nationality find summer jobs, applications for which must be received before the end of February. For further information about the official German employment service and other aspects of work there consult the free fact sheet *Working in Germany* published by Jobcentre Plus. This is available from the European and International Jobsearch Advice Team, Jobcentre Plus, Yorkshire & The Humber Regional Office, Whitehall II, Whitehall Quay, Leeds LS1 4HR; (☎+44 (0) 113 307 8090; e-mail international-jobsearch-advice@jobcentreplus.gsi.gov.uk). and Jobcentre Plus offices throughout the UK.

In addition to those listed in this chapter there are opportunities for voluntary work in Germany; British applicants can apply through International Voluntary Service, UNA Exchange, Youth Action for Peace and Concordia; CIEE and Service Civil International (see the IVS entry) can help US residents; their entries can be found in the *Worldwide* chapter.

An advertisement in a German newspaper may bring an offer of a job; *Rheinische Post* is published at Zulpicher Strasse 10, 40196 Dusseldorf, Germany (☎+49-211-505 2880). The following weekly newspapers might also be of interest: The *Süddeutsche Zeitung*, Sendlicher Str. 80331 München; ☎+49 89 21830; fax +49 89 2183 787; www.sueddeutsch.de; the *Bayernkurier* Nymphenburger Str. 64, D-80005 München, Germany (☎089-120040; fax 089-1293050; e-mail redaktion@bayernkurier.de), *Die Welt* at Axel-Springer Strasse 65, GKP 20350, Brieffach 2410/10888 Berlin (fax 030-3591 71606), or the *Frankfurter Allgemeine Zeitung*, which can be found at Hellerhofstr. 2-4 60327 Frankfurt/Main (☎069-75910; fax 069-7591 1743), can also sell you an advertisement promoting your availability to work.

# RED TAPE

**Visa Requirements:** a visa is not required by citizens of EU/EEA nations or Iceland or Norway. British citizens should hold a 'European Community' passport. Members of other countries who wish to go to Germany to do paid work need a Visa/Residence Permit before entering Germany.

**Residence Registration:** this applies to everyone including Germans. Within a week of finding permanent (i.e. not hotel accommodation) you should register your address (and any subsequent change of address) with the registration office (Einwohnermeldeamt), usually found in the town hall.
**Residence Permit:** a residence permit is required for any visit of more than three months or where employment is intended. Applications should be made to the Visa Section of the nearest Embassy or Consulate General of the Federal Republic of Germany. Or in the case of EU Nationals already in Germany, to the Foreign Nationals Authority *(Ausländerbehörde)* in the town or district *(Kreis)* of intended residence. Nationals of Switzerland, the USA, Australia, New Zealand, Japan, Canada and Israel can apply for a residence permit after arriving in Germany unless they have secured a job before arriving. A residence permit is usually furnished within two weeks of application and is provided free of charge.
**Work Permits:** To find work in Germany it is essential to speak some German. The regulations for work permits are the same as for visas. EEA Nationals intending to look for work for more than 3 months might have to show the local authority that they are self-supporting while conducting a job hunt.
**Au Pair:** Agencies in Germany no longer have to be licensed so there are now lots of private agencies. Agencies in Germany include IN VIA Germany (Ludwigstr. 36, Postfach 420, 79004 Freiburg; 0761-200208; invia@caritas.de; www.aupair-invia.de) with 40 branches, and Verein für Internationale Jugendarbeit, Goetheallee 10, 53225 Bonn (0228-698952/fax 0228-694166; au-pair.vij@netcologne.de/ www.vij-Deutschland.de). The German YWCA (VIJ) has more than 20 offices in Germany and places both male and female au pairs for a preferred minimum stay of one year. Pocket money is paid. Au Pairs must be between 17 and 24 years of age. From January 2006, the monthly pocket money will be 260 euros.
**Voluntary Work:** there are no restrictions on work of this nature.

# Hotel Work and Catering

**HOTEL ALTE THORSCHENKE:** Brueckenstrasse 3, 56812 Cochem (Mosel), Brückenstrasse (☎+49 (0)2671 7059; fax +49 (0)2671 4202; e-mail alte-thorschenke@ t-online.de; www.castle-thorschenke.com).
A medieval hotel built in 1332 with positions for chambermaids, waiting staff, receptionists and kitchen staff. Jobs available between April and October.
For more information *contact* Geschäftsfürer Herr Dudeck.


**HOTEL BAYERISCHER HOF/HOTEL REUTEMANN/HOTEL SEEGARTEN:** Seepromenade, D-88131 Lindau, Germany (☎08382-9150; fax 08382-91 55 91; e-mail hotel@bayerischerhof-lindau.de; www.bayerischerhof-lindau.de).
**Waiting Staff (9).** Must speak reasonable German.
**Kitchen Assistants (8).** Knowledge of German not essential.
**Chambermaids (8).** Knowledge of German not essential
    Wage approx. € 860 (£595) net per month for 8 hours work per day, 5 days per week. Board and accommodation available at a small charge. Minimum period of work 3 months. Applicants must be students.
    *Applications* to the above address.


**BERGHOTEL JOHANNESHOEHE:** Wallhausenstr. 1, D-57072 Siegen 1, Germany (e-mail hoeffkes@johanneshoehe.de; www.johanneshoehe.de)
**Buffet Assistants** (2). Wage approximately £460 per month plus free board and

lodging. To work a 40 hour week. To work for at least 12 weeks; period of work by arrangement. Applicants must speak German.
*Applications* should be sent to the above address from April 6th.

**HOTEL BRUDERMUHLE BAMBERG:** Schranne 1, D-96049 Bamberg, Germany (☎09-51 955 220; fax 09-51 955 2255; e-mail info@brudermuehle.de; www. brudermuehle.de).
**Hotel Managers, Waitresses (2)** with knowledge of German and relevant professional training to work 5 days a week, 8-10 hours a day at varying times during the day. Those working in the restaurant will serve food, drinks and wine. Applicants should be prepared to work for a minimum of 3 months. Wage of about £775 per month provided.
**Cook (1)** with cooking qualifications and knowledge of German is required to help prepare food with the French cook. Wage of about £840 a month provided.
Subsidised board and accommodation is available at around £100 per month.
*Applications* are invited at any time to the above address.

**HOTEL BOLD, RINGHOTEL OBERAMMERGAU:** Konig-Ludwig Strasse 10, D-82487 Oberammergau, Germany.
**Commis de Rang (1/2).** £350 per month. Must be experienced.
**Chambermaid (1/2).** Salary as above. Must be neat and clean.
**Dishwasher (1/2).** As above.
To work 8-9 hours per day, 5 days per week. Board and accommodation provided free. Minimum period of work from 30 May to 30 September.
*Applications* before May to the above address.

**HOTEL-RESTAURANT BURGFRIEDEN:** J. M. Muhlental 62, D-56814 Beilstein/ Mosel, Germany (☎026 739 36 39; fax 026 73 93 63 88).
**Restaurant Staff** to work in a buffet, serving food and drink and cleaning. Approx. £320 per month. To work a 48 hour week from 8am-6pm or 2-9pm. Free board and lodging provided. Minimum period of work 2 months. Knowledge of German necessary.
*Applications* to Frau Sprenger-Herzer at the above address before the end of April.

**BURGHOTEL AUF SCHONBURG:** D-55430 Oberwesel am Rhein, Germany (☎+49-6744 93930; fax 06744-1613; e-mail huettl@hotel-schoenburg.com; www. hotel-schoenburg.com). Schönburg Castle is a beautiful medieval castle in the romantic Rhine Valley with a superior hotel-restaurant and interntational guests. This is a small and friendly hotel with a young and enthusiastic staff.
**Chambermaid (1)** to work part-time in the morning, or full-time from 8am-4.30pm. Duties include cleaning rooms.
To work 5 days per week: full-time staff work 8 hours per day (salary €500 (approx £337), and part-timers work 4-5 hours per day (salary €300 (approx £202). Board and accommodation provided free. Minimum period of work two months. Applicants should speak good German.
*Applications* should be sent to the Familie Hüttl at the above address in March.

**CITYHOTEL-METROPOL:** D-56068 Koblenz am Rhein, Germany (☎0261-350-60; fax 0261-160366).
**Musicians (1-3)** to perform folk and popular music for evening entertainment: must already have a wide repertoire of songs. Wages by arrangement. To work around 8 hours per day, 5 or 6 days per week. Board and accommodation available. Period of work by arrangement.
*Applications* to the above address at any time.

**HOTEL DEUTSCHES HAUS:** D-91550 Dinkelsbuhl, Weinmarket 3, Bavaria, Germany (☎+49-(0)9851 6058; fax+49-(0)9851 7911; info@deutsches-haus-dkb.de.) **Kitchen Assistants** (2). Pay negotiable. Hours: 09.00-14.00, 18.00-21.00, 6 days per week. Free board and accommodation. Minimum period of work 2 months.
*Applications* until April to the address above.

**EUROTOQUES:** Winnender Str 12, D-73667 Ebnisee/Schwäbischer Wald, Germany (☎+49-7184-91055; fax 07184-91053; e-mail secretary@eurotoques.de; www. Eurotoques.de).
**Kitchen Assistants, Waiting Staff** for placements in the restaurants of some of Germany's top cooks all over Germany. No wage, but free board and lodging is provided. To work 9 hours per day, 5 days per week. Minimum period of work three months at any time of year. Applicants should speak German.
*Applications* to the above address.

**FAMILIEN UND SPORTHOTEL ALLGAEUER BERGHOF:** D-87544 Blaichach, Southern Bavaria, Germany (☎08321-8060; fax 08321-806219; e-mail m.neusch@allgaeuer-berghof.de; www.allgaeuer.berghof.de). A 180 bed hotel with 50 staff situated in a hill-top ski resort, with access to world-cup races, hiking, tennis and mountain biking.
**Chambermaids:** knowledge of German required.
**Buffet, Kitchen Assistants** and **Restaurant Assistants:** knowledge of German required.
Wages €720 (£480) approx. net per month by arrangement for 40 hours work per week. Free board and lodging. No previous hotel experience required. Minimum age 18.
*Enquiries* to Mrs Neusch at the above address.

**RESTAURANT FRIEDRICHSHOF:** D-76596 Forbach/Murgtal, Landstrasse 1, Germany (☎+49(0)7228 2333).
**Kitchen Assistant** (female). £335 approx. per month. Hours: 9am-2pm and 6-9pm, 5½ days per week. Free board and accommodation. Minimum period of work 2½ months between June and the end of September. Those with allergies should note that there are cats in the hotel.
*Applications* should be sent with a photo to the above address.

**GASTHOF UND PENSION ADLER:** Ehlenbogen 1, D-72275 Alpirsbach Schwarzwald, Kreis Freudenstadt, Germany (☎+49-7444-2215; fax 07444-4588; e-mail adler@alpirsbach.com). Family run hotel restaurant and farm in the black forest between Stuttgart and France.
**Chambermaid.** Around £400 per month plus board and lodging. Work includes helping with the laundry.
**Waiter/Waitress.** Approximately £400 per month including tips plus board and lodging. Must have a knowledge of German and the ability to get on with people.
**Kitchen Assistant** to prepare vegetables and wash up (using machine). Around £400 per month plus board and lodging.
**Farmhand/Groom** to work around the farm and/or help with the horses. Wage c. £340 plus board and lodging.
To work eight to ten hours a day, 5½ days per week, in shifts. Time off by arrangement. Salaries quoted are net, deductions having been made for board and accommodation. Staff should be prepared to help in other departments. Minimum period of work 2 months.
*Applications* throughout the year to Georg Dietel at the above address.

**HOTEL GOGGL:** H.V. Herkomer Strasse 19/20, D-86899 Landsberg-Lech, Germany (☎08191 3240; fax 08191 324-100; e-mail info@hotel-goggl.de).
**Chambermaid, Waitress, Receptionist** to work five days per week, eight hours per day. Waitress to serve breakfast. Knowledge of German essential for Receptionist position.
*Applications* to the above address.

**HOTEL GROSSFELD:** Schlosstrasse 4-6, D-48455 Bad Bentheim, Germany (☎ 05922-77770; fax 05922-4349; e-mail hotel@grossfeld.com). A 120 bed hotel with spa, sauna, Turkish bath and restaurant/café.
**General Assistants (4)** to work in a hotel and cafe. Wage approximately £115 per month net with free board and lodging. To work 8 hours per day, 5 days per week between 9am and 5pm. Minimum period of work 2 months. Some knowledge of the Dutch language would be an advantage.
*Applications* with a passport photo should be sent to Herr Johannes Grossfeld from the beginning of the year until 1 April.

**HOTEL HAMM:** D-56068 Koblenz, St. Josef Strasse 32-34, Germany (☎0261-34546; fax 0261-160972).
**Chambermaids (2).** 5 day week, 5 hours per day.
**Waitress** to serve breakfast and dinner and do some reception work. 5 day week, 8 hours per day.
**Night Porter** to man the reception desk between 7.30pm and 3am, 6 nights a week. Knowledge of German essential.
Wages on application. Free board and accommodation provided. Applicants must be available for at least 3 months (5 or more preferred) between May and September.
*Applications* to the above address.

**HOLIDAY INN FRANKFURT AIRPORT-NORTH:** Isenburger Schneise 40, D-60528 Frankfurt, Germany (☎069-67840; fax 069-678 4190; e-mail info.hi-frankfurt-airportnorth@queensgrappe.de). Set in Germany's largest stretch of urban woodland near the old city, the Holiday Inn Frankfurt Airport-North is one of Frankfurt's premier hotels.
**Serving Staff** required for the hotel's restaurant, bar and beer-garden. To work a seven and three-quarter hour shift per day not including a 30 minute break, over a 5-day week. The hours worked will vary according to the shifts. Board and lodging are available at a cost of c.£28 per month for board. Wages by negotiation. Staff should speak English and German.
*Applications* to Frau Sonia Thierer at the above address.

**INTERNATIONALES HAUS SONNENBERG:** Clausthalerstr. 11, D-37444 St Andreasberg, Germany (☎+49-05882-9440; fax +49-05582-944100; e-mail info@ sonnenberg-international.de).
**Domestic Assistants (6)** needed from 1st August for at least 3 months. The work is in the Housekeeping department and involves working in the dining hall, washing up, and cleaning in the kitchens, accommodation and conference rooms. The hours of work are 7.30am-1.45pm and 4.45-7.30pm, up to a total of 38 and a 1/2 hours per week. Within each four-week period there are eight days off which will not necessarily fall on weekends. Overtime is available and can be accumulated and taken as time off. Wages are £430 approx. per month and accommodation is provided at a cost of around £54 per month.
Applicants should be over 18, no previous experience is necessary but a basic

knowledge of German and any requisite work permits are required. Staff may also take part in a conference towards the end of their stay.
For further details *contact* Reception at the centre.

**HOTEL JAKOB:** Schwarzeweg 6, D-87629 Fussen-Bad Faulenbach, Germany (fax 08362-913270; e-mail info@kurhotel-jakob.de; www.kurhotel-jakob.de).
**General Assistants:** around €1350 per month, hours by arrangement. Free board and lodging provided. Period of work from mid-May to mid-October. A basic knowledge of German is necessary.
*Applications* to Frau G. Jakob at the above address.

**KLOSTER HORNBACH:** Loesch GmbH Im Klosterbezirk, D-66500 Hornbach, Germany (☎0049-6338 91010-0; fax 0049-6338 91010-99; e-mail info@kloster-hornbach.de; www.kloster-hornbach.de). Kloster Hornbach is a former monastery founded in 742, and rebuilt over the last 6 years into a 4-star hotel with 34 rooms, 2 restaurants, a large garden restaurant and several banqueting rooms.
**Hotel and Restaurant Staff** required.
*Applications* by e-mail to Christiane und Edelbert Loesch at the above address.

**HOTEL KONIGSSEE-BETRIEBE:** Seestrasse 29, D-83471 Konigssee-Berchtesgaden, Upper Bavaria, Germany. This hotel company is one of the largest in Bavaria. Konigssee is in the Alps, in a region famous for its beautiful landscape, mountains, forests, lakes and castles. It is thirty minutes from Salzburg Airport.
**Ice-Cream Sellers (3).** £285 per month net. Moderate knowledge of German required.
**Chambermaids (3-4)** to clean rooms and make beds. £285 per month net. Moderate knowledge of German required.
**Assistant Waiters/Waitresses (2)** to serve meals. £285 per month net. Moderate knowledge of German required.
**Kitchen Assistant** to wash vegetables, prepare food and assist cooks. £285 per month net. Moderate knowledge of German required.
To work 8½ hours per day, 5 days per week. Minimum period of work 2½ months. Free board and lodging provided.
*Applications* to the above address at any time.

**POSTHOTEL:** Obermarkt 9, D-82481 Mittenwald/Karwendel, Germany (☎+49 8823 93 82 333; fax +49 8823 93 82 999; e-mail info@posthotel-mittenwald.de; www.posthotel-mittenwald.de).
**Chambermaids (2)** to clean guest rooms, corridors, toilets, swimming pool etc. To work from 6.30am-4pm, with one hour break.
**Kitchen Assistants/Washers Up (2)** to wash tableware and cooking utensils, peel potatoes, clean vegetables, etc. To work from 7am-2pm and 5.30-9pm with 1½ hour break.
£650 per month, approximately. To work 8-9 hours per day, 5 days per week. Board and lodging available for around £100 per month. Minimum period of work 2½ months between July and October and between 20 December and 31 March.
Some knowledge of German an advantage: other languages are not essential.
*Applicants only accepted from students holding EU passports or those studying in Germany who have the relevant work permit from the employment office.*
*Applications,* enclosing proof of student status from school, college or university stating that you are a full-time student there (International Student Identity Cards will not suffice) to the above address.

**HOTEL PRINZ-LUITPOLD-BAD:** D-87541 Hindelang/Allgäuer Alpen, Germany (☎08324-8900; fax 08324-890379; e-mail info@luitpoldbad.de; website www.luitpoldbad.de). A 110 bedroom spa hotel built in 1864 in a quiet mountain location with glorious views of the Allgäu in the Bavarian Alps. Features include their private mud baths and their sulfur spring, which is the highest in Germany. The hotel is 70km from Lake Constance and 45km from the king's castle Neuschwanstein/ Füssen.
**General Assistants (2).** Should speak fluent German.
**Chambermaids (3), Kitchen Helps (3).** £400 net per month, approx., plus around £50 net bonus per month. To work 5 days a week. Free board and accommodation provided. Minimum period of work 3 months all year round. Raise of £30 per month from the fourth month onwards.
    *Applications* from EU passport holders only to the above address.

**MONCH'S POSTHOTEL:** Doblersk.2, 76328, Bad Herrenalb, Germany (☎070-837440; fax 070-8374-4122)
**Waiting Assistant, Room Attendant, General Assistant.** Wages approx. £240 per month. To work 9 hours per day, 5 days per week. Board and accommodation provided free. Knowledge of low German or English or French needed.
    *Applications* to the above address in spring.

**RHEINHOTEL LORELEY:** Rheinallee 12, D-53639 Königswinter 1, Germany (☎02223-9250; fax 02223-925100; info@hotelloreley.de). A tourist and conference hotel open all year, set beside the Rhine. Family-run with employees of various nationalities.
**Chambermaids (1-2)** to tidy rooms and change the beds. Approx. €500 (approx £337) per month. Must have previous relevant experience and knowledge of German.
**Waiters (1-2)** to serve food. Around €500 (approx £337) per month. Previous experience of waiting desirable. Must have knowledge of German.
    To work 9 hours per day, 5 days per week. Working days variable. Applicants must be friendly people who are willing to work for at least three months. Food and lodgings free.
    *Applications* to Manfred Maderer at the above address between 1 March and 15 March only.

**ROMANTIK HOTEL FASANERIE:** Fasanerie 1, D-66482 Zweibrücken/ Rheinland-Pfalz, Germany (☎+49-6332-9730; fax 06332-973111; e-mail info@ landschloss-fasanerie.de; www.landschlossfasanerie.de).
Two hotels in Zweibrücken require **Waiting Staff** to work in a restaurant and buffet. Wages around £246 per month, with accommodation and meals included. To work 8-10 hours per day between 6.30am and midnight, 6 days per week. Period of work by arrangement between April and October.
    Applicants should speak German and be flexible and adaptable; additional knowledge of French and English would be helpful.
    *Applications* should be sent to Doris Heiden at the above address 2-3 months before the desired start of work.

**HOTEL SCHASSBERGER EBNISEE:** Winnenderstr. 10, D-73667 Ebnisee, Germany (☎07184-292-0; fax 07184-292-204; e-mail info@schassberger.de; www. schassberger.de). The hotel is one of the most attractive resorts in Germany, in the heart of the Swabian forest northeast of Stuttgart.

**Kitchen Assistants, Waiting Staff, Housekeeping Staff** to work for a spa and health resort hotel situated in the Swabian forest nature park, 40 km from Stuttgart specialising in short sporting/relaxation breaks.

Ages 18-30. Knowledge of German required. Some previous experience desirable. Minimum period of work 2 months. Board and accommodation provided. Initially no salary, but wage will be paid from the 4th month depending on performance. To work 9 hours per 5 day week. On days off there are a variety of activities available to staff both in and outside the hotel, including a Finnish sauna, tennis, swimming, hiking, fishing, horse riding and continuing education classes.

*Applications* should be sent to Iris Schassberger at the above address at any time of year.

**HOTEL SCHLOSS HUGENPOET GmbH:** August-Thyssen-Strasse 51, D-45219, Essen (☎02054-120436; fax 02054-12045; e-mail personal@hugenpoet.de; www. hugenpoet.de). The Hotel Schloss Hugenpoet is a beautiful building, not far from Düsseldorf. It belongs to the Relais and Chateaux Hotel Group.
**Gardeners, General Assistants, Chambermaids, Laundry Assistants** needed. Applicants should be flexible, friendly and polite, and should have a little German and/or English. Wages €600 (£405) approx. gross, monthly. Staff work eight hours per day over a five-day working week during the summer months. Accommodation is provided at €105-€120 (£70-£80) (per room) per month and food is provided free of charge.

*Applications* are invited from six months prior to starting date if possible.

**HOTEL SCHLOSS PETERSHAGEN:** Schlosstrasse 5-7, D-32469 Petershagen, Germany. (☎+49-05707-9313-0; fax 05707-2372; jobs@schloss-petershagen.com; www.romantikhotels.com/petershagen).
**Kitchen Assistant, Waiter/Barman, Housekeeping Assistant:** To work 5 hours per day over a 5 day week. Wages £63 approx. (€103) per week plus free board and lodging. Basic knowledge of spoken German required. Applications to the above address 3 months before desired period of starting work.

E-mail *applications* preferred.

**SCHLOSSHOTEL LISL & JAGERHAUS:** Neuschwansteinstr. 1-3, D-87645 Hohenschwangau, Germany (☎08362-8870; fax 08362-887201; e-mail info@ hohenschwangau.de).
**Seasonal Staff** for jobs including chambermaids, dishwashers, buffet assistants, restaurant assistants and waiting staff. Minimum wage €400 per month, approximately. To work 8 hours per day, 5 days per week: no night work required. Free board and lodging provided.

Some knowledge of German required. Minimum period of work 3-4 months from April to November. Students preferred.

*Applications* to G. Meyer, Manager, at the above address until 31 March: replies will only be sent if a job is offered.

**SCHLOSS REINHARTSHAUSEN:** Hauptstrasse 41, Erbach m Rheingau, D-65346 Eltville, Germany (☎06123-676355; fax 06123-676490; e-mail info. reinhartshausen@kempinski.com; www.schloss-hotel.de).
Small, leading 5-star hotel with 54 rooms, 11 conference rooms, 3 restaurants, a beautiful terrace and a winery. Run by a young team.
**Waiting Staff (3)** required to prepare or serve food, clear tables, etc. To work for about 5 hours a day, 5 days a week. Salary approx £550 per month Must be open

minded, guest-orientated, friendly and enjoy serving.
**Banqueting Set-Ups (3)** required to prepare meeting rooms, serve food etc. To work 5 days a week. Salary £460 per month approx.
**Kitchen Helpers (2)** required to prepare food, especially for breakfasts and buffets. Cooking ability an advantage. 5 days work a week. Salary around £550 per month.
Working time ranges from 5-10 hours a day for banqueting set-ups and kitchen helpers. Applicants must be prepared to work for at least 3 months, and must speak German and English. Accommodation and board may be available, depending on the number of requests, for approx £150 per month.
*Applications* to the above address from December.

**GASTHOF & HOTEL VIKTORIA:** D-87561 Rubi bei Oberstdorf, Allgäu, Germany (☎8322-977840; fax 8322-9778486).
**General Assistant** for buffet and housework. Wage over £320 per month. Free board and accommodation. Minimum period of work 3 months between beginning of June and mid October.
*Applications* not later than mid April to Frau Julia Ess.

**WARNER BROS. MOVIE WORLD GmbH & Co KG:** Warner Allee 1, D-46244 Bottrop-Kirchellen, Germany (☎02045-8990; fax 02045-899505; e-mail www. sixflagseurope.com). Hollywood movie styled theme and entertainment park in the west of Germany.
**Caterers (420)** for food and concession stands in the theme park. Previous experience would be useful, as staff will be serving in restaurants, bakeries, and at hamburger and ice-cream stalls. To work 20-40 hours per week according to post, from around 9am to 7pm or sometimes to 9pm and later. Applicants should be able to speak Dutch, German and English. Wages are approx £4 per hour net. Accommodation is not available but a staff canteen is provided where meals cost around £2.
*Applications* should be sent to the above address.

**HOTEL-WEINHAUS-OSTER:** Moselweinstrasse 61, D-56814 Ediger-Eller 2, bei Cochem/Mosel, Germany (☎02673-1748; fax 02673-1649; e-mail hotel-oster@t-online.de). A family hotel facing the magnificent river Mosel, with many attractions including the local wine festivals and wine-tastings arranged by the owner's brother.
**Waiting Assistant, General Assistant.** Wages approximately £320 per month plus tips and free board and accommodation. To work 7 hours per day, six days per week. Minimum period of work 3 months between May and October. Applicants must speak German.
*Applications* to Mrs M.L. Meyer-Schenk at the above address from January.

**WALDHOTEL FORELLENHOF:** D-76534 Baden-Baden, Gaisbach 91, Germany (☎07221-974-221; 07221-974299; e-mail info@forellenhof-baden-baden.de).
**House Assistants/Chambermaids/Waitresses (2).** Salary by arrangement. Hours from 6.30am-5.30pm (with 1½ hours free for meals) 5 days per week. Free board and accommodation. Knowledge of German required. Minimum period of work 5 months between 1 May and 30 September.
*Applications* to Georg Huber at the above address in January.

**HOTEL WITTELSBACHER HOF:** Prinzenstrasse 24, D-87561 Oberstdorf, Germany (☎08322-605 0; fax 08322-605 300; e-mail info@wittelsbacherhof.de; www.wittelsbacherhof.de)
**Chambermaids, Dishwashers, Kitchen Assistants, Restaurant Assistants** (male

and female) to work in a 120 bed hotel. Wages €650 (£442) net approx. per month plus help with travelling expenses. 8 hours per day, per 5-day week. Knowledge of German preferable. Board and lodging provided free of charge. Minimum period of work 2 months from May to July, July to October or December to March. Positions also available from 20 December to 10 January, or for both the summer and winter seasons.

*Applications* from *EU citizens only* to the above address enclosing a photograph, CV and proof of student status.

**HOTEL WOLF:** Dorfstr. I, D-82487 Oberammergau, Germany (☎08822-9233-0; fax 08822-9233-33; e-mail info@hotel-wolf.de; www.hotel-wolf.de).
**Waiter/Waitress/Chambermaid/Kitchen Assistant**. £400 to £600 per month, 5 days per week. Free board and lodging. Period of work May-October.
*Applications* to the above address before May.

**HOTEL SCHASSBERGER:** Wimenash 10, D-73667, Florisce, Germany (☎+49-7184-2920; fax +49-7184-292204; e-mail info@schassberger.de; www.schassberger. de). This luxury hotel is near Stuttgart. For more information see the website.
**Assistants (1-2)** to help serve food, in kitchen and with maintenance.
Should speak basic German. €50, (approx £33.70) free board and lodging. €100 (approx £67.40) after three months, or upon performance.
*Apply* to the above e-mail address.

# Sports, Couriers and Camping

**BENTS BICYCLE & WALKING TOURS:** The Blue Cross, Orleton, Ludlow, Shropshire SY8 4HN (☎01568-780800; fax 01568-780801; e-mail info@bentstours. com; www.bentstours.com).
**Company Representatives (4-5)** for a tour operator offering cycling and walking holidays in Germany, Austria and France. Duties to include meeting clients at the airport, maintaining bicycles, transporting luggage between hotels and generally taking care of the needs of clients. Wages of around £600 per month with board and accommodation provided. To work varied hours as needs of work dictate, but generally around 40 hours per up to 7-day week.
Minimum period of work 8 weeks between the end of May and end of September. Applicants should have a reasonable grasp of either spoken German or French and, fluent English. They must also possess a full valid driving licence.
*Applications* should be sent, with a photograph, to Stephen Bent at the above address from January.

**CANVAS HOLIDAYS:** GVN Camping Recruitment, East Port House, Dunfermline, KY12 7JG (☎01383-629012; fax 01383-629071; e-mail campingrecruitment@ gvnrecruitment.com; www.gvnrecruitment.com). Canvas Holidays provide luxury mobile home and tent holidays at over 100 campsites.throughout Europe.
**Campsite Courier.** Involves cleaning accommodation, welcoming families to the site and showing them to their accommodation. Visiting customers, providing local information and basic maintenance are very important parts of the job. Campsite Courier Opportunities are also available for couples to work on site together. For details of management positions, see website.
*Please call* the Recruitment Department for more information and an application form, or *apply online* at www.gvnrecruitment.com.

**EUROCAMP:** Overseas Recruitment Department (Ref SJ/07) (☎01606-787525). Eurocamp is a leading tour operator in quality self-drive camping and mobile home holidays in Europe. Each year the company seeks to recruit up to 1,500 enthusiastic people for the following positions:

**Campsite Courier:** job involves cleaning and preparing customer accommodation, providing assistance, acting as an information service and performing some administrative duties. Couriers need to be flexible to meet the needs of the customer to provide them with excellent service. Minimum age 18 years. Applicants should be independent with plenty of initiative and relish a challenging and rewarding position. They should also possess a friendly and helpful personality. Previous customer service experience would be an advantage. Applicants should be available to work from April/May to September.

**Children's Courier:** work involves organising a wide range of exciting activities for children aged 4-13. Applicants should possess initiative, imagination and enthusiasm along with good safety awareness. Previous childcare experience is essential. Minimum age is 18 years and applicants should be available from April/ May to September. Languages are not a requirement but would be an advantage (in particular German). Successful candidates will be asked to apply for an Enhanced Disclosure.

**Senior Couriers:** required to work alongside a team of Campsite Couriers and organise their daily workload, as well as carrying out the normal day-to-day duties of a Campsite Courier. Applicants should have good language skills and experience of leading a team.

**Site Managers:** required to lead a large team of Campsite Couriers, organising their daily workloads and ensuring they provide the very best customer service. Applicants should be 21 or over, have proven managerial experience, excellent communication skills and language ability.

**Montage/Demontage:** for a period of approximately 6-8 weeks at the beginning/end of season to erect/dismantle equipment.

Comprehensive training is provided together with a competitive salary, insurance, return travel and accommodation. Applications are accepted from September/October and *can only be accepted from UK/EU passport holders*. Interviews will be conducted in Hartford, Cheshire between October and April.

*Applicants should apply on-line* at **www.holidaybreakjobs.com** or telephone 01606-787525 for an Application Pack.

**KEYCAMP HOLIDAYS:** Overseas Recruitment Department (Ref: SJ/07), Hartford Manor, Greenbank Lane, Northwich CW8 1H (☎01606-787525; www. holidaybreakjobs.com).

**Campsite Couriers:** to look after British, Dutch and Scandinavian customers on campsites in Germany. Duties include welcoming customers, providing local information, organising social activities on site and ensuring that all accommodation is prepared prior to arrival.

**Children's Courier:** to organise and provide up to 24 hours of activities per week for children aged 4-13 years, to advertise the club activities and visit families on arrival.

**Senior Courier:** incorporating the role of campsite courier with the additional responsibility of organising and managing the team and ensuring the smooth running of the Keycamp operation on site.

**Montage/Demontage:** for a period of approximately 6-8 weeks at the beginning/end of season to erect/dismantle equipment.

Minimum age 18 years. Accommodation, uniform, competitive salary and return travel and training provided. A working knowledge of German would be an advantage.

Period of employment between March and July/October.
*Applicants* should apply on-line at **www.holidaybreakjobs.com** or telephone 01606-787525 for an Application Pack.

**RIECHEY FREIZEITANLAGEN GMBH:** D-23769 Wulfen-Fehmarn, Germany (☎04371-86280; fax 04371-3723).
**Kitchen Helpers:** Duties include washing dishes, salad preparation and serving food. Must speak German.
**Sales Assistants for Golfshop:** Knowledge of German and competence with cash handling essential.
**Catering Staff:** to order and sell food. Knowledge of German and competence with cash handling essential.
**Golf-teacher's Assistant.**
All staff to work approximately 195 hours per month. Wages approximately £780 net per month plus free board and lodging or approximately £920 gross. Minimum period of work 8 weeks. Certificate of university-registration necessary.
*Applications* from 15 January to the above address.

# Voluntary Work and Archaeology

**ARBEITSKREIS DENKMALPFLEGE e.V:** Goetheplatz 9B, D-99423 Weimar, Germany (☎+49-3643 502390; fax +49-3643 851117; e-mail info@openhouses.de; www.ak-denkmalpflege.de).
**Building Assistants (25), Carpenters (7), Joiners (4), Bricklayers (5), Students of Architecture (6-12), Civil Engineers (3), Office Assistants (4), Unskilled Staff (25)** for voluntary work with an organisation conducting **restoration work on historic monuments** in eastern regions of Germany. This project involves mainly young people, mainly from abroad. No payment, but accommodation is provided; for students the work may be recognised by their place of study as practical work experience. 4-8 hours of work a day will be expected for 3-6 days per week; the normal minimum period of work is one week. Most of the projects take place between May and October, but help is needed in the office around the year. A basic knowledge of German is desirable, but English, French, Russian or Czech may be acceptable.
*Applications* should be sent to Bert Ludwig at the above address.

**AKTION SUHNEZEICHEN FRIEDENSDIENSTE (ASF, ACTION RECONCILIATION SERVICE FOR PEACE):** Auguststr. 80, 10117 Berlin, Germany (☎+49-30-28395-184; fax +49-30-28395-135; e-mail asf@asf-ev.de; www. asf-ev-de). ASF works for reconciliation and peace through long-term and short-term volunteer service.
Volunteers for the 'Sommerlager' programme in Belarus, Belgium, Czech Republic, France, Germany, Great Britain, Israel, the Netherlands, Norway, Poland, Russia, Slovakia and the United States. For volunteers from West Europe, USA and Israel, the cost is €100 (approx £67.40). Volunteers must pay travel expenses. To **help with the maintenance of Jewish cemeteries and memorial centres, work in social facilities and involve themselves in projects that support intercultural experiences.** In addition there is much discussion concerning historical and current issues. To work on the Summer camps (two weeks long) between 1st July and 1st October. All nationalities are welcome: Short -term volunteers do no need a visa or work permit.
*Applications* to the above address.

**CAMPHILL SCHULGEMEINSCHAFT BRACHENREUTHE:** D-88662, Uberlingen, Germany (☎+49-7551-80070; fax+49-7551-800750; e-mail info@ brachenreuthe.de; www.brachenreuthe.de).
Volunteers to work as helpers in a residential community for mentally handicapped children. Pocket money of approx. €260 per month plus insurance, board and lodging in a shared room. Most vacancies exist for a period of 6 months or longer around the year; the school is closed for July and much of August. The ideal candidates for the school would work from the end of August to the end of the following July. Minimum age 18. A knowledge of German is essential.
For further details please *contact* the above address.

**CONCORDIA:** 19 North Street, Portslade, Brighton, BN41 1DH (☎01273-422218; fax 01273 421182; e-mail info@concordia-iye.org.uk; www.concordia-iye.org.uk).
Concordia offers volunteers aged 16+ the opportunity to take part in international short-term volunteer projects in over 60 countries worldwide. The work is community based and ranges from **nature conservation, renovation, construction and social work including children's play schemes and teaching**. Volunteers pay a registration fee of £110 and fund their own travel. Board and accommodation are free of charge.
For further information on volunteering or coordinating please check the website or *contact* the International Volunteer Coordinator at the above address.

**INTERNATIONALE BEGEGNUNG IN GEMEINSCHAFTSDIENSTEN eV:** Schlosserstrasse 28, D-70180 Stuttgart 1, Germany (☎0711-6490263; fax 711-6409867; e-mail info@ibg-workcamps.org; www.ibg-workcamps.org).
Volunteers to attend international youth workcamps in Germany. Projects include **restoring an old castle, environmental protection, children's playschemes and media projects**. Each workcamp consists of a group of about 15 people aged 18-30 from all over the world living and working together for the public benefit.
There is a registration fee of approximately £55; food and accommodation are provided free on the camps. IBG's new programme is published in March.
*Applications* to the above address. British volunteers should apply through Concordia or another UK organisation.

**IJGD INTERNATIONALE JUGENDGEMEINSCHAFTSDIENSTE eV:** Kaiserstrasse 43, D-53113 Bonn, Germany (☎228-2280011; fax 228-2280024; www. ijgd.de).
**Volunteers (300)** to work on summer projects such as **environmental protection, the restoration of educational centres, and to assist with city fringe recreational activities**. 30 hours per week of work for periods of 3 weeks at Easter or between June and September. Free board and accommodation provided. Applicants should be aged between 16-26. British volunteers should apply through Concordia or another UK organisation. Knowledge of German required on social projects.
*Applications* should be made to the above address as early as possible.

**NIG EV:** (☎+49-381 4922914; fax+49-381 4900930; e-mail NIGeV@aol.com; www.campline.net).
Volunteers to work for a non-profit organisation, which organises 20 workcamps, for people aged 18-30, in Germany and various countries. The camps focus on **environmental protection, nature conservation, archaeology and cultural projects**. Some projects are aimed at conserving the remains of concentration camps and developing museum projects there to educate people about the Jewish holocaust.
Accommodation and food are provided free, but volunteers will need to pay a

registration fee of approximately £60. British volunteers should apply through Concordia or another UK organisation.
*Further details* can be obtained from the address above.

**NOTHELFERGEMEINSCHAFT DER FREUNDE eV:** Post Fach 10 15 10, D-52349 Düren, Germany (☎02421-76569; e-mail info@nothelfer.org; www.nothelfer.org).
Volunteers for spring and summer work camps arranged by the organisation. The work may involve **building, gardening or social work.** 35 hours per week approximately. Special workcamp with German language courses normally held mid July-mid August. Work is unpaid but free board and accommodation and insurance against sickness, accident and liability are provided.
Applicants should be aged 16-20 years. Camps normally last for 1 month. Volunteers are responsible for their own travel costs.
*Applications* in April or May at the latest to the above address.

**PRO INTERNATIONAL:** Bahnhofstrasse 26 A, D-35037 Marburg, Germany (☎06421-65277; fax 06421-64407; e-mail pro-international@lahn.net; www.pro-international.de).
Following the concept of 'Peace through Friendship' Pro International organises international vacation work camps during the Easter and summer vacations. On these camps, which last for up to 3 weeks, 10 to 15 people aged between 16 and 26 years old from different countries participate. The participants work about 5 hours a day on **public or social projects** and spend their time together. Accommodation and food supply are free; the participants pay only their tickets and €65 (approx. £40) to cover administration. Volunteers should apply through Concordia or another UK organisation.
*Applications* have to be sent to the above address.

# Other Employment in Germany

**FAMILIENWEINGUT OSTER & FRANZEN:** Calmonstrasse 96, D-56814 Bremm/Mosel am Calmont, Germany (e-mail oster-franzen@rz-online.de).
A small family business set in the beautiful surroundings of the Mosel Valley offering a wonderful opportunity to learn about wine and vineyards.
**Two people** (preferably a couple) to work in vineyards, and cellars, and also to do housework, 8 hours per day, 6 days per week. Minimum age normally 24, although younger, if mature, applicants may be considered. The ability to speak English or German is essential. A driving licence would be an advantage. Full board and lodging provided in the family home, with a family atmosphere. Periods of work: two months between May and July and September to November. For further details contact the above address enclosing an International Reply Coupon.
*Applications* to the above address will be considered from February onwards. *EC passport holders preferred.*

**WEINGUT FREIHERR VON LANDENBERG 'SCHLOSKELLEREI':** Moselweinstr. 60, D-56814 Ediger-Eller (Mosel), Germany (☎02675-277; fax 02675-207; e-mail info@mosel-weinproben.de; www.mosel-weinproben.de). 500-year-old vineyard and cellars in the heart of the Mosel wine region. Many connoisseurs of wine, young and old, buy direct from the estate because of its quality.
**Sales Woman** to sell wines and gifts in this award winning vineyard and castle's shop. To work 8 hours per day over a 6 day week for approx. £270, with free board

and lodging. Applicants must speak German. Dates of work are variable between May and October.

*Applications* in writing to Frau H. Trimborn von Landenberg at the above address.

**ZENTRALSTELLE FUR ARBEITSVERMITTLUNG:** ZAV, 212.12 Internationale Nachwuchsförderung Studentvermittlung Postfach, 53107 Bonn, Germany (☎+49 228 713 1330; fax +49 228 713 270 1037; e-mail bonn-zav.info-auslaendische-studenten@arbeitsagentur.de)
This is the official government labour agency which places German-speaking students in summer jobs throughout Germany. Applicants must be at least 18 years old, have a good command of German, (how good it must be depends on the individual job) and agree to work for at least two months. Work is available in hotels and restaurants, as chambermaids or kitchen helpers, or in agriculture. Contact the ZAV at the above address for application forms and further information; there is no fee for this service.
*Apply* before March.

## Au Pairs, Nannies, Family Helps and Exchanges

**IN VIA:** Katholische Mädchensozialarbeit, Deutscher Verband eV, Karlstrasse 40, 79104, Freiburg, Germany (+49 761-200 206; fax +49 761-200 638; e-mail invia@caritas.de; www.aupair-invia.de).
**Au Pair** positions in Germany; with regional offices in 40 cities IN VIA can arrange to place au pairs between 18 and 24 years with German families. Minimum length of stay 6 months, but stays of 1 year preferred.
For *further information* please contact the above address.

**VEREIN FÜR INTERNATIONALE JUGENDARBEIT:** Goetheallee 10, 53225 Bonn, Germany (☎+49-228 698 952; fax +49-228 694 166; e-mail au-pair@vij-bundesgeschaeftsstelle.org; www.vij-deutschland.de; www.au-pair-vij.de).
**Au Pairs:** girls and boys between 18 and 24 years can be placed as au pairs with families in Germany. Length of stay varies from 6 months to a year. Pocket money of around £180 per month (€260); season ticket for local transport also provided. Applicants must have a reasonable command of German.
Those interested should *contact* the above address.

# Great Britain

There are so many opportunities for summer work in Great Britain that the opportunities are collected together in the separate title *Summer Jobs in Britain*; for details see the *Useful Publications* chapter at the end of this book. However, a number of the employers and voluntary organisations listed in the *Worldwide* chapter can place people in the UK.

US students seeking temporary work in the UK can benefit from the *Work in Britain Program*. This allows full-time US college students and recent graduates over the age of 18 to look for work in Britain, finding jobs through programme listings or through personal contacts. Jobs may be pre-arranged, though most participants wait until arrival in Britain to begin their job hunt. They must first obtain a *British Universities North America Club (BUNAC) blue Card*, which is recognised by the British Home Office as a valid substitute for a work permit; this BUNAC Card must be obtained before leaving the US for Britain, as it acts as an entry document. It allows the holder to work for a maximum of six months at any time of year: extensions are never granted, but it is possible to hold two cards in a lifetime. The BUNAC card is available for a fee of approx. $275 (£153) from BUNAC (toll free ☎1-800-GO BUNAC) or by applying online after reading their brochure – full details at www.bunac.org/usa/ or e-mail info@bunacusa.org.

A similar programme, called the Student Work Abroad Programme (SWAP), is organised for Canadian students, graduates and young people, with varying age restrictions applying. It is administered by the Canadian Universities Travel Service, which has over 40 offices in Canada. For details see www.swap.ca where you can apply online or see a listing of the numerous Travel Cuts offices, including Granville Island, 1516 Duranleau St, Vancouver, BC V6H 3S4, (604) 659-2820 where applications can be made in person.

# Greece

Every year Greece receives around ten million foreign tourists, and it is the tourist trade with employers such as those listed in this chapter that offers the best chances of finding temporary work to the foreigner. One reason for this is that in the tourist industry having a native language other than Greek is an asset rather than a liability. Such work is best found by making opportunistic enquiries once at the main tourist destinations. Even so, most Greek proprietors, in defiance of EU guidelines on male/female parity in the workplace, prefer to employ girls.

Other opportunities for foreigners involve domestic work with Greek families, helping with the housework and perhaps improving the family's English. Wages in Greece are generally low, but are enough to permit an extended stay. In recent years wage levels for unskilled work have been depressed in some areas because of the large number of immigrants – legal and otherwise – from Albania and other countries in Eastern Europe who are willing to work for low rates. Unemployment remains constantly high at around 10%.

British, Irish and other EU nationals are permitted to use the Greek national employment service: local branches are called offices of the *Organisimos Apasholisseos Ergatikou Dynamikou*, or OAED (the Manpower Employment Organisation: Ethnikis Antistasis 8 str., GR-17456 Alimos, Greece; ☎+30-1-9989000; www.oaed.gr). For further information consult the free booklet *Working in Greece* published by the UK Employment Service. Jobs are also advertised in the local major newspapers such as *Ta Nea*, *Eleftheros Typos*, *Eleftherotypia* and *Apogevmatini*.

Although people have succeeded in finding casual farm work, such as picking oranges and olives, it is almost impossible to arrange this from outside Greece. The large number of foreigners from Eastern Europe who are already present in Greece usually fill these jobs, so it is just as difficult to arrange this kind of work on arrival. Oranges are picked between Christmas and March, especially south of Corinth. Grapes are grown all over the mainland and islands, and growers often need casual help during the September harvest. Those who are prepared to take a chance on finding casual work in Greece will find further information on harvests in the book *Work Your Way Around the World* (see *Useful Publications*).

There are opportunities for voluntary work in Greece arranged by International Voluntary Service, Youth Action for Peace, Concordia and UNA Exchange for British applicants and Service Civil International and for other nationalities: see the *Worldwide* chapter for details.

It may be possible to obtain a job by means of an advertisement in one of the English language newspapers in Athens. The *Athens News* is a weekly newspaper published every Friday whose classified department is at 9 Christou Lada str, 102 37 Athens, Greece (☎ 010 3333404; fax 010 3223746; e-mail an-classified@ dolnet.gr). The minimum charge for an advertisement is €8 (approx £5) for 15 words. You can check the classified advertisements in the Athens News on the internet on www.athensnews.gr.

# RED TAPE

**Visa Requirements:** citizens of the UK and other EEA countries and Australia, Canada, New Zealand, Japan, Israel and the USA do not require a visa to travel to Greece providing that they stay no more than 90 days.

**Residence Permits:** those wishing to stay in Greece for longer than three months require permission to do so from the Aliens Department *(Grafeio Tmimatos Allodapon)* or Tourist Police in the area along with your passport and a letter from your employer. The permit is normally granted on the spot. By the time of publication EU citizens should be able to file their application at the nearest KEP (Cititzen's Advice Centre). The European Parliament has already approved the scrapping of residence permits for EU citizens within the EU and Greece will go down this route eventually. Residence formalities may be maintained in Greece for longer than in other countries because of the influx of Eastern Europeans whose countries border Greece. A summary of recent immigration regulations for Greece appears on the *Athens News* website at www.athensnews. gr/Directory2005/1dir40.htm.

**Work Permits:** a permit must be obtained by a prospective employer on behalf of a non-EEA national prior to arrival in Greece. Failure to follow this procedure may result in refusal of entry to the country. EEA nationals do not require a work permit to work in Greece. For more information see the Greek Embassy in London's website: www.greekembassy.org.uk.

**Au Pair:** allowed; a work permit must be obtained for non-EEA citizens.

# Hotel Work and Catering

**HOTEL AGHIOS GORDIS:** St George South, Paleokastritsa, and Pelekas Regions, Corfu, Greece; email rizosresorts@sympnia.com (Subject line ATTN HR – Dr Paul Rizos).

**Cooks (4)** to prepare food for around 400 people daily. From £400 per month. Should have previous experience of professional cooking of international specialities, with an emphasis on Italian cooking. 8 hour day, 6 day week. No accommodation provided. Minimum period of work 4 months between 10 April and 1 October.

*Applications* to Dr Paul Rizos, Manager, at Rizos hotels, PO Box 70, Corfu, Greece, 491500 or email.

**ARISTOTELES HOTEL:** 15 Acharnon Street, GR-104 38 Athens, Greece (☎+30-1-522 8126; fax +30-1-523 1138).
**Cleaners, Bar Staff, Couriers** are needed for a three star hotel. Wage £250 per month (plus commission for courier) with free accommodation and breakfast provided. Most vacancies are for the Summer, but some exist all year round. Minimum age 24.
*Applications* to Mr Vakis Ovvadias at the above address.

**HOTEL ASTIR:** 16 Agiou Andreou Street, 26223 Patras, Greece (☎+30 2610 279 812; fax +30 2610 271 644; e-mail astir@pat.forthnet.gr; www.greekhotel.com).
**Catering Manager, Chef Cook.** To work eight hours a day, six days a week. No accommodation is provided. Previous employment and knowledge of English is required. Minimum period of work eight months from 15 October to 15 June.
*Applications* to the above address.

**HOTEL CAPRI:** 6, Psaromilingou Street, Athens, Greece (☎01-3252091/3252085; fax 01-3252091).
**Cleaners, Bar Staff, Couriers** and **Nannies** are needed for a three star hotel. Wage £250 per month (plus commission for couriers), free accommodation and breakfast. Most vacancies are for the summer but some exist around the year. Minimum age 24.
*Applications* to Mr Vakis Oadias.

**COLOSSOS BEACH HOTEL:** PO Box 105, 85100 Faliraki, Rhodes, Greece (☎+30 2241-85502; fax +30 22410-85679; e-mail colossos@louishotels.com; www. colossosbeach.gr).
The hotel has vacancies for work and training in the kitchens, restaurants and bars. These vacancies are only open to students who can prove their student status. Period of work is May to October; staff staying the whole period will receive a refund to cover their normal fare ticket.
In return for working 8 hours a day per 6 day week, staff will receive approximately €140 (approx £95) a month, full board and accommodation, training and free medical/ hospital insurance. Applicants should preferably speak English and German or Italian and have previous experience or qualifications in hotel/restaurant work.
*Applications* with a recent photograph to Mr D. Rozalis at the above address before the end of March.

**CORINA'S PLACE-IL GIARDINO:** Logaras, Paros, Greece (☎30 22840-28451; fax 30 22840-41942; info@corinasplace.com).
**Kitchen Porter, Commis Chefs (2), Chef de Partie, Waitresses (2)**. Salary at Greek rates with eventual possibility of free accommodation. Period of work 1 April to 15 October. Split and straight shifts; 5 day week during low season, 6 day week during high season.
Applicants for kitchen work should be male, while applicants for waitressing should be female. *All applicants should be EU nationals*, hard-working, of neat appearance and have at least 2-3 years previous experience.
*Applications: send* curriculum vitae and references, enclosing a recent photo, to Miss Corina Harcourt at the following address between November and March: 10 rue Carnot, Versailles 78000, France; at the above address after April or telephone the above number after 9pm.

**DORETA BEACH HOTEL:** Theologos, 85100 Rhodes, PO Box 131, Greece (☎ +30 22410 8254363; fax +30 22410-82446; e-mail alexia-doreta@otonet.gr).
**Barman, Barmaid, Waitresses**. Around £450 per month. Knowledge of German required.

*Applications* to Michalis A. Yiasiranis, Manager, at the above address.

**HOTEL ERI:** Parikia Paros Island, Greece (☎ +30 22840 23360; fax +30 22840 24562; e-mail rivolli1@otenet.gr; www.erihotel.gr).
**Bar Staff, Couriers** needed to work in this hotel in the Cyclades, on the Island of Paros.
*Applications* to the above address.

**RESTAURANT KAMARES:** 80100 Kapsali, Kythira, Greece (☎/fax +30-736-31-064; mobile 0944-363732).
**Kitchen Helps (2-4).** Some knowledge of Greek would be an advantage.
**Waiters/Waitresses (4).** Some knowledge of Greek is essential, and applicants should have some restaurant experience.
  Wages starting at £290 per month approx. with food and accommodation provided; to work shifts of 9-10 hours per day. Period of work from 1 July to 15 September.
  *Applications* with a full-length photo should be sent to Antonis Magiros at the above address.

**KIVOTOS CLUB HOTEL:** Ornos Bay, GR-84600 Mykonos, Greece (☎+30-289 10300-330; fax 289 220785) H/O: 10 Thetidos St., GR 11528 Athens (☎ 1-7246766/7; fax 1-7249203; e-mail Kivotos_1@hol.gr; www.agn.hol.gr/hotls/Kivotos/Kivotos/. htm). Kivotos Club Hotel is a member of the Small Luxury Hotels Group.
**Receptionists (2).** Must have a relevant qualification in the hospitality industry. Wage approx. £330-£360 per month. Will work 7 days a week either from 7am to 3pm or from 3 to 11pm.
**Waiters/Waitresses (3)** required to serve breakfast, lunch and dinner at the main restaurant or serve at the restaurant by the pool. Must have a relevant qualification in the hospitality industry. Wage approx. £330 to £360 per month in return for 9 hrs work a day, 7 days a week.
**Maitre'D** to be responsible for running the food and beverage departments of the hotel. To work 11-12 hours a day, 7 days a week. Wage approx. £450 a month. Must have graduated with a qualification relating to the hospitality industry.
  Board and accommodation is available for all positions. Applicants should be prepared to work for a minimum of 3 months (6 months for the Maitre'd). Knowledge of English, German, Italian or French is useful.
  *Applications* are invited from November to the address given above for the head office for work in the following summer.

**HOTEL PORTO LOUTRO:** Loutro, Sfakia, Crete, Greece 73011 (☎+30 28250 91433; fax +30-2825091910; e-mail portolou@otenet.gr; www.hotelportoloutro. com). The hotel is in a village on the South coast of Crete with no cars or roads and is only accessible by foot or ferry.
**Breakfast/Bar Staff** for duties including evening bar work and serving breakfasts in a small English/Greek family beach hotel. Wage around €500 (approx £337) per month plus shared tips and accommodation. To work shift work 9 hours per day, i.e. 7.30am-3.30pm or 3.30pm-midnight. Staff should only apply if they can work from April 1st until mid-October.
  Applicants should be aged 24-28; no experience is necessary but should be enthusistic, honest, reliable and outgoing. *Applications* enclosing a photo and telephone number from November to February, the earlier the better, to Alison Androulakakis at the following address: 21 Papanastasiou, Hania 73100, Crete (☎/fax 0821-43941).
  *Applications* from November for the next season, to Captain Stavros Androulakis,

21 Papanastasiou, Hania 73100, Crete (0030-821043941/0030-825091433/44), enclosing a photo and telephone number and e-mail address.

**SANI RESORT:** Kassandra 63077 Chalkidiki, Greece (☎+30 23740 99447; fax +30 23740 99441; e-mail info@saniresort.gr; www.saniresort.gr ).
Sani Resort is one of the most unique resorts in Europe, comprising of two luxury 5* hotels, two up-scaled 4* hotels and the recently renovated biggest Marina in North Greece. This long established ecological resort, on the Haldiki peninsula, guarantees its guests' enjoyment by focusing on the training and motivation of its staff.
Training placements are available for 18-20 year-old Hotel, Catering and Tourism trainees in this popular Greek resort. The training programme includes financial, social and cultural elements, so that this is as much a cultural exchange as a working environment. Trainees are offered the following package: free accommodation (3 or 4 bed shared rooms), full board, one or two free tourist excursions and free transfers from accommodation to resort. Employees are expected to stay for five or six months and to work minimum 5 days per week. Those staying five months will receive €16 (approx £10) per 8 hour working day, while those staying for six months will receive €18 (approx £12) per 8 hour working day, overtime is paid extra.
Places are available from 15th May to 15th Oct (Asterias Suites), 15th March to 1st April and 1st April to 30th October (Porto Sani Village), 15th May to 30th October (Sani Beach Club) and 1st April to 30th October (Sani Beach Hotel). For more details *contact* Georgia Routsou at the above address.
*Applications* in English to Georgia Routsou at the above address.

**VILLAGE INN:** 400 Laganas St., Mouzaki, Zakynthos 29092, Greece (☎+30-2695-51033; fax +30-2695-52387; e-mail info@villageinn.gr). Medium size self-catering accomodation on the Greek island of Zakynthos.
**Entertainers/Bar Staff (2)** to plan, organise and perform entertaining events such as music quizzes, karaoke nights etc, and to work as bar staff in the resort's pool bar. Wages c. €550 (approx £365) per month according to qualifications.
**Mates/Housekeeping (2)** to work in the resort. Wages €500 (approx £330) per month.
Staff work 8 hour days in 6 day weeks. Work is available between 1 May and 20 October. Board and lodging is available, and candidates should speak English.
*Applications* to the above address are invited from 15 March.

# Sports, Couriers and Camping

**HILLWOOD HOLIDAYS:** Lavender Lodge, Dunny Lane, Chipperfield, WD4 9DD (☎01923-290-700; fax 01923-290-340; e-mail sales@hillwood-holidays.co.uk; www.hillwood-holidays.co.uk) This family tour operator have a child care club and crèche and sailing boats.
**Children's Representatives (4)** to work six hours a day, six days a week. Should have NNEB or equivalent. Wages of about £100 per week plus free accommodation (food is extra).
**RYA Sailing Instructors (2)** to work six hours a day, six days a week. Should be an RYA Instructor. Wages of £100 per week plus free accommodation (food is extra).
Positions are in the Crete resort of Bali. Minimum period of work is six weeks between 1st June and September.
*Apply* from February to the above address.

**MARK WARNER:** 20 Kensington Church Street, London, W8 4EP (☎08700 330750 or 08700 330760 for children's places); e-mail recruitment@markwarner. co.uk; www.markwarner.co.uk/recruitment.
**Accountants, Receptionists, Watersports Instructors, Tennis and Aerobics Instructors, Chefs, Kitchen Porters, First Aid, Nannies, Handymen, Nightwatchmen** and more are required to work in hotels in Corsica, Sardinia, Greece and Turkey during the summer from April to October and Egypt, and Sri Lanka and Mauritius year round. Wages from £50 per week plus full board, medical insurance, travel expenses and free use of watersport and activity facilities. Some reserve staff also needed throughout the season. Requirements for languages, experience, qualifications etc. vary according to the job applied for.
   For further details, please *contact* the Resorts Recruitment Department on the above number.

**MASTERSUN HOLIDAYS:** Thames House, 63-67 Kingston Road, New Malden, Surrey, KT3 3PB (☎020-8942 9442; fax020-8949 4396; e-mail lynette@mastersun. co. uk; www.mastersun.co.uk). Mastersun is a Christian holiday company that organises holidays in prime Mediterranean watersports centres including Greece and France. Holidays are hotel-based and the package includes watersports and other activity programmes.
**Resort Managers, Waterfront Managers/RYA Windsurfing and Sailing Instructors, Waterfront Assistants, Resort Representatives, Bar Assistants, Children's and Teen's Workers**; about 100 staff needed over the summer season. There are winter ski jobs as well.
   *Applications:* ask for a job pack from the above address or e-mail, or download both pack and an application form from the website. Applications welcome at any time.

**OLYMPIC HOLIDAYS** 1 Torrington Park, Finchley, London N12 9SU (☎0870-499 6742; fax 0870-429 4142; e-mail julian@olympicholidays.com; www. olympicholidays.com). Olympic Holidays was one of the first tour operators in Greece over 40 years ago and they are now the leading independently owned tour operator to both Greece and Cyprus. They cover most resorts from young and lively to upmarket, and ethnic. In recent years they have added Bulgaria, Tunisia and Turkey to their portfolio. They also feature a range of more exotic destinations such as Egypt, The Gambia, the Dominican Republic, Mexico and India.
**Overseas Resort Representatives: (250)** Minimum age 21 by 1st April 2007. Act as ambassadors of the company. Applicants must be professional, hardworking and possess unlimited stamina. Duties involve airport transfers, hotel visits, guiding excursions, administration, health and safety checks, complaint handling, welcome meetings. Applicants should have customer service experience, and sales experience is preferable. Maturity, a calm manner and good organisation are all necessary skills. Wages are approx. £110 per week (tax free), plus generous commission (tax free), return flights, insurance and accommodation (meals not included). Representatives work six days per week with variable hours and may be on call 24 hours a day, seven days a week. Applications should have at least 12 months direct customer service experience, and sales experience is preferable. Maturity, a calm manner and good organisation are all necessary skills. Wages are approximately £110 per week (tax free), plus generous commission, return flights, insurance and accommodation (meals not included). Representatives work six days per week with variable hours and may be on call 24 hours a day, seven days a week.
**Overseas Transfer and Guiding Representatives: (20)** Minimum age 20 by

1<sup>st</sup> April 2007. Applicants will be responsible for accompanying guests to and from the airport and their holiday accommodation. They will also guide day and evening resort excursions and assist the representatives whenever required. Wages are approximately £350 per month (tax free), return flights, insurance and accommodation (meals not included). Transfer/Guiding Representatives work 6 days a week with variable hours.

**Overseas Administrators: (30)** Minimum age 22 by 1<sup>st</sup> April 2007. For office based administration work, arranging flights and transfers, accommodation allocation and guest related reports along with accompanying guests on transfers. Applicants should be able to use Word, Excel, and possess advanced PC skills along with good organisational skills. Wages are approx. £600 per month (tax free) and flights, insurance and accommodation (but not food) are provided. Employees work six days a week. Hours are variable.

The season begins in March/April until October, but high season positions (June to September) are also available. For both types of positions, Greek language skills are an advantage, but not essential.

*Applications* can be made via the online application form on the Olympic website. Alternatively, applicants should call the above number to request an application form. Interviews start in November 2006.

**PAVILION TOURS:** Lees House, 21 Dyke Road, Brighton, East Sussex, BN1 3GD (☎0870-241 0425/7; fax 0870-241 0426; e-mail info@paviliontours.com). An expanding, specialist activity tour operator for students, with bases in Greece and Spain. Watersports include: windsurfing, dinghy sailing, water skiing and canoeing. Keen to recruit highly motivated staff.

**Watersports Instructors** required to instruct sailing/windsurfing etc. and to assist with evening entertainments. Hours of work variable, 7 days a week. Wages approx. £115 per week. Minimum period of work 1 week between May and October. Board and lodging provided free.

*Applications* from November to the above address, please include current instructor qualifications.

**SKYROS:** 92 Prince of Wales Road, London NW5 3NE (☎020-7284 3063; fax 020-7284 3063; e-mail john@skyros.com or office@skyros.com). Skyros offer holistic holidays: They combine a holiday in a Greek island with the chance to participate in over 200 courses from yoga to sailing and cooking.

**Work Scholars** to assist in the smooth running of Atsitsa, a holistic holiday centre on Skyros island. Duties include **Cleaning, Bar Work, Laundry, Gardening and General Maintenance.** Allowance of around £50 per week plus full board and accommodation. Variable working hours, but normally between 6 and 8 per day, 6 days per week.

Period of work about three months; either April to July or July to October. Work scholars live as part of the community; in exchange for their hard work they may participate in the courses (such as yoga, dance and windsurfing) where their duties allow. Applicants should be 21+: qualified nurses, chefs and Greek speakers preferred.

*Applications* should be sent to the above address between January and February to office@skyros.com or john@skyros.com.

# Work at Sea

**SETSAIL HOLIDAYS:** Setsail Holidays, PO Box 5224, Sudbury, CO10 2GD. (☎01787 310445; fax: 01737 378078; e-mail boats@setsail.co.uk; www.setsail.

co.uk). Setsail Holidays are a specialist tour operator providing flotilla sailing and bareboat charter holidays to Greece, Turkey and Croatia.

**Skippers, Hostesses and Engineers** required to coordinate and run the flotilla sailing holidays which can consist of up to 12 yachts.

Must have sailing experience and/or qualifications and the ability to work well with people. Pay range is £120-£140 per week depending on job and experience. Accommodation is provided on the 'lead yacht'. From May to Sepember 2007.

*Applications* to John Hortop at the above address by fax or e-mail. Applications must include a CV.

# Voluntary Work and Archaeology

**ARCHELON SEA TURTLE PROTECTION SOCIETY OF GREECE:** Solomou 57, GR-104 32, Athens, Greece (☎/fax +30-210 523 1342; e-mail stps@archelon. gr).

Archelon is a non-profit-making NGO founded in 1983 to study and protect sea turtles and their habitats as well as raising public awareness. Each year over 300 volunteers participate in STPS projects.

Volunteers are required for summer fieldwork on the the islands of Zakynthos, Crete and Peloponnesus, where the Mediterranean's most important loggerhead nesting beaches are to be found. Volunteers will participate in all aspects of the projects including **tagging turtles and public relations,** and receive on-site training. The work can involve long nights in the cold or long days in the heat, so a resilient, positive and friendly attitude is essential, especially as the Society's work requires constructive co-existence with local communities.

The projects run from mid-May to mid-October, with free accommodation provided at basic campsites. Volunteers will need to provide their own tents and sleeping bags; warm clothing will be required for night work as the temperature can get quite cold and smart clothes are needed when working in hotels and information stations. The minimum period of participation is 4 weeks, and there are greater needs for volunteers at each end of the project (May, June, September, October).

Volunteers are also required to **work at the Sea Turtle Rescue Centre near Athens.** This is a new centre set up on the coast 20km from Athens to help treat and rehabilitate turtles caught in fishing nets or injured by speedboats. Volunteers will **help in the treatment of injured turtles, assisting the ongoing construction of the site and carry out public relations work with visitors.** A basic knowledge of animal care is helpful but not essential. Free accommodation is provided in converted railway carriages.

Would-be volunteers for either project need to be over 18 and willing to work in teams with people from other nationalities and backgrounds. Volunteers will have to provide a participation fee of around £50 which goes towards supporting the project and includes a one year membership of the Archelon, including 3 issues of 'Turtle Tracks', their newsletter. Archelon cannot provide any financial assistance but estimates that volunteers will need to allow about £6 per day to cover food costs. Volunteers should be able to communicate in English and have their own health insurance. Successful applicants will be informed within one month of application.

*Application forms* can be obtained by contacting the above address including an International Reply Coupon.

**CONSERVATION VOLUNTEERS GREECE:** Veranzerou 15, 106 77 Athens, Greece (☎+30-210 382 5506; e-mail 1987@cvgpeep.gr; www.cvgpeep.gr). Volunteers required for projects in Greece between April and September. Volunteers will be **working on projects that have a strong emphasis on Greek culture** and the protection of Greek environment and take place in several areas of the country from remote villages to big cities. Volunteers will work a 5-6 hour day over a 6-day week, minimum period of work two weeks. CVG provides food, shared accommodation, and accident insurance.

*Applications* can be sent to the above address from the beginning of April; prospective volunteers from the UK can also apply through UNA Exchanges and Concordia (see *Worldwide* chapter).

**GREEK DANCES 'DORA STRATOU' THEATRE:** 8 Scholiou Street, GR-10558 Athens Plaka, Greece (☎+30 (0)1 03244395; fax +30 210 324 6921; e-mail mail@ grdance.org; www.grdance.org). The official government-sponsored organisation for Greek folk dance, music & costume. The theatre provides: daily performances, courses, workshops, field research programmes, books, CDs, CD-roms, tapes, videos costumes and more, related to Greek dance and folk culture.

Voluntary trainee assistants **(2) to learn theatre management, costume maintenance** or **computer production of cultural CD-Rom** between May and October. No accommodation provided, but help may be given in finding it: the cost will be around £20 per day. No previous experience is necessary.

Also trainees **(2)** to learn dance research.

For further information *contact* Dr A. Raftis, President, at the above address.

**MEDASSET (MEDITERRANEAN ASSOCIATION TO SAVE THE SEA TURTLES):** 1c Licavitou Str. 106 72 Athens, Greece. (☎+30-21-0-361 3572; email mesasset@medasset.org.; www.medasset).

Conservation volunteers needed to work in central Athens for a minimum of three weeks **in the office providing administrative back-up** .

Volunteers pay for their own transport costs etc. but free accommodation is provided in central Athens. For further details *contact* the above web/address/e-mail.

**SEA TURTLE PROJECT RHODES ISLAND:** CHELON, Viale val Padana 134B, I-00141 Rome, Italy(☎+39-6-812 5301; e-mail chelon@tin.it). CHELON is a research group working to protect and obtain in-depth knowledge of marine turtles. Volunteers **(12)** to help protect rare loggerhead turtle nest sites on Rhodes; until recently it was assumed that the beaches of southern Rhodes were no longer suitable for turtles to nest on. Volunteers take part in **nest censuses, the protection and observation of nesting behaviour, as well as helping researchers tag turtles for ongoing observation studies.** The work also involves beach vegetation studies and conservation awareness raising among local people and tourists. English, Italian and Greek language skills will therefore prove useful, but no previous experience or skills are required.

Volunteers provide their own tents for accommodation, as well as meeting travel and insurance costs. The registration fee of approx £380 covers the cost of meals. The project runs between June and September and the minimum stay is two weeks, but volunteers can stay longer subject to approval. CHELON also runs projects in Italy and Thailand.

*Contact* CHELON at the above address for further information and an *application form.*

## Au Pairs, Nannies, Family Helps and Exchanges

**NINE MUSES AGENCY:** Thrakis 39 and Vas. Sofias 2, 17121 Nea Smyrni,Athens, Greece (☎210-931 6588; www.ninemuses.gr).
**Au Pairs:** to assist families with housework and look after children for about 30 hours a week. Summer placements from 1 to 3 months possible. Hotel positions sometimes also available. The owner Kalliope Raekou prides herself on her after-placement service, meeting regularly with au pairs at coffee afternoons. No fee is charged to au pairs.

*Applicants* should be young European or American women. Can also place candidates after arrival in Athens.

For further details *contact* the above address.

# Iceland

The island of Iceland has a tiny population of about 300,000 inhabitants and has an unemployment rate that is low by European standards at 3%. Iceland is a member of the European Economic Area (EEA) and thus EEA citizens as well as European Union (EU) citizens have the right to live and work in Iceland without a work permit. Foreign nationals (not citizens of the EEA/EU) who wish to work and live in Iceland can only do so if they have arranged a contract of engagement with an Icelandic employer prior to entering Iceland; the employer will arrange for a limited Work and Residence Permit. Summer is really the only time to get paid and unpaid temporary work as it gets much colder after that. Demand is greatest in the fish, farming, tourism and construction industries. The minimum period of work is usually three months.

There are eight regional Employment Offices in Iceland and EURES advisors can be consulted at the main VMH (Jobcentre), Firdi, Fjardarjötu 13-15, 220 Hafnardjordur (554 7600;eures@svm.is). Efforts to recruit tend to be focused on the Scandinavian countries through the Nordjobb scheme (www.nordjobb.norden. no), which arranges summer jobs for citizens of Scandinavia aged 18-25 able to work in Iceland for at least four weeks.

## RED TAPE

**Visa Requirements:** a visa is not required by citizens of most European countries, if they are entering Iceland as a visitor or as tourists.
**Residence Permits:** those planning a stay of over three months must register with the Icelandic Directorate of Immigration (Utlendingastofnun),Skogarhlid 6, 105 Reykjavik, Iceland (☎+354 510 5400; e-mail utl@utl.is; www.utl.is)
**Work Permits:** are not needed by nationals of the United Kingdom or any other EEA country. If you are planning to take advantage of the freedom of all EEA nationals to go to Iceland to look for work, take plenty of funds with you to cover the notoriously high Icelandic cost of living.

**NINUKOT:** Skeggjastadir 861, Hvolsvöllur (☎487 8576; ninukot@ninukot.is; www. ninukot.is). This private employment agency originally found **horticultural and agricultural jobs** throughout Iceland but now also finds jobs **babysitting, fisheries work, gardening, horse training and tourism.** The website is in English and so offers the opportunity to pre-arrange a working holiday in Iceland.

*Applications* to the website at the above address.

**WORLDWIDE FRIENDS:** Hafnarstraeti 15, 101 Reykjavik (☎551 8222; fax 561 4617; wf@wf.is; www.wf.is).
Worldwide Friends offers an interesting **range of two-week projects** which are open to international volunteers. Many of these are related to the environment and others revolve around a national festival which starts on the first weekend in August when Icelanders celebrate the granting of national sovereignty to their country in 1874. Volunteers can join in preparation work for and during the festival in several towns including Heimaey on the Vestmannaeyjar islands. Participation costs €50, €120 or €150 depending on the project and its duration.
   *Applications* to the above address or e-mail.

# Ireland

The rapid growth of the Irish economy in recent years has produced an astonishing turnaround in the fortunes of a country which historically was one of the most poverty-stricken nations of Europe. It enjoys one of the lowest rates of unemployment in the European Union (4.4%), and the rapid development of the economy has even resulted in shortages of skilled employees in some sectors such as information and computing technologies, construction and nursing. Ireland offers a number of opportunities for seasonal work. The greatest demand for summer staff is in the tourist industry, which is concentrated around Dublin and in the West, South West and around the coast. Dublin is a boomtown at present for the tourist industry and the rash of construction there shows no sign of abating. Unlike several other EU countries, Ireland has not imposed restrictions on the arrival of immigrants from the new (2004) member countries of Eastern Europe. Consequently, seasonal jobs are rapidly filled by workers from these countries. Ireland is however a notoriously expensive country to live in and has high taxes but without the correspondingly high wages to compensate for such costs. Wages are however rising steadily.
   There is a fair chance of finding paid work on farms and also scope for organising voluntary work. Two organisations can help those wishing to work voluntarily on Irish farms or who are interested in learning organic farming techniques; World Wide Opportunities On Organic Farms and the Irish Organic Farmers and Growers Association. WWOOF Ireland is no longer listed by other WWOOF organisations because of communication problems. About 80 Irish hosts can now be found on the WWOOF independents list; this can be found at www.wwoof.org. For information on the Irish Organic Farmers and Growers Association, contact them at Main Street, Newtownforbes, Co Longford, Ireland (☎+353 043-42495; www.irishorganic.ie/services/placelist.htm).
   FAS is Ireland's Training & Employment Agency. In addition to accessing details of Irish vacancies on their website www.fas.ie, job seekers can also register their CV and state what type of job they would like to do. Job seekers with a work permit in Ireland can call to the local FAS EURES office for details of vacancies. The main one for foreigners is the Dublin office (27-33 Upper Baggot Street, Dublin 4, ☎+353-1-6070500; e-mail info@fas.ie). Jobseekers from outside Ireland can also gain access to vacancies by using the European Commission's internet EURES placement system – http://europa.eu.int/jobs/eures. There are also listings of private employment agencies in the Irish Golden Pages.
   Those seeking temporary work in Ireland's hospitality and leisure industry who don't want to be based in Dublin can try the main tourist regions including most of the South-West and Co. Kerry. Some vacancies can be found on EURES where

prospective employees can leave their details. Potential employers can then access the website's database and contact you to invite you to apply for jobs they are offering.

Foreign students are under certain employment restrictions in Ireland with the exception of students from the USA, Canada, Australia and New Zealand, which have reciprocal agreements with Ireland. Students from other nations studying in Ireland may work up to 20 hours per week in term and full-time in vacations only if they are attending a full-time course of at least a year leading to a recognised qualification. As their primary cause for being in Ireland is study, work permits are not required but working beyond the above limits will be construed as a breach of the students' study visa. This change in the availability of casual work for students does not remove the financial support requirements for student visas.

In addition to the opportunities listed in this chapter voluntary work can be arranged by International Voluntary Service for British applicants and Service Civil International for Americans: see the *Worldwide* chapter for details.

Placing an advertisement in an Irish newspaper may lead to a job. The *Irish Times* can be contacted at 10-16 D'Olier Street, Dublin 2; the *Irish Independent* and *Evening Herald* are based at 90 Middle Abbey Street, Dublin. Several newspaper websites carry information on job vacancies. You might also try the websites for job listings; these include the *Irish Examiner* (www.examiner.ie), the *Irish Independent* (www.loadza.com), the *Irish Times* (www.ireland.com), the *Sunday Business Post* (www.sbpost.ie) or the *Sunday Tribune* (www.tribune.ie).

# RED TAPE

**Visa Requirements:** If you are a citizen of an EU/EEA member state, you do not require a tourist visa to travel to Ireland. A number of other nationalities can enter Ireland without applying for a visa in advance including Australians, Canadians, New Zealanders and Americans. The full list of countries that do not require a visa in advance of entering Ireland is available on the Department of Justice, Equality and Law Reform website, www.justice.ie .

**Residence Permits:** EU citizens do not require residence permits. However, nationals of the other EEA countries and Switzerland still need residence permits to stay in Ireland. On arrival in Ireland these citizens do not have to report their presence in the country immediately. However they must register within three months of their arrival and apply for a residence permit. If resident in Dublin, they should register with the Garda National Immigration Bureau. In other areas, they should register at the local Garda District Headquarters.

**Work Permits:** A work permit is granted by the Department of Enterprise, Trade and Employment to an employer in order to employ a non-European Economic Area national in a specific position in their company or organisation for a specific period of time. For further information contact Work Permits, Enterprise, Trade and Employment, Davitt house, 65a Adelaide Road, Dublin 2, Ireland, (+353 1 6313333; fax +353 1 6313268; e-mail workpermits@entemp.ie; www.entemp.ie/labour/workpermits.

**'Work in Ireland Scheme' for Americans and Canadians:** 'Work in Ireland is a reciprocal programme which allows US students to work in Ireland for up to 4 months, and Canadian students to work in Ireland for up to 12 months. For further information contact: BUNAC USA, PO Box 430, Southbury, CT 06488; (☎+1 203-264 0901; fax +1 203-264 0351; e-mail info@bunacusa.org; www.bunacusa.org) or SWAP (www.swap.ca) for Canadians.

**Working Holiday Permit for Australians and New Zealanders:** Working Holiday Permits are available to Australians and New Zealanders for one year. For further

information contact: Embassy of Ireland, 20 Arkana Street, Yarralumla, A.C.T. 2600, Canberra, (☎+612 6273 3022; fax +612 6273 3741; e-mail irishemb@ cyberone.com.au or Honorary Consul General, PO Box 279, Auckland 1001, New Zealand, (☎+65 9900 2252; fax +64 9977 2256; e-mail consul@ireland.co.nz)
**Au Pair:** only nationals of EEA countries, Iceland and Switzerland can be accepted as au pairs in Ireland without a work permit.
**Voluntary Work:** Only nationals of EEA countries, Iceland and Switzerland can become voluntary workers in Ireland without a visa.

# Hotel Work and Catering

**ANGLO CONTINENTAL PLACEMENTS AGENCY:** 9 Wish Road, Hove, East Sussex, BA3 4LL (☎01273-776660; fax 01273-776634; e-mail sharon@ anglocontinentalplacements.com; www.anglocontinentalplacements.com). Established 1985.
**Chefs, Receptionists, Waiters, Waitresses, Chambermaids, Kitchen Porters** for hotel work in Ireland and the UK. Applicants must be EU nationals, or must have a Visa for the appropriate country.
*Applications* enclosing 4 International Reply Coupons. to Mrs Sharon Wolfe at the above address.
Anglo Continental Placements are also advertising for **Chefs, Sous Chefs, Chefs de Partie, Commis Chefs, Wine Waiters, Receptionists, Waiters, Waitresses, Chambermaids, kitchen Porters, Porters.** Jobs available in 2 star, 3 star, 4 star and 5 star hotels. Accommodation provided for all jobs.
*Applications* to the above address: *EU nationals, Austrians, and South Africans may apply.*

**ARDAGH HOTEL:** Clifden, Co. Galway, Ireland (☎095-21384; fax 21314; e-mail ardaghhotel@eircom.net).
**Chambermaids, Waiting/Bar Staff, Chefs, Kitchen Porters, Reception/Bar Staff.** Wages according to experience: accommodation provided. Period of work from April to October. Applicants must speak English, have experience in the hotel trade and be flexible and have an interest in catering.
*Applications* to Mr and Mrs Bauvet at the above address.

**BLUE HAVEN HOTEL:** 3 Pearse Street, Kinsale, Co. Cork, Ireland (☎00-353-21; fax 00353-21; e-mail info@bluehavenkinsale.com; www. bluehavenkinsale.com). The Blue Haven is a small family owned and run, 18-bedroom hotel. They pride themselves on friendliness and efficiency.
**Bar/ Restaurant Staff (5-6).** Responsible for service and hygiene. €7.50 (approx £5) per hour. Relevant experience desirable.
**Kitchen Junior Chefs (2-3).** Preparation, presentation and service of food. Cleanliness in the kitchen. Experience preferred. €7.50 (£5) per hour.
**Receptionist (1-2).** Greeting, administration, hospitality. Computer skills required. Wages of €8 (£5.50) per hour.
**Accommodation Assistants (1-2).** Cleaning of all bedrooms and public areas. Wages of €7.50 (£5) per hour. Computer skills required.
To work 39 hours per week, five days a week. Minimum period of work is three months between 1st May and 31st October. Accommodation is not provided (about €80 (approx £54) per week locally).
*Apply* to the above address with CVs and a recent photograph.

**CARRIG HOUSE:** Carrig House, Caragh Lake, Killorglin, Co. Kerry (☎+353-66 9769100; e-mail info@carrighouse.com; www.carrighouse.com)
Staff to work in the restaurant and hotel of Carrig House, a family-run hotel, renowned for its hospitality.
   *Applications* to Frank and Mary Slattery at the above email or postal address.

**CASTLE LESLIE:** Glaslough, Co Monaghan, Ireland (☎+353-47-88109; fax +353-47-88256; e-mail info@castleleslie.com; www.castleleslie.com). Irish country castle with specialist accommodation catering to local and international clientele.
**Commis Chef** to work in the restaurant kitchens under the supervision of a senior chef, preparing meals for guests. Wages £150 per week.
**Restaurant Staff** (3) to wait on tables under the supervision of the restaurant manager. Previous experience required but further training will be given. Wages £120-£160 per week, depending on experience.
**Front of House Staff** to process check-in and check-out of guests and generally look after guests' needs. Should be computer literate, with some telephone skills, further training provided. Wages £160 per week.
   Restaurant and front of house staff should be fluent English speakers. Staff work a 40 hour, 5 day week, and work is available any time of year. The minimum period of work varies according to position, between 3 months (kitchen) and 6 months (restaurant/front of house). Board and lodging is available.
   *Applications* are invited at any time to Samantha Leslie at the above address.

**EVISTON HOUSE HOTEL:** New Street, Killarney, Co. Kerry, Ireland (☎+353 64 31640; fax +353 64 33685; e-mail evishtl@eircom.net. The Eviston House is a family run hotel in the centre of beautiful Killarney. It comprises 75 rooms, the 'Colleen Bawn' restaurant, the famous 'Danny Mann' Pub and 'Scoundrels' nightclub. Staff are admitted free to pub and nightclub when off duty.
**Bar Staff**. Minimum age 18 years. Wages on application.
**Chefs** all grades of chef required.
**Receptionists** experience preferred.
**Waiter/Waitress**. Wages on application. Preferably with experience. Minimum age 18 years.
   Minimum period of work 4 months between May and September.
   *Applications* during March/April to the above address.

**GOLF LINKS HOTEL:** Glengariff, Co. Cork, Ireland.
**Waitresses** (3). Wages on application. Average 55 hours per week. Minimum age 17 years.
**Barmaid**. Wages and hours as above. Minimum age 19 years.
**Hall Porter**. Wages and hours as above. Minimum age 18 years.
**Laundry Maid**. Wages as above. Average 40 hours per week. Minimum age 18 years.
**Housemaids (2)**. Wages and hours as above. Minimum age 17 years.
**Chef/Cook**. Wages and hours as above. Must have some experience of commercial catering. Free board and accommodation. Minimum period of work 5 weeks between mid-May and September.
   *Applications* from April to the above address.

**THE OLDE RAILWAY HOTEL:** The Mall, Westport, County Mayo, Ireland (☎+ 353-98-25166; fax+353-98-25090; e-mail railway@anu.ie; www.theolderailwayhotel. com). Charming 18th Century coaching inn, situated alongside the Carrowbeg river in the centre of the pretty town of Westport on the West Coast of Ireland. Plenty to do in time off; new town swimming-pool and leisure centre, cinema, beaches, walks, fishing, golf etc.

**Cooks, Chefs, Waiting Staff (4)** required to work 40 hours per five-day week and **Resident Pianist** (five nights, 4 hours a night). Pay from €300 per week gross with free board and lodging (provided if available) plus gratuities. Must have relevant experience/qualifications. Minimum period of work 2 months; staff required from March through to November. Full knowledge of English essential.

*Applications* to Karl Rosenkranz at the above address.

**SINNOTT HOTELS:** Furbo, Co. Galway, Ireland 9 (☎091-592108;e-mail sinnott@ iol.ie; www.sinnotthotels.com). This is quality employer hotel is a leading four star property in the west of Ireland, and is part of a progressive group. There is a strong emphasis on professional customer service.

**Chefs/Commis Waiting Staff, House Assistants, Bar Staff, Porters.** Wages by arrangement, depending on experience. For shift work, five days per week. Minimum period of work three months between April and October. Applicants should be able to speak English; previous experience is desirable but not essential.

*Applications* to the above address from January.

**ZETLAND COUNTRY HOUSE HOTEL:** Cashel Bay, Connemara, Co Galway, Ireland (☎095-31111; fax 095-31117; e-mail zetland@iol.ie; www.connemara.net/ zetland/). A 4-star country house hotel on Ireland's west coast.

**Receptionist** for reception desk work, welcoming guests etc.

**Commis Chefs (2)** for breakfast and dinner catering.

**Waiting staff (4)** to serve guests at breakfast and dinner.

**Housekeeper** to oversee upkeep of house and guest rooms.

**Chambermaids (4)** to clean and tidy guest rooms.

**Kitchen Porter (2)** for general kitchen duties.

Apart from the kitchen porter and chambermaid positions, some previous hotel/ catering experience is necessary. Staff wages are £480 (except for Housekeeper £600) per month live in. Hours of work are 8-10 hours per day within a 5½ day week. Period of work 1 April-31 October, with a minimum period of work of one month. All staff should speak English.

*Applications* from 1st March to the above address.

# Sports, Couriers and Camping

**ERRISLANNAN MANOR:** Clifden, West Galway, Ireland (☎353-95-21134; fax 353 95 21670; e-mail errislannanmanor@eircom.net). The manor is situated on Ireland's western seaboard, where the Gulf Stream allows palm trees and fuchsia to grow. The local habitat of sandy beaches and rock pools is home to wonderful seabirds, sea shells and wildflowers.

**Assistant Gardener:** €80 (approx £55) per week. To work between July and August. Flat provided.

**Junior Trek Leaders (2)** and **Instructors** €100 (£67) per week. Flat provided. Knowledge of languages essential.

To work with 30 Connemara ponies on a trekking and riding centre mainly for children, the manor also breeds and schools ponies. Hours from 8.30am-5.30pm daily. Minimum period of work 3 months between March and the end of September. Saturday afternoon and Sundays free. Knowledge of French or German an advantage.

*Applications* to Mrs S. Brooks at the above address during January and February.

# Voluntary Work and Archaeology

**THE BARRETSTOWN GANG CAMP FUND:** Barretstown Castle, Ballymore Eustace, Co. Kildare, Ireland (☎+353-45-864115; fax +353-45-864711; e-mail recruit@barretstowngc.ie; www.barretstown.org). The Barretstown Gang Camp was founded by Hollywood Actor Paul Newman in 1994 to help children with serious illnesses to rediscover their childhood. The organisations mission is to provide a powerful, activity-based therapeutic recreation programme for children with serious illnesses and their families both from Ireland and 22 other European countries.

**Activity leader:** responsible for designing, planning and directing one or more activities. Will have overall responsibility for the safety and age appropriateness of the activities. Applicants must possess experience in people guidance and group work.

**Summer Carer:** to be responsible for supporting and encouraging each child to participate fully in all aspects of camp to ensure they have the best experience possible and to look after their day and night time needs.

**Volunteer Carer:** required throughout the day to accompany the children in their Activity Group to scheduled activities and to look after their night time needs.

Applicants must be 18 years of age or over and must be fluent in English. Some experience with children or young people, particularly in terms of social, creative or sporting activities would be an advantage.

Barretstown runs seven ten-day sessions each summer. There is no typical working day with contact hours varying, but staff can expect to work quite long days. Staff are given 3/4 days off between sessions with some time off every day during sessions including one 24-hour block.

**Summer Carer and Activity Leader:** paid positions (approx €400/£270 per week) with a training period of one week before sessions start, length of contract is approximately end of May to end of August. The closing date for these positions is 31st January 2007.

**Volunteer Carer:** nine or twelve day volunteer positions are available throughout the summer and 3 or 4 day weekends during our Spring and Autumn programmes.

All posts are residential, full shared accommodation and all food is provided. Travel costs are to be met by the applicant.

*Application forms* can be downloaded from the website or had by request from The Barretstown Gang Camp.

**CONSERVATION VOLUNTEERS IRELAND:** The Steward's House, Rathfarnham Castle, Dublin 14; ☎495 2878; fax 495 2879; e-mail info@cvi.ie). Conservation Volunteers Ireland is an agency that coordinates, organises and promotes **environmental working holidays**. Volunteers are required to work on the conservation of Ireland's natural and cultural heritage: no previous experience is required as full training is provided on site, but a knowledge of English is essential. Volunteers work 8 hours per day. Please note that this work is unpaid; board and lodging are provided at a reasonable cost. Work ranges from 3 days to 2 weeks all year round.

CVI also has a 4-week programme beginning in autumn in Donadea forest park, County Kildare. Volunteers will be repairing sections of a rare and heritage protected walled stream. The forest park has 14th century castle, walled gardens, loads of forest and gallons of history.

The project will involve clearing vegetation from the walls near where the repairing takes place, mixing limestone mortar, replacing the dislodged stones and mortaring them back in place. The projects will run from Monday to Friday starting the 6th

September to the 1$^{st}$ October. Call or e-mail CVI for bookings and enquiries. *Applications* to the above address for further information and a booking form.

**SIMON COMMUNITIES OF IRELAND:** St Andrew's House, 28-30 Exchequer Street, Dublin 2, Ireland (☎+353 1 671 1606; +353-1 671 1098; e-mail simon@ simoncommunity.com).
Volunteers required for **work alongside the homeless** in Ireland. The main duties of the volunteer include befriending residents and general housekeeping.
Volunteers work shifts and receive full board and lodging. In addition, they receive £50 per week allowance and regular holidays. A minimum commitment of six months is required. Applicants must be 18 years of age.
For more information contact the above address.

**VOLUNTARY SERVICE INTERNATIONAL:** 30 Mountjoy Square, Dublin 1, Ireland (☎855-1011; fax 855-1012; e-mail info@vsi.ie; www.vsi.ie).
Volunteers to work with VSI (the Irish branch of Service Civil International). The aim of the organisation is to promote peace and understanding through voluntary service in Ireland and throughout the world. VSI organise 30 short-term voluntary **workcamps** in Ireland each summer and welcome the participation of volunteers from other countries.
Enquiries and applications must go through your local SCI Branch or workcamp organisation.

# Other Employment in Ireland

**AILLWEE CAVE CO. LTD:** Ballyvaughan, Co. Clare, via Galway, Ireland (☎+353-65-7077036; fax+353-65-7077107; e-mail info@aillweecave.ie.; www.aillweecave. ie). Ireland's premier show cave, Aillwee Cave is situated in a remote rural area of the famous region the 'Burren'. It is a place of wonder, beauty and discovery. From the terrace there are breathtaking views of Galway Bay and the Connemara Mountains.
**Cave Tour Guides (5)** to lead a maximum of 35 persons on a 45 minute tour through the caves. Wages are (€1100) £650 approx. per month gross, plus tips. Training will be given. Knowledge of geology a help but not essential.
**Catering Staff (6)** to work as counter hands for the salad bar, fast food outlet and potato bar. From (€1100) £650 gross per month. Experience necessary.
**Sales Staff (2)** to work in the gift shop. From €1200 (approx £809) per month. Previous sales experience an advantage.
**Sales Staff (2)** to work in a farm shop in which cheese is made daily on the premises. Wage as above.
For all positions, hours of work are 40 hours over 5 days a week. Minimum period of work 2 months; work commences March, majority of staff needed by the end of April. Board and shared accommodation are available at the staff hostel at a cost to be arranged. Proficiency in English essential and a genuine wish to work in tourism.
Work is also now available from mid-November to end of December for people with some drama/acting/singing experience to act as cave guide for the Santa Claus Project. *Applicants from outside the EU must be in possession of a current work permit and health insurance.*
Applications to Fiona at the above address.

# Italy

The rate of unemployment in Italy has fallen to under 8%. This can be misleading however as there is a sharp divide between northern and southern Italy in this respect. In the industrial powerhouse of the north, unemployment is low (about 4%), while in the far south it can be as high as 20% in some regions. The best chances of obtaining paid employment in Italy are probably with the tour operators in this and the *Worldwide* chapter at the beginning of the book. Other possibilities involve teaching English as a foreign language, though most who get jobs have a TEFL qualification and are prepared to stay longer than a few months of the summer. If you want to try and find this sort of job once you are in Italy look up *Scuole di Lingue* in the *Yellow Pages*. Those with special skills are most likely to find work: for example an experienced secretary with a good knowledge of English, Italian and German would be useful in a hotel catering for large numbers of German, British and American tourists. Otherwise it is surprisingly difficult to find work in hotels and catering as there are many Italians competing for the jobs and now also people from Eastern European countries that joined the EU in 2004. People looking for hotel work while in Italy should do best if they try small hotels first: some large hotel chains in northern resorts take on staff from southern Italy, where unemployment is especially high, for the summer season and then move them on to their mountain ski resorts for the winter season.

Although Italy is the world's largest producer of wine, a similar problem exists with the grape harvest (*vendemmia*): vineyard owners traditionally employ migrant workers from North Africa and other Arab countries to help the local work force. Opportunities are best in the north west of the country, for example in the vineyards lying south east of Turin in Piemonte, and in the north east in Alto Adige and to the east and west of Verona. The harvest generally takes place from September to October. For details of the locations of vineyards consult the *World Atlas of Wine* by Hugh Johnson and Jancis Robinson (£24.50 from Amazon) or in a public library; the same publishers also produce the useful *Touring in Wine Country: Tuscany* (£12.99).

There are other possibilities for fruit picking earlier in the year, but again there will be stiff competition for work. Strawberries are picked in the region of Emilia Romagna in June, and apples are picked from late August in the region of Alto Adige and in the Valtellina, which lies between the north of Lake Como and Tirano. More information about finding casual farm work is given in *Work Your Way Around the World* (see *Useful Publications*). When in Italy you should be able to get information on local harvest work from *Centri Informazione Giovani* (Youth Information Offices) which exist throughout the country for the benefit of local young people: consult telephone directories for their addresses.

EU nationals are allowed to use the Italian state employment service when looking for a job in Italy. To find the addresses of local employment offices in Italy either look up *Centro per L'Impiego* in the telephone directory of the area where you are staying, or go to www.ufficiodicollocamento.com. Note that these offices will only deal with personal callers. For further information consult the free booklet *Working in Italy* published by the UK Employment Service.

International Voluntary Service (IVS), Youth Action for Peace, UNA Exchange and Concordia can assist British applicants to find voluntary work in Italy, and Service Civil International can aid Americans; see the *Worldwide* chapter for details.

An advertisement in an Italian newspaper may produce an offer of employment. Smyth International, 1 Torrington Park, London N12 9GG (www.smyth-international.

com) deal with *La Stampa* (Turin daily), and other provincial papers. The Milan paper *Il Giornale* is published at Via Gaetano Negri 4, I-20123 Milan. The Friday edition of *Corriere della Sera* has a large section of employment adverts.

# RED TAPE

**Visa Requirements:** full citizens of the United Kingdom, of the United States, Australia, New Zealand and most western European countries do not require a visa for visits of up to 3 months.

**Residence Permits:** visitors staying in a hotel will be registered with the police automatically. Those intending to stay for more than 3 months should apply to the local police at the *Questura* (local police headquarters) for a *permesso di soggiorno* which is valid for 90 days. If you arrive with the intention of working, EEA nationals must first apply to the police *(questura)* for a *Ricevuta di Segnalazione di Soggiorno* which allows them to stay for up to three months looking for work. Upon production of this document and a letter from an employer, you must go back to the police to obtain a residence permit – *Permesso di Soggiorno*. Then in some cases you will be asked to apply for a *Libretto di Lavoro* (work registration card) from the *Ispettorato del Lavoro* and/or *Ufficio di Collocamento* (although, in theory, this should not be necessary for EU nationals).

**Special Schemes for Australians and New Zealanders:** Australians and New Zealanders aged 18-30 are eligible for a working holiday visa for up to 12 months in Italy. Further details can be obtained from www.ambitalia.org.au in Australia or the Italian Embassy in Wellington (www.italy-embassy.org.nz).

**Work Permits:** a work permit is issued by the local authorities to the prospective employer, who will then forward it to the worker concerned. Non-EU citizens must obtain the permit before entering Italy.

**Au Pair:** no problem for EEA citizens but very difficult for others (except Australians and New Zealanders – see scheme above). Some Italian au pair agencies encourage their non-European au pairs to tell the authorities that they are in Italy as house-guests or on a cultural exchange rather than face the bureaucracy. Other agencies simply do not accept non-Europeans onto their books.

# Hotel Work and Catering

**DARWIN SRL:** Piazza Del Pesce 1, 50122 – Firenze, Italy (tel: +39 (0)55 292114; fax: +39 (0)55 292114; e-mail darwinstaff@yahoo.it; www.darwinstaff@yahoo. it) Darwinstaff is a recruitment organisation dealing with hotels, resorts and tourist villages all over the world.

**Entertainment director (10)** responsible for the organisation of all entertainment activities. Wages €1500 (approx £1014) per month

**Mini Club Animators (150)** responsible for organisation of children's activities. Wages €750 (approx £507) per month.

**Sports Animators (70)** responsible for the organisation of all sports activities. Wages €500 (approx £337) per month plus extra earned from private lessons.

**Hostess (70)** Must have an interest in PR. Wages €450 (approx £304) per month.

**DJ / sound engineer (50)** Wages €800 (approx £548) per month.

**Dancers (80)** Wages €500 (approx £337) per month.

**Live musicians (30)** Wages €1200 (approx £811) per month.

All applicants must have experience in their chosen field. Staff work between 8 and 10 hours per day, 6 days a week. Dates of work are from April to September, minimum period of work 3 months. Board and lodging is available for €150 (approx

£100) a month. Knowledge of English, Italian or Dutch is important. *Applications* by e-mail.

**THREE HOTELS ON ITALY'S LAGO D'ORTA:** Hotel L'Approdo, Villa Crespi, Hotel Giardinetto: for address see below. The Lake D'Orta is a popular tourist destination, full of marvellous gardens and green meadows in a Mediterranean haven. Attractions on offer include water sports, horse-riding, golf and tennis.
**Assistant Receptionists (2-3)** required for hotel reception tasks, language skills helpful.
**Chambermaids (2-3)** to clean hotel rooms.
**Waiting Staff (2-3)** to serve meals and beverages.
**Kitchen Staff (2-3)** to help prepare food for meals and desserts.
Staff required for all posts from May until September, minimum period of work 3 months. Staff work 8-9 hours per day over a 5 1/2 day week. All posts come with board and accommodation in addition to wages varying between £130-£190 approx. according to position. Applicants should speak at least English and Italian.
To apply *contact* Caterina Primatesta at the Hotel Giardinetto, Via Provinciale 1, Pettenasco, Italy (☎+39-323-89118; fax +39-323-89219; e-mail hotelgiardinetto@ lagodortahotels.com).

**RELAI CA' MASIERI:** I-36070 Trissino, Italy (☎445-490122; fax 445-490455; e-mail info@camasieri.com; www.camasieri.com).
**Waiters/Waitresses, Kitchen Staff.** Wages around £80 per week. To work 8-12 hours a day, 5-6 days a week. Free board and accommodation provided. Period of work 3-6 months between end of March and end of October. Knowledge of German, Italian or French required.
*Applications* as soon as possible to Mr Vassena Angelo.

**ALBERGO RISTORANTE COLIBRI:** Via Cristoforo Colombo 57, I-17024 Finale Ligure (Savona), Italy; (☎019 692681; fax 019 694206) .
Located in a pleasant sea resort, situated 110km from Nice and 65km from Genoa. The hotel's guests are mainly German, Italian and French.
**Commis Waiters** to set and clear tables and clean dining room. Some hotel experience an advantage.
**Chambermaids** for general cleaning duties and room service. Experience and some knowledge of languages an advantage.
**Dishwashers** to operate dish washing machine, assist cooks and clean the kitchens.
Salaries for all positions approximately £650 per month. To work 9 hours per day, 6 days per week. Free board and accommodation provided. Applicants must be available for at least 4 months between March and October and be at least 18 years of age.
*Applications* as soon as possible to the above address.

**RELAIS IL CANALICCHIO**: Via della Piazza 4, 06050 Canalicchio, Italy (☎+39 075 870 7325; fax +39 075 870 296; e-mail relais@relaisilcanalicchio.it; www. relaisilcanalicchio.it). Elegant relais just south of Perugia with 50 rooms. Friendly, international environment, vacation clients, multi-lingual.
**Restaurant** and **Bar Staff (2)** for table service. €720 (£505) plus tips and free board and lodging. To work 8 hours per day, 6 days a week for a minimum of 2 months from 1 May to 30 Sept. Staff should speak basic Italian, good English, good French and basic German.
*Apply* anytime from March onwards to Diane Kunst, Manager.

**HOTEL CANNERO:** I-28821 Cannero Riviera, Lake Maggiore, Italy (☎+390-323-788046; fax +390-323-788048; e-mail info@hotelcannero.com; www.hotelcannero.com).
**Receptionist**. To work 10 hours per day, 6 days per week. Free board and accommodation. Knowledge of English, basic German and Italian required. Period of work 3-5 months between April and September.
**Chambermaid**. To help in the bar and the garden. Working hours and period of work approximately as for receptionist
  *Applications* at the above address.

**HOTEL CAPO SUD:** Lacona 57031 Capoliveri, Isola d'Elba, Italy; (☎+39 0565 964021; info@hotelcaposud.it; www.hotelcaposud.it).
**Waiter**. Knowledge of Italian and German required.
**Receptionist**. Knowledge of Italian and German required. Applicants must be of good appearance.
  *Applications* from January to the above address.

**HOTEL CAVALLINO D'ORO:** I-39040 Castelrotto (BZ), Sudtirol, Dolomite, Italy (☎0-471-706337; fax 0-471-707172; e-mail cavallino@cavallino.it; www.cavallino.it). This carefully renovated hotel in the old village square of Kastelruth, dates from 1326, thus it has a history of hospitality spanning 680 years.
**Assistant Manager**, **Waiters (2)**, **Kitchen Helps (2)**, **Dish Washers (2)**, **Chambermaids (2)**. Wage depends upon experience and qualifications. To work 7 hours per day, 6 days per week. Minimum period of work 10 weeks. Free board and lodging provided. Knowledge of German and/or Italian would be an advantage, and is essential for the managerial position.
  *Applications* to the above address from January.

**GRAND HOTEL CESENATICO:** Piazza A. Costa, 47042 Cesenatico (FO), Italy; (☎+39 0547 80012; fax +39 0547 80270; e-mail info@grandhotel.cesenatico.fo.it; www.grandhotel.cesenatico.fo.it).
**Secretary**. Duties include bookkeeping and reception work. Knowledge of several languages required.
**Waiters:** duties by arrangement.
8 hours per day. Wages by arrangement, with free board and accommodation provided. Must have knowledge of French and German. Minimum period of work 3 months between 1st June and 20th September.
  *Applications* in February to the address above.

**HOTEL EDEN GIGLI:** Viale Morelli 11, I-60026 Numana (AN), Riviera del Conero, Italy (☎071-9330652; fax 071-9330930; www.giglihotel.com).
This 35 bed, family-run hotel is situated by a sheer drop overlooking the sea, near Mount Conero. The hotel places emphasis on peace and restfulness, and the owners aim to meet the needs of their employees as well as their customers.
**Bar Staff**. Male or female applicants must have a good knowledge of Italian and experience in mixing cocktails (at least two years). To work 12.30pm-9pm/9.30pm-. Wages €930-1035 (approx £627-£700) depending on experience.
**Receptionist**. To work 8pm-2am/3am with a good knowledge of Italian. Wages €930-1000 (approx £627 - £675).
  The company also has a restaurant-pizzeria (self-service, American bar) called La Rotonda Gigli which needs **bar staff** to work 4pm-1am/3am (wages c. €1500 (£1011) and **waiting staff** (wages €930-1500/ £627-£1011). La Rotonda staff get

accommodation included.

Employees for all positions will work eight to nine hours per day, seven days a week. Minimum period of work is three months between 10th June and 10th September. Board and accommodation is provided free of charge.

*Applications* accepted from March onwards.

**COUNTRY HOTEL FATTORIA DI VIBIO:** Doglio, I-06057 Montecastello di Vibio (PG), Italy (☎075-874 9607; fax 075-878 0014; e-mail info@fattoriadivibio. com; www.fattoriadivibio.com). A family-run country house.
**Barman/Waiter** required to serve at tables in the restaurant/bar.
**Chambermaid** required to clean rooms and carry out other general cleaning jobs.

Salary approximately £265 per month, board and accommodation provided. Applicants should have relevant experience, be 20 to 35 years of age and have a basic knowledge of spoken Italian and English. Minimum 2 month stay required between 15 June and 15 September, working 8 hours a day, 6 days a week.

*Applications* are invited to the above address from February.

**HOTEL FRANCESCO:** Via Santa Maria 129, 56126 Pisa, Italy (☎/fax +39 050 555 453; fax 050 556 145; info@hotelfrancesco.com; www.hotelfrancesco.com).
**Receptionist** (also waits tables) needed from 2 June to 1 August and 1 August to 31 September. Wages approximately €100 (approx £67.50) per week.

*Apply* to Giovanni Bragna.

**HOTEL DES GENEYS SPLENDID:** Via Luigi Einaudi 21, 10052 Bardonecchia, Casella Postale 45, Italy (fax +39-122-999295; e-mail geneys@libero.it). A hotel with a youthful and family atmosphere. An ideal place to learn Italian, to study and to rest in a beauty spot. Porters: **(2)**. One for day and one for night needed. Wages by arrangement. 6 day week of 48 hours. Free board and accommodation. Minimum period of work July and August.

*Applications* from May to the above address.

**HOTEL MORANDI ALLE CROCETTA:** Via Laura 50, 50121 Firenze, Italy (☎+39 055 2344747; fax +39 055 2480954; e-mail welcome@hotelmorandi.it; www. hotelmorandi.it). Small, three-star hotel in the centre of Florence.
**Reception/Breakfast Clerk** to take care of the reception in the hotel cafeteria. Must be well-groomed, have fluent Italian and English and knowledge of French and/or German. €6 (£4.20) per hour. Board and lodging not provided. to work seven and a half hours a day 3/4 days per week for a minimum of 2 months.

*Apply* to Paolo Antuono at the above address.

**IL PARETAIO:** Strada delle Ginestra 12, Barberino Velsa-Firenze, Italy (☎+39 (0) 55 8059218; fax +39 (0)55 8059; il paretaio@tin.it; www.ilparetaio.it). Country house accommodation and horse riding school half an hour from Florence and Siena.
**Grooms (2)** to look after horses. Salary negotiable plus lodging, food and horse riding. Must be experienced with horses.
**Chambermaid** to clean 10 rooms. Salary negotiable.
**Waiter/kitchen help** to be in charge of breakfast and serving dinner for 20 people. No cooking, just serving and cleaning. Salary negotiable plus board and lodging.

Staff work 8 hours a day, six days a week (Mon-Sat).

*Applications* at any time to Giovanni de Marchi at the above address or e-mail.

**ROMANTIK HOTEL TENUTA DI RICAVO:** Ricavo, 53011 Castellina in Chianti, Italy (☎0577-740221; fax 0577-741014; e-mail ricavo@ricavo.com; www.ricavo.com). A four-star hotel amidst typical Chianti landscape half an hour from both Siena and Florence.

**Dishwasher** to work morning or night shifts. Pay is €1000 (approx. £674).Dish and pan washing, kitchen cleaning, carrying suitcases.

**Waiter** to work at breakfast, lunch, dinner as service, filling up stock, stocking minibar, cleaning restaurant. €1000 (approx £674).

**Restaurant and Reception Assistant** for morning, afternoon and evening shifts. Besides English two languages requested, preferably French, German or Italian. €1000 (approx £674).

Staff work 40 hours a week, six-day week. Work period is from April to September/October and from July to September/October and minimum period is two months.

*Apply* January/February, May/June to the above address or e-mail. Apply from October onwards for reception.

**PARKHOTEL VILLA GRAZIOLI:** Via Umberto Pavoni 19, I-0046 Grottaferrata, Rome (☎ +39 06 9454001; fax +39 06 9413506; e-mail info@villagrazioli.com; www.villagrazioli.com). This historic sixteenth century hotel, sited 20km from Rome, belongs to the international association, 'Relais and Chateaux'.

**Waiting Staff (2).** To work in restaurant and bar. Some English and French required. Wages c. €500 (£310) per month.

**Reception Clerk.** Must speak English and French. Wages c.€ 500 (£310) per month.

**Chambermaid.** Wages c. €400 (£245) per month.

All employees to work eight hours per day, five days a week between 1ˢᵗ June and the end of August. Board and accommodation is provided.

*Applications* should be sent to the above address from December.

**HOTEL ZIRMERHOF:** Oberradein 59, 39040 Radein, South Tyrol, Italy (☎+39 0471 887215; fax +39 0471 887335; info@zirmerhof.com; www.zirmerhof.com).

**Waiting Staff (2)** and **Room Maid** to work from 9am to 6pm, 6 days a week. Board and accommodation are free. Period of work is mid-May to 9 November. Minimum period of work is six months. Knowledge of German and Italian are required.

Apply in January to Sepp Perwanger at the above address.

# Industrial, Sales and Office Work

**TRENKWALDER SRL:** Via Santi G/6, 4100 Modena, Italy (☎+39 059 82 22 09; fax +39 059 82 13 04; www.trenkwalder.it). Trenkwalder is an employment bureau supplying temporary workers to companies. It has 25 branches in Italy.

**IT Manager** to work on maintenance of Net, PC, printers and server. Wages are €400 (approx £269) monthly plus accommodation. To work 8 hours a day, five days a week. Minimum period of work is one month. Must speak Italian and English or German.

*Apply* from 1 May to the above address.

# Sports, Couriers and Camping

**ASSOCIAZIONE NAZIONALE ANIMATORI:** Via Sicilia 166/B, 00187 Rome, Italy (☎+39 06 6781647; fax +39 330 636836; e-mail associazionenazionaleanimatori@hotmail.com; www.ilportaledegliartisti.it/ana.htm).

Thousands of **Animateur, Sports Animateurs** and **Baby & Mini Club Animateurs** to work in a professional association organising all types of free time activities (social, cultural, ecological, tourist, events etc) for all ages and abilities and disabilities, all over Italy. Salaries: from €300/£210 (baby and Mini Club) to €800/£560 maximum (general animateurs). No experience needed for animateurs and baby/mini club, but sports diploma needed to lead sports. Hours are 8/10 daily for 6/7 days per week for a minimum of one month between 1 May and 31 October. Board and lodging is provided free. Italian-speaking essential.

*Applications* to the above address or e-mail accepted all year.

**BOLERO INTERNATIONAL HOLIDAYS:** Bolero House, Roseberry Court, Stokesley Industrial Estate, Stokesley TS9 5QT (☎01642-714000; fax 01642-712711; e-mail info@boleroholidays.co.uk; www.boleroholidays.co.uk). Bolero Holidays was established in 1984 and is a small family business specialising in family holidays to Spain and Italy.

**Campsite Courier (6)** to carry out cleaning and maintenance and entertainment. £120 per week.

**Children's Campsite Courier (4)** for running Kids Club for ages 4-14 and cleaning duties. £120 per week. Children and craft skills preferable.

**Coach Courier (4)** to travel on coaches to and from Spain and Italy and loading bike trailer, and on board entertainment, quizzes, videos etc.

Hours of work are 9am-1pm and 3pm-6pm, 6 days per week for a minimum of 3 months between April and October. Lodging provided but not board. Knowledge of Italian required.

*Apply* from January.

**CAMPING LIFE:** GVN Camping Recruitment, East Port House, Dunfermline, KY12 7JG (☎01383-629012; fax 01383-629071; e-mail campingrecruitment@gvnrecruitment.com; www.gvnrecruitment.com). Camping Life provide good value mobile home and tent holidays at large family campsites in France, Spain and Italy.

**Campsite Courier.** Involves cleaning accommodation, welcoming families to the site and showing them to their accommodation. Visiting customers, providing local information and basic maintenance are very important parts of the job. Campsite Courier opportunities are also available for couples to work on site together. Senior courier positions available. For more details see website.

**Children's Courier.** Camping Life has its own full-time Children's Club which is open from May to the beginning of September. Couriers plan and deliver an exciting and fun-packed programme of varied activities for children aged 4 to 12. Must be enthusiastic, energetic, and have good communication skills. A tent is provided as a Club venue and for equipment storage. Children's couriers also help out with campsite duties as needed.

Package includes competitive salary, tent accommodation, medical insurance, uniform and return travel from a UK port of entry. Full season positions start in March, April or May and end in September/October. High season staff needed to work at least two months during the peak season.

*Please call* the Recruitment Department for more information and an application form, or *apply online* at www.gvnrecruitment.com.

**CANVAS HOLIDAYS:** GVN Camping Recruitment, East Port House, Dunfermline, KY12 7JG (☎01383-629012; fax 01383-629071; e-mail campingrecruitment@gvnrecruitment.com; www.gvnrecruitment.com). Canvas Holidays provide luxury mobile home and tent holidays at over 100 campsites throughout Europe.

**Campsite Courier.** Involves cleaning accommodation, welcoming families to the site and showing them to their accommodation. Visiting customers, providing local information and basic maintenance are very important parts of the job. Campsite Courier Opportunities are also available for couples to work on site together. For details of management positions, see website.

**Children's Courier.** Needed to work at Hoopi's Club. Applicants must have formal experience of working with children. Children's couriers should be energetic, enthusiastic and have good communication skills. A tent is provided as a Club venue and for equipment storage; this has to be kept safe, clean and tidy. Visiting new arrivals on site is an important and fun part of the job. Children's couriers also help with other campsite duties as needed. Visit recruitment website for information about working with teenagers (Buzz Courier) and wildlife and the environment (Wild & Active Courier).

Package includes competitive salary, tent accommodation, medical insurance, uniform and return travel from a UK port of entry. Full season positions start in March, April or May and end in September/October. High season staff needed to work at least two months during the peak season.

*Please call* the Recruitment Department for more information and an application form, or *apply online* at www.gvnrecruitment.com.

**COLLETT'S MOUNTAIN HOLIDAYS**: Harvest Mead, Great Hormead, Buntingford, Herts, SG9 0PB (☎01763-289660; fax: 01763-289690; e-mail admin@ colletts.co.uk; www.colletts.co.uk/work).

Collett's Mountain Holidays offers specialist holidays to the Italian Dolomites and South Tyrol for walkers, climbers, wildflower enthusiasts and painters. Each year it recruits people for the summer to join its small resort teams to do a variety of jobs based in three Alpine villages in the central dolomites. A rich and unforgettable five-month experience spent in Europe's most spectacular mountains.

**Walk & Via Ferrata 'Organisers' (20)** required to organise and accompany guests on high and low level walks or Via Ferratas in the area. Advising guests on suitable walking and/or Via Ferrata routes. Domestic commitment involving chalet cleaning, kitchen work and hosting assistance. Also involved with airport transfer driving. Walk organisers must have excellent map reading and navigational skills. A summer mountain leader award is a bonus as well as a first aid course. Via Ferrata organisers must have extensive climbing experience. First aid qualification advantageous. Wages are €480 (approx £324) per month.

**Resort Managers (4)** must be German or Italian speakers; couples welcome as well as individuals. Required to perform various management tasks in one of our three Alpine Resorts. Includes hospitality, staff support and general management. Overseeing the day-to-day running of the resort. Food and laundry ordering, accounts, cleaning rotas, airport transfers. Would participate in the organised walk programme with guests. Must have a good level of spoken Italian or German. Must have experience of managing people, excellent interpersonal skills and the ability to think on their feet, as well as the experience and interest needed for the Walk Organiser role. Wages are €600 (approx. £385) per month.

**Resort Representatives (2)** must be an Italian speaker. Required for office management, accounts, food and laundry ordering and management and supplier liaison. Participation in organised walks and/or Via Ferrata. Caring for well-being of guests, assistance, advice and suggestions. Booking restaurants and activities etc. Domestic tasks, cleaning and kitchen assistance. Applicants must have an excellent level of spoken Italian and a good manner with people. Must have a patient and helpful personality. Experience of accounting and/or Microsoft Excel a bonus. Wages €480 (approx £324) per month.

**Chalet Hosts/Cooks (10)** Couples and individuals welcome to apply. Required to provide breakfast and an excellent three-course evening meal six days a week in an Alpine Chalet hosting between ten and twenty guests. Hosting and hospitality. Must have a warm, engaging sociable and efficient manner. Responsible for domestic management of the chalet such as room cleaning, food ordering, chalet accounts, kitchen hygiene procedures etc. Applicants must have a good amount of cooking experience, but not necessarily professional. A passion for food and sharing it with other people is very important. Food hygiene certificate is a bonus. Wages are €600 (approx. £385) per month.

**Artists (2)** to give casual 'on-location' watercolour tuition four days a week. Keen walker with interest in the mountains and the outdoors. Optional participation in organised walks programme. Involvement with domestic tasks, cleaning, helping at dinner, kitchen assistance etc. Responsibility for general care and well-being of guests. Must have qualifications up to degree level or experience of teaching art in some capacity. Untrained but talented individuals welcome to apply.

Dates of work are from mid-May to late October. Applicants are preferred who are willing to work a full season. Employees work between 7 and 10 hours a day, 6 days a week; board and lodging is provided free of charge. Knowledge of Italian and German is required for managerial and administration positions.

*Applications* invited at any time. Contact Phil Melia at phil@colletts.co.uk or telephone 01763-289660. Interviewing from September 2006 for 2007 positions.

**ESPRIT ALPINE SUN:** 185 Fleet Road, Fleet, Hants GU51 3BL (☎01252-618318; fax 01252-618328; e-mail recruitment@esprit-holidays.co.uk; www.esprit-holidays. co.uk) Esprit Alpine Sun run Alpine holidays (France, Italy and Austria) for families in catered chalets and hotels and provide childcare in nurseries and Alpine adventure clubs for children aged 4 months to 12 years old.

**Resort Managers.** Minimum age 23: should be French, German or Italian speakers, with some management, customer care and accountancy experience.

**Chalet Hosts and Hostesses** for various grades of responsibilities: minimum age 21, Cordon Bleu/City and Guilds 706/HND/OND or equivalent or experience in cooking professionally required.

**Nannies** should be aged 18 or over with NNEB, NVQ3, BTECH or RGN qualification.

**Nanny Assistants** aged 18 or over with NVQ2 or equivalent.

**Alpies Rangers** with experience as play scheme leaders, children's sports coaches or trained teachers required to run adventure actvity clubs. Minimum age 18. Should have a mature, fun loving personality.

All staff must be EU passport holders available from mid-June to mid-September. Ideal for anyone who has an interest in alpine activities, i.e. mountain walking and biking, white water rafting etc. All staff assist with chalet cleaning, babysitting and hosting guests. EU holders essential. Weekly wage, with food and accommodation, uniform, activities allowance and transport provided.

*Applications* to the above address.

**EQUIPE SMILE SRL**: Via Fioravanti, 5/f, 40129 Bologna, Italy (☎+39 (0) 51 370774; fax: +39 (0) 51 368518, e-mail equipesmile@libero.it; www.equipesmile. com). Equipe Smile is one of the leading Tourist Agencies in Italy. Established 20 years ago and functioning all around the world but predominantly in Italy. Equipe Smile specializes in the training of animators, with most jobs taken by Europeans. A job with Equipe Smile requires reliability, seriousness, responsibility but is a lot of fun too!

**Animators/Entertainers (150)** required for entertaining in high quality Italian resorts such as Lake Garda and the Adriatic Coast in the North, Sardinia and Latium in central Italy and Apulia in the South. Candidates must have artistic and/or sporting skills and a natural affinity for public relations. Must be open-minded and have a sunny disposition and enjoy interaction with guests.

Animators have the opportunity to work as Sport-animators (tennis, swimming, organising archery tournaments), dance-animators, choreographers, fitness-animators (aerobic, step, trainer, water-gym, yoga), childcare-animators, scenographers, customer care/public relations, the are also opportunities for musicians, DJs and clowns! The minimum wage for an animator is €350/€400 (approx £236/£270) per month up to €1200/€1300 (approx £812/£880) per month there are no upper limits to earnings. Free board and accommodation are provided.

Dates of work are from Easter (April/May) to 30th September, minimum period of work is usually 2 months. Shorter one-month jobs are available but board and lodging will be charged at a small fee.

Knowledge of German, Dutch, French and/or English is essential.

*Applications* are invited from January. Candidates should fill in the application form on the website and send their cv with photos by post or e-mail.

**EUROCAMP:** Overseas Recruitment Department (Ref SJ/07) (☎01606-787525). Eurocamp is a leading tour operator in quality self-drive camping and mobile home holidays in Europe. Each year the company seeks to recruit up to 1,500 enthusiastic people for the following positions:

**Campsite Courier:** job involves cleaning and preparing customer accommodation, providing assistance, acting as an information service and performing some administrative duties. Couriers need to be flexible to meet the needs of the customer to provide them with excellent service. Minimum age 18 years. Applicants should be independent with plenty of initiative and relish a challenging and rewarding position. They should also possess a friendly and helpful personality. Previous customer service experience would be an advantage. Applicants should be available to work from April/May to September.

**Children's Courier:** work involves organising a wide range of exciting activities for children aged 4-13. Applicants should possess initiative, imagination and enthusiasm along with good safety awareness. Previous childcare experience is essential. Minimum age is 18 years and applicants should be available from April/May to September. Languages are not a requirement but would be an advantage (in particular German). Successful candidates will be asked to apply for an Enhanced Disclosure.

**Senior Couriers:** required to work alongside a team of Campsite Couriers and organise their daily workload, as well as carrying out the normal day-to-day duties of a Campsite Courier. Applicants should have good language skills and experience of leading a team.

**Site Managers:** required to lead a large team of Campsite Couriers, organising their daily workloads and ensuring they provide the very best customer service. Applicants should be 21 or over, have proven managerial experience, excellent communication skills and language ability.

**Montage/Demontage:** for a period of approximately 6-8 weeks at the beginning/end of season to erect/dismantle equipment.

Comprehensive training is provided together with a competitive salary, insurance, return travel and accommodation. Applications are accepted from September/October and *can only be accepted from UK/EU passport holders*. Interviews will be conducted in Hartford, Cheshire between October and April.

*Applicants* should apply on-line at **www.holidaybreakjobs.com** or telephone 01606-787525 for an Application Pack.

**G & D GRUPPO VACANZE:** Via del Portonaccio 1, 47100 Forlì, Italy (☎+39 0543 26199; fax +39 0543 379784; e-mail info@gedgruppovacanze.com; www.riscoweb. it).
**Camp Activity Organiser** *(20)* to organise activities including sports, mini club, lifeguard, choreography, dancing, music and theatre activities. Pay starts at €430 (about £300) per month; more for experienced applicants. Free board and lodging. To work 8 hours, six days a week. Minimum period of work 3 months. Knowledge of Italian, German or French required.
    *Apply* to Giuliano de Astis at the above address.

**HEADWATER HOLIDAYS:** The Old School House, Chester Road, Castle, Northwich, Cheshire, CW8 1LE (☎01606-720033; fax 01606-720001; e-mail info@ headwater.com; www.headwater.com). Headwater offers relaxed discovery and adventure holidays; their hallmarks are personal service, warm friendly hotels and good regional cuisine. Headwater guides and information packs help clients make their own discoveries off the beaten track.
**Overseas Representatives** to work in France, Italy, Spain and Austria. Duties include meeting clients at airports and stations, supervising local transportation for them and their luggage, hotel and client liaison, bike maintenance and on the spot problem solving. Good, working knowledge of the language and full, clean driving licence required. Organisational skills, resourcefulness and cheerfulness essential. Minimum age 21 years.
**Canoeing Instructors:** duties etc. as for Overseas Representatives but also include giving canoe instruction.
    Wages from £140 per week; accommodation provided. To work hours as required. Staff required for full season from April to October.
    Further information and an *on-line application* form can be found on the website, or an application form can be requested from the above address.

**KEYCAMP HOLIDAYS:** Overseas Recruitment Department (Ref: SJ/07), Hartford Manor, Greenbank Lane, Northwich CW8 1H (☎01606-787525; www. holidaybreakjobs.com).
**Campsite Couriers:** to look after British, Dutch and Scandinavian customers on campsites in Italy. Duties include welcoming customers, providing local information, organising social activities on site and ensuring that all accommodation is prepared prior to arrival.
**Children's Courier:** to organise and provide up to 24 hours of activities per week for children aged 4-13 years, to advertise the club activities and visit families on arrival.
**Senior Courier:** incorporating the role of campsite courier with the additional responsibility of organising and managing the team and ensuring the smooth running of the Keycamp operation on site.
**Montage/Demontage:** for a period of approximately 6-8 weeks at the beginning/end of season to erect/dismantle equipment.
    Minimum age 18 years. Accommodation, uniform, competitive salary and return travel and training provided. A working knowledge of Italian would be an advantage. Period of employment between March and July/October.
    *Applicants* should apply on-line at **www.holidaybreakjobs.com** or telephone 01606-787525 for an Application Pack.

**ROSSODISERA S.r.l.:** Via M. Pagano 9, 71100 Foggia, Italy; tel/fax +39 (0)881 709951; info@rossodiseranimazione.it; www.rossodiseranimazione.it Holiday resort that offers activities, conferences, events, touristic services and much more.
**Instructors/Animators (50)** to be *animatori turistici* to instruct holidaymakers at

the resort in one or more of the following fields: sports, tennis, windsurfing, aerobics, dancing and theatre. Must be very friendly and open with people and have some experience with children as well as adults. Wages are €500-€1000 monthly depending on qualifications and experience. Work is 8 hours per 6-day week. Posts are from June to September or one month during August only. Board and lodging provided free.
*Applications* are invited from March to August to the above address.

**SIBLU HOLIDAYS:** Recruitment Team, Bryanston Court, Selden Hill, Hemel Hempstead, HP2 4TN (☎ 01442-293231; recruitment@siblu.com; www.siblu.com). Siblu Holidays exclusively own holiday parks in France, and also operate on 16 fantastic parks in France, Spain and Italy. The following roles are offered in Italy for seasonal work:
**Park Representatives:** duties include cleaning and maintaining accommodation, welcoming new arrivals, reception duties, paperwork and administration.
**Children's Club Representatives:** duties include creating and running a daytime entertainment programme for children between the ages of 5 and 12 years old, associated paperwork and assisting Park Representatives. Experience of working with children is desirable.
**Assistant Park Representatives:** duties include cleaning and preparation of accommodation, welcoming new arrivals and reception duties.
Team members will receive a competitive salary, accommodation on park, uniform, medical cover and travel costs to park. The season runs between March and October, with varying contract dates. Limited high season positions are available.
Please telephone the above number for a recruitment pack or visit the website to *apply* online.

# Teaching & Language Schools

**ACLE**: via Roma 54, 18083 Sanremo (IM), Italy (☎+39 184 506070; fax +39 184 50 9996; e-mail info@acle.org; www.acle.org). ACLE are looking for young, enthusiastic and dependable people to work at English Camps throughout Italy for Summer 2007. Applicants must be native English speakers, between 20 and 30 years of age, love working with children and preferably with some experience living and travelling abroad . Italian language skills are not necessary.
**Summer Camp English Tutors (150+)** No qualifications are needed but experience of teaching and/or working with children is an advantage. Applicants must be native English speakers and aged between 18 and 30. Wages are €180 to €200 (approx £125 to £140) per week. Teachers work 40+ hours per week, 5-7 days a week depending on type of camp. Minimum period of work is 2 weeks.
**Short-term Teaching Placements (30)** ACLE also provide opportunities to teach English at Summer Camps in Italy on short-term placements from the 21st August-8th September. Training is provided in San Remo and applicants will receive an Introductory TEFL certificate. Transport, accommodation, meals, insurance and €190 a week are all provided. After a week of training, teachers will be sent to teach English in a fun creative way to groups of about 10 children. Games, songs, sport and drama will be an important part of the learning process. Applicants are sent all over Italy, including the Dolomites, Rome, Milan, Venice, Verona, Bologna, Pisa, Siena, Naples and Sicily.
Each Year ACLE sends English-speaking counsellors to around 50 camps in Italy. Their camps are located all over Italy from the Dolomites to Sicily. Camps are either

city based or residential. Previous camps have been held in Rome, Milan, Sicily, Bologna, Dolomites, Pisa, Siena and Naples to name but a few. It's a great summer experience with fantastic benefits for you and the children you meet.

ACLE is the only programme in Italy recognised by the Italian Ministry of Education to use drama in education. English lessons are combined with games, songs, sports and drama to make English interesting and accessible to children.

We provide accommodation, meals, transport between camps and a bonus. It's an experience not to be missed.

*Applications* should be made before April 1$^{st}$. *Apply* online at www.acle.org.

**KEEP TALKING:** Via Roma 60, 33100 Udine, Italy (☎+39 (0)432 5015256; tel/ fax: +39 (0)432 228216; e-mail info@keeptalking.it; www.keeptalking.it).
English teachers: **(12)** for 2 schools. All applicants must have a university degree and CELTA or equivalent plus minimum one year of experience. No nationality is preferred but all applicants must be native English speakers. All teachers will have 9-month contracts (*contratto a progetto*) and will be working minimum of 700-800 hours per year, 25 hours a week. Lessons are taught mostly at lunchtimes, evenings till 9.30pm and Saturday mornings. Starting hourly wage of €13.40-€15/ £9-£10 (net); monthly €1,100-€1,240 / £741 -£758) depending on qualifications and experience.

Teachers are given training seminars once a month. Excellent facilities. Package includes income tax, pension, medical/accident insurance all paid by employer. Accommodation provided.

**LINGUE SENZA FRONTIERE:** 104 Via de Amicis, 18038 Sanremo, Italy (☎+39 (0)184 50 86 50; fax: +39 (0)184 540 584; e-mail info@linguesenzafrontiere.org; www.linguasenzafrontiere.org).
**Camp Tutors: (25)** for full-immersion summer camps run by an Italian cultural association. All applicants must be fluent English speakers, over 21 and have experience teaching or working with children. Applicants should be able to lead sports, crafts or drama activities. Tutors work from mid-June for two, four or six weeks during the day at the residential camp. In the morning children do worksheets and classroom games; in the afternoons arts, crafts and sports (all in English). At the end of the two week courses the children put on a show in English. The association provides board and accommodation, insurance, all materials, 3-day orientation and travel to and from the camps. Travel to Italy not included.

*Applications* to Helen Clarke at the above address/e-mail.

**SMILE:** v.Vignolese 454, I-41100 Modena, Italy (☎+39-059-363868; fax 059-363868).
**Tutors** required to take **Classes in English and Supervise Games** and sporting activities involving groups of 10-12 children. Applicants should be between 20 and 25 years old, well-behaved and cheery with an interest in culture, be keen and able sportsmen and should play a musical instrument. Experience of working with children and any relevant special abilities would be an advantage. Applicants will work from 9am to 5pm from Monday to Friday and for two hours on Saturday morning. There will be a day of training in Modena before the placement begins.

Applicants should be prepared to work between 25 Aug and 14 Sept. Free accommodation and food will be provided, as will a wage of between £130 and £150 per week. There will also be the opportunity to travel in Italy; SMILE may be able to pay for a part of the cost of a flight to Italy.

*Applications* to the above address.

**SUMMER CAMPS:** Via Roma 54, 18038 San Remo, Italy (☎/fax +39-0184-506070; e-mail info@acle.org; www.acle.org). Summer Camps is a non-profit association which was the first in Italy to teach English through theatre in Education and organise drama courses recognised by the Italian Ministry of Education.

**Summer Camp Counsellors/Tutors** required in camps throughout Italy. Working in association with the Italian Ministry for Education, ACLE provides full immersion English camps for Italian children. Staff would be expected to work eight to ten hours a day, at residential and non-residential camps, providing fun and exciting programmes in English for children between 5 and 16. Applicants must be between the ages of 20 and 30, preferably with some experience of living and travelling abroad. They should be native English speakers and have the ability to create English lessons involving songs, games, sport, art and drama. Successful applicants will be invited to San Remo for full training and introductory TEFL course prior to working between 2 and 10 weeks. Applicants must love working with children and have energy and enthusiasm.

Application forms and details on the web site; *applications* accepted between January and April.

**THEATRINO:** Via Roma 54, 18038 San Remo, Italy (☎/fax +39-0184-506070; e-mail camps@acle.it; www.acle.org). Theatrino is part of ACLE, a non-profit organisation, which was the first to teach English to children and teenagers through Theatre in Education (TIE), and to organise drama courses recognised by the Italian Ministry of Education for Teachers. This small touring English language theatre company and the small routing French language theatre company both recruit from January to April, April to June and September to December (auditions one month prior to tour start).

**Native English Speaking TIE Actors** required. Also **French-speaking TIE Actors**. Should be young, enthusiastic actors with plenty of energy to work in Italy on a 'Theatre in Education' tour.

Actors tour Italian schools in groups of three and present graded interactive English Language shows. These are followed by workshops consisting of sketches adapted for a particular age group focusing on a particular theme and grammatical point. The overall emphasis is on promoting spoken English in a fun way.

Applicants must be flexible, able to work in a team, be able to handle being 'on the road' and love working with children. ACLE provides accommodation, transport, your flight to Italy ex-London, and a weekly wage. It's a great opportunity.

*Applicants* must visit the website for details and an application form. Auditions are held in London throughout the year.

**WINDSOR SCHOOL OF ENGLISH:** Via Molino delle Lime 4/F, 10064 Pinerolo (TO), Italy. (tel/fax: +39 (0)121 795555; Mobile: 348 3914 155; e-mail info@ windsorpinerolo.com).

**English teachers:** (15-20). Teachers with minimum CTEFL certificate to teach for 9-10 months in Italy.

British or EU applicants only. Wages according to experience. Accommodation is provided. Interviews can be carried out in UK.

*Applications* to Sandro Vazon Colla, Director.

# Voluntary Work

**ABRUZZO NATIONAL PARK:** Viale Tito Livio 12, 00136 Rome - Italy (☎06-35403331; fax 06-35403253; e-mail info@parcoabruzzo.it; www.parcoabruzzo.it). Volunteers to spend 15 days working with other young people who are interested in protecting flora and fauna in an outpost of the Abruzzo National Park. Participants **collaborate with the operators, researchers, technicians and guards of the Park in activities such as assisting and educating visitors, maintenance and research.** Volunteers should have experience in the field of nature and be able to spend time in the mountains even in tough living conditions. Minimum age 18. Accommodation and a contribution towards food expenses are provided.

For more information *contact* the above address or e-mail.

**AGAPE:** Centro Ecumenico, I-10060 Prali (Torino), Italy (☎+39-0121-807514; fax +39-0121-807690; e-mail ufficio@agapecentroecumenico.org). AGAPE is situated in the village of Prali in the Germanasca valleys, about eighty miles from Turin. The centre organises national and international one week seminars on theological, political, female, male and homosexuality issues. Its isolated position provides the opportunity to experience life away from modern stresses, although this means that the volunteers should be good at entertaining themselves.

AGAPE is an 'ecumenical centre', where believers of different faiths and denominational backgrounds can meet with non-believers in an open and relaxed atmosphere.

Volunteers for manual work alongside the permanent staff. Job **includes helping with cooking, cleaning, laundering etc.** Board and lodging provided. To work for from 20 days to five weeks between the middle of June and September. Shorter workcamps are also held at Christmas and Easter. Applicants must be aged at least 18; knowledge of Italian or English an advantage.

*Applications* should be sent to the above address.

**CHELON MARINE TURTLE CONSERVATION & RESEARCH PROGRAMME:** Viale val Padana 134B, I-00141 Rome, Italy (☎+39-06-8125301; e-mail chelon@inwind.it). Founded in 1992 CHELON is a research group within the Tethys Institute; its researchers work to obtain in-depth knowledge of the biology of marine turtles and aid their conservation.

Volunteers to help researchers studying loggerhead turtles in the Mediterranean (Greece, Italy) between June and September. Volunteers will assist in **gathering data on nesting behaviour, tagging turtles for observation and taking part in conservation awareness raising among local people and tourists.** English and Italian language skills in particular will prove useful.

Volunteers contribute about £380 per two weeks; this covers food and accommodation. Travel and insurance costs are not included. The minimum stay is two weeks, but volunteers can stay longer subject to approval. CHELON also runs projects in Thailand.

*Contact* CHELON at the above address for further information and an application form.

**CONCORDIA**: 19 North Street, Portslade, Brighton, BN41 1DH (☎01273-422218; fax 01273 421182; e-mail info@concordia-iye.org.uk; www.concordia-iye.org.uk). Volunteers aged 16-30are needed for international volunteer projects lasting 2-4 weeks from May to September. Work is mainly on **nature conservation, renovation,**

construction and social work including children's play schemes and youth work. Basic food and accommodation provided. Volunteers pay a registration fee of £110 and organise their travel and insurance.

*For further information* on volunteering or co-ordinating please check the website or contact the International Volunteer Co-ordinator at the above address.

**LA SABRANENQUE:** Centre International, rue de la Tour de l'Oume, F-30290 Saint Victor la Coste, France (☎466-50-05-05; e-mail info@sabranenque.com).
La Sabranenque is a non-profit organisation working with volunteers toward the preservation of traditional Mediterranean architecture. Participants learn skills, share experiences within a diverse group and live in these beautiful villages.
Volunteers (10) to help with the restoration of villages, sites and simple monuments, using traditional building methods, in Altamura, Southern Italy and the hamlet of Gnallo, Northern Italy. Work includes **restoration of walls, paths or the reconstruction of small houses.** Period of work 2-3 weeks between early July and August.

Board and accommodation is included in the project cost, which is equivalent to £180 per 3 week project. At least one day during each 2-3 week session is spent visiting the region. Applicants must be at least 18 years old and in good health.

*Applications* to the above address at any time.

## Au Pairs, Nannies, Family Helps and Exchanges

**ARCE:** Attività Relazioni Culturali con l'Estero, Via XX Settembre, 20/124, 16121 Genova, Italy (☎010-583020; fax 010-583092; e-mail info@arceaupair.it; www.arceaupair.it). Their Italian families are well selected and applicants can choose placements between large and small towns, as well as being able to rely on A.R.C.E. for support.
**Au Pairs (100)/Mothers' Helps (50)** for placements in Italy; to babysit and perform a little light housework. Au pairs work 6 hours a day, mothers' helps work 8 hours a day, 6 days a week. Wages approximately € 240 (approx £160) per month for Au Pair and €420 (approx £275) per month for Mother's Help. Board and accommodation provided. Applicants should be aged between 18 and 30. Minimum period of work 1 month from June/July to end of August/September. Childcare experience essential. Knowledge of English and possibly Italian required.

A.R.C.E can also offer positions for native English speakers to teach English to children.

*Applications* (male or female) from April to the above address.

# Luxembourg

The official language in Luxembourg is Luxembourgish but German and French are spoken and understood by almost everyone, and casual workers will normally need a reasonable knowledge of at least one of these. Unemployment is low, but has climbed from 2.8% in 2002 to 5.3% (June 2006). EU citizens can use the State Employment Service when they are looking for work and can get general information on the current work situation from them: *Administration de l'Emploi (ADEM)*, 10 rue Bender, L-1229 Luxembourg (☎352-478 53 00; www.etat.lu/ADEM/adem.htm). ADEM also operates an employment service for students and young people (Services Vacances; info.jeu@adem.public.lu) offering jobs in warehouses, catering etc. There is also useful information in the free booklet *Working in Luxembourg* published by the UK Employment Service (see the *Useful Publications* chapter towards the end of this book).

Employment agencies specialising in temporary work include *Manpower-Aide Temporaire*, 42 rue Glesener, L-1630 Luxembourg (☎352-48 23 23; fax 352-40 35 52; e-mail manpower.lux@manpower.lu). Employment agencies are listed in the yellow pages under *Agences de Travail*.

In March or April of each year, a special forum for summer jobs is organised by the Youth Information Centre in Luxembourg City, where students can meet employees and firms offering summer jobs and be informed about their rights. The centre also runs a special service for summer jobs from April to August. The Youth Information Centre can be found at *Centre Information Jeunes*, 26 place de la Gare, L-1616 Luxembourg (☎352-26 29 32 00; fax 352-26 29 32 03; e-mail cij@info.jeunes.lu; website www.cij.lu).

The internet can be used for obtaining contact details of hotels in Luxembourg, for instance the directory www.hotels.lu or the website of the Luxembourg tourist office www.luxembourg.co.uk.

People are sometimes needed to help with the grape harvest, which normally begins around the 20th September and continues for four or five weeks.

To advertise in newspapers contact *Tageblatt* at 44 rue du Canal, L-4050 Esch-Alzette (☎352-54 71 31; fax 352-54 71 30; www.tageblatt.lu) who also publish a French weekly called *Le Jeudi* aimed at foreigners living in Luxembourg.

# RED TAPE

**Visa Requirements:** no visa is necessary for entry into Luxembourg by members of an EEA country or citizens of the USA, Canada, Australia or New Zealand.

**Residence Permits:** if you wish to stay in Luxembourg for longer than three months, you must obtain permission in advance from the Administration Communale of the Municipality of Residence unless you are an EU national. Non-EU nationals must produce a medical certificate and radiographic certificate issued by a doctor established in Luxembourg as well as the other documents required by all applicants: proof of identity and proof of sufficient means of support or a *Déclaration Patronale*.

**Work Permits:** are necessary for any non-EEA national wanting to work in Luxembourg. Permits (*Déclaration Patronale*) are issued by the *Administration de l'Emploi* to the prospective employer. Non-EEA nationals must obtain a job and a0 work permit before entering Luxembourg.

**Au Pair:** The information Youth Centre of Luxembourg can give information to young people from Luxembourg who want to go abroad as au pairs. However, as Luxembourg does not recognize the legal status of au pairs, any person who wishes to au pair within Luxembourg will have to pay social security. Furthermore, people coming from outside the European Union are unlikely to receive permission to work or stay as au pairs in this country.

**Voluntary Work:** foreigners are free to carry out voluntary work for recognised international bodies.

# Hotel Work and Catering

**HOTEL DE L'ABBAYE:** 80 Grand'rue, L-9711 Clervaux, Luxembourg.
**Waiting staff (1/2).** £440-£550 per month, plus tips and share of service charge. A little cleaning work. Knowledge of French or German required. Minimum period of

work 3 months under contract.
**General Assistants (1/2)**. £470-£530 per month plus tips. To help in the kitchen and with cleaning.

8-12 hours per day, 6/7 days per week. Free board and accommodation. The order of the house must be accepted by those wishing to live in. A married couple would be acceptable. Minimum period of work 3 months between 15 March and 15 October. Training may be given.

*Applications* to Mr Paul Wagner, Director.

**HOTEL LE ROYAL:** 12 Boulevard Le Royal, L-2449 Luxembourg, Luxembourg (☎+352-2416161; fax +00352-24-16-16-782; e-mail humanresources@hotelroyal.lu; www.hotelroyal.lu). Located in the heart of Luxembourg City, this 5 star hotel has 210 rooms and suites, and prides itself on the attentive but discreet service of its staff.
**Stagiares (2)** required to take up six month placements in this leading hotel. Successful candidates may be employed as restaurant and banquet waiting staff or assistant receipt controllers and auditors. Staff will earn around £170 per month for working 40 hour weeks, with board and lodging available. Applicants should ideally speak French. As a trainee, staff will earn: 1-2 months, €150 (£101); 2-4 months, €200 (£134); 4-6 months, €300 (£202); 6-12 months, €450 (£300).

*Applications* are invited immediately and should be sent to Albanse Millot-Royer, Human Resources Manager at the above address.

**SHERATON AEROGOLF HOTEL LUXEMBOURG:** Executive Hotels Sarl, BP 1973, L-1019 Luxembourg (☎+352 340571; fax +352 340217; Sheraton. Luxembourg@Sheraton.com; www.Sheraton.com).
**Waiter:** should be able to ensure a high degree of customer satisfaction through prompt, courteous and efficient food and beverage service.
Chambermaid: Duties include changing linen and making beds daily, ensuring the cleanliness of guest rooms and hotel corridors. Wages approximately €1200 per month net. To work 8 hours per day, 5 days per week. Employees have a hotel room and a reduced rate. Period of work from 1 June to 30 September. Applicants must speak English; French or German would be an advantage. EU work permit essential.

*Applications* should be sent to Gunnar Ormalm, Personnel Manager, at the above address.

# Sports, Couriers and Camping

**CANVAS HOLIDAYS:** GVN Camping Recruitment, East Port House, Dunfermline, KY12 7JG (☎01383-629012; fax 01383-629071; e-mail campingrecruitment@ gvnrecruitment.com; www.gvnrecruitment.com). Canvas Holidays provide luxury mobile home and tent holidays at over 100 campsites.throughout Europe.
**Campsite Courier.** Involves cleaning accommodation, welcoming families to the site and showing them to their accommodation. Visiting customers, providing local information and basic maintenance are very important parts of the job. Campsite Courier Opportunities are also available for couples to work on site together. For details of management positions, see website.

Package includes competitive salary, tent accommodation, medical insurance, uniform and return travel from a UK port of entry. Full season positions start in March, April or May and end in September/October. High season staff needed to work at least two months during the peak season.

*Please call* the Recruitment Department for more information and an application form, or *apply online* at www.gvnrecruitment.com.

**EUROCAMP:** Overseas Recruitment Department (Ref SJ/07) (☎01606-787525). Eurocamp is a leading tour operator in quality self-drive camping and mobile home holidays in Europe. Each year the company seeks to recruit up to 1,500 enthusiastic people for the following positions:

**Campsite Courier:** job involves cleaning and preparing customer accommodation, providing assistance, acting as an information service and performing some administrative duties. Couriers need to be flexible to meet the needs of the customer to provide them with excellent service. Minimum age 18 years. Applicants should be independent with plenty of initiative and relish a challenging and rewarding position. They should also possess a friendly and helpful personality. Previous customer service experience would be an advantage. Applicants should be available to work from April/May to September.

**Children's Courier:** work involves organising a wide range of exciting activities for children aged 4-13. Applicants should possess initiative, imagination and enthusiasm along with good safety awareness. Previous childcare experience is essential. Minimum age is 18 years and applicants should be available from April/May to September. Languages are not a requirement but would be an advantage (in particular German). Successful candidates will be asked to apply for an Enhanced Disclosure.

**Senior Couriers:** required to work alongside a team of Campsite Couriers and organise their daily workload, as well as carrying out the normal day-to-day duties of a Campsite Courier. Applicants should have good language skills and experience of leading a team.

**Site Managers:** required to lead a large team of Campsite Couriers, organising their daily workloads and ensuring they provide the very best customer service. Applicants should be 21 or over, have proven managerial experience, excellent communication skills and language ability.

**Montage/Demontage:** for a period of approximately 6-8 weeks at the beginning/end of season to erect/dismantle equipment.

Comprehensive training is provided together with a competitive salary, insurance, return travel and accommodation. Applications are accepted from September/October and *can only be accepted from UK/EU passport holders*. Interviews will be conducted in Hartford, Cheshire between October and April.

*Applicants should apply on-line* at **www.holidaybreakjobs.com** or telephone 01606-787525 for an Application Pack.

# Malta

It may be possible to arrange a holiday job in Malta with the Malta Youth Hostels Association mentioned below. Otherwise, jobs are likely to be mainly in the tourism sector. You can contact hotels in Malta via the Malta Tourism Authority (mta.com.mt) or contact hotel chains such as Hilton (www.hiltonmalta.com.mt), Dolmen (www.dolmen.com.mt).

## RED TAPE

**Visa Requirements**: Citizens of the following countries do not need a visa to travel gain entry: UK, other EU countries, USA, Australia, Japan and Canada. Stays must not exceed 3 months. Visitors must not attempt to gain employment whilst they stay unless they are EU citizens who have applied for a work permit.

**Work Permits for EU Citizens**: Malta joined the EU on 1 May 2004. However since it is a small island, it fears a disproportionate influx of labour from elsewhere in the EU. Therefore EU citizens still have to apply for a work permit until at least 2012 so that Malta can keep control of its labour market. An Employment Licence is obtained with a signed Employment Engagement Form from the employer which is submitted to the Employment and Training Corporation, Head Office, Hal Far (etc@etc.org.mt). Information about opportunities to work in Malta for EU citizens can be obtained by sending an e-mail to eures@etc.org.mt or looking on the website www.etc.mt.

**Non EU Citizens**: will find it is very difficult to get a permit to work in Malta, however in exceptional circumstances permits can be provided for a year.

**MALTA YOUTH HOSTELS ASSOCIATION (MYHA):** 17 Triq Tal-Borg, Pawla PLA O6, Malta (☎+356 2169 3957; e-mail myha@keyworld.net).
The MYHA offers temporary, free accommodation to persons needing social assistance. It also receives young travellers and workcamp volunteers to assist in the achievement of this aim. The MYHA operates workcamps all round the year, whereby volunteers are accommodated in return for a minimum of 3 hours per day of unpaid work as directed by the MYHA.
**Volunteers** to work on a Short-term Workcamp. Volunteers, (aged 18-25) who must be from EU countries may stay for between two weeks and three months. Accommodation is in the youth hostels.
  *Apply sending three International Reply Coupons* (or two US dollars if IRCs not available). Forms should be received three months before the camp is due to start.

# The Netherlands

The Netherlands has one of the lowest unemployment rates in the EU at only 3.8%. Most Dutch people speak excellent English, and so knowledge of Dutch is not essential for those looking for unskilled seasonal jobs. The tourist industry employs large numbers of extra workers over the summer: it is worth noting that the bulb fields attract tourists from spring onwards, and so the tourist season begins comparatively early for Europe. Early application is therefore important. Information on living and working in The Netherlands can be found on the Dutch Embassy's website (www.Netherlands-embassy.org.uk)
  Although this chapter lists only details of paid employment in the Netherlands, there are in fact a number of opportunities for voluntary work. International Voluntary Service, Youth Action for Peace, Concordia and UNA Exchange recruit Britons and Service Civil International (see the IVS entry) in the USA recruits Americans for camps there; see the *Worldwide* chapter for details.
  Holland has many private employment agencies (*uitzendbureaus*) which are accustomed to finding short term jobs for British and Irish workers. These jobs normally involve unskilled manual work, such as stocking shelves in supermarkets, working on factory production lines, or washing up in canteens. Most of the agencies will only help people who visit them in person. To discover nearby addresses look up *uitzendbureaus* in the *Gouden Gids* (Yellow Pages); Randstad, ASB, Unique and Manpower are among the best known names.
  Some agencies handle vacancies for work in flower bulb factories, which need large numbers of casual workers from mid-April to October to pick asparagus,

strawberries, gherkins, apples and pears: the peak period is between the middle of June and the beginning of August. At the same time of year there are jobs in greenhouses and holiday parks. These jobs are popular with locals and usually can be filled with local jobseekers. From the end of September/beginning of October until January of the following year, jobs might be available in the bulb industry (bulb picking and in factories). Although bulbs are grown elsewhere in Holland, the industry is concentrated in the area between Haarlem and Lisse, especially around the town of Hillegom. There are also a limited number of jobs every year in the fruit and vegetable producing greenhouses of the 'Westland' in the province of Zuid-Holland.

EU (EEA) nationals can make use of the service of the European Employment Services (EURES) represented in their own Public Employment Service and in the Netherlands. EURES provides jobseekers with information and advice about living and working in another country of the EEA. The Euroadvisers also have an overview of temporary and permanent vacancies available in the Netherlands. Contact the nearby local employment office for more information. In the Netherlands addresses of local Dutch Euroadvisers can be obtained through the *Landelijk Bureau Arbeidsvoorziening*; look up *Arbeidsbureau* in a telephone directory. For further information consult the free booklet *Working in The Netherlands* published by the UK Employment Service (Jobcentre Plus).

Those wishing to place advertisements in Dutch newspapers may contact De Telegraaf, a major Dutch newspaper, at Basisweg 30, 1043 AP Amsterdam, The Netherlands (☎010-20-5852208; e-mail com.bin@telegraaf.nl; www.telegraaf.nl).

# RED TAPE

**Visa Requirements:** citizens of the United Kingdom, United States, EEA countries, Canada, Australia, New Zealand, Switzerland and Japan do not need a visa. Members of countries needing a visa will have to apply for one at the Netherlands embassy. The application will need to be accompanied by full details of means of support, accommodation and prospective employment.

Entry may be refused to all travellers who are unable to show that they have the means to support themselves whilst in the Netherlands and to buy a return onward ticket.

**Residence Permits:** Members of those countries not requiring a visa who intend to stay for more than three months must acquire a sticker in their passport from the local aliens police (*Vreemdelingenpolitie*) or Town Hall, normally over-the-counter, within 8 days of arrival. Non-EEA members may be required to undergo a medical check for tuberculosis, take out comprehensive medical insurance, submit evidence of suitable accommodation and means of support, and sign a statement that they do not have a criminal record. Short-Term Residence Permits can be authorised for paid employment and au pair placements.

**Work Permits:** Subjects of the EU or EEA do not need work or employment permits. North Americans, Antipodeans and others who require no visa to travel to the Netherlands are allowed to work for less than three months, provided they report to the Aliens Police within three days of arrival and they and their employer have obtained a *tewerkstellingsvergunning* (employment permit) (the employer may do this for them). In practice, the *tewerkstellingsvergunning* is unlikely to be issued for casual work. Non-EU nationals wishing to work for longer than three months must obtain a work permit before arrival in the Netherlands from the local labour exchange in the Netherlands.

**Working Holiday Scheme.** The scheme is open to Australians, New Zealanders

and Canadians who are aged between 18 and 30. They may obtain temporary work for up to a year to finance their holiday in the Netherlands. Applications must be made in person for a provisional residence permit (MVV) to the Dutch Embassy from which further details of personal requirements are available.
**Au Pair:** such arrangements are allowed, subject to the conditions outlined above.
**Voluntary Work:** permission to take work of this type may be obtained on your behalf by the sponsoring agency in the Netherlands.

# Hotel Work and Catering

**HOTEL MALIE:** Malienstraat 2, N-3581 SL Utrecht, The Netherlands (☎+31-30-2316424; fax 030-2340661; e-mail info@maliehotel.nl)
**Chambermaids** wanted for June, July, August to work 8 hours per day per 5 day week. Wages by arrangement, with board and lodging available according to space. Staff should speak a foreign language: English, French, German, Italian or Spanish and if possible Dutch. The minimum period of work is three months.
*Applications* are invited from January marked for the attention of Mr E R van Driel at the above address.

**GRAND HOTEL & RESTAURANT OPDUIN-TEXEL:** Ruyslaan 22, 1796 AD De Koog, Texel, The Netherlands (☎+31-222-317445; fax +31-222-317777; e-mail info@opduin.nl; www.opduin.nl). A luxurious 4 star hotel with 100 rooms, 50 employees, gourmet restaurant, and swimming pool. It is just 200 metres from the beach on a beautiful island in 'the top of Holland'
**Kitchen Porters (2)** for general kitchen work including dishwashing and cleaning. No previous experience necessary.
**Assistant Waiters (2)** for general work in their service department during breakfast, lunch and dinner. Previous experience is recommended but not necessary. Good appearance essential.
**Chambermaids (2)** for general cleaning work in the hotel. Good health essential.
Applicants for these positions must be available for at least 3-4 months during the period March to November.
*Applications* with photograph from January to Mr C den Ouden Esq. at the above address .

**HOTEL WILHELMINA/HOTEL KING:** Koninginne Weg 167-169, NL-1075 CN Amsterdam, The Netherlands.
**Receptionists (2), Chambermaids (3)**. Approximately £700 gross per month. To work 4-8 hours per day, 5 days per week. No accommodation available. Applicants must speak English.
*Applications*, enclosing a processing fee of £10, to the above address as soon as possible.

# Sports, Couriers and Camping

**CANVAS HOLIDAYS:** GVN Camping Recruitment, East Port House, Dunfermline, KY12 7JG (☎01383-629012; fax 01383-629071; e-mail campingrecruitment@gvnrecruitment.com; www.gvnrecruitment.com). Canvas Holidays provide luxury mobile home and tent holidays at over 100 campsites.throughout Europe.
**Campsite Courier.** Involves cleaning accommodation, welcoming families to the site and showing them to their accommodation. Visiting customers, providing local

information and basic maintenance are very important parts of the job. Campsite Courier Opportunities are also available for couples to work on site together. For details of management positions, see website.

Package includes competitive salary, tent accommodation, medical insurance, uniform and return travel from a UK port of entry. Full season positions start in March, April or May and end in September/October. High season staff needed to work at least two months during the peak season.

*Please call* the Recruitment Department for more information and an application form, or *apply online* at www.gvnrecruitment.com.

**EUROCAMP:** Overseas Recruitment Department (Ref SJ/07) (☎01606-787525). Eurocamp is a leading tour operator in quality self-drive camping and mobile home holidays in Europe. Each year the company seeks to recruit up to 1,500 enthusiastic people for the following positions:

**Campsite Courier:** job involves cleaning and preparing customer accommodation, providing assistance, acting as an information service and performing some administrative duties. Couriers need to be flexible to meet the needs of the customer to provide them with excellent service. Minimum age 18 years. Applicants should be independent with plenty of initiative and relish a challenging and rewarding position. They should also possess a friendly and helpful personality. Previous customer service experience would be an advantage. Applicants should be available to work from April/May to September.

**Children's Courier:** work involves organising a wide range of exciting activities for children aged 4-13. Applicants should possess initiative, imagination and enthusiasm along with good safety awareness. Previous childcare experience is essential. Minimum age is 18 years and applicants should be available from April/May to September. Languages are not a requirement but would be an advantage (in particular German). Successful candidates will be asked to apply for an Enhanced Disclosure.

**Senior Couriers:** required to work alongside a team of Campsite Couriers and organise their daily workload, as well as carrying out the normal day-to-day duties of a Campsite Courier. Applicants should have good language skills and experience of leading a team.

**Site Managers:** required to lead a large team of Campsite Couriers, organising their daily workloads and ensuring they provide the very best customer service. Applicants should be 21 or over, have proven managerial experience, excellent communication skills and language ability.

**Montage/Demontage:** for a period of approximately 6-8 weeks at the beginning/end of season to erect/dismantle equipment.

Comprehensive training is provided together with a competitive salary, insurance, return travel and accommodation. Applications are accepted from September/October and *can only be accepted from UK/EU passport holders*. Interviews will be conducted in Hartford, Cheshire between October and April.

*Applicants should apply on-line* at **www.holidaybreakjobs.com** or telephone 01606-787525 for an Application Pack.

# Volunteer Work

**ACTIVITY INTERNATIONAL:** PO Box 694, NL-7500 AR Enschede, the Netherlands (☎+31-53 4800 382; fax+31-53 4880 801; e-mail info@ activityinternational.nl; www.activityinternational.nl).

**Dutch Citizens** (hundreds) for several work and volunteer placements in the Netherlands. Includes work on farms, in national parks, in hotels, in orphanages, as au pair etc.

Applicants should *contact* the above address for details.

# Norway

Norway voted not to join the European Union, but it is a member of the European Economic Area (EEA) which means that EU nationals can enter and look for work for up to 6 months. They can seek work through local offices of the Norwegian employment service Aetat (www.aetat.no), and work without needing work permits. Citizens of other Scandinavian countries are also free to enter Norway. The majority of other foreign nationals are required to get a visa once they have entered Norway. For full details check with the Norwegian Embassy (www.Norway.org.uk).

You can try the telephone job line of the Aetat Servicecenter which is toll-free within Norway; ( ☎ +47 800-33166), or if using their website use the search word '*sommer*'.Aetatprovides information on vacancies registered with the Employment Service throughout Norway. Summer jobs are advertised as early as February.

Unemployment in Norway seems to be going down again and in 2006 it was running at just under 4%, which means it may be less difficult for prospective job-hunters to find jobs. There are a number of well-paid jobs available in Norwegian hotels over the summer. English is widely spoken but knowledge of Norwegian is advantageous. As elsewhere in Europe, the tourist industry appreciates people who can speak more than one language. People who are in Norway may also be able to find unpleasant but lucrative work in fish processing factories in such towns as Bergen, Vardes and Bodes area, but over-fishing has reduced the possibilities of finding such work. When looking for work it is worth bearing in mind that Norwegian students are on vacation between 15 June and 15 August (approximately), and so there will be more opportunities before and after these dates. Those aged 18-30 can take advantage of a 'Working Guest' programme whereby visitors can stay with a Norwegian family in a working environment such as a farm or in tourism or as an au pair; details can be found on their www.atlantis.no or under the Atlantis Youth Exchange Entry under *Agricultural Work*: an application form and further details can be obtained from Concordia in the UK or Interexchange in the US (see the *Worldwide* chapter for details) see and at other outlets in other countries.

The Norwegian employment service is unable to help people looking for summer jobs. British citizens may be able to find voluntary work in Norway through Concordia or International Voluntary Service and Americans through Service Civil International (see the *Worldwide* chapter for details). A booklet entitled *Norway_ A Guide to Living and Working in Norway* is published by NAV (www.nav.no). Apply for a copy to: Directorate of Labour, PO Box 8127 Dep, N-0032, Oslo, NORWAY(www.aetat.no) or to your nearest Norwegian Embassy.

Oslo has a Use It office (*Ungdomsinformasjonen*), one of whose aims is to find work and accommodation for young visitors while offering a range of services, which are all free of charge, as in Copenhagen. Use It is located at Møllergata 3, 0179 Oslo (22 41 51 32/fax 22 42 63 71; e-mail Post@unginfo.oslo.no) and is open year round from 11am to 5pm with longer opening hours during the summer. Their website www.unginfo.oslo.no/streetwise in English carries tips for living and working in Oslo.

Those wishing to advertise in Norwegian newspapers may contact Crane Media Partners Ltd, 20-28 Dalling Road, Hammersmith, London W6 OJB (020-8237 8601; fax 020-8735 9941), who handle the national daily *Dagbladet* (www.dagbladet.no). *Aftenposten* (www.aftenposten.no/english) has a job section and is published at Biskop Gunnerusgt 14A, 0051 Oslo.

# RED TAPE

**Visa Requirements:** a visa is not required by citizens of most EEA countries for a visit of less than three months, provided that employment is not intended.
**Residence Permits:** this permit may be obtained before entering Norway through a Norwegian foreign service or in Norway at the local police station for any stay of more than three months – your passport, two photographs and proof that you are financially self-supporting are required. Even if obtained before entering the country, you must report to the local police with a 'Confirmation of Employment' within 3 months of arrival. EEA nationals, with the firm intention of taking up employment, may enter and stay in Norway for up to 3 months (extendable to six months, if you are financially self supporting) while seeking work. Should you obtain long-term work during this period you must apply for a residence permit and report to the local police. If you are from the EEA and you take up short-term employment for a period not exceeding 3 months, you do not need a residence permit, nor do you need to report to the police.
**Work Permits:** British, Irish and nationals of other EU/EEA/EFTA countries do not need work permits in Norway. Non-EEA citizens must obtain a work and residence permit before entering Norway. Permits should be applied for at least 3 months before you intend to arrive in Norway. Having been offered a job and a place to live, you should obtain application forms for a work permit from the nearest Norwegian Embassy or Consulate General, which will send the completed applications to the Directorate of Immigration in Oslo for processing. Applicants may not enter Norway during the period in which the application for a work-and-residence permit is under consideration.
**Permits for Skilled and Seasonal Workers.** Skilled workers with higher level training whose position cannot be filled by Norwegian nationals or EEA members may be provided with a work permit for at least one year. Non-EEA nationals looking for seasonally-determined work may be granted a work permit for a period of usually no greater than 3 months. Applications for such permits should be made to the Norwegian Embassy.
**Working Holiday Visas.** A working holiday visa scheme exists between Norway and Australia; applicants must be Australian nationals, intend primarily to holiday in Norway for up to a year, be aged between 18 and 30 years at time of application, possess reasonable funds and travel insurance. Applications can be made through the consular offices of the Royal Norwegian Embassies in Australia or London.
**Au Pair.** Atlantis runs a programme for 100-150 incoming au pairs who must be aged 18-30, able to speak English and willing to stay at least six months but preferably 8-12 months. Details are available on their website www.atlantis-u.no and also see their entry under *Agricultural Work*. Atlantis charges a registration fee, non-refundable if the placement doesn't go ahead. See entry for Atlantis under farming. Au pairs from an EEA country can obtain the residence permit after arrival whereas citizens of non-EU countries must arrange the paperwork before arrival.
**Voluntary Work:** this is permitted, but is subject to the regulations outlined above.

## Agricultural Work

**ATLANTIS YOUTH EXCHANGE:** Rådhusgt 4, 0151 Oslo, Norway (☎+47-22 47 71 70; fax+47-22 47 71 79 e-mail atlantis@atlantis.no; www.atlantis.no).
Atlantis, the Norwegian Foundation for Youth Exchange, arranges stays on Norwegian farms for people of any nationality who are aged 18-30 and speak English. Participants

share every aspect of a farmer's family life, both the work and the leisure; free board and lodging are provided. The work may include **haymaking, weeding, milking, picking berries, fruit and vegetables, caring for animals** etc.. Pocket money of approx. £56 per week is paid for a maximum of 35 hours work a week.

Stays are for between eight and twelve weeks all round the year. EU applicants can apply for up to twenty-four weeks though. *Applications* must be received 3-4 months before desired date of starting work for non-EU applicants: EU applicants may be accepted closer to the arrival date. The registration fee is approx. £100 (£200 for a placement of 12-24 weeks); if not placed all but approximately £20 is returned.

*Prospective applicants* should contact the above organisation direct for details of partner organisations in their own country.

**INTEREXCHANGE:** 161 Sixth Avenue, New York, NY 10013, USA (☎212-924-0446; fax 212-924-0575; e-mail info@interexchange.org; www.interexchange.org). Inter-Exchange is a non-profit organisation dedicated to promoting cultural awareness through a wide range of work and travel, language, volunteer, professional, training, internship and au pair programes within the United States and around the world. In the USA they offer J-1 Visa programs and an H-2B Visa program.

**Working Guest in Norway:** this program gives participants the opportunity to experience life in Norway Working Guests are placed on family farms throughout the Norwegian countryside. Participants live with the farm owners in their house and are considered an invited guest and part of the family, while performing a variety of farm duties.

For further details contact Inter-Exchange at the above address.

# Hotel Work and Catering

**FRETHEIM HOTEL:** Post Box 63, 5742 Flåm, Norway (☎57636300; fax 57636400; e-mail mail@fretheim-hotel.no; www.fretheim-hotel.no.

**Waiting Staff (15)** for silver service, buffet and à la carte. Wages Nkr. 17,445+ per month. Must be qualified with good knowledge of wine an advantage.

**Bar Staff (2)** for hotel bar seating 80 persons. Wages: same as waiting staff. Must have good knowledge of drinks, familiar with micros system and speak Scandinavian language.

**Chefs (10)** all grades for buffet, à la carte, lunches and breakfast. Nkr. 18,500 per month. Must have NVQ level and 2 or C&G 7061 and 2.

**Chamberstaff (12)** for cleaning rooms and other parts of the hotel. Nkr. 17,000 per month.

**Café Personnel (4)** to make salads/sandwiches/speciality coffee and to work in bar two nights per week. Wages Nkr. 17,445 per month.

All staff get board and accommodation (cost Nkr. 650 for room and Nkr. 1878 for food per month), work 35.5. hours per week, 5 days per week. Period of work is from May/June to August/September. Minimum period of work is 2 months.

*Applications* in Jan/Feb/Mar to the above address or e-mail.

**HOVRINGEN HOGFJELLSHOTEL:** N-2673 Hovringen, Norway.

**Waitresses (2).** Wages according to experience.

**Chambermaids (2).** Wages according to experience.

**Kitchen Assistants (2).** Wages according to experience.

A 7 hour day, 6 day week is worked. Board and accommodation provided at NKr. 2400 per month. Minimum period of work 6 weeks between 1 July and 30 September. This is a small family hotel in the mountains.

*Applications* from mid-April to the above address.

**KVIKNE'S HOTEL:** Box 24, 6898 Balestrand, Norway (☎+47 57 69 42 00; fax +47 57 69 42 01; booking@kviknes.no; www.kviknes.no). One of Norway's largest tourist hotels with 210 rooms, 400 guests, conference facilities.
**Chamber staff (10), Waiting staff (15), Bartender (5), Chef (10), Kitchen Help (8), Luggage Porters (3), Night Porters (2).**
Staff work 152 hours per month, 5/6 days a week. Accommodation and board are provided for NOK 1190 per month. Minimum period of work 1 June to 31 August. Previous experience is an advantage as are languages (German, French, Scandinavian).
Apply to the above address from 1 February.

**LINDSTROM HOTEL:** N-5890 Laerdal, Norway. ☎+47 (0) 57 666 202; fax +47 (0) 57 666 681.
**Hotel Staff (20)** to work in the kitchen, dining room and cafeteria and to clean rooms. Payment on an hourly basis at £8.50 per hour. Board and lodging available at a charge. To work 8 hours per day, 5 days per week. Minimum period of work 6 weeks between 1 May and 30 September. Applicants should be aged at least 18 and speak English.
*Applications* to Knut Lindstrom at the above address from January.

**STALHEIM HOTEL:** N-5715 Stalheim, Norway (www.stalheim.com; info@ stalheimhotel.hl.com). This busy first class, family run hotel is beautifully situated in the Fjord country of western Norway, 140km from Bergen. It has an international clientele and is open from May to October.
**Chefs (8).** Wages approx. £1,650 per month, must be fully trained, experienced, and hold appropriate certificates.
**Chambermaids (8), Waiters/Waitresses (10), Pantry Boys/Girls (8), Cooks (5).** All paid approximately £1,500 per month. Previous experience a plus.
**Sales Girls (5)** for the gift shop. £1,500 per month. Must be sales minded.
All staff work 7½ hours per day, 5 days a week, occasional overtime required. Salaries taxed at approximately 25%. Board and accommodation provided at approximately £184 per month. Uniforms available. Minimum period of work 3 months between 10 May and 25 September.
*Applications* giving date of birth and details of education, experience, references and dates available and enclosing a recent photograph should be sent to Ingrid Tonneberg, Managing Director, at the above address or e–mail.

**HOTEL ULLENSVANG:** N-5787 Lofthus, Hardanger, Norway (☎+47 53 67 00 00; fax +47 53 67 00 01; e-mail ullensvang@hotel-ullensvang.no; www.hotel-ullensvang. no).
**Waiters, Waitresses, Chambermaids, Kitchen Assistants, Cooks.** Wages by arrangement according to qualifications. 38 hours per 5 day week. Board and accommodation available at £60 per month. Period of work 1 May to 1 November.
*Applications* as soon as possible to the above address.

**HOTEL VORINGFOSS:** N-5783 Eidfjord i Hardanger, Norway (☎+47-5367 4100; +47-5367 4111).
**Waiters/Waitresses** and **Chambermaids**. Board and accommodation available. Experience preferred but not essential. Minimum period of work 3 months between April and October.
*Applications* in March-April to the above address: a reply is not guaranteed.

## Teaching and Language Schools

**BERLITZ A/S:** Akersgate 16, 0158 Oslo. (☎+47-2200 3360; e-mail info@berlitz. no; www.berlitz.no).

Berlitz A/S employs energetic, outgoing and creative graduates and students to teach English in Norway.

Teachers are employed on a freelance basis. Instructors choose their hours of availability between 8am and 9pm. Trainee teachers receive an initial training course in the Berlitz Direct Method. Other employment openings for people willing to sell language courses. Wages are to be negotiated. No assistance with accommodation given.

*Applications* to Instructional Supervisor.

# Portugal

Unemployment in Portugal is not one of the highest rates in Europe, although it stands at 7.4%. The best chances of finding paid employment are in the tourist industry. Tour operators (see below and the organisations in the *Worldwide* chapter), or teaching English as a foreign language, or in hotels and bars etc. in tourist areas such as the Costa do Sol and the Algarve are normally good starting points. A drawback is that the minimum wage in Portugal is one of the lowest in the EU and approximately half that of Britain or France and that living costs, once correspondingly low, are rising faster than wages. Private employment agencies such as Manpower may however be able to provide casual jobs for which knowledge of Portuguese is necessary.

American and British citizens can arrange some voluntary work places through International Voluntary Service/Service Civil International, see their entry in *Worldwide* for details.

British and Irish citizens and other EU nationals are permitted to use the Portuguese national employment service: look under *Centro do Emprego* in a telephone directory. The website of Portugal's national employment institute (*Instituto do Emprego e Formação Profissional*), is currently developing an English version of their website (www.iefp.pt). There are also a number of private employment agencies, principally in Lisbon and Oporto: for agencies specialising in temporary work look under *Pessoal Temporàrio* in the yellow pages (*Pàginas Amarelas*). For further information consult the free booklet *Working in Portugal* published by the Employment Service.

Short-term voluntary work can be arranged for British travellers by UNA Exchange and Youth Action for Peace. Their entries in the *Worldwide* chapter give more details about their organisations.

An advertisement in the English language *Anglo Portuguese News (APN)* may lead to an offer of a job; its address is Apartado 113, P-2766-902 Estoril, Portugal (☎ +351-21-466 1551; fax 21-466 0358; e-mail apn@mail.telepac.pt). *Expresso* is published at Rua Duque de Palmera 37-2, P-1296 Lisbon (☎21-526141; fax 21-543858).

## RED TAPE

**Visa Requirements:** for holiday visits of up to three months a visa is not required by full citizens of EEA countries. A visa is not required for either US or Australian citizens for holiday visits of up to three months.

**Residence Permits:** for stays longer than three months a residence permit should be obtained from the nearest immigration office (*Serviço de Estrangeiros e Fronteiras*) in the area of residence. The addresses of the regional offices are: Lisbon: Avenida Antònio Augusto Aguiar 20 (☎21-315 9681); Oporto: Rus D. João IV, 536 (☎22 510 4308); Faro: (Algarve): Rua Luis de Camões, 5 (☎289 888 300); Coimbra: Rua Venãncio Rodrigues, 25-31 (☎239 824 045); Funchal (Madeira): Rua Nova da Rochinha, 1-B (☎291 229 589) and Ponta Delgarda (Azores): Rua Marquês sda Praia e Monforte, 10 (☎296 302 230). To obtain a residence permit, you must be able to provide a letter from your employer in Portugal confirming your employment. Non-EU nationals must provide a residence visa obtained from the Portuguese Consulate in their home country.

**Work Permits:** EU/EEA nationals do not require work permits to work in Portugal, only a residence permit as above. Non-EU nationals must provide an array of documents before they can be granted a work visa, including a residence visa obtained from the Portuguese Consulate in their home country, a document showing that the Ministry of Labour *(Ministerio do Trabhalho)* has approved the job and a medical certificate in Portuguese. The final stage is to take a letter of good conduct provided by the applicant's own embassy to the police for the work and residence permit.

**Au Pair:** permitted but not customary; a work permit is required.

**Voluntary Work:** there are no restrictions applied to work of this nature.

# Hotel Work and Catering

**HOTEL ESTALAGEM VALE DA URSA:** Cernache do Bonjardim, P-6100-302 Serta, Portugal (☎274- 802 981; fax 274-802 982; info@hotelvaledaursa.com; www.hotelvaledaursa.com).

**Waitresses/Restaurant Assistants (1/2), Kitchen Porters (1/2)** to help in the dining room, bar and kitchen. Some experience in the catering industry would be an advantage.

*Applications* should be sent to the Manager at the above address in April and May.

**LAWRENCES HOTEL:** Rua Consiglieri, Pedroso, 38-40, Vila de Sintra,Sintra, Portugal (☎21-910-5500; fax 21-910-5505; e-mail geral@lawrenceshotel.com; www.lawrenceshotel.com). A five star hotel and restaurant situated in the beautiful heritage town of Sintra.

**Kitchen Staff (3), Restaurant Staff (3), Receptionists (3)** required to work 5 days a week for a minimum of three months between 1 May and 15 October. Salary £150 per month approx. Knowledge of English is required. Some knowledge of French, Portugese or German would be advantageous.

*Applications* are invited from February to the above address.

**MAYER APARTMENTS:** Praia Da luz, 8600-157 Luz Lagos, Algarve, Portugal (☎00351-282-789313; fax 00351-282-788809).

**Bar Person.** Outgoing, hardworking, independent individual to serve drinks and snacks at a busy poolside bar. No experience necessary since full training is given. To work 10am to 7pm, 6 days a week from 1st May to 31st October. Accommodation is included. Applicants must speak English

*To apply* send CV and photo to Mr Adrian Mayer at the above address from February onwards.

**QUINTA DO BARRANCO DA ESTRADA:** 7665-880 Santa Clara A Velha, Portugal (☎+351 283-933065; fax +351-283-933066; e-mail paradiseinportugal@

mail.telepac.pt; www.paradiseinportugal.com; www.birding-in-portugal.com). This small, family-run hotel is in some of the most remote and unspoilt countryside in Europe. On the shore of a vast freshwater lake, the hotel is ideal for nature lovers and anyone wanting to get away from it all.

**Bar Staff, Gardeners, Entertainers, Waiters/Waitresses, Cooks**. Board and accommodation are provided; some paid positions and some volunteer ones. A knowledge of Portuguese, English, French and German would be useful. Driving licence, and knowledge of ornithology or nature are also useful.

*Apply* early in the year to Frank McClintock.

## Sports, Couriers and Camping

**OPEN HOLIDAYS:** The Guildbourne Centre, Chapel Road, Worthing, BN11 1LZ (☎01903-201864; fax 01903-201225; e-mail personnel@openholidays.co.uk; www.openholidays.co.uk). Open Holidays offers unpackaged, tailor-made villa and apartment holidays in the Algarve and various locations in Spain.

**Overseas Representatives** required between March/April and October. Staff look after holidaymakers staying with the company, hosting welcome meetings, checking properties. The working week is 43 hours over 6 days. Wages vary according to experience, but start at £824 per month + performance bonus. This sum includes an accommodation allowance of £150 per month. Applicants must have a full driving licence and be over 21.

To *apply* telephone the number above and ask for the Personnel Manager, or e-mail personnel@openholidays.co.uk.

## Voluntary Work and Archaeology

**INSTITUTO DA PORTUGUES JUVENTUDE:** Av. Da Liberdade 194, 1269-051 Lisbon, Portugal;Apartado 4586, P-4009 Porto Codex, Portugal (☎+351 21 317 9200; geral@juventude.gov.pt; www.juventude.gov.pt).

**Volunteers** are needed by Portugal's main government agency for volunteer workcamps including archaeology. Applications are usually made to a partner organisation in your own country. In the UK these are Concordia and UNAExchange.

# Spain

Unemployment has dogged the Spanish economy in recent years mainly due to regulations restricting fluidity in the job market. However, annual growth rates in GDP indicate a stable economy and unemployment hovers at around 8.5% having been in double figures for all the previous years since Spain joined the EU. Thus there are reasonable opportunities for finding temporary work. For foreigners these are best sought in the tourist industry or teaching English, both of which count knowledge of another language as an asset.

Many jobs in the tourist industry are described both in this chapter and in the chapter at the beginning of the book. Some of the best opportunities for work in Spain are in hotels so that applications to hotels in tourist areas could result in the offer of a job. Since many of these hotels cater for tourists from Northern Europe, a good knowledge of languages such as German, Dutch, French and English will be a great advantage to foreign workers. The website www.gapwork.com has information about working in Ibiza and provides the web addresses for clubs and other potential employers. It is estimated that about 6,000 Britons try to find work on Ibiza each year so it is important to offer a relevant skill.

It should be remembered that hotel workers in Spain work very long hours during the summer months and foreign workers will be required to do likewise. In many cases at the peak of the tourist season hotel and restaurant staff work a minimum of 10 hours per day and bar staff may work even longer hours. A 7-day week is regarded as perfectly normal during the summer. Despite these long hours, salaries are generally somewhat lower than elsewhere in Western Europe.

English and Spanish may help an experienced secretary to get bilingual office work with companies in large cities. There are also a number of jobs for teachers of English: the definitive guide to this type of work is *Teaching English Abroad* (see *Useful Publications*).

British and Irish citizens and other EU nationals who are in Spain and confident of their knowledge of Spanish may use the Spanish national employment service: look under *Oficina de Empleo* in a telephone directory. Private employment agencies are known as *Empresas de Trabajo Temporal:* for addresses consult the Yellow Pages (*Páginas Amarillas*). For further information consult the free booklet *Working in Spain* published by the UK Jobcentre Plus (see the *Useful Publications* chapter towards the end of this book). Alternatively you can contact your nearest embassy: the Spanish Embassy in London produces information leaflets, one of which is entitled *Working in Spain* which gives a general guide to the travelling employee. Others are aimed at students and voluntary workers.

It is always worth checking the English language press for the sits vac columns which sometimes carry adverts for cleaners, live-in babysitters, chefs, bar staff, etc. Look for SUR in English (www.surinenglish.com) which has a large employment section and is used by foreign and local residents throughout southern Spain. It is published free on Fridays and distributed through supermarkets, bars, travel agencies, etc. If you want to place your own ad, contact the publisher Prensa Malaguena, Avda. de Maranon 48, 29009 Malaga or this can be done through the website. Advertisements can be placed in Spanish newspapers including El Mundo, a national daily, which is handled by Smyth International, Archgate Business Centre, 825 High Road, London N12 8UB (☎020-8446 6400; fax 020-8446 6402; e-mail alastair@smyth-international.com; www. smyth-international. com). El Pais, the leading national daily, is published at Prisa, Miguel Yuste 40, E-28037 Madrid.

There are also opportunities for voluntary work in Spain arranged by Concordia, UNA Exchange, Youth Action for Peace and International Voluntary Service for British citizens, and Service Civil International for US nationals; see the *Worldwide* chapter for details.

# RED TAPE

**Visa Requirements:** a visa is not required by citizens of the United Kingdom, United States and of EEA countries for non-working visits to Spain. Non-EEA nationals taking up a paid job must obtain a visa from the Spanish Consulate before travelling to Spain: this can take 3 months to process. To avoid delay, anyone requesting information or visa forms should write stating their nationality and the purpose of their intended stay, enclosing a stamped addressed envelope.

**Residence Permits:** Since March 2003, it has not been necessary for British and other EU/EEA citizens to apply for a residence card to reside in Spain. Residence cards can however be applied for on a voluntary basis (apply direct to the local

*Comisaria de Policia* or *Oficina de Extranjeros*. Further details on the Ministry of the Interior's website (www.mir.es).

Non-EEA citizens who intend to stay more than three months must apply for a residence card *(Tarjeta de Residencia)* within 30 days of arrival. Application should be made to the local police headquarters *(Comisaria de Policia)* or to a Foreigners' Registration Office *(Oficina de Extranjeria)*. The documents necessary for the *residencia* are a contract of employment, three photos, a passport and (sometimes) a medical certificate. This information can be confirmed with the Spanish General Consulates your own country or at www.mtas.es/consejerias/reinounido. You may also wish to register your stay in Spain with your country's consulate in Spain.

Further information on residing in Spain can also be obtained from the Spanish Consulates General in London, Manchester and Edinburgh and with the British Consulate-General in Spain (c/ Marqués de la Ensenada 16-2°, 28004 Madrid; 91-308 5201). Their notes *Settling in Spain* include detailed advice on sorting out red tape as well as the addresses of all 14 British Consulates in Spain.

**NIE Number:** all foreign nationals need to apply for a foreigner's identification number *(numero de identificación de extranjeros)* from the police as soon as they start work. The NIE is a tax identification number that allows you to undertake any kind of employment or business activity in Spain.

**Work Permits:** are not required by EEA nationals. The immigration situation for non-EU citizens has become increasingly difficult forcing employers of non-Europeans to embark on an expensive, complex and lengthy process. Non-EU nationals must first obtain a *visado especial* from the Spanish Embassy in their country of residence after submitting a copy of their contract, medical certificate in duplicate and authenticated copies of qualifications. In some cases a further document is needed, an *antecedente penale* (certificate proving that they have no criminal record). The employer must obtain a work permit on your behalf from the Spanish Ministry of Labour through the relevant *Delegacion Provincial de Trabajo y Seguridad Social*.

**Au Pair:** The status of an au pair is between that of a worker and a student. If from a non-EEA country au pairs should apply for a student visa before leaving their country of residence. Once in Spain, they should report to the local police authorities and show a letter from the family and another one from the school where they are studying Spanish.

**Voluntary Work:** there are no restrictions applied to work of this nature.

# Hotel Work and Catering

**HOTEL ANCORA:** Lloret de Mar, Costa Brava, Spain (☎+34-972 364 589).
**Receptionist**. Wages on application. Hours approximately 9am-1pm and 4-8pm, shift work. Board and accommodation provided free of charge. Knowledge of Spanish and English essential, German useful. Must be able to work minimum of 3 months, between May and end of September.

*Applications* from February to the Director.

**HOTEL BON SOL RESORT & SPA:** Paeso de Illetas 30, 07181 Illetas, Mallorca (☎971-4021-11; fax 971-40-25-59; e-mail ILABonSol@ila-chateau.com; www.ila-chateau.com). This family run hotel has 92 rooms and three restaurants.
**Nannies (2)** to care for and entertain children. Must be kind and be able to care for babies. Wages £525 (€760) per month.
**Beach Boys (2)** to look after the pools, beach and garden. Applicants must be qualified pool attendants, and should be friendly, professional and kind. Wages £545 (€790) per

month.
**Waiters (2)** to serve meals and drinks. Must be friendly, kind and professional. Wages £545 per month.
**Commis Waiters (2)**. To assist the waiter. Wages £525 per month.
**Dish washers (2)** should be clean and professional. Wages £525 per month.
**Trained Cooks (2)** to organise the working of the kitchen. Should be professional with good experience of working in a kitchen. Wages c. £930 (€1,350) per month.
**Buffet and Snack Kitchen Helper (2)** to prepare food and assist with buffet. Should be clean, with a knowledge of cooking. Wages £545 per month.For all positons, employees will work 40 hours over a five day week. Minimum of two months work betwen June and October. Accommodation is shared and costs £100 (€145) per month. For all positions except kitchen staff, a knowledge of German, English and Spanish is necessary.
*Applications* from March onwards.

**HOTEL BON REPOS:** Calella, Costa Del Maresme (Barcelona), Spain; (☎+34 937690512)
**Receptionist.** Wages on application. Must be able to type. Average 10 hours work per day. Board and accommodation provided free of charge. Knowledge of Spanish and English essential, of German or French helpful. Minimum period of work 3 months between beginning of May and end of September.
*Applications* from February to the above address.

**HOTEL-RESTAURANT CAN BOIX DE PERAMOLA:** Can Boix, S/N, E-25790, Peramola, Spain (☎+34-973 470266; fax +34-973 470281; e-mail hotel@canboix. com; www.canboix.com). A small hotel situated in the low Catalan Pyrenees run by the Pallarès family for many generations. Hotel has 41 rooms, well-known restaurant, wide range of facilities and an official rating of four stars.
**Waiter(s) (1/2)** to work in the restaurant or in the bar. Wage depending upon skills.
**Cook.** Wage depending upon ability.
**Chambermaids (1/2)** required to clean and prepare the rooms, public areas and laundry service. Wage depending upon ability.
To work for a minimum of six months between April and October. 6 days a week, 9 to 10 hours a day. Board and accommodation are available free of charge. A good knowledge of both English and Spanish is required.
*Applications* are invited at any time to Mr. Joan Pallares at the above address.

**HOTEL CAP ROIG:** 17250 Playa de AroCtr, Spain (☎+34-972 652000; fax 972-650850). The hotel is situated directly over the sea. It is frequented by international clients and is open all year round.
**Waitresses (2), Waiters (3), Bar Assistants, Bar and Pool Assistants (2), Chambermaids (3)** with relevant experience required. Salary approx. £500 per month.
**Assistant Cook** with relevant experience required. Salary approx. £575.
6-8 hours work a day, 6 days a week, either between 8am and 4pm or between 2pm and 10pm. All applicants must be prepared to work for a minimum of 6 to 8 weeks between June and September. Board and accommodation is included. Those who can speak relevant languages such as Spanish are preferred. All applicants must have a valid EU passport.
*Applications* are invited as early as possible to Peter Siebauer at the above address.

**CASAS CANTABRICAS**: 31 Arbury Road, Cambridge CB4 2JB (tel: 01223-328721; fax: 01223-322 711; e-mail mail@casas.co.uk; www.casas.co.uk). Casas Cantabricas is the leading tour operator in Northern and Western Spain. It is a family run business with 2 of their 4 partners living in Northern Spain.
**Holiday Rep/Support Staff (2)** would suit two friends or a couple on a job-share basis. Required to visit clients in their properties and advise them on local area. To deal with practical problems that may arise e.g. plumbing, electrics or illness (all necessary contacts provided). Occasional cleaning, laundry and checking houses between lets. Involves some office work; answering phone, occasional paperwork. Job requires an outgoing personality and a readiness to deal with whatever situation arises. Wages negotiable depending on hours and experience. Local accommodation provided, accommodation will be taken into account when negotiating wages. Applicants must be good Spanish speakers and hold a full, clean driving licence. Hours of work are variable, maximum 6 days a week. Period of work June to September; minimum period of work 2 months.
*Applications* are invited from January 2007.

**HOTEL CASTILLO DE MONZON S.L.:** Carretera Santander, Monzon de Campos 34410, Palencia, Spain.
**General Assistants (2)** to work in a hotel as cleaners and waitresses. Approximately £165 per month. Board and accommodation provided. Period of work from 2 to 6 months. Applicants should have an experience of hotel work and be able to speak Spanish and French.
*Applications* to Jose Diez Sedano at the above address in June.

**HOTEL CUEVA DEL FRAILE:** Ctra. Buenache, 7km, E-16001 Cuenca, Spain (☎+34-969 211571/72; fax 969 256047; reserves@hotelcuevadelfraile.com; www. hotelcuevadelfraile.com).
Waiters (5), Cooks (2) to work in a restaurant and at an outside barbecue. Wages depend upon qualifications, experience etc.; free board and lodging provided. To work 8 hours per day, 5-6 days per week. Minimum period of work 2 months between 1 June and the end of September. Knowledge of Spanish, English and French would be advantageous.
*Applications* should be sent to Mr Borja Garcia at the above address from March.

**HOTEL CASTILLO EL COLLADO:** Paseo el Collado, 1, E-01300 Laguardia, Alava, Spain (☎+34 945 62 12 00; fax +34 945 60 08 78; e-mail collado@elcollado. com).
**Waiting Staff (3)** to help the head waiter, lay tables, clean cutlery, and serve and help in the bar/coffee shop. Should have experience of restaurant and bar service.
**Cook Assistant (2)** to help the chef, and clean his/her job area. Must have basic knowledge of kitchen work.
All staff get wages €600 (£420) per month. Minimum period of work 3 months during the season June to October. 4-6 hours per day, 6 days per week. Must speak Spanish. Board and lodging available for about €300 (£210) in village hostel.
*Applications* to Javier Arcillona Santa Maria at the above address.

**EASY WAY ASSOCIATION:** Calle Gran Via 80 Of. 1017, E-88013 Madrid, Spain (☎+34-9154 88679; fax +34-9154 88919; e-mail info@easywayspain.com; www. easywayspain.com).
**Restaurant Staff** to work in Madrid and Barcelona as fast-food staff, waiters and commis waiters. Full and part-time work available. Accommodation is available in

shared flats. Minimum period of work is two months at any time of year. Applicants can be with or without relevant qualifications but should be aged 18-28.
*Applications* to the above address.

**EMILIO'S BAR & APARTMENT RENTALS:** Apartado de Correos no 80, El Puerro de Santa Maria, 11500 Cadiz, Spain (☎956 540112; fax 01643-702134; e-mail mail@emiliosbar.com; www.emiliosbar.com). Busy beach bar and apartment rentals in the Puerto Sherry complex in El Puerto de Santa Maria on the Costa de la Luz.
Live-in bar staff and chambermaids required. Shared accommodation provided within walking distance of the beach; knowledge of Spanish is essential. Would suit gap year students or Spanish language students. Staff expected to work 6 hours a day, 6 days a week, €100 (approx £64) per week pocket money plus tips, accommodation is free of charge.

Please e-mail or telephone us for *further information* or send a CV with a full-length photo.

**HOTEL FESTA BRAVA:** Avenue Vila de Blanes 23, Lloret de Mar (Costa Brava), Spain; (☎972 364550)
**Receptionist.** Wages on application plus commission and tips. Knowledge of Spanish and English essential, German useful.
**Chambermaids.** Wages as above.

Board and accommodation provided free of charge. Minimum period of work 3 months between May and end of September.
*Applications* from February to Sr Angel Panes Rius, Director, at the above address.

**HOTEL FLAMINGO:** Av. Just Marlés 27, Lloret de Mar 17310 (Costa Brava), Spain.
**Assistant Receptionist.** Salary on application. Average 9-10 hours daily, shift work. Free board and accommodation. Knowledge of Spanish, English and German essential. Minimum period of work beginning of May to beginning of October.
*Applications* from February to the above address.

**HOTEL LA RESIDENCIA:** 07179 Deia, Mallorca, Spain (☎+34 971 639011; fax +34 971 63 83 70; e-mail reserves@hotel-laresidencia.com; www.hotellaresidencia. com). Part of Orient-Express Hotels, 'Small leading hotels of the world'; 160 staff to 110 guests maximum.
**Waiters/Assistant Waiters (2 of each)** to work in beverages and restaurant. €1001 (£702).
**Chef de Rangs, Cooks, Assistant Cooks** and **Chefs de Partie (2 of each).** Must be experienced and have good CVs. Minimum salaries from €931 (£650) to €1074 (£750), but are negotiable depending on CVs and experience.

There is a charge for accommodation. Staff work 40 hours; five-day week for a minimum period of six months from April to October. Knowledge of Spanish and English required.
*Apply* all year round to Jacinta Escalas, Human Resources Manager at the above address.

**HOTEL MONTE CARLO:** Sant Jordi 7, 17310 Lloret de Mar, Costa Brava, Spain.
**Waiters (2).** Wages on application plus tips. Hours: 8-10am, 1-3pm and 8-10pm. Board and accommodation provided free of charge. Knowledge of Spanish and English essential. Must be able to work for a minimum of 5 months, from April to October.
*Applications* from March to the address above.

**HOTEL MONTEMAR:** Calle Puntaires 20, Pineda de Mar (Barcelona), Spain (☎+93-767 00 02; fax +93-767 15 79).
**Assistant Animateur.** Must be Dutch.
**Receptionist.** £550 per month. Must be Dutch.
To work 7 hours per day, 6 days per week. Board and accommodation provided free of charge. The ability to speak Dutch, Spanish and German is essential and some knowledge of French is required. Applicants must be Dutch and available for at least 4 months from May to October.
*Applications* from February to the above address.

**HOTEL-RESTAURANT MONT SANT:** Xativa, Valencia, Spain (+34 96 2275031; fax +34 96 2281905; e-mail mont-sant@mont-sant.com; www.mont-sant.com ). Small (17 bedrooms) purpose-built on the site of an ancient farmstead and situated in its own landscaped gardens with Michelin recognised restaurant, gymnasium and swimming pool.
**Chefs (2)** for cold starters, desserts, hot meals, sauces etc. €800-1200 (£560-840) per month to work 8 hours a day, 5-day week .
**Waiting staff (2)** serving food in a good restaurant, banquet work. €750-1000 (£525-700) per month.
There is a charge of about £30 approx per month for board and lodging. Staff work 8 hours a day, five days per week. The work period is from three to six months. Should speak English, French or German.
*Apply* to Javier Andrés Cifre, Director from February.

**NICO-HOTEL:** CN-II km 150, 42240 Medinaceli (Soria) Spain (☎975-326111; fax 975-326474; e-mail jacinto.3017@cajazuzal.com). This hotel is in an historic village 150km from Madrid, with a high class Spanish clientele. There is a staff of fifty, aged between 20 and 40. Customers are mainly Spanish, although other nationalities often visit in summer.
**Kitchen Staff** needed all year round. Wages on application. To work 7 hours per day, 6 days per week.
**Waitresses (5).** Wages on application. To work 8 hours per day, 6 days per week. Previous experience preferred. Some knowledge of Spanish required. Minimum period of work 3 months.
**Chambermaids (4).** Wages and conditions as above, although slightly shorter hours are worked.
**Secretary.** Wages on application. To work 6 hours per day, 6/7 days per week. Some knowledge of Spanish required. Minimum period of work 2 months.
Free board and accommodation provided. All applicants must be at least 18 years of age. The work period is April to October. The Manager of this hotel wishes to stress that Medinaceli is not situated on the coast. There are also vacancies at the Hotel Duque de Medinaceli, CN-II 150, Medinaceli (Soria), Spain.
*Applications* from February to the Manager at the above address, enclosing a full-length photograph.

**HOTEL PICASSO:** Platja de la Gola 17257 Torroaella de Montgeri, Girona, Spain.
**Waiters, Maids.** £400 per month.
To work at least 5 hours per day, 7 days per week. Board and accommodation available. Minimum period of work between July and August. Experience required.
*Applications* to J.M. Ferrer at the above address in spring.

**HOTEL RIGAT:** Avd America 1, Playa de Fenals, Lloret de Mar, Costa Brava, Spain; ☎972 365200. (e-mail info@rigat.com; www.rigat.com) A 5 star Mediterranean hotel located on the sea, 68km from Barcelona. Those with or without hotel work experience are welcome to apply.

**Waiter/Assistant/Receptionist/Barmaid:** must be able to type. Wages by arrangement according to type of job and qualifications. 8 hours per day, 6 day week. Free board and accommodation. Age 19-28. A knowledge of French and German is required. Applicants must be considerate, polite and in good health. Girls should take a blue knee-length skirt and white blouses. Minimum period of work July and August but there are vacancies from June to September.

*Applications* from February to Mr Sebastian Gispert, Cadena Hotelera Rigat, c/o Ave de America No.1, Lloret de Mar (17), Spain (Cost Brava).

**HOSTAL DEL SENGLAR:** Plaça Montserrat Canals 1, 43440 L'Espluga De Francoli, Spain (☎+34-977-870-121; fax +34-977-870-127; e-mail recepcio@hostaldelsenglar. com; www.hostaldelsenglar.com). This two star hotel has a well-known restaurant and is situated in an attractive location, 90 minutes from Barcelona and 30 minutes from the beach. The restaurant seats 600 people, while the hotel itself has 40 rooms.

**Receptionist** for administration and client check-in. Wages €750 (£525) net. Should be a PC user. To work eight hours per five day week for a minimum of two months between June and October. Board and lodging is provided. Must speak Spanish.

*Applications* to the Manager at the above address.

# Sports, Couriers and Camping

**BOLERO INTERNATIONAL HOLIDAYS:** Bolero House, Roseberry Court, Stokesley Industrial Estate Stokesley TS9 5QT (☎01642-714000; fax 01642-712711; e-mail info@boleroholidays.co.uk; www.boleroholidays.co.uk). Bolero Holidays was established in 1984 and is a small family business specialising in family holidays to Spain and Italy.

**Campsite Couriers (6)** to carry out cleaning and maintenance and entertainment. £120 per week.

**Children's Campsite Couriers (4)** for running Kids Club for ages 4-14 and cleaning duties. £120 per week. Children and craft skills preferable.

**Coach Couriers (4)** to travel on coaches to and from Spain and Italy and loading bike trailer, and on board entertainment, quizzes, videos etc.

Hours of work are 9am-1pm and 3pm-6pm, 6 days per week for a minimum of 3 months between April and October. Lodging provided but not board. Knowledge of Spanish required.

*Apply* from January.

**CAMPING GLOBO ROJO:** Barangé-Brun C.B., Carretera Nacional II, km 660,9 08360 Canet de Mar (Barcelona), Spain (tel/fax 93-794 1143; e-mail camping@ globo-rojo.com; www.globo-rojo.com).

**Receptionist, Waiter/Waitress, Qualified Swimming Pool Guard** required for this campsite near Barcelona (40km). All staff should be polite, with relevant experience. The wages are c. £375 per month for 8-9 hour days over a 7 day week, with free board and lodging. Ideally applicants should speak English, German, and some Spanish, while the job provides an excellent chance to improve Spanish.

The work is available between 1 July and 30 August; *applications* are invited from April onwards.

**CAMPING LIFE:** GVN Camping Recruitment, East Port House, Dunfermline, KY12 7JG (☎01383-629012; fax 01383-629071; e-mail campingrecruitment@gvnrecruitment.com; www.gvnrecruitment.com). Camping Life provide good value mobile home and tent holidays at large family campsites in France, Spain and Italy.
**Campsite Courier.** Involves cleaning accommodation, welcoming families to the site and showing them to their accommodation. Visiting customers, providing local information and basic maintenance are very important parts of the job. Campsite Courier opportunities are also available for couples to work on site together. Senior courier positions available. For more details see website.
**Children's Courier.** Camping Life has its own full-time Children's Club which is open from May to the beginning of September. Couriers plan and deliver an exciting and fun-packed programme of varied activities for children aged 4 to 12. Must be enthusiastic, energetic and have good communication skills. A tent is provided as a Club venue and for equipment storage. Children's couriers also help out with campsite duties as needed.

Package includes competitive salary, tent accommodation, medical insurance, uniform and return travel from a UK port of entry. Full season positions start in March, April or May and end in September/October. High season staff needed to work at least two months during the peak season.

*Please call* the Recruitment Department for more information and an application form, or you can apply online at www.gvnrecruitment.com.

**CANVAS HOLIDAYS:** GVN Camping Recruitment, East Port House, Dunfermline, KY12 7JG (☎01383-629012; fax 01383-629071; e-mail campingrecruitment@gvnrecruitment.com; www.gvnrecruitment.com). Canvas Holidays provide luxury mobile home and tent holidays at over 100 campsites throughout Europe.
**Campsite Courier.** Involves cleaning accommodation, welcoming families to the site and showing them to their accommodation. Visiting customers, providing local information and basic maintenance are very important parts of the job. Campsite Courier Opportunities are also available for couples to work on site together. For details of management positions, see website.
**Children's Courier.** Needed to work at Hoopi's Club. Applicants must have formal experience of working with children. Children's couriers should be energetic, enthusiastic and have good communication skills. A tent is provided as a Club venue and for equipment storage; this has to be kept safe, clean and tidy. Visiting new arrivals on site is an important and fun part of the job. Children's couriers also help with other campsite duties as needed. Visit recruitment website for information about working with teenagers (Buzz Courier) and wildlife and the environment (Wild & Active Courier).

Package includes competitive salary, tent accommodation, medical insurance, uniform and return travel from a UK port of entry. Full season positions start in March, April or May and end in September/October. High season staff needed to work at least two months during the peak season.

*Please call* the Recruitment Department for more information and an application form, or *apply online* at www.gvnrecruitment.com.

**EUROCAMP:** Overseas Recruitment Department (Ref SJ/07) (☎01606-787525). Eurocamp is a leading tour operator in quality self-drive camping and mobile home holidays in Europe. Each year the company seeks to recruit up to 1,500 enthusiastic people for the following positions:
**Campsite Courier:** job involves cleaning and preparing customer accommodation, providing assistance, acting as an information service and performing some

administrative duties. Couriers need to be flexible to meet the needs of the customer to provide them with excellent service. Minimum age 18 years. Applicants should be independent with plenty of initiative and relish a challenging and rewarding position. They should also possess a friendly and helpful personality. Previous customer service experience would be an advantage. Applicants should be available to work from April/May to September.

**Children's Courier:** work involves organising a wide range of exciting activities for children aged 4-13. Applicants should possess initiative, imagination and enthusiasm along with good safety awareness. Previous childcare experience is essential. Minimum age is 18 years and applicants should be available from April/May to September. Languages are not a requirement but would be an advantage (in particular German). Successful candidates will be asked to apply for an Enhanced Disclosure.

**Senior Couriers:** required to work alongside a team of Campsite Couriers and organise their daily workload, as well as carrying out the normal day-to-day duties of a Campsite Courier. Applicants should have good language skills and experience of leading a team.

**Site Managers:** required to lead a large team of Campsite Couriers, organising their daily workloads and ensuring they provide the very best customer service. Applicants should be 21 or over, have proven managerial experience, excellent communication skills and language ability.

**Montage/Demontage:** for a period of approximately 6-8 weeks at the beginning/end of season to erect/dismantle equipment.

Comprehensive training is provided together with a competitive salary, insurance, return travel and accommodation. Applications are accepted from September/October and *can only be accepted from UK/EU passport holders*. Interviews will be conducted in Hartford, Cheshire between October and April.

*Applicants should apply on-line* at **www.holidaybreakjobs.com** or telephone 01606-787525 for an Application Pack.

**KEYCAMP HOLIDAYS:** Overseas Recruitment Department (Ref: SJ/07), Hartford Manor, Greenbank Lane, Northwich CW8 1HW (☎01606-787525; www. holidaybreakjobs.com).

**Campsite Couriers:** to look after British, Dutch and Scandinavian customers on campsites in Spain. Duties include welcoming customers, providing local information, organising social activities on site and ensuring that all accommodation is prepared prior to arrival.

**Children's Courier:** to organise and provide up to 24 hours of activities per week for children aged 4-13 years, to advertise the club activities and visit families on arrival.

**Senior Courier:** incorporating the role of campsite courier with the additional responsibility of organising and managing the team and ensuring the smooth running of the Keycamp operation on site.

**Montage/Demontage:** for a period of approximately 6-8 weeks at the beginning/end of season to erect/dismantle equipment.

Minimum age 18 years. Accommodation, uniform, competitive salary and return travel and training provided. A working knowledge of Spanish would be an advantage. Period of employment between March and July/October.

*Applicants* should apply on-line at **www.holidaybreakjobs.com** or telephone 01606-787525 for an Application Pack.

**OPEN HOLIDAYS:** 29 Guildbourne Centre, Worthing, West Sussex BN11 1LZ (☎01903-201864; fax 01903-201225; e-mail personnel@openholidays.co.uk; www. openholidays.co.uk). Unpackaged, tailor-made villa, apartment and hotel holidays, specialising currently in Andalucia, Costa Blanca, Majorca and Menorca in Spain and the Algarve in Portugal.

**Resort Representatives** to assist clients and work 8 hours per day, 6 days per week with no excursion sales. Salary from £824 per month + performance bonus. An accommodation allowance of £150 per month is included in this sum. Minimum period of work 6 months from April to October. Minimum age 21. Knowledge of Spanish preferred. Must hold a full UK driving licence, car provided.

*Applications* from November-December to the Personnel Manager at the above address or e-mail personnel@open4holidays.co.uk; successful applicants must attend a training course in the UK during March.

**PAVILION TOURS:** Lees House, 21 Dyke Road, Brighton, East Sussex, BN1 3GD (☎0870-241 0425/7; fax 0870-241 0426; e-mail info@paviliontours.com). An expanding, specialist activity tour operator for students, with bases in Greece and Spain. Watersports include: windsurfing, dinghy sailing, water skiing and canoeing. Keen to recruit highly motivated staff.

**Watersports Instructors** required to instruct sailing/windsurfing etc. and to assist with evening entertainments. Hours of work variable, 7 days a week. Wages approx. £115 per week. Minimum period of work 1 week between May and October. Board and lodging provided free.

*Applications* from November to the above address, please include current instructor qualifications.

**PGL TRAVEL:** Alton Court, Penyard Lane, Ross-on-Wye, Herefordshire HR9 5GL (☎0870 401 4411; recruitment@pgl.co.uk; www.pgl.co.uk/recruitment). With 27 activity centres located in the UK, France and Spain, PGL Travel provides adventure holidays and courses for children. Each year 2,500 people are needed to help run these adventure centres.

**Children's Group Leaders** required to take responsibility for groups, helping them to get the most out of their holiday. Minimum age 18. Previous experience of working with children is essential.

**General positions available** in catering, administration, driving (car or D1 towing), stores, site cleaning.

**Children's Activity Instructors** qualified or personally competent in canoeing, sailing, windsurfing, or multi-activities.

From £65-£100 per week plus full B & L. Vacancies available for the full season (February – October) or shorter periods between April and September. Overseas applicants eligible to work in the UK welcome.

*Applications* can be made online or a form obtained from the above address.

**SIBLU HOLIDAYS:** Recruitment Team, Bryanston Court, Selden Hill, Hemel Hempstead, HP2 4TN (☎ 01442-293231; recruitment@siblu.com; www.siblu.com). Siblu Holidays exclusively own holiday parks in France, and also operate on 16 fantastic parks in France, Spain and Italy. The following roles are offered in Spain for seasonal work:

**Park Representatives:** duties include cleaning and maintaining accommodation, welcoming new arrivals, reception duties, paperwork and administration.

**Children's Club Representatives:** duties include creating and running a daytime entertainment programme for children between the ages of 5 and 12 years old, associated paperwork and assisting Park Representatives. Experience of working with children is desirable.

**Assistant Park Representatives:** duties include cleaning and preparation of accommodation, welcoming new arrivals and reception duties.

Team members will receive a competitive salary, accommodation on park, uniform, medical cover and travel costs to park. The season runs between March and October, with varying contract dates. Limited high season positions are available.

Please telephone the above number for a recruitment pack or visit the website to *apply* online.

**SOLAIRE HOLIDAYS:** 43 Milcote Road, Solihull, B91 1JN (☎0870 054 0202; fax 0121-778-5065; e-mail jobs@solaire.co.uk; www.solaire.co.uk). Solaire Holidays provides self-drive, self-catering holidays to Spain and France.

**Site Couriers (20)** to look after clients and prepare accommodation. Knowledge of French desirable. Wage £280-£400 per month.

**Children's Couriers (4)** to run a children's club. Previous experience of working with children is required. Wage £280-£400 per month.

Applicants can apply for work between April and October, May and September or July and August. Hours of work vary according to demand, but applicants can expect to work for six days a week, on a rota system. Accommodation is provided as part of contract. Food is not provided.

*Applications* are invited from October onwards to the above address.

**TJM TRAVEL:** 40 Lemon Street, Truro, Cornwall TR1 2NS (01872-272767; fax 01872-272110; e-mail jobs@tjm.co.uk; www.tjm.co.uk). TJM run hotels and activity centres in France, Spain and the UK in the summer months, and they operate ski holidays from French Alpine hotels in the winter.

**Hotel Managers (3)** required to run hotels in France and Spain, must have experience in the field. Wages from £600 per month.

**Water Sports Instructors (20)**: to teach watersports to children, must hold instructor qualification. Wages from £300 per month. Required are qualified **Sailing (RYA), Canoe (BCU), Windsurfing** and **Snorkelling Instructors**, as well as **Beach Lifeguards**.

**Support Staff (10)** to help run hotels; no previous experience necessary. Wages from £260 per month.

**Hotel Staff; Manager, Chef, 2nd Chef, Reps, Waiting, Chamber & Kitchen Staff, Handypersons.**

All required for hotel or activity centre work in France, Spain or the UK, all staff must have appropriate qualifications, experience and skills. Wages vary between £300 and £800 per month according to job and experience. Board and lodging provided. Staff work 7 hours a day; 6-day week. Working periods are (summer) May to August and (winter) December to April.

*Applications* must include passport photos, current CV and copies of any relevant certificates (including driving licence); apply by post or e-mail.

# Teaching and Language Schools

**ABC ENGLISH:** Calle Sol de Abajo 3, Antoñana, 01128 Alava, Spain (tel/fax 945-41045; e-mail tulio@thefarmfun.com; www.thefarmfun.com)

ABC English organise summer English language camps in the Basque country. They are not a language academy.

**Summer Camp Staff (20)** required in July to organise activities for Spanish children aged between 8-14. Applicants must be at least 18 years old and should have outdoor skills, a creative nature and complete proficiency in English.

*Applications*, from *EU citizens* only, should be sent to Tulio Browning at the above address no later than 28th February.

**CASTRUM LENGUAS CULTURAS Y TURISMO**: Arda. Ramón Pradera no.10-12 A, 47009, Valladolid, Spain (tel/fax +34 983 355 343; mob. +34 6354 15265; e-mail info@castrum.org). Castrum is a youth organisation operating language, business and cultural exchange programmes in France and Spain. Programmes include: au pairs in Europe; European cultural and language exchange; living and working in Spain; placements in industry; short group stays for cultural and linguistic exchange; international summer camps.

Further *details* of Spanish programmes from Jesús G. Marciel, Director of Castrum in Spain at the above address, or email garcia.marciel@castrum.es or see the websites www.castrum.org; www.castrum.es.

**CPN AZTERLARIAK:** Apartado nùmero 3191, 01002 Vitoria-Gasteiz, Spain (☎945-281794; e-mail azterlaria@euskalnet.net; www.euskalnet.net/azterlariat). C.P.N. Azterlariak, run nature camps in sessions of two weeks during the summer to provide a balanced programme of leisure activities for children and teenagers aged 8-18. The camps take place near Urbion's beautiful mountains.

**Volunteer Monitors** are required to work for two weeks 15th-30th July. To be responsible for the children 24 hours a day; overseeing activities, looking after their personal belongings, planning their outdoor activities. Monitors should be energetic, imaginative patient and sensitive. Being an extrovert is not necessary. Monitors will also be involved in general cleaning/camp maintenance duties. Some knowledge of Spanish is essential and Monitors are required to attend a short training course preceding the camp.

**Cooks (1-2)**. Experience of cooking for large numbers is useful, and applicants will preferably hold a relevant qualification. Cooks must be prepared for outdoor cooking.

For all positions, employees receive full board, accommodation in tents and liability insurance. Monitors are unpaid volunteers: Cooks receive £130-£185 depending on numbers attending.

*Apply* by e-mail, or to the address above.

**ENGLISH EDUCATIONAL SERVICES:** c/ Alcalá 20-2°, 28084 Madrid (☎34-91-531-4783; fax 34-91-531-5298; e-mail movingparts@wanadoo.es).

**English Teachers (80-110)** with recognised EFL qualification such as CELTA or TESOL Trinity College required by recruitment specialists for EFL in Spain. Positions available in various parts of the country including Madrid. Standard length of contact is 9 months; teaching mainly in the evenings from 5pm onwards. Salary depends on the client school the teacher is employed by, as does provision for accommodation. Most client schools will help their teachers find a place to live.

There is also an English-speaking theatre company operating October-June, which has opportunities for candidates with a native speaker's standard of English. EU citizens are preferred. Interviews may be carried out in the UK and Ireland at peak times.

*Applications* should be made to the above address.

**INSTITUTO HEMINGWAY:** Bailen 5, 2 Dcha, 48003 Bilbao, Spain (☎ 94-4167901; fax 94 4165748; e-mail info@institutohemingway.com; www.institutohemingway.com).

**Assistant** to work in a Spanish language school. To work 20 hours per week; duties to include some administration, marketing and helping with tours. Accommodation and pocket money and/or Spanish lessons provided. Period of work to be arranged; minimum period of work 3 months. Applicants should be aged 18-30 and extroverts.
Applications to Jose A. Lopez, Director, at the above address.

**NEW MANGOLD CENTRE:** Marques de Sotelo 5, Pasaje Rex, Valencia E-46002, Spain (☎96-352-77-14 or 96 351-45-56; fax 96-351-45-56; e-mail newmangold@ newmangold.com; www.newmangold.com).
**Teachers**. To teach general English including the technical aspects of the language. 30-34 hours work per week for wages of £550-£750 per month. No accommodation available. Applicants must be university graduates and hold an E.F.L. certificate or similar. They should be dynamic and outgoing. Minimum period of work 9 months, October to June.
*Applications* in May to the above address or come in person.

**RELACIONES CULTURALES INTERNACIONALES:** Callez Ferraz no. 82, Madrid E-28008, Spain (☎91-541-71 03; fax 91-559-11-81; spain@clubrci.es; www. clubrci.es).
**Supervisors, Language Assistants**. Approx. £100 per month. 5-8 hours per day. 5 to 6 days per wk. Should like children and have studied at higher education establishment. Teaching and/or sport orientated applicants preferred. Minimum period of work 1 to 2 months around the year.
**English Language Teachers** for private Spanish colleges and kindergartens. Wages from £130 per month. To teach English and look after children aged from 4 years onwards. Should be qualified teachers, preferably with EFL experience. Minimum period 1 month all year round.
**Au Pairs** to live and help with light household chores in a Spanish family, or take care of children and help teach English. Ages 18-28 years. Placements all over Spain and over the whole year. Full social assistance during the stay is provided by RCI. Summer stays from one to three months, or around the year for 6 to 12 months. No special requirements are necessary. Paying stays are also arranged.
**Counsellors** (80) to supervise and teach English sports on 3 summer camps.
*Applications* to the above address as soon as possible.

# Voluntary Work

**VAUGHANTOWN:** Virgen de Nuria, 11, 28027, Madrid, Spain (☎+34-914 057080; fax 914-048862; www.vaughantown.com). VaughanTown is the brainchild of an established English Language school in Spain, Vaughan Systems. Founded by American Richard Vaughan in 1977, Vaughan Systems is the largest in-company language training firm in Spain, with over 300 teachers providing more than 350,000 hours of language training per year to over 5000 executives and technical personnel in more than 520 national and international companies. In VaughanTown, native English-speaking volunteers spend a free week at a four-star hotel, near the Gredos mountain range in Spain together with a number of Spaniards who have paid for the privilege of speaking English and interacting with them. During the week everyone will be involved in games and group dynamic exercises, amongst many other activities, all to help the Spanish participants practice their language skills. So, if you have the gift of the gab and you are set for an adventure, check out the website where you will find all the necessary information and an application form.
*Applications* via the website; click on 'sign-up'.

**SUNSEED DESERT TECHNOLOGY:** Apdo. 9, E-04270 Sorbas, Almeria, Spain (☎+34-950 525 770; e-mail sunseedspain@arrakis.es; www.sunseed.org. uk). Sunseed Desert Technology aims to develop, demonstrate and communicate accessible, low-tech methods of living sustainably in a semi-arid environment. It is a registered Spanish Association and a project of the registered UK charity The Sunseed Trust.

Short and longer-term volunteers are required year round. Work includes **gardening, dryland management, appropriate technology, cooking including solar cooking, construction, publicity and more**. Longer-term volunteers can carry out their own projects in this field which may be suitable as dissertation projects.

Year round sunshine, beautiful rural location, friendly community and delicious vegetarian food. Volunteers make a weekly contribution of between £49 and £98 (depending on length of stay and hours worked).

*Applicants* see website or contact the project directly for further details.

# Au Pairs, Nannies, Family Helps and Exchanges

**ABB AU-PAIR FAMILY SERVICE:** Via Alemania 2, 5ºA, E-07003 Palma de Mallorca Spain (☎+34-971-752027; fax +34-971-298001; abbaupair@ono. com). Friendly au pair agency with high quality services and carefully chosen host families.

**Au Pairs** required to help families look after children and carry out general housekeeping work. Applicants should have a mature outlook, be responsible and have a love of children. Au pairs normally work 25-30 hours over a 5-6 day week. Placements are available all year, with a minimum stay of 2 months in the summer. Applicants should speak either English or Spanish, English and French or English and German.

Applications accepted all year, and should be sent to Clara Mangin at the above address and please remember to mention your telephone number.

**CENTROS EUROPEOS GALVE SA:** C/Principe 12, 6A 28012 Madrid, Spain (☎+34-91 532 72 30; fax +34-91 521 60 76; e-mail centros-principe@telefonica.net; www.centrosprincipe.com).

This is a small agency with many years of experience, dealing with all types of linguistic programmes. There is supervision in all centres.

**Au Pairs** to work 30 hours per week; pocket money of around €65 (approx. £43) per week. Placements of 2/3 months are possible over the summer, but it is easier to arrange placements of 9/10 months for the whole school year, or for 6 months from January or April.

**Paying Guests** for stays in Madrid, Alicante, Segovia, Salamanca, Valencia, Toledo, Barcelona, Cordoba, Granada, Seville or Santander.

**Exchanges** also arranged between Spanish and British students aged 12-25 for 2-4 weeks.

In addition there are Spanish courses all year round and accommodation for independent or work placement students.

*Applications* to the above address.

# Other Employment in Spain

**SPAINJOY:** Madrid, Spain (☎+34 620 78 29 36; e-mail info@spainjoy.com) Young, motivated people required for a sales job in Madrid that combines travelling with sales of oil paintings all over Spain. Positions available throughout the year, minimum period of work 8 weeks. Hours of work 10am-2pm and 7pm-9pm, 5 and a half days a week. Language skills are not essential although Spanish can be helpful. Accomodation is usually available at the cost of €40 (approx £26) per week. Applications welcome throughout the year.

# Sweden

Unlike its neighbour Norway, Sweden is a fully integrated EU member, and EU and EEA countries are free to enter to look for and take up work. The rate of unemployment in 2006 was 5.9%, and there are strict limits on the number of foreigners allowed to work in Sweden.

The Swedish Public Employment Service cannot help jobseekers from non-EEA countries to find work in Sweden. General information and addresses of local employment offices may be obtained from *Arbetsmarknadsstyrelsen* at Vattugaten 17 45, S-113 99 Stockholm, Sweden (☎46-8-5860 6000; e-mail arbetsmarknadsstyrelsen@ams.amv.se; www.amv.se) which is in English and www.sweden.se). It is up to the individual to get in touch with employers. Long-term vacancies and summer jobs can now be sought by those with a knowledge of the Swedish language on the internet: http://jobb.amv.se.

There are also opportunities for voluntary work in Sweden arranged by International Voluntary Service for British people and Service Civil International for Americans: see the *Worldwide* chapter for details.

Advertisements in Swedish newspapers may be placed through Crane Media Partners Ltd, 20-28 Dalling Road, Hammersmith, London W6 OJB (☎020-8237 8601; fax 020-8735 9941), who handle *Dagens Nyheter, Goteborgs Posten* and *Sydsvenska Dagbladet*.

## RED TAPE

**Visa Requirements:** a visa is no longer required by many countries including all EU/EEA countries, the USA, Canada, New Zealand and Japan. Nationals of these countries are allowed to visit Sweden for up to 3 months. Visa information is available from the embassy website www.swedenabroad.com/London.
**Residence Permits:** Required if you are to live and work in Sweden for more than 3 months. EU citizens can apply for residence permits from within Sweden by contacting the Swedish Migration Board (Migrationsverket), 60170 Norrköping; ☎011-156000; e-mail migrationsverket@migrationsverket.se; www. migrationsverket.se) and completing the application forms. Applicants should note that the procedure of obtaining a Residence Permit can take between 2 and 5 months but that EU citizens are given preference over those from outside the EU.

Non-Europeans must submit to their local Swedish Embassy a written offer of work on form AMS PF 101704, at least two months before their proposed arrival. The procedure involves an interview at the Embassy. Immigration queries should be addressed to Migrationsverket, the Swedish Migration Board (601 70 Norrköping; 11-15 60 00; www.migrationsverket.se). Full details are posted in English on their web pages or you can request printed leaflets.
**Work Permits:** Citizens of EU countries do not need work permits in order to work in Sweden. For others a work permit requires an offer of employment to have been

obtained, application forms for the necessary permit should then be obtained from your nearest Swedish Embassy. The application will be processed by the Swedish Migration Board and the procedure can take 1-3 months. Applications for work permits are not accepted from foreign visitors who are already in Sweden.
**Au Pairs:** Au pairs are subject to the same regulations as all other foreign employees so non-EU nationals must obtain a work permit before leaving their home country. The Scandinavian Institute in Malmö (Box 3085; 040-93 94 40/fax 040-93 93 07; info@scandinavianinst.com) makes au pair placements in Swedish families and throughout Scandinavia.

## Agricultural Work

**CARL-HENRIK NIBBING:** Skillinggrand, 9, S-11120 Stockholm, Sweden, (e-mail segretaria@intercultural.it).
**Farm Assistant**. Wages by arrangement: free travel. Board and lodging provided; helper lives as member of the family. General duties around summer residence/farm in southern Sweden. Age 14-19 years. Applicants should be competent and good natured. Period of work June to August.
*Applications* to C.H. Nibbing.

## Hotel Work and Catering

**PENSIONAT HOLMHALLAR:** S-62010 Burgsvik, Sweden (☎0498-4980-30; fax 0498-498056; holmhallar@brevet.nu; www.holmhaller.se).
**Hotel Workers** (2) to clean rooms and work in the kitchen. Wages £1000 approx. per month. To work 40 hours per week of hotel work between May and September.
*Applications* to Carl Hansen at the above address in February/March.

## Teaching and Language Schools

**THE BRITISH INSTITUTE:** Hagagatan 3, 11348 Stockholm (☎+46 8 341200; fax: +46 8 344192; e-mail corporate@britishinstitute.se; website: www.britishinstitute. se).
**English teachers:** (12) for centres in Stockholm and Göteborg. Applicants must have CELTA or DELTA qualifications and British citizens only. Teachers are employed on either short-term or permanent contracts. Permanent staff get paid an annual salary; termly staff earn less. Deductions of 30%-35% for tax and contributions or made.
No assistance with accommodation is provided. Training is given. A local interview is essential.
*Applications* should go to Principal on above contact information.

# Switzerland

Switzerland has managed to maintain one of the lowest unemployment rates in the world at 3.8% in 2006 and to preserve that state it has traditionally imposed strict work permit requirements on all foreigners who want to work there. It is significant that unlike most of the other non-EU members of Western Europe, Switzerland did not join the EEA a few years ago, although there are long-term plans for it to do so. However, a bilateral treaty on free movement of persons was concluded with the EU and the main obstacles to free movement of labour were removed in

2004. In the same year the seasonal worker category of permit was abolished. As a result,EU job-seekers are able to enter Switzerland to look for work for up to three months.Permits are extendable for a potential period of up to five years, depending on the contract. Information on this can be found on-line at www.europa.admin.ch or www.auslaender.ch.

Switzerland has always needed extra seasonal workers at certain times of the year. The tourist industry in particular needs staff for both the summer and winter seasons (July to September and December to April). Jobs in the tourist industry are described both in this chapter and the Worldwide chapter at the beginning of the book (for example see entry for Village Camps). Students looking for hotel work should note the entry below for the *Schweizer Hotelier Verein* (Swiss Hotels' Association). Hotel work can be hard going: in the past some workers have found they have been expected to work longer hours than originally promised without any compensation in the form of overtime payments or extra time off, or be asked to do jobs other than those specified in their contracts. In return, however, wages should be higher than average for hotel work in the rest of Europe.

Farmers also need extra help at certain times of the year: see the entry below for the Landdienst-Zentralstelle, which can arrange working stays on Swiss farms. Opportunities in the short but lucrative grape harvest in October (particularly in the Lausanne area) are also worth seeking out although this takes place usually in October rather than summer. Some knowledge of German or French is normally needed, even for grape-picking. Italian is also spoken, particularly in the canton of Ticino.

Placing an advertisement in a Swiss paper may lead to the offer of a job. Tribune de Geneve is published at 11 rue des Rois, CH-1211 Geneva (www.tdg.ch – go through Google to translate the site into English).

There are opportunities for voluntary work in Switzerland with the organisations named at the end of this chapter and British applicants can also apply through Concordia and International Voluntary Service, and Americans through Service Civil International; see the *Worldwide* chapter for details.

# RED TAPE

**Visa Requirements:** citizens of the United Kingdom, the United States, Canada, Australia, New Zealand and most other European countries do not normally require visas for tourism. Nationals of most other countries need a visa.

**Residence/Work Permits:** Seasonal Workers who are EU nationals, are issued with an L-EU permit (*Kurzaufenhalter/autorisation de courte durée*), issued for 4, 6, or the maximum of 12 months.

For non-EU citizens the situation is now trickier as employers in Switzerland have to deal with sponsorship paperwork on their behalf and try harder to prove to the authorities that they need to employ a foreigner from outside Europe. An L permit has to applied for by the employer in Switzerland and has be issued in advance to the employee by the Swiss embassy in the employee's own country.

The L permits cover both the right of abode and employment. These are required for all persons entering to take up employment and entitle the holder to live in a specific canton and work for a specified employer. They also entitle the worker to join the state insurance scheme and enjoy the services of the legal tribunal for foreign workers, should they require an arbitrator in a dispute with their employer. Accident insurance is compulsory and is largely paid by the employer. This does not obviate the need of the temporary foreign employee to take out their own health insurance policy.

Perks of having a Swiss L permit include discounts on public transport and discounted lift passes in mountain resorts.
**Au Pairs** also require a work permit as above.
**Voluntary Work:** a work permit is required as above.

# Agricultural Work

**LANDDIENST-ZENTRALSTELLE:** Postfach 728, CH-8025 Zurich, Switzerland (☎1-261-44-88; fax 1-261-44-32; e-mail admin@landdienst.ch; www.landdienst. ch). Landdienst is a non-profit making, publicly subsidised organisation which each year places around 3,000 Swiss and 500 foreign farmers assistants.
**Farmers' Assistants** to work on family farms. Wages £200 per month plus free board and lodging. To work 8 hours per day, 6 days per week. Minimum period of work 3 weeks between the spring and autumn; maximum period is two months. Knowledge of German and/or French essential. Individual applicants should be aged 18-25.

Danish applicants should contact EXIS, Postboks 291, DK-6400 Sonderborg; Dutch applicants through Travel Active Programmes, Postbus 107, NL-5800 AC Venray; Portuguese applicants through International Friendship League, R. Ruy de Sausa Vinagre 2, P-2890 Alcochete. A six-week group stay for applicants from Eastern Europe will also be arranged from mid-August to late September: contact the above address for contact addresses in Poland, the Czech Republic, Slovakia and the Baltic States.

*Applications* are invited at least 4 weeks prior to desired starting date. Individual applicants must be nationals of a country in western Europe and pay a registration fee.

# Hotel Work and Catering

**CHALET-HOTEL ADLER:** Fam.A & E Fetzer, CH-3718 Kandersteg, Switzerland (☎033-675 8010; fax 033-675 8011; e-mail info@chalethotel.ch; www.chalethotel. ch). This hotel is set in the mountains of Switzerland, with rail access allowing excursions across the country.
**Barmaids, Chambermaids, Waitresses** to work from 8½ hours, 5 days a week. Net salary approx. £690 per month. Minimum period of work 2½ months from May/June to September/October. Accommodation provided. Knowledge of German required.

*Applications*, with a photo, from April to the above address.

**HOTEL ALPENBLICK:** Oberdorf, CH-3812 Wilderswil, Switzerland (☎+33-828 3550; fax +33-828 3551). The hotel is situated in the Ferienort Wilderswil near the Jungfrau. It has an excellent reputation for the high standard of its cooking, and a friendly, co-operative and cosy atmosphere.
**Cook** to prepare meals for the à la Carte restaurant and also prepare the menu and meals for half-board hotel guests. Good cooking abilities, and the ability to cope with the stresses of a busy restaurant are prerequisites.
**Waiting Staff** to serve breakfast, evening meals and light afternoon snacks. Applicants should have a sound knowledge of German, experience of waiting on tables and a well-groomed appearance.
**Housekeeper** to clean the hotel and restaurant and to look after children; the applicant should have a love of order and a way with children.

All posts pay £940 gross per month, for 45-48 hours per week; board costs c.£190 and lodging c.£90 per month. Period of work is from early June to mid September, with the minimum period of work being 2-3 months. All staff should speak German.

*Applications* are accepted from October onwards, addressed to Richard Stöckli at the above address.

**HOTEL BAHNHOF:** Bahnhofstrasse 46, CH-8200 Schaffhausen, Switzerland (☎52-630 35 35; fax 52-630 35 36; mail@hotelbahnhof.ch; www.hotelbahnhof.ch).
**Hotel Staff (2)** for housekeeping and work in the dining room. Wages up to £1,500 per month. 8 hours per day, 5 days per week. Knowledge of German required. Minimum period of work 4 months between 1 June and 30 September.
*Applications* from the spring to Arnold P Graf at the above address.

**HOTEL BELLEVUE:** CH-3901 Simplon-Pass, Switzerland (☎027-979 1331; fax 027-979 1239).
**Secretary** to work on reception desk and take care of all correspondence. Knowledge of German, French and Italian essential. Good secretarial and hotel experience required.
**Chambermaid**. Knowledge of German, French and Italian an advantage.
**Waiters/Waitresses (4)**. Must have experience in similar work. Knowledge of some German, French and Italian required. Suit trainee wishing to widen experience.
Wages on application. Free board and accommodation provided. Minimum age 18 years. Minimum period of work 2 months during the summer season.
*Applications* from January to the above address.

**BEST WESTERN HOTEL BERNINA SAMEDAN:** CH-7503 Samedan, St Moritz, Switzerland (☎081-852 12 12; fax 081-852 36 06; e-mail hotel-bernina@bluewin.ch; www.hotel-bernina.ch).
The Hotel Bernina is a traditional hotel for holiday-makers (in the summer outdoor activities such as hiking, biking and mountain climbing are available) with 100 beds, an à la carteItalian restaurant, bar, park, tennis courts and sun-terrace.
**Porters, Waiters/Waitresses (3)** with experience in hotel/restaurant work. Wages about £1,400 per month. To work 42 hours per day, 5 days per week. Minimum period of work is three months between June and October. Board and accommodation are available at a cost of £250 per month. Must have previous experience and knowledge of German and Italian.
*Applications* to Giuseppe Lagrotta at the above address before May.

**HOTEL CASA BERNO:** CH-6612, Ascona, Switzerland (☎091-791-3232; hotel@ casaberno.ch; www.casaberno.ch). This four star hotel is situated above Ascona, with magnificent panoramic views.
**Kitchen/Office Staff. (2)** No special qualifications nor languages necessary.
**Laundry Staff** for light work/ironing. No special qualifications necessary, nor languages.
For both positions, the minimum period of work is 2 months between 15th March and 31st October. Board and accommodation available for approx. £310 per month. Wages are approx. £1,100 per month.
*Apply* to Pierre Goetschi, the Director, at the above address.

**HOTEL CLUB:** 71 rue du Parc, CH-2300 la Chaux-de-Fonds, Switzerland (☎041-32 914 15 16; fax 041-32 914 15 17).
**Bar Assistant** to serve drinks and attend to customers; training will be given.
**Trainee Receptionist** to welcome clients, take reservations, operate the telephone switchboard and computer, run the front office, and help serve breakfasts when things are quiet.

**Breakfast Assistant** to prepare a buffet breakfast, serve tea and coffee and generally clean up.
**Chambermaids** for general cleaning duties in all parts of the hotel, work in the laundry and to perform general errands. Wages approx. £920 per month. To work a 42 hour, 5 day week; working hours will vary according to need. Board and lodging available for around £100 per month. Period of work by arrangement between July and August and December and January. Applicants who can speak French are preferred; knowledge of Swiss-German, German, French, English and/or Italian would be advantages. The hotels' clients tend to be businessmen so efficiency of service is of importance.

*Applications* to Madame J. Koegler, Director, at the above address at any time; due to large number of applications only candidates who might be hired will receive replies.

**CONTINENTAL PARKHOTEL:** Via Basilea 28, CH-6900 Lugano, Switzerland (☎91-966-11-12; fax 91-966-12-13). This holiday hotel set in a sub-tropical park, overlooks Lake Lugano and the mountains.
**Waitress** £700 net or more, depending on previous experience, per month. 45 hour, 5 day week. Free board and accommodation provided. Season from 1 April to 30 October. Knowledge of German or experience of hotel work necessary to get a working permit (citizens of EU only).

*Applications* to E. Fassbind at the above address.

**HOTEL CRISTALLO:** Poststrasse, CH-7050 Arosa, Switzerland (☎081-377 2261; fax 081-377 4140; cristalloarosa@swissonline.ch; www.cristalloarosa.ch).
**Waiter/Waitress (1-2).** £1,500 per month. Must have previous experience. Staff work about 9 hours per day, 5 days per week. Board and accommodation provided at £300 per month, deducted from gross salary. Knowledge of German essential. Minimum period of work 12 weeks between the middle of June and the end of September.

*Applications* to the above address in March and April.

**HOTEL FORNI:** Marzio Forni, CH-6780 Airolo, Switzerland (☎91-869 12 70; fax 91-869 15 23; e-mail INFO@forni.ch).
**Kitchen Staff and Waitress** to serve in the bar and restaurant. Must be presentable. Approximately £1,100 per month. To work 9 hours per day, 5 days per week. Board and accommodation available for £340 per month.

*Applications* to the above address.

**BERGHAUS GFELALP:** CH-3718 Kandersteg, Switzerland (☎+41-33-6751161). This hotel is situated in Kandersteg, an area of outstanding beauty, and renowned for its hiking possibilities.
**Waiting and Chamber Staff:** required between 15th July and 15th September, to work 45 hours per week over 5-6 days. The posts are available as either 2 female or 2 male jobsharers, or one male/female working full-time. Job sharing would mean both employees working at weekends with one free during the week to travel or go sightseeing. Wages are £405 approx. per month and free accommodation is provided. Employees must be able to speak German.

To *apply* write to Kathrin Fankhauser or Fam Schärer at the above address.

**GRAND HOTEL BELLEVUE:** CH-3789 Gstaad, Switzerland (☎033-748 31 71; fax 033-724 21 36; info@Bellevue-gstaad.ch; www.Bellevue-gstaad.ch).
**Waiting Assistants** (2). Wage approx. £900 per month. To work 42 hours per week,

with board and lodging available for around £285 per month. Period of work by arrangement between Christmas/New Year and July/August. Applicants should speak German, English and French.

*Applications* to Mr Ferdinand D. Salverda, General Manager, at the above address.

**THE HIKING SHEEP AUBERGERIE:** Villa La Joux, CH-1854 Leysin, Switzerland (☎/fax +41(0)24-494 3535; e-mail info@hikingsheep.com; www.hikingsheep. com). A guesthouse in the Swiss French Alps nestled beside forest and snow-capped mountains, looking towards the Trient Glacier and the Mont Blanc massif.
**General Staff** required to assist in the running of the guest house. Should speak basic French and English; speaking German would be an asset. Applicants must be outgoing, friendly, flexible and trustworthy. To work 4-5 hours a day 7 days per week, all year round; minimum period of work 1 month. Board and lodging can be provided but iare not guaranteed.

*Applications* may be made by e-mail or fax at any time of year to Paul-Henri at the above address.

**HOTEL HIRSCHEN:** Passhöhe, CH-9658 Wildhaus, Switzerland (e-mail info@ hirschen-wildhaus.ch; www.hirschen-wildhaus.ch).
**Counter Assistants/Waiting Staff (1/2)** to serve hotel guests at mealtimes, present buffets, wash glasses, prepare coffee, breakfast etc. Wages approx. £1,100 per month. 9-9½ hours work per day, 5 days per week. Board and lodging provided. Minimum period of work 3 months between June and October. Knowledge of German and previous experience of hotel work essential.

*Applications* to S. Walt at the above address from February.

**JOBS IN THE ALPS (EMPLOYMENT AGENCY):** 17 High Street, Gretton, Northants NN17 3DE (e-mail info@jobs-in-the-alps.co.uk; www.jobs-in-the-alps.co.uk).
**Waiting Staff, Porters, Kitchen Porters and Housekeepers** (200 in the winter, **150** in summer) for Swiss and French hotels, cafes and restaurants at mountain resorts. Wages of circa £500 per month for a 5-day week with free board and accommodation. Good French and/or German required for most positions. Experience is not essential, but a good attitude to work and sense of fun are definite requirements. Periods of work: June to mid-September (minimum period three months including July and August), or December to April.

*Applications* should be sent by 30th April for Summer and 30th September for winter.

**HOTEL JUNGFRAUBLICK UND BEAUREGARD:** Haupstrasse, CH-3803 Beatenberg, Switzerland (☎41-33 841 15 81; fax 41-33 841 20 03; e-mail mail@ casagrande-beo.ch).
**Waiting Staff.** Wages £825 per month, approximately. To work 8½ hours per day, 5 days per week. Board and lodging available for £270 per month. Period of work at least 4 months from June to October or November. Knowledge of German required. Applicants should be reliable workers who can take pleasure in their work.

*Applications* to Herr Heinrich at the above address.

**HOTEL LANDHAUS:** CH-7265 Davos Laret, Switzerland (hublis.landhaus@ bluewin.ch; www.hublis.ch).
**Waitress** for general dining room duties. £500-£600 per month. Preferably with previous experience and some knowledge of French and German.

**Stillroom Maid** for general and buffet duties. £150-£180 per month. Some knowledge of French and/or German an advantage.

8½ hours per day, at least 5 days per week. At the height of the season a 7 day week may be worked. Free board and accommodation. All applicants must be available for the whole of the period 1 July to mid September and be over 18 years old.

*Applications* with recent photograph and an international reply couponfrom April to the above address.

**HOTEL MEIERHOF:** CH-7260 Davos-Dorf, Switzerland (☎41-81 416 82 85; fax 41-81 416 39 82; e-mail info@meierhof.ch or kathrin.frey@meierhof.ch; www. meierhof.ch). Traditional and charming mountain resort-hotel with 80 rooms, set in the heart of the village next to all the attractive sport and leisure facilities of Davos. **Waiter/Waitress** £900 per month, for a 44 hour week, 9 hours per day. Board and accommodation provided. Knowledge of German essential. Must be able to start work on the 15 June.

Applications in March and April to Mrs Kathrin Frey, at the above address or e-mail.

**HOTEL MEISSER:** CH-7545 Guarda, Switzerland (☎81-862-21-52; fax 81-862-24-80; e-mail info@hotel-meisser.ch; www.hotel-meisser.ch). A medium-sized hotel, 2½ hours from Zurich, led by a young dynamic team.
**Service Workers (1-2)** Wage about £775 per month. Should have relevant experience.
**General Workers (1-2)** Wage around £775 per month.

Both positions involve 8-9 hours work a day, 5 days per week. To work from 15 June to 31 August or as contracted. Board and accommodation are available, the cost to be deducted from wages. Ability to speak German and English is important; knowledge of German, French or Italian would also be useful.

*Applications* are invited to Benno Meisser at the above address from January onwards.

**HOTEL MOND:** Dorfstrasse 1, CH-6375 Beckenried, Switzerland (☎+41-620 1204; fax +41-620 4618; e-mail info@hotel-mond.ch; www.hotel-mond.ch). The 'Mond' hotel was built in 1870. Since then it has been owned and run by the same family. The hotel has 60 beds, 2 restaurants and a bar and is located at Beckenreid, on the edge of Lake Lucerne.
**Buffet Assistants** to serve drinks.
**Waiting Staff** to serve in a la carte restaurant.

Wages approximately £1,300 per month gross. To work 8-9 hours per day, 5 days per week. Period of work from the beginning of June to the end of September: minimum period of work 2 months. Applicants must speak German.

*Applications* to Monica Amstad at the above address before the end of January.

**MOTEL-RESTAURANT MON ABRI:** Seestrasse 580, 3658 Merligen, Switzerland (☎033-2511380; fax 033-2513671; info@mon-abri.ch; www.mon-abri.ch).
**Temporary Waiting Assistant** to work in a good standard *à la carte* restaurant. Wage according to turnover, with a minimum of £950 per month. To work 8 hours per day, 5 days per week. To work shifts either from 7am-3.30pm or from 3.30pm-midnight, each with a 30 minute meal break. Accommodation available for approx. £130 per month. Minimum period of work three months. Applicants should be friendly and speak English and German; knowledge of French would be an advantage.

*Applications* to Fam. C. Rijke-Wyler at the above address in April and May.

**MOTOTEL POSTILLON:** CH-6374 Buochs, Switzerland (☎+41 620 54 54; fax +41 620 23 34; info@postillon.ch; www.postillon.ch).
**Waiting Staff** to work in a busy restaurant on a motorway. Approximately £940 per month. To work 8½-10½ hours per day, 5 days per week. Board and accommodation available for £95-£115 per month approx. Knowledge of German and English is necessary.
*Applications* to Rene Ulrich, Director, at the above address.

**PARKHOTEL BAD RAGAZ:** CH-7310 Bad Ragaz, Switzerland (☎081-302 22 44; fax 081-302 64 39).
**Waiting Staff (2), General Assistants (2).** Wages by arrangement. 42 hours per 5 day week. Minimum period of work 5 months between April and October. Board and accommodation available for around £200 per month. Applicants should speak German and have some previous experience.
*Applications* to the Manager at the above address as soon as possible.

**PARK HOTEL WALDHAUS:** CH-7018 Flims-Waldhaus, Switzerland (☎+41-81-928 4848; fax 81-928 4858; e-mail info@parkhotel-waldhaus.ch; www.park-hotels-waldhaus.ch). The Park Hotel Waldhaus have 140 rooms and 20 junior suites and apartments.
**Assistant Waiters/Waitresses:** must have previous experience of serving and speak German and French or Italian. Net wages approximately £900 per month, with board and lodging provided for approx. £300 per month.
*Applications*, with a photograph, should be sent to the above address from February; *only applicants from EEA countries will get work permits for Switzerland.*

**RESIDENCE AND BERNERHOF HOTELS:** CH-3823 Wengen, Switzerland (☎+41-33 855 27 21; fax +41 33 855 33 58; e-mail bernerhof@wengen.com; www.wengen.com/hotel/bernerhof).
**Waiters/Waitresses, Buffet Assistants, Laundry Maids, General Assistants.** Monthly salary payment. Staff work 9 hours per day, 5 days per week. Accommodation (30) days. Meals: lunch/dinner (no breakfast) for 22 days. 2 hotel restaurants; à-la-carte, and pizzeria. Guests almost always English, German, US, and Swiss. In the centre of Wengen. Period of work from December to April, and June to October. Knowledge of German required; knowledge of French an advantage.
*Applications* to Rudolph Schweizer at the above address.

**RESTAURANT BLAUES ROSSLI:** CH-3668 Utzigen, Switzerland (☎+41- (0)31 839 2438; fax (0)31 839 9036; e-mail blaues.roessli@bluewin.ch; www.motel.ch).
**General Assistants (2),** preferably female to help clean rooms, serve in the restaurant and help at the counter coffee bar, wash dishes, help with the laundry. To work 5 days per week. Salary approximately £400, net, per month. Board and accommodation provided free of charge. Minimum period of work 8 weeks, although preference will be given to those who can work for the whole season, April to October. Knowledge of German preferable.
*Applications* to Mrs Kilchör at the above address at any time.

**HOTEL RIGIBLICK AM SEE:** Seeplatz 3, CH-6374 Buochs, Switzerland (☎41-41-624 4850; fax 41-41-620 6874; e-mail info@rigiblickamsee.ch; www.rigiblickamsee.ch). A 4-star hotel and restaurant on the lakeside.
**Trainee Assistant (Waiter/Waitress), Trainee Chef** to work 44 hours, 5 days a week. Wages approx. €1800 (£1,260) per month. Period of work May/June-August/

September. Board and accommodation provided for €600 (£420) per month. *Applicants must hold an EU passport* and have a very good knowledge of German. *Applications* as soon as possible to the above address.

**ROMANTIK HOTEL SÄNTIS:** CH-9050 Appenzell, Switzerland (☎0041-71 788 11 11; fax 0041-71 788 11 10; e-mail info@saentis-appenzell.ch; www.saentis-appenzell.ch). A traditional family-run 4-star hotel in one of the most beautiful areas of Switzerland; Appenzell is in the German-speaking region. The staff are mostly young people of various nationalities.
**Waiter/Waitress,** gross salary approx. SFr 3000 (approx £1310) per month. To work 9 hours per day, 5 days per week. Board, accommodation available for SFr 540 (approx £235) per month. Minimum period of work is 4 months between June and October. Applicants must have experience and speak German. Temporary residence permits are only available for EU/EFTA nationals.
*Applications* to Stefan A. Heeb at the above address.

**ROMANTIK HOTEL SCHWEIZERHOF:** CH-3818 Grindelwald, Switzerland (☎+41 33 854 5858; fax +41 33 854 58 59); e-mail info@hotel-schweizerhof.com). The Schweizerhof, a truly traditional hotel in Grindelwald, world famous holiday and winter sports centre at the foot of the Eiger in the Bernese Oberland.
**Chambermaids (4-5)** to clean rooms and do laundry.
**Maintenance Assistants (3)** to carry out general maintenance tasks on house and in garden.
**Assistant Cooks (2)** to assist in the kitchen with preparation and washing-up.
**Laundry Assistants (2)**
Wages about £1,400 per month. To work a 42-hour 5-day week. Period of work is from 1 June to 15 October. Board and accommodation is available at a cost to be arranged. Knowledge of German is required.
*Applications* to the above address between January and March at the latest.

**SCHWEIZER HOTELIER-VEREIN:** Monbijoustrasse 130, Postfach, CH-3001 Bern, Switzerland (☎41-31-370-43-33; e-mail hoteljob.be@swisshotels.ch; www. hoteljob.ch). The 'Swiss Hotel Association' has around 2500 hotels and restaurants as members.
**General Assistants** from EU and EFTA countries to work in hotels in German-speaking Switzerland. Wages approximately £1,100 per month. Duties include helping with cooking, service and cleaning. Wages by arrangement. Period of work 3-4 months between June and September.
Board and accommodation available at a cost of approximately £325 per month. Good knowledge of German essential. Please note that jobs in the French and Italian speaking parts of Switzerland can not be arranged. Applicants must possess valid passports etc.
*Applications* to the above address.

**SEEHOTEL WILERBAD:** CH-6062 Wilen am Sarnersee, Switzerland (☎041-662 70 70; fax 041-662 70 80; e-mail wilerbad@tic.ch; www.wilerbad.ch).
**Waiters/Waitresses (1-2)** for lido and terrace restaurant. Must speak fluent German. Wages of around £450 per month. All staff to work 8½ hours per day, 5 days a week. Board available at approx. £110 per month; accommodation in a double room costs approx. £58 per month. Minimum period of work 3 months.
*Applications* in the autumn to Herr Bruno Odermatt, Director, at the above address.

**HOTEL SONNE:** CH-9658 Wildhaus, Switzerland (e-mail beutler-hotels@bluewin.
ch; www.beutler.hotels.ch).
**Waiters/Waitresses (3).** £700, net, per month. Good knowledge of German
required.
**Buffet Staff (2).** £600, net, per month. Good knowledge of German required.
   Staff work 8½ hours per day, 5 days a week. Board and accommodation available
at £216 per month. Minimum period of work 10 weeks. Winter season December to
March and Summer season July to October.
   *Applications* as soon as possible to the proprietor, Paul Beutler, at the above
address.

**TRUMMELBACH FALLS:** Gletscherwasser-Fälle, CH-3822, Lauterbrunnen,
Switzerland.
**Restaurant Assistant** to work in the self-service restaurant at the entrance to the falls.
The position calls for an all-rounder as duties include assisting behind the counter,
operating the cash register, clearing tables and cleaning.
**Elevator Operator/Restaurant Assistant** to operate a funicular lift inside a mountain,
taking people to see the waterfalls. Time to be divided between operating the lift 2-3
days per week and working in the restaurant.
Wages of £800-£900 per month for working a 5 day week. To work approximately
8-10 hours a day with a half hour lunch break. Applicants must speak fluent English
and some basic German; knowledge of French would be an advantage. Must hold an
EU passport and be aged at least 22.
   *Applicants should send* a full CV and a passport photo to Herr Urs von Almen at
the above address by January.

**HOTEL WALDHAUS:** CH-7514 Sils-Maria, Engadin, Switzerland (☎081-838
5100; fax 081-838 5198; e-mail staff@waldhaus-sils.ch; www.waldhaus-sils.ch). A
five-star family hotel with up to 70% regular guests from all over the world.
**General Assistants (2)** to play an extensive role in service for the guest-rooms, lounge
and terraces, and to see to the welfare of 220 guests as well as taking responsibility for
their meals, under the direction of a superior. Wages £715-£858 per month. Must have
knowledge of German, and the ability to take pleasure in working for guests.
   To work 8-9 hours per day, 5 days per week. Minimum period of work is 3-4
months in the summer or winter seasons. Food and accommodation are available at
the following prices; a double-room costs about £70 per person per month.
   *Applications* are invited up until mid-March for the summer season, or mid-
August for the winter, and should be sent to Irene Ryser, Personnel Manager, at the
above address.

**HOTEL ZUM WEISSEN ROSSLI:** CH-6487 Goschenen, Switzerland (☎+41-886
80 10; fax 886 80 30).
**Waiting Assistants, Buffet Assistants, Chambermaids**. Wages and hours of work by
arrangement. Board and lodging provided. Period of work by arrangement, minimum
contract of 6 months. Good knowledge of German required.
   *Applications* to the above address 8 weeks before the desired beginning of work.

# Sports, Couriers and Camping

**CANVAS HOLIDAYS:** GVN Camping Recruitment, East Port House, Dunfermline,
KY12 7JG (☎01383-629012; fax 01383-629071; e-mail campingrecruitment@
gvnrecruitment.com; www.gvnrecruitment.com). Canvas Holidays provide luxury

mobile home and tent holidays at over 100 campsites.throughout Europe.
**Campsite Courier.** Involves cleaning accommodation, welcoming families to the site and showing them to their accommodation. Visiting customers, providing local information and basic maintenance are very important parts of the job. Campsite Courier Opportunities are also available for couples to work on site together. For details of management positions, see website.

Package includes competitive salary, tent accommodation, medical insurance, uniform and return travel from a UK port of entry. Full season positions start in March, April or May and end in September/October. High season staff needed to work at least two months during the peak season.

*Please call* the Recruitment Department for more information and an application form, or *apply online* at www.gvnrecruitment.com.

**EUROCAMP:** Overseas Recruitment Department (Ref SJ/07) (☎01606-787525). Eurocamp is a leading tour operator in quality self-drive camping and mobile home holidays in Europe. Each year the company seeks to recruit up to 1,500 enthusiastic people for the following positions:

**Campsite Courier:** job involves cleaning and preparing customer accommodation, providing assistance, acting as an information service and performing some administrative duties. Couriers need to be flexible to meet the needs of the customer to provide them with excellent service. Minimum age 18 years. Applicants should be independent with plenty of initiative and relish a challenging and rewarding position. They should also possess a friendly and helpful personality. Previous customer service experience would be an advantage. Applicants should be available to work from April/May to September.

**Children's Courier:** work involves organising a wide range of exciting activities for children aged 4-13. Applicants should possess initiative, imagination and enthusiasm along with good safety awareness. Previous childcare experience is essential. Minimum age is 18 years and applicants should be available from April/May to September. Languages are not a requirement but would be an advantage (in particular German). Successful candidates will be asked to apply for an Enhanced Disclosure.

**Senior Couriers:** required to work alongside a team of Campsite Couriers and organise their daily workload, as well as carrying out the normal day-to-day duties of a Campsite Courier. Applicants should have good language skills and experience of leading a team.

**Site Managers:** required to lead a large team of Campsite Couriers, organising their daily workloads and ensuring they provide the very best customer service. Applicants should be 21 or over, have proven managerial experience, excellent communication skills and language ability.

**Montage/Demontage:** for a period of approximately 6-8 weeks at the beginning/end of season to erect/dismantle equipment.

Comprehensive training is provided together with a competitive salary, insurance, return travel and accommodation. Applications are accepted from September/October and *can only be accepted from UK/EU passport holders*. Interviews will be conducted in Hartford, Cheshire between October and April.

*Applicants should apply online* at **www.holidaybreakjobs.com** or telephone 01606-787525 for an Application Pack.

**SWISS TRAVEL SERVICE:** Tabley Court, Victoria Street, Altrincham, Cheshire, WA14 1EZ (www.swisstravel.co.uk).
Swiss Travel Services is a UK market leader for holidays to Switzerland with over 50 years of experience. Posts are available both in summer and in winter.

**Resort Reps (22)** required to meet and greet clients, liaise with suppliers and sell tickets for excursions. Ability to speak German, Italian or French would be advantageous.

During the summer season the minimum period of work is 4 months between 1$^{st}$ April and 30$^{th}$ September; generally working from 8:30am to 7:30pm, 6 or 7 days a week. Board, accommodation and a competitive wage are provided.

Applicants should be at least 21 years old, have good client handling skills and experience of dealing with a wide selection of the public.

*Applications* can be made through the above website and are invited from EU nationals or those who have a visa to work in Switzerland.

**VENTURE ABROAD:** Rayburn House, Parcel Terrace, Derby, DE1 1LY (☎01332-342 050; 01332-22-49-60; e-mail joannek@rayburntours.co.uk; www.ventureabroad. co.uk). Venture Abroad organise package holidays for scout and guide groups to the continent. They arrange travel and accommodation and provide representatives in the resort.

**Resort Representatives (2-3)** to work in Belgium and Switzerland; checking in groups, dealing with accommodation enquiries, organising and accompanying local excursions etc.

Applicants should be practical, resourceful and calm under pressure. Speaking German an advantage. To work six days a week, flexible hours. Five weeks minimum work from June to August.

*Applications* to the above address.

# Work with Children

**THE HAUT LAC INTERNATIONAL CENTRE:** CH-1669 Les Sciernes, Switzerland (☎+41-26-928 4200; fax +41-26-928 4201; e-mail stevie@haut-lac. ch; www.haut-lac.com). The Haut Lac Centre is a family-run business organising language and activity courses for an international clientele. A high client return rate is due to the Centre's work and play philosophy.

**Language Teachers; French (4), English (4), German (1)** to take four 40-minute classes (Monday, Tuesday, Thursday, Friday) and one 40 min. study per day, supervise one test per week and have two days off per week. Candidates should have a degree and a TEFL qualification or equivalent, or be studying for a Language or Teaching degree.

**Sports Activity Monitors (6)** to organise and run a wide variety of sports and excursions. One day off per week.

**Maintenance Person** to carry out garden upkeep, decorating tasks and repair work, should have previous experience.

**House Staff** for Cleaning Work.

Wages for all positions are from £120 per week according to qualifications and experience. Board and accommodation are included as is laundry. Staff work 45-54 hours per 5-6 day week. Period of work mid-June until mid-August, with a minimum requirement of 4 weeks work.

Applicants should speak English, French or German, and *applications* are invited at any time to the above address.

**VILLAGE CAMPS INC:** Recruitment Office, Dept 808 14 Rue de la Morâche, 1260 Nyon, Switzerland. (☎+41 22 990 9405; fax +41 22 990 9494; e-mail personnel@ villagecamps.ch; www.villagecamps.com). Village Camps has been organising educational and activity camps for children from all over the globe for over 25 years with a serious commitment to client and staff alike. Offering opportunities for outdoor education and specialist instructors at the spring and fall residential camps across Europe. Domestic and kitchen assistants are required during the winter season in Switzerland. Nurses, receptionists, French/ TEFL/German teachers, chefs, house counsellors, domestic and kitchen assistants are also required for Village Camps summer programmes. Contract periods vary from 3 to 8 weeks between May and October.

The Outdoor Education Programme occurs from May to June in Switzerland and France and in the Autumn, August to October in Switzerland. The Summer Residential and Day Camps occur from June to August in Switzerland, UK, Holland, France and Austria. Room and board, accident & liability insurance and a generous allowance are provided, allowances are paid in local currency.

Applicants must be a minimum of 21 years of age to apply (over 18 years for domestic/kitchen staff and house counselors) and have relevant experience and/or qualifications. A second language is desirable. A valid first aid and CPR certificate is required while at camp. Much is expected of staff but the rewards are generous. Motivated staff are required for short seasonal positions.

Recruitment starts in December and ends in August. There is no deadline to submit applications but positions are limited. Interviews are by telephone. Please specify department 808 on application.

For more information on dates, locations and positions available and to download an application form, visit the website or *contact* organisation at above address.

# Voluntary Work and Archaeology

**GRUPPO VOLUNTARI DALLA SVIZZERA ITALIANA:** CP 12, CH-6517 Arbedo, Switzerland (☎079-3540161 (NATEL) 091-8574520 (office); fax 071-6829272; e-mail Fmari@vtx.ch; www.gvsi.org).
Volunteers **(15 per camp)** to take part in work camps in Maggia, Fusio and Borgogne **helping mountain communities, cutting wood, help the aged, in the orchards, etc.** 4 hours work per day. Board and accommodation available. Minimum period of work one week between June and September.

*Applicants* should speak Italian, German or French. Minimum age, 18.

*Applications* to the above address. Volunteers must be able to present valid documents and a residence permit.

**INTERNATIONALE BEGEGNUNG IN GEMEINSCHAFTSDIENSTEN eV:** Schlosserstrasse 28, D-70180 Stuttgart 1, Germany (☎0711-6491128; fax 711-6409867; info@ibg-workcamps.org; www.ibg-workcamps.org).
Volunteers to attend international youth workcamps in Switzerland. Typical projects might include **restoring an old castle, environmental protection, children's play schemes and media projects.** Each workcamp consists of a group of about 15 people aged 18-30 from all over the world living and working together for the public benefit.

There is a registration fee of approximately £55; food and accommodation are provided free on the camps. The annual programme is published in March. British volunteers should apply through Concordia or another UK organisation.

*Applications* to the above address.

**INTERNATIONALE UMWELTSCHUTZ STUDENTEN:** IUS-AWSR, Postfach 1, CH-9101 Herisau, Switzerland (tel/fax 071-351 5103).
**International Student Exchange Placements** for voluntary work during the summer.

Volunteers aged between 18 and 28 to help on mountain clearing and conservation projects. The projects last 10-20 days in the Alps around Davos, Zermatt and Engelberg. The work involves **clearing rubbish from ski slopes and footpath networks and repairing footpaths.** Volunteers receive pocket money of £2 per day and accommodation is offered in tourist camps offering traditional Swiss food.

Volunteers must meet their own travel costs, and obtain health, accident and third-party insurance before arriving. A registration fee is also required and details of that are in the application form. In addition to being in good physical condition applicants should be surefooted with some mountain experience. The nature of the work is such that applicants must be German speakers, willing to participate in camp life and over 18.

Further details and an *application form* are available from IUS at the above address.

**MOUNTAIN FOREST PROJECT: STIFTUNG BERGWALDPROJEKT:** Hauptstrasse 24, CH-7014 Trin, Switzerland (+41 81-630-4145; fax +41-81-630-4147; e-mail info@bergwaldprojekt.ch; www.bergwaldprojekt.ch). An organisation of workcamps for volunteers from 18 to 80, working in the mountain forests of Switzerland, Austria and Germany.

Volunteers: 15-20 places per week available in over 60 camps per year. **Work involves reforestation and forest maintenance, building footpaths for access and fences.** No experience is necessary. Camps run from April to October. Volunteers may stay for one week per year. Free board and lodging is provided. Volunteers should have a basic knowledge of German.

Programme details will be available from January and *applications* will be accepted from then onwards. Apply online if possible.

# Au Pairs, Nannies, Family Helps and Exchanges

**PRO FILIA:** 16 Beckenhofstr., Postfach, 8035 Zürich (☎/fax +41 (0)1 361 53 31; info@profilia.ch; www.profilia.ch).
**Au Pairs** can be placed with families in the regions of Switzerland for stays of a minimum of 12 months. A list of branches of Pro Filia around Switzerland can be found on the above website.

For further details *contact* the above address.

**PERFECT WAY:** Hafnerweg 10, 5200 Brugg, Switzerland; (e-mail info@perfectway.ch or perfectway@bluewin.ch; www.perfectway.ch). Au pair, domestic help and nanny agency that offers placements in Swiss, American and other international families in Switzerland.

Applicants should be aged 18-29 (**au pair**) or 18+ (**nanny and domestic help**) and if possible available for at least six months. Good manners, common sense and references required. Sfr. 700 per month approximately, plus other perks.

For further details *contact* the above address.

# Central and Eastern Europe

## Armenia

The chances of finding paid summer work in Armenia are slim. In addition to the entry below, the voluntary organisations in the *Worldwide* chapter may be able to find placements.

**ASSOCIATION FOR EDUCATIONAL, CULTURAL AND WORK INTERNATIONAL EXCHANGE PROGRAMS (AIEP).** 28 Isahakstan St, 3$^{rd}$ floor, Room 19, Yerevan, 375009 Armenia (☎+374 10 58 47 33; fax +374 10 52 92 32; e-mail aiep@arminco.com); www.aiep.am.
   **Internship Training Program Short-term Volunteers** required to work on a science technology training programme and to run an internship programme.

## Belarus

Short-term voluntary work in Belarus can be obtained for UK nationals through the International Voluntary Service, UNA Exchange, Youth Action For Peace and Concordia; US nationals need to contact Service Civil International or CIEE; see their entries in the *Worldwide* chapter for details. The following organisation can also act as an advisory service for those interested in finding voluntary work in Belarus.

**INTERNATIONAL EXCHANGE CENTER:** 20 Kalku Street, 1050 Riga, Latvia (☎ 722 8228; fax 783 0257; info@iec.lv).
English teachers with a TEFL qualification for summer language camps in Russia and Belarus. Between 20 and 40 hours of teaching in return for a salary equivalent to local rates or free board and lodging. Application fee is $150.
   For further information in the UK *contact* the partner organisation, International Youth Exchange Centre, (89 Fleet Street, London EC4Y 1DH; 020-7583 9116; fax 020 7583 9117; www.isecworld.co.uk).

## Croatia

The chances of finding paid summer work in Croatia are not very good although its tourist industry is burgeoning. The following organisation does offer paid employment.

## Sports, Couriers and Camping

**CANVAS HOLIDAYS:** GVN Camping Recruitment, East Port House, Dunfermline, KY12 7JG (☎01383-629012; fax 01383-629071; e-mail campingrecruitment@ gvnrecruitment.com; www.gvnrecruitment.com). Canvas Holidays provide luxury mobile home and tent holidays at over 100 campsites.throughout Europe.
**Campsite Courier.** Involves cleaning accommodation, welcoming families to the site and showing them to their accommodation. Visiting customers, providing local information and basic maintenance are very important parts of the job. Campsite Courier Opportunities are also available for couples to work on site together. For details of management positions, see website.

Package includes competitive salary, tent accommodation, medical insurance, uniform and return travel from a UK port of entry. Full season positions start in March, April or May and end in September/October. High season staff needed to work at least two months during the peak season.

*Please call* the Recruitment Department for more information and an application form, or *apply online* at www.gvnrecruitment.com.

## Voluntary Work

**ECO-CENTRE CAPUT INSULAE-BELI:** Beli 4, 51559 Beli, Island of Cres, Croatia (☎+385-51-840-525; +385-51-840-525; e-mail caput.insulae@ri.htnet.hr; www.caput-insulae.com).
Conservation Volunteers to help with a variety of projects including the **conservation of the Eurasian griffon vulture; cleaning and feeding griffons in the bird sanctuary, repairing dry stone walls, saving small ponds, interpretation centre, picking olives and helping local shepherds.**
Applicants should be healthy, able to swim and speak English. Minimum age 18. To work a minimum of one week between 15th January and 15th December. Volunteers have to pay a volunteer fee, travel expenses to and from Croatia, and food expenses. Accommodation is provided.

*Apply* to the address above.

# The Czech Republic

The chances of finding paid summer work in the Czech Republic and Slovakia are low with the possible exception of TEFL, but voluntary work can be arranged for British people by International Voluntary Service, UNA Exchange, Youth Action For Peace and Concordia; Americans can be placed there by the CIEE and also Service Civil International (see the International Voluntary Service entry). Details of the above organisations can be found in the *Worldwide* chapter.

## RED TAPE

**Visa Requirements:** the Czech Republic became a member of the EU on 1$^{st}$ May 2004. EU Citizens are entitled to stay in the Czech republic on a temporary or permanent basis without any permit, irrespective of the purpose of the stay. Those unsure about whether they require a visa should check with their nearest Czech consulate. For Non-EU Citizens a Visa for stays over 90 days must be obtained. When applying for a visa, applicants must be able to present a passport valid for at least 15 months (or 9 months for a short-term stay) from the date of issue of the visa, two passport-sized photographs, a document proving the purpose of the stay (e.g. a work permit or a Long Term Residence visa) confirmation of available accommodation, proof of health insurance and proof that they have sufficient funds to cover their living expenses in the country.

**Residence Permits:** A new Residency Law came into force in 2000 making it necessary to apply for a long-stay Czech visa before arrival in the country. EU Citizens can obtain a Permanent Residence Permit by applying to the Alien and Border Police, to gain a PRP applicants will require: an application form completed and signed by the applicant, valid passport, 2 recent passport photographs and a document proving the applicant's compliance with the PRP. Full details are available from the Czech Embassy in your country (in Britain phone 020-7243 1115/fax 020-7243 7988 or in the USA www.czech.cz/washington). Anyone who intends to work or for any other reason stay in the Czech Republic for longer than 90 days must obtain the visa in advance. Necessary documents include a work permit issued by the employer, proof of accommodation, etc. all presented in the original or a notarised copy.

**Work Permits:** Must be obtained by your future employer from the local employment office *(Urad práce)*. They will need a signed form from you plus a photocopy of your passport and the originals or notarised copies of your education certificates. Work Permits will only be granted where the employer can prove that they cannot find a suitable Czech candidates to carry out the job. All of this takes at least three months.

# Teaching and Language Schools

**CALEDONIAN SCHOOL:** Vltavská 24, 15000, Prague 5, Czech Republic (☎ (+420 257 313 650; fax +420 251 512 528); jobs@caledonianschool.com; www.caledonianschool.com.

**Teachers (250)** with TEFL background to teach English in a large Prague language institute.

**KMC:** Karoliny Svetle 31, 110 00 Prague 1, Czech Republic (Tel/fax +420-2222-20347; e-mail kmc@kmc.cz; www.kmc.cz).
Providing assistance with accommodation in youth hostels in the Czech Republic for incoming individuals and groups including package tours with a Prague Card and Go As You Please programmes

**Volunteers (25)** to take part in various work camps lasting approx. two weeks each in the Czech Republic between June and September. Typical projects might involve **gardening, cleaning and renovation work in centres for handicapped children, castles or zoo gardens, or taking part in ecological projects in the mountains.** Board and lodging provided free of charge; to work 6-7 hours per day, Monday-Friday. Applicants should be aged 18-30.

*Applicants* should apply through partner voluntary organisations in their own country: in Britain these are UNA Exchange in Cardiff (☎02920-223088; www.unaexchange.org) and Concordia in Brighton (☎01273-422535; www.concordia-iye.org.uk): in the US contact Volunteers for Peace (☎802-259 2759; www.vfp@vfp.org).

# Hungary

In addition to the opportunities listed below there are also opportunities for voluntary work arranged by Youth Action for Peace, International Voluntary Service and UNA Exchange for UK nationals, and for US nationals through the CIEE and Service Civil International: see the *Worldwide* chapter for details. Although the residence procedure for some foreigners has been much simplified, there is a considerable downside to working full-time in Hungary as EU nationals are subject to the same social security and pension deductions as Hungarians, namely 12.5% of wages. Employers' contributions total nearly 30%. This means employers are handing out fewer long-term contracts, which may increase the opportunities for summer teaching jobs and freelance work.

## RED TAPE

**Visa Requirements:** Hungary joined the EU on 1 May 2004. Citizens of the EU along with nationals of the USA, Australia, New Zealand, Norway and Canada do not require a visa to enter Hungary. Nationals of non-EU countries not listed above, wishing to transit at Hungarian Airports may need an airport transit visa.

**Work Permits**: Non-EU citizens must arrange work permits before leaving their own country. Nationals of some EU countries including Holland will still be required to have a work and residence permit. UK citizens need only register their address and employment details. Further details on the Hungarian Ministry of Foreign Affairs (www.mfa.gov.hu) and the expat website www.ercglobal.com.

## Teaching English

**CENTRAL EUROPEAN TEACHING PROGRAMME/CETP:** 3800 NE Portland, OR 97213, USA (503 287 4977;cetp@comcast.net ; www.ticon.net/~cetp). CETP has a large presence in Hungary.

*Applicants* must be university graduates, and have either a teaching certificate or a TEFL certificate (it may be earned online). Contracts are for five or ten months and paid at approximately $500 per month.

# Latvia

The following organisation can help people to find employment in Latvia. In addition UK nationals can arrange voluntary work there through International Voluntary Service, Youth Action for Peace or UNA Exchange and US nationals through Service Civil International (see the *Worldwide* chapter for details).

## RED TAPE

**Visa Requirements:** Visas are not required by the following for stays of up to 90 days: holders of Latvian, Estonian & Lithuanian passports, citizens of (and holding a passport valid for two months from arrival) Andorra, Austria, Belgium, Croatia, Czech Rep, Denmark, Estonia, Finland, France, Germany, Greece, Hungary, Iceland, Ireland Rep, Italy, Japan, Liechtenstein, Lithuania, Luxembourg, Malta, Netherlands, Norway, Poland, Portugal, Slovakia, Slovenia, Spain, Sweden,

Switzerland, the United Kingdom, United States.
**Work and Residence Permits for EU citizens:** Latvia joined the EU on 1 May 2004, but is still allowed to require expatriates from other EU countries to apply for work and residence permits if they come from EU countries that have not yet opened up their labour markets fully to Latvian job seekers. You should therefore check with the Latvian embassy in your country as to whether or not you need these permits.
**Work & Residence Permits for non-EU citizens:** in order to obtain a residence permit for Latvia an applicant must submit an application form, a photocopy of a valid travel document and an invitation certified by the Department of Migration and Citizenship Affairs (www.ocma.gov.lv). If an applicant intends to work in Latvia, an invitation approved by the State Labour Department must be obtained. For assistance obtaining residency permits, special visas or work permits call the visa section of the Citizenship and Migration Board, Raina 5, (☎721 94 24, fax 782 03 06).

**INTERNATIONAL EXCHANGE CENTER:** 89 Fleet Street, London EC4Y 1DH (☎020-7583 9116; fax 020-7583-9117; e-mail isecinfo@btconnect.com; www. isecworld.co.uk). The center works to promote positive, enjoyable cultural exchanges. Overseas work is offered in various countries for various types of work. See website for details. Non-students welcome. No language requirement.

**English Teachers** to work on EFL teaching programme. English teachers are placed at language schools, summer language centres in Latvia, Russia and Ukraine. Some teaching experience/qualifications desirable. Placement fee of £100. Students must arrange their own medical insurance and visas must notify IEC of their arrival dates at least one week before arrival.

*Applications* must be submitted at least 3 months before the earliest program start date for those wishing to be placed through IEC and 1½ months for those wishing to find their own job.

# Poland

Poland's unemployment rate has gone down slightly since it joined the EU, but that does not prevent it from having the highest unemployment in the EU (18%). While Polish professionals and the under 24s are leaving Poland to work in the richer EU countries including Ireland and Britain, TEFL teachers can find relatively abundant employment and reasonable working conditions in Poland. Teaching work in Poland can be found with the organisations listed below. In addition, voluntary work in Poland can by arranged through Youth Action for Peace, UNA Exchange and International Voluntary Service for British people, and the CIEE and Service Civil International for Americans: see the *Worldwide* chapter for details.

## RED TAPE

**Visa Requirements:** Poland joined the EU on 1 May 2004. EU and EEA nationals and those from the USA, Canada and New Zealand do not require visas to enter Poland but their stay is limited to anything from 14 to 90 days depending on country of origin. For stays of longer than three months EU citizens have to apply for a residence permit. The residence permit for EU citizens is renewable for periods of up to five years at a time. The website of the Polish Foreign Ministry is www.msz.

gov.pl.
**Work Permits:** these are not required by EU/EEA citizens. Other nationalities should contact the Polish embassy in their home country for further details. For instance, American citizens should enquire at the Polish Embassy in Washington.

# Language Schools

**APASS UK NORTH, ANGLO-POLISH UNIVERSITIES TEACHING PROJECT:** 93 Victoria Road, Leeds LS6 1DR (☎043- 275 8121; fax 020-7498 7608; no website) Placements are for either four or eight weeks in July/August. The students are from grammar schools, roughly of the same age and ability. The course will be two and a half hours English instruction in the morning (mainly conversational) followed by only two hours recreational activities either in the afternoon or evening. Weekends are free. Generous pocket money given.

Accommodation and food are provided free, as well as leisure/sporting facilities (swimming, walking, barbecue, horse riding, discos, visits to places of interest etc). Some placements include a weekend trip to Prague. After three weeks out at the summer school, a week's 'grand tour of Poland' is organised; visiting Warsaw, Krakow, Auschwitz and the Tatra Mountains – all expenses paid by the Polish host. Applicants of all ages from 16+ are welcome (16-17-year-olds need written parental permission), as are parents with children (maximum two) aged 10+.

For a comprehensive information pack, please *send* a 50p A5 stamped, addressed envelope plus a £3 postal order to the above address.

**THE ENGLISH SCHOOL OF COMMUNICATION SKILLS (ESCS):** Attn. Personnel Department, ul. Wałowa 233-100 Tarnów, Poland (tel/fax +48 14 627 01 57; e-mail personnel@escs.pl).
**Teachers of English (60)** wanted for full-time positions at ESCS schools in: Tarnòw, where the locals are reputedly the friendliest people in Poland; Nowy Targ, where they take their skiing seriously; Myslenice, the best of both worlds, close to the big city and in the beautiful countryside; Sulowice and Limanowa.

Period of work from October to June. Job involves teaching English to Polish students of all ages. Salary according to experience and qualifications. Applicants must hold an EFL methodology certificate and have a degree level of education. ESCS holds EFL training courses in September.
**Summer School teacher** same working conditions as above for August in Tarnòw, . Minimum age 21. Applicants should be educated to degree level, with bright, confident personalities and be enthusiastic about sport.
*Applications* to the above address.

**OVERSEAS WORKING HOLIDAYS:** Level 1, Fife Road, Kingston, Surrey, KT1 1SF (0845 344 0366; fax 0870 460 4578; e-mail info@owh.co.uk; www.owh.co.uk)
Working holidays in various countries. Summer resort work in Canada and France and paid English teaching placements in Thailand, China, Poland and Korea.

Placements are for gap years or shorter placements. All jobs, visas and accommodation are arranged. Programme fees are from £299 to £599. Also available, African Experience Volunteer placements. Job interviews for all programmes are carried out pre-departure.
*Applications* through the website above or telephone 0845-344 0366.

**PROGRAM-BELL:** AUL. Fredry 1, 61-701 Poznan, Poland (☎ +48 61 8519 250; fax +48 61 855 18 06; e-mail office@program-bell.edu.pl).

**Teachers of English/Sports Monitors** wanted for summer language camps for 6 weeks from the end of June. Should have Cambridge Cert. And experience of teaching young children. Winter possibilities also. Salary of 1900 zloties net per month. Accommodation provided.

*Applications* to the above address or e-mail Anna Gebka-Suska at the above e-mail address.

# Romania

Romania, with a population of about 23 million (over 47% of these are classed as rural) is one of the largest, former communist countries still waiting to join the European Union. The following organisation offers voluntary work in Romania.

**DAD INTERNATIONAL UK-ROMANIA:** 1 Camil Petrescu, 705200 Pascani Iasi, Romania (☎+40 788 473 523; fax +40-726 164 039; e-mail dad@dad.ro; www.dad. ro).

**Volunteer English Teachers/Activity Leaders (50)** to teach English for 4-6 hours a day to Romanian students through informal classes, games and fun. Applicants must pay for their own fare to Romania but receive a benefits package including full board, insurance, 24 hour support and assistance, transfers to the place of work, training, internet access, a phrasebook and excursions to Transylvania, Moldavia etc. Periods of work are from June 17-July 11, 8-31 July, 28th July-20th August or 17 August-9 September.

Applicants must be aged at least 17; no previous teaching experience or special qualifications are required.

*Applications* to Professor Dorin Apopei at the above address.

# Russia

While there are occasional opportunities for finding paid temporary work in Russia it is still easier to find voluntary than paid work there. Even the English teachers in language schools are mostly home grown non-native speakers, although there are still sufficient high grade schools who are prepared to go to the expense of hiring foreign teachers with appropriate qualifications for TEFL. Don't forget that wages in Russia are shockingly low by Western standards, but those inspired by a genuine fascination with Russia will not be put off by this. In addition to the opportunities listed below British people should contact Youth Action for Peace, International Voluntary Service, UNA Exchange and Concordia while Americans should contact the CIEE and Service Civil International; for details see the *Worldwide* chapter. The Russian state body 'Goskomtrud' is responsible for the hiring of manpower from abroad. The address of the Department is: The Goskomtrud of Russia, 1 Square Kuibysheva, 103706, Moscow, Russia.

## RED TAPE

**Visa Requirements**: Any person wising to travel to Russia must obtain a visa and register it within three working days of their arrival in the country (this does not apply to visits of 3 days or under). The visa is valid for three months but does not entitle the holder to gain work in Russia.

Work Permits: Russian countries wishing to employ foreign labour have to gain special permission to do so. As this takes time, money and effort very few companies have been granted the power to do so legally. However there are certain categories of visitor such as students on internships that are not covered by this law. In general it is much easier to enter Russia to work on an established exchange programme than to try to find work independently. In order to gain a work permit the foreign national must be able to produce a work contact from a company with permission to employ foreign citizens and the results of an HIV test. In certain cases a three-month stay can be lengthened to a year.

**INTERNATIONAL SCIENTIFIC PROJECTS:** Laboratory of Geoarchaeology (Institute of Geology, Acad. Sciences, Kaz), State Institute for Scientific Research and Planning on Monuments of Material Culture (Min. Culture Kaz), Tole Bi 21, Room 31, 480100 Almaty, Kazakhstan (☎+7-3272 914386; fax +7-3272 917931; e-mail ispkz@nursat.kz).
**Volunteers** for archaeological fieldwork, to take part in four programmes of summer fieldwork based mainly on geoarchaeological survey and documentation. Under instruction from specialists from several Kazakh institutes, volunteers will receive training in steppe archaeology, paleoecology, methodology, aerial surveying and documentation. Programme costs are between US$250-300 (£175-£210 approx.) per week, in return volunteers will be provided with food and accommodation.
   For more details *contact* Renato Sala or Jean-Marc Deom at the Institute or consult the following fieldwork opportunities webpagesL www. archaeological.org/webinfo. php or www.cincpac.com/afos/testpit.html.

**INTERNATIONAL EXCHANGE CENTER:** 89 Fleet Street, London EC4Y 1DH (☎020-7583 9116; fax 020-7583-9117; e-mail isecinfo@btconnect.com; www. isecworld.co.uk). The International Exchange Center works to promote positive, enjoyable cultural exchanges. Overseas work is offered in various countries for various types of work. See website for details. Non-students welcome. No language requirement.
**Camp Counsellors Programme:** Camp Leaders/Activity Instructors/Language Teachers needed to work in children's summer camps in Russia and Ukraine, looking after children aged 8-15 years old. Energetic and friendly personality and a genuine desire to work with kids is essential; specialists in sports, music etc. are especially welcome. Free board and accommodation. Pocket money is low by western standards but is equivalent to the basic wage of local camp staff. Placement fee of £100.
**English Teachers** to work on EFL teaching programme. English teachers are placed at language schools, summer language centres in Latvia, Russia and Ukraine. Some teaching experience/qualifications desirable. Placement fee of £100.
**Work and Study Experience Russia.** This programme allows foreign participants to get involved in Russian daily life and culture. Participants are enrolled into 4 week language courses (10 hours per week) based at universities in Moscow, followed by work experience in a company in Moscow and other cities in Russia for a period of 2-4 months. Whenever possible. The programme cost of £240 (US$350) includes the cost of 4 weeks of study and accommodation in a University dormitory room, pick up on arrival to Moscow and a work placement. Salary may be low by Western standards – £34-£138 (US$50-200) per month. Participants can extend their study period while they are in Russia by paying directly to the University £82 (US$120 for 4 weeks of study). Jobs are at entry level; positions mainly in hospitality but may be in other areas. Participants can also choose to find a job themselves while studying at language

courses: however they need to be aware that unemployment rate is Russia is high. IEC will provide informational support but will not find an actual job for such participants. (If finding own job, the programme costs $330/£184). Students must arrange their own medical insurance and visas must notify IEC of their arrival dates at least one week before arrival.

*Applications* must be submitted at least 3 months before the earliest program start date for those wishing to be placed through IEC and 1½ months for those wishing to find their own job.

## Teaching and Language Schools

**BENEDICT SCHOOL:** 23 ul. Pskovskaya, St. Petersburg 190008. ☎+7 812 113 85 68/114 10 90; fax: +7 812 114 44 45; e-mail info@benedictinternational.co.uk; www. benedictinternational.co.uk).

**English teachers (40-60)** for Russia including 18-20 for St. Petersburg (main franchise holder) and others in Novosibirsk (see above), Tomsk, Murmansk and Kemerovo (see entry). British, American, Canadian and Australian applicants preferred. No TEFL background needed for Work-Study programme. TEFL graduates needed for teaching.

Teachers work 3-12 months, 15-25 hours per week. Wages US$400-800 (approx £220-440) per month (net). Work-Study participants pay £399 for package: two-week orientation in St. Petersburg including Introductory TEFL course, placement in a school and board and lodging in student hostel or with local family.

Work permits not needed for Work-Study Programme; otherwise full assistance given (visa costs £89); UK office can assist only British applicants. In-house training course (10-30 lessons) results in international Benedict teachers' certificate.

*Applications* via Benedict International Ltd in the UK: 74 Baxter Court, Norwich NR3 2ST (01603 301522; fax 01603 787618; info@benedictinternational.co.uk). Also via universities, careers centres and websites.

# Serbia

Serbia's status as an independent state is very recent. Serbia and Montenegro, two former provinces of former Yugoslavia, existed in a state union until Montenegro voted for separation from Serbia in June 2006. Short-term volunteer projects in Serbia can be arranged for British citizens by Youth Action for Peace and in Serbia by UNA Exchange. See their entries in the *Worldwide* chapter for more details. The following organisation offers opportunities to work in these states.

## RED TAPE

**Visa Requirements**: the citizens of most EU countries as well as the United States of America, Canada, Singapore, the Republic of Korea, Australia and New Zealand do not need a visa to travel to Serbia.

**GALINDO SKOLA STRANIH JEZIKA (SAVA CENTAR & VOZDOVAC):** Milentija Popovica 9, 11070 Novi Beograd, Serbia (☎11-311 4568; fax 11-455785; e-mail galindo@net.yu). The first private language school in the country, located in Novi Beograd's congress and shopping centre. Excellent working atmosphere, with

students from pre-school to executives.
**English Teachers (3)** to work with children, adolescents and adults. Minimum wage approximately £280 per month, working 6 or 7 hours per day, 5 days per week.

Applicants should be enthusiastic and responsible, and have a BA in English and TEFL, TESL or TESOL qualifications. Knowledge of some Serbo-Croatian would be an advantage. *Applications* should be sent to Nada Gadjanski at the above address.

# Slovenia

Slovenia is a great country to work in with a high standard of living. Most of the short-term possibilities for foreigners revolve around teaching English or voluntary work. The British Council in Ljubljana (www.britishcouncil.si) has a list of private language schools that may take teachers for summer schools.

The following organisation organises voluntary work in Slovenia. British people can also find this type of work there through International Voluntary Service or UNA Exchange, while US citizens can apply to Service Civil International; see the *Worldwide* chapter for details.

## RED TAPE

**Visa Requirements:** the citizens of a majority of countries may travel to The Republic of Slovenia without obtaining a visa, including those from the USA, New Zealand, Canada, Japan and Australia. Slovenia joined the EU on 1 May 2004. EU/ EEA citizens are able to work in Slovenia under the same conditions as Slovenes. EU citizens also have the right to live in Slovenia, but for stays of longer than 3 months a residence permit is obligatory. For EU citizens working in Slovenia, the employer has to register their employment with the Slovenian Employment Service. Nationals of other countries may stay up to 90 days in any half a year depending on their country of origin. For more information go to www.ess.gov.si.

**ZAVOD VOLUNTARIAT:** Service Civil International Slovenia, Breg 12 Sl-1000 Ljubljana, Slovenia (☎+386-1-2417620; fax +386-1-2417626; e-mail placement@ zavod-voluntariat.si or irena@zavodvoluntariat.si; www.zavod-voluntariat.si). Voluntariat is a non-profit and non-governmental organisation which coordinates voluntary work and international work camps in Slovenia. Voluntariat aims to promote social justice, sustainable development and solidarity through voluntary service.
**International Work Camp Volunteers**. Voluntariat organises between 15 and 20 work camps in Slovenia every year. Most work camps are held from June to September and last two or three weeks. The main topics of the work camps are: ecology, Bosnian refugees, children and handicapped people. Most work camps do not require any special skills. Accommodation and food is provided.
**Long and medium-term voluntary work:** projects of LTV and MTV are based mostly in Ljubljana and they include: refugee projects, projects for youngsters from underprivileged backgrounds and projects for elderly people. Voluntariat also offers long and medium-term voluntary work abroad.

*Applications* should be made through the applicant's nation branch of SCI.

# Turkey

Opportunities for paid work in Turkey usually involve either teaching English or working for a tour operator. There are opportunities for volunteer work with the organisations listed below or through UNA Exchange, Youth Action for Peace, International Voluntary Service and Concordia for British citizens, or the CIEE and Service Civil International for Americans; see the *Worldwide* chapter for details.

Please note that those who enter Turkey as tourists with or without a tourist visa are not permitted to take up employment in the country.

## RED TAPE

See the website www.turkconsulate-london.com for up-to-date information.

**Visa Requirements:** All British, Australian, US, Canadian and Irish nationals can obtain a 3 months/multiple-entry visa at their point of entry to Turkey. New Zealand citizens do not need visas for stays of up to 3 months as tourists. Any UK national entering Turkey is advised to have a minimum of 6 months validity on their passports from the date of their entry into Turkey. In the UK up-to-date details of visa and permit requirements can be obtained by telephoning 09068-347348 (calls cost 60p per minute). No paid work of any kind may be undertaken with only a tourist visa; in order to gain employment a working visa must be obtained.

**Residence Permits:** If you wish to reside in Turkey longer than the normal period allowed to tourists, you need to apply to the relevant Turkish consulate for a residence visa. After obtaining a residence visa, you must apply to the local police headquarters of the area where you are residing within a month following arrival in Turkey to be issued a residence permit. Nationals of European Union countries and nationals of Australia, Canada, Iceland, New Zealand, Norway, Switzerland and USA may be issued a one-year resident visa in a week.

**Work Permits:** Work permit applications are always for a specific position and they are employer driven. Prospective employers must apply to the Turkish Ministry of Labour and Social Affairs in Ankara (www.csgb.gov.tr), for a work permit for their UK employees. Once this has been approved the person seeking employment must apply for a work visa through the Embassy of the Republic of Turkey (www. turkishconsulate.org.uk). Prospective English teachers must have a degree and TEFL certificate. Should the employer be related to the tourism business, a letter of approval should be obtained from the Turkish Ministry of Tourism before visa application. The application should be made from the country of origin, unless the applicant is the holder of a residence permit. Applications for an extension of a given work permit can be made if accompanied by a valid residence permit.

The visa procedure in Turkey requires a double application - from the employee in their country of origin, and from the employer in Turkey who must submit a file to the Ministry of Labour and Social Security, Department for Work Permits for Foreigners (www.yabancicalismaizni.gov.tr). There should not be more than 3 working days between the two applications. It usually takes 2 months for the applications to be processed. Foreigners who enter Turkey on the basis of a work visa are expected to get a residence permit within 30 days of arrival.

**Au Pair:** work permits are required.

**Voluntary Work:** work permits are required.

# Agriculture

**THE BUGDAY ASSOCIATION FOR SUPPORTING ECOLOGICAL LIVING:** (☎ +90 (0) 212 252 5255, fax; fax 212 252 5256; e-mail portal@bugday.org; www. bugday.org/).

This is the new WWOOF exchange known as TaTuTa (an acronym of Agro Tourism and Voluntary Exchange, in Turkish). The number of participating farms taking volunteer workers on their organic enterprises is small at the moment (about two dozen), but is set to increase.

# Sports, Couriers and Camping

**MARK WARNER:** 20 Kensington Church Street, London, W8 4EP (☎08700 330750 or 08700 330760 for children's's places); e-mail recruitment@markwarner. co.uk; www.markwarner.co.uk/recruitment.

**Accountants, Receptionists, Watersports Instructors, Tennis and Aerobics Instructors, Chefs, Kitchen Porters, First Aid, Nannies, Handymen, Nightwatchmen** and more are required to work in hotels in Corsica, Sardinia, Greece and Turkey during the summer from April to October and Egypt, and Sri Lanka and Mauritius year round. Wages from £50 per week plus full board, medical insurance, travel expenses and free use of watersport and activity facilities. Some reserve staff also needed throughout the season. Requirements for languages, experience, qualifications etc. vary according to the job applied for.

For further details, please *contact* the Resorts Recruitment Department on the above number.

**SAVILE TOURS**: 8 Southampton Place, London WC1A 2EA (☎020-7242 8488; fax 020-7242 6166; e-mail info@saviletours.com; www.saviletours.com). Savile Tours is an up market tour operator specialising in holidays to Turkey and Northern Cyprus.

**Overseas Representatives (3-4)** to escort clients between airport and accommodation and assist them during their holidays. Pay negotiable depending on experience. Previous experience preferred. Working hours are variable and the minimum period of work is 6 months from May to October.

*Applications* to Ozgur Sav at the above address.

# Teaching English

**GENCTUR:** Istiklal Cad. No 212, Aznavur Pasaji, K: 5 34430, Istanbul, Turkey (☎+90 212 244 62 30; fax +90 212 244 62 33; e-mail workcamps.in@genctur.com; www.genctur.com).

Genctur is Turkey's leading youth and student travel organisation. Their main activities are **international voluntary workcamps** in Turkey. Camps last 2-3 weeks. Project volunteers are needed for mostly manual work including repairing and painting schools, digging water trenches, constructing schools or health care centres, gardening and environmental development works or social schemes such as helping handicapped people or practising English with children. Projects take place mostly in small villages and towns where the traditional way of life can be seen through contact with the local people. Full board and accommodation is provided. The language spoken at the camps is English. Age group: 18+.

*Applications* are only accepted through the following partner voluntary organisations: UNA Exchange, Concordia, IVS and YAP UK.

# Work at Sea

**SETSAIL HOLIDAYS:** Setsail House, Christopher Lane, Sudbury, Suffolk CO10 2GE (☎01787 310445; fax: 01737 378078; e-mail boats@setsail.co.uk; www.setsail. co.uk). Setsail Holidays are a specialist tour operator providing flotilla sailing and bareboat charter holidays to Greece, Turkey and Croatia.

**Skippers, Hostesses and Engineers** required to coordinate and run the flotilla sailing holidays which can consist of up to 12 yachts.

Must have sailing experience and/or qualifications and the ability to work well with people. Salary range £120-£140 per week. Accommodation is provided on the 'lead yacht'. Minimum period of work, six months.

*Applications* to John Hortop at the above address, fax or e-mail. Applications must include a CV.

# Voluntary Work and Archaeology

**CONCORDIA:** 19 North Street, Portslade, Brighton, BN41 1DH (☎01273-422218; fax 01273 421182; e-mail info@concordia-iye.org.uk; www.concordia-iye.org.uk). Volunteers aged 16+ are needed for international volunteer projects lasting 2-4 weeks from May to September. Work is mainly on **construction and manual projects in villages.** Basic food and accommodation are provided. Volunteers pay a registration fee of £110 and organise their own travel and insurance.

*For further information* on volunteering or coordinating please check the website or contact the International Volunteer Coordinator at the above address.

**GSM YOUTH SERVICES CENTRE:** Bayindir Sokak, No.45/9 Kizilay, 06450 Kizilay-Ankara, Turkey (☎+90-312-417-11 24/417-29-91; fax +90-312-425-81-92; e-mail gsm@gsm-youth.org; www.gsm-youth.org).

GSM organises around 20 workcamps throughout Turkey in co-operation with the local municipalities and universities. The projects, usually taking place in towns or on campus sites, can involve **environmental protection, restoration and/or festival organisation.**

The age limits are: 18-28 in all of the projects. The projects last for 2 weeks from July until the end of September. Volunteers work 5 hours a day, weekends are free with organised excursions available. Board and lodging are provided in dormitories, small hotels/pensions, camp houses or with families. Volunteers pay their own travel costs and pay a contribution fee of approx. £45.

*Applications* through partner organisations including Concordia, Quaker International Social Projects and the United Nations Association (Wales): see the *Worldwide* chapter for details.

**GENCTUR** Istiklal Cad. No 212, Aznavur Pasaji, K: 5 34430, Istanbul, Turkey (☎+90 212 244 62 30; fax +90 212 244 62 33; e-mail workcamps.in@genctur.com; www.genctur.com). Contact (Mr) Zafer Yilmaz, Workcamps Coordinator. Genctur is Turkey's leading youth and student travel organisation. Their main activities are international voluntary workcamps in Turkey. Camps 2-3 weeks.

**Project volunteers** for mostly manual work including repairing and painting schools, digging water trenches, constructing schools or health care centres, gardening and environmental development works or social schemes such as helping handicapped people or practising English with children. Projects take place mostly in small villages and towns where the traditional way of life can be seen through contact with the local people. Full board and accommodation is provided. Camp language is English. There is also one French speaking and one Japanese speaking camp each year. Age group is 18 and over.

*Applications* are only accepted through the partner organisations below:
GREAT BRITAIN
    *UNA Exchange*, Temple of Peace Cathays Park CARDIFF CF10 3AP; ☎+44 (0)2920-223 088; fax +44 (0)2920-665 557; e-mail : unaexchange@btinternet.com.
    *Concordia,*-UK 19 North Street, Portslade, Brighton BN41 1DH; ☎/fax +44 (0)1273-422218; e-mail info@concordia-iye.org.uk.
    *IVS-GBS Old Hall*, East Bergholt Colchester CO7 6TQ; ☎44 +(0)1206.298215; fax +44 (0)1206.299043; e-mail ivs@ivsgbsouth.demon.co.uk; www.ivs-gb.org.uk.
    *IVS-GBN*, Castlehill House, 21 Otley Road, Headingley GB Leeds LS6 3AA; ☎44.1132.304600; fax: + 44 (0)1132-304610; e-mail ivsgbn@ivsgbn.demon.co.uk; www.ivsgbn.demon.co.uk .
    *IVS-SC*, 7 Upper Bow, Edinburgh EH1 2JN; ☎+44 (0)1312-266722; fax +44 (0)1312-266723 e-mail ivs@ivsgbscot.demon.co.uk; www.ivsgbn.demon.co.uk .
    *YAP-UK*, POB 43670, London SE22 0XX (☎08701 657 927; e-mail action@yap-uk.org; www.yap-uk.org).

# Ukraine

Until recently the political situation in Ukraine has been so unstable that it has been difficult for foreign organisations trying to operate there efficiently. Following the election of a pro-Western government in late 2004, there is likely to be a rise in demand for teachers of English. In some cases it will be possible to work on three-month contracts for the summer; although 9 months to a year is more usual minimum. The British-based organisation Teaching and Projects Abroad run an English-teaching project in Ukraine while the American organisation Ukrainian National Association (2200 Route 10, PO Box 280, Parsippany, NJ 07054; 973-292-9800; www.unamember.com) recruits volunteer teachers for short periods, from the USA), see entry below. The American website www.volunteerabroad.com lists 13 projects that Americans can apply for in Ukraine ranging from workcamps to underwater archaeology. Apart from the voluntary work available in Ukraine through the Latvian-based International Exchange Centre (see chapter on Latvia), short-term voluntary work can be arranged for UK nationals through Concordia, International Voluntary Service and UNA Exchange. US citizens can arrange placements through the CIEE and Service Civil International. Voluntary work can also be obtained through the organisation listed below.

## RED TAPE

**Visa Requirements**: Since 2005, EU citizens have been able to travel in the Ukraine without a visa for up to 3 months. Similarly, US, Canadian and Japanese, Norwegian and Swiss citizens can travel visa-free for up to 3 months.

**UKRAINIAN NATIONAL ASSOCIATION (UNA):** 2200 Route 10, PO Box 280, Parsippany, New Jersey 07054, USA (☎973-292-9800; fax: +973 292-0900; e-mail una@unamember.com; www.unamember.com).
UNA is an American association for Ukrainian immigrants to the US. It recruits volunteers from the USA, Canada and English native speakers from Europe, who

are qualified teachers, to teach English for an average of four weeks between May and August. 5-days a week, 4 hours per day. Teachers can be sent to any region of the Ukraine. Homestay and board are provided but no stipend. Students are normally adolescents and adults from varied backgrounds.

*Applications* to the above address.

**YOUTH VOLUNTARY SERVICE:** 11/60 Lystopadna, LVIV, 290034, Ukraine (☎/ fax 00-380-322 423658).

**Volunteers (15)** required to take part in short term social projects (2-3 weeks) from late June until the end of August. To work 5 hours a day, Monday-Friday. Board and accommodation provided.

*Applications* through national organisations or directly to the above address.

# Africa and the Middle East

# Egypt

Chances of finding a paid summer job in Egypt are slight but there may be possibilities in the tourist industry for example in the diving resort of Dahab. Otherwise opportunities for temporary work are normally restricted to voluntary work. There is also a need for English teachers to teach summer schools to Egyptian children and adults. Prospective teachers can advertise in the Egyptian expat press *Egypt Today* (www.egypttoday.com).

## Teaching and Language Schools

**INTERNATIONAL HOUSE:** International Language Institute Heliopolis, 2 Mohamed Bayoumi Street, Off Merghany Street, Heliopolis, Cairo, Egypt (☎202-291295/418 9212; fax 202-415 1082; e-mail ili@idsc.net.eg or affiliates@ihworld.co.uk; www.ihworld.com).
Heliopolis is an affluent neighbourhood near the airport, downtown Cairo and the Pyramids. IH was established in 1976 and is well known for its teacher development in English and Arabic language programmes.

**Teachers of English (6)** required to teach intensive English courses to adults and young learners aged 5-15. Applicants should be Cambridge/RSA or CELTA qualified and preferably have experience of working with young learners. 20-25 hours of work per week between June and September, minimum period of work 6 weeks. Wages c.£300 per month with free accommodation. Depending on the length of contract worked there is a bonus of a percentage paid towards the cost of the flight to Egypt, e.g. 50% for 12 weeks worked, up to a limit of £380.
*Applications* to the above address from February.

## Voluntary Work and Archaeology

**WIND SAND & STARS:** 6 Tyndale Terrace, Islington, London, N1 2AT (☎020-7359 7551; e-mail office@windsandstars.co.uk; www.windsandstars.co.uk). Wind Sand & Stars is a small specialist company that organises a wide range of journeys and projects within the desert and mountain areas of South Sinai, Egypt.
Participants for work on an annual **environmental, scientific, historical expedition operated during August in the desert and mountains of Sinai.** There is a fee attached for travel to the area. All applicants must be over 16 years of age.
*Applicants should* contact *the above address any time.*

# Ghana

Voluntary work for Britons in Ghana can be organised by Concordia, UNA Exchange and Youth Action for Peace. A summary of their work is listed along with their addresses in the *Worldwide* chapter. The Student and Youth Travel Organisation in Accra (www.sytoghana.com) works with many partner organisations to bring volunteers to Ghana, but individuals can also apply to them direct via the website though this has to be done ten weeks in advance. The organisations below also offer opportunities to work in Ghana.

# RED TAPE

**Visa Requirements**: the citizens of most countries are required to apply for a visa before travelling to Ghana.

# Voluntary Work and Archaeology

**AFRICATRUST NETWORKS:** Africatrust Chambers, P.O Box 551, Portsmouth, Hampshire, PO5 1ZN (UK tel/fax 01873-812453; e-mail info@africatrust.gi; www. africatrust.gi).

Africatrust Networks offers 3 to 6 month periods of **tropical work experience** in North and West Africa with disadvantaged young people in Cameroon (French/ English speaking), Ghana (English speaking) and in the southern parts of Morocco (French and Arabic speaking).

Africatrust Networks is looking for volunteers who can work as part of a team, wish to learn as well as to give, can cope with limited resources and adapt their skills to a very different and difficult work situation overseas.

The UK office carries out the selection, interviewing, pre-departure briefings and helps with the fund-raising for self-funded volunteer programmes. Each in-country director then leads the post-arrival and in-country two-week induction course; acclimatisation, language, health, security, culture, music, history, geography, experimental living etc. Volunteers then choose from selected programmes and meet their host family. The in-country director then presides over the regular volunteer/host review meetings throughout the programme.

Donations raised by volunteers are grouped and then distributed by the same team of volunteers. One vote per person not per pound raised. There are no deductions unlike the 22% expense deductions made by organisations such as Oxfam.

Teams consist of 6 or 8 volunteers who are usually graduates, university gap year students, or students on placements – seeking supervised work experience in tropical development environments with the possibility of using French or Arabic. Such field experience might lead to careers with the British Council, UN, Save the Children, Oxfam, CNN/BBC or World Bank.

*For more information* visit www.africatrust.gi or *contact* Africatrust Network at the above address.

**FIOH/WWOOF GHANA:** PO Box TF 154, Trade Fair Centre, Accra, Ghana (tel/fax 23321-716091; e-mail kingzeeh@yahoo.co.uk). WWOOF is concerned with organic farming and FIOH runs tree planting and environmental projects. Both organisations require a large number of participants for their annual WORKCAMPS. Their schools help train children from poor families, participants get to experience traditional and proverbial Ghanaian hospitality. The founder is a former school teacher who has founded four international organisations in Africa.

Voluntary farm workers to **work on both organic and traditional farms in Ghana. Work includes weeding with a hoe or cutlass and harvesting of food and cash crops including maize, cassava, oranges, cocoa etc.** Volunteers with experience of organic farming especially welcome.

Volunteers to **work in a bicycle repair workshop** currently being set up; no wage paid at present but there is the possibility of pocket money in the future. Two volunteers needed every six months. No particular qualifications are necessary, but applicants should be have experience of repairing bicycles.

Other schemes are also operated such as: summer workcamps on which volunteers work on construction conservation projects and tree planting activities in rural areas; placement schemes for qualified teachers are also organised. Practical lessons in traditional African drumming and dancing are available too.

*For further information* send two International Reply Coupons; *contact* Mr Kenneth Nortey-Mensah, Coordinator, at the above address.

**RURAL UPGRADE SUPPORT ORGANISATION (RUSO):** P O Box CE 11066, Tema, Ghana (☎+233 21 513149 e-mail benxzola@africanus.net; www.ruso. interconnection.org)
RUSO is a non-political, non-sectarian and non-governmental organisation that aims to assist community upgrading using sustainable and environmentally friendly means. It employs volunteers to help with it implement community-based solutions after a thorough environmental impact assessment and total commitment to the 'green' approach. Projects include providing **healthcare, education and small scale business management, cultural exchange and social development**.

Refer to the website for details of volunteer costs. *Apply* direct, or via email, but not through the website.

**SAVE THE EARTH NETWORK:** Save the Earth Network, PO Box CT 3635, Cantonments-Accra, Ghana, West Africa ☎ 233-27-7743139; e-mail ebensten@ yahoo.com or eben_sten@hotmail.com; www.worldvoices.no). Save the Earth Network is an organisation dedicated to promoting sustainable development, agro-forestry, environmental conservation and cultural exchange through voluntary work in Ghana. Volunteers to **teach English language and mathematics in primary and junior secondary schools for under-privileged communities. Caring for orphans, destitutes and abandoned children** in foster homes and orphanages, **assisting in giving free basic education to street and financially disadvantaged children and HIV/AIDS education. Reforestation and environmental conservation, agro-forestry, organic farming, primary health care and community development programmes.** Volunteers mostly work alongside staff and volunteers from the local community. Special skills, professional qualifications or previous experience is not essential, however, some of the volunteers may undergo a short (one week) training in Ghana, prior to the volunteering work.

Volunteers work four or more hours a day. Period of work 4 weeks to a year or longer. There is a monthly fee for participation, which covers board and lodging with local families: $595/ £328 (4 weeks); $995/£550 (8 weeks) and $1,395/£770 (12 weeks). Payment is made a day after beginning in Ghana. Volunteers must be aged 18 or above.

Other programmes run by the same organisation are Visitor/Cultural Exchange Programme and General Tour Programme.

**SOFT POWER EDUCATION:** 55 Guildhall Street, Bury St Edmunds, Suffolk IP33 1QF (e-mail info@softpowereducation.com; www.softpowereducation.com, www. kutunza.com).
Soft Power Education is a British registered, non-religious charity based in Junja, Uganda. The organisation works at improving the educational facilities within

primary schools with the help of international volunteers. Soft Power Education has successfully built, and continues to maintain, two pre-schools for AIDS orphans and since November 2003 they have worked at refurbishing the 20 government primary schools, bringing them up to government standard. They are completing targets through the continued support of visiting tourists, long-term volunteers and inspired donors who have spent anything from one day to three months working on our projects – with their help Soft Power Education has also built a health clinic, a working pottery and an inspiring Education Centre. Volunteers get to see that the local communities and their children not only benefit from Soft Power Education working within their schools, but that they employ trained and skilled builders and foremen from the villages to help in the venture. Soft Power is extending into other areas of Uganda with the help of Ku Tunza Travel – who offer tours within East Africa – enabling volunteers to see more of the country whilst making a difference.

*For further information* please *visit* www.softpowereducation.com and www.kutunza.com or e-mail info@softpowereducation.com

**VOLUNTARY WORKCAMPS ASSOCIATION OF GHANA (VOLU):** PO Box 1540, Accra, Ghana (☎233-21-663486; fax 233-21-665960; voluntaryworkcamp@yahoo.com; www.volu.org/).
VOLU organises workcamps in the rural areas of Ghana for international volunteers. Tasks involve mainly manual work; **construction projects, working on farm and agro-forestry projects, tree planting, harvesting cocoa and foodstuffs, working with mentally disabled people, teaching,** etc. Around 1,500 volunteers are needed for workcamps at Easter, Christmas and from June to October. Volunteers can stay throughout each period.

No special skills or experience are required but volunteers should be over 16 years old and fit to undertake manual labour. Volunteers pay their own travelling costs and an inscription fee of approximately £120 but accommodation and food are provided at the camps. VOLU supplies official invitations to enable volunteers to acquire visas before leaving for Ghana.

*Applications* to the above address.

**VOLUNTEER IN AFRICA:** 10 Tackie Tawiah Avenue, Adabraka, Accra, Ghana (☎+233-244761050; e-mail Ghanaprograms@yahoo.com; www.volunteeringinafrica.org).
Volunteer Africa organises programmes in Ghana, mainly in conjunction with its partner institutions. Volunteer programmes include **educational, social and environmental and health projects**. Health projects are mainly for medical students and health care professionals.

Volunteers can participate in most of the programmes at any time of year. Special skills and professional qualifications are not required for most of the projects. Volunteers work 4 or 5 days a week for 4 or 5 hours a day. Host families provide accommodation.

Participation fees: £377 (1-4 weeks), £537 (6 weeks), £697 (8 weeks), £857 (10 weeks), £1,017 (12 weeks).

*Applications* can be filled in online at the above website.

**VOLUNTEER GHANA:** BUNAC, 16 Bowling Green Lane, London EC1R 0QH (☎020-7251 3472; fax 020-7251 0215; e-mail volunteer@bunac.org.uk).
BUNAC runs a *Volunteer Ghana* programme which enables recent graduates aged 18 or over to spend between three and six months working and travelling in West Africa. Placements range from teaching positions or development projects to administrative

roles. Departures are all year round.

Placements on these programmes are unpaid and participants will be expected to make a small weekly contribution towards living costs.

For further details about this programme *contact* BUNAC at the above address or visit www.bunac.org.

# Israel

The number of foreigners wishing to work in Israel has dwindled considerably since the explosive conflict between the Israelis and Palestinians that goes on interminably and seems irresolvable, at least to foreigners' eyes. Even more recently, the conflict between Israel and Lebanon has made travelling to this region an extremely dangerous prospect. The Foreign and Commonwealth Office advises against all travel to Israel and Occupied Territories (www.fco.gov.uk). However, even so, tourists flock to Israel each year, and almost all visits are trouble-free. If you do decide to visit Israel, maintaining a high level of vigilance and taking security precautions for your personal safety is essential.

A special visa exists for volunteers to Israel to work on kibbutzim and moshavim, and there are organisations sending volunteers to Palestine though it is becoming increasingly difficult for such organisations to operate there because of the instability of the Palestinian territories.

There are some opportunities for paid employment in the tourist industry, especially around the resort of Eilat on the Red Sea and the Old City in Jerusalem. However, most people who wish to work in Israel for a few months choose to work on kibbutzim or moshavim. These are almost wholly self-sufficient settlements which take on volunteers for a normal minimum of eight weeks. The main difference between the two is that the property is shared on a kibbutz, while most houses and farms are privately owned on a moshav. So on one volunteers work and share the farm tasks with permanent staff, while on the latter they are paid and there is less communal spirit. However, the whole kibbutz system has undergone so many dramatic changes since from its origins in socialist, pioneering communities to the transfer of kibbutzim from state to private ownership. In the moshavim movement private ownership of land has always been the norm.

On a kibbutz the work may consist of picking olives, grapes or cotton in the fields, domestic duties, or factory work; on a moshav the work is usually agricultural. In return for a six-day week volunteers receive free accommodation, meals, laundry and cigarettes. Volunteers are normally given pocket money on kibbutzim, while on a moshav a small wage is paid but the working hours are liable to be longer. Other programmes available on kibbutzim include Kibbutz Ulpan (which is intensive Hebrew study) and Project Oren Kibbutz Programmes (which is intensive Hebrew study, as well as travel and study of Israel).

Kibbutz Representatives, Golders Green, London which, for decades, arranged for Britons to work on kibbutzim has shut up shop due to lack of demand and commercialization within the the the kibbutz movement. Anyone interested in working on a kibbutz is advised to contact the Kibbutz Programmes Centre in Israel (e-mail: kpc@volunteer.co.il). Americans can contact Kibbutz Program Center at 21st Floor, 633 Third Ave., New York, NY 10017 (☎ 1-800247 7852 or 212-318-6130; fax 212-318-6134; e-mail kpc@jazo.org.il or ulpankad@aol.com); volunteers need to bear in mind that with this organisation they must be prepared to make a commitment of at least six weeks. Registration costs $150 +$80 for insurance.

There are many other placement offices around the world: Israel's diplomatic missions should be able to advise on the nearest one to you.

The following organisation may be able to place people who are actually in Israel. In recent years the authorities have been discouraging volunteers from travelling to Israel on one way tickets without having a written assurance of a place on a kibbutz, and with insufficient money for their fare home: the official line is that volunteers must have a return ticket and a reasonable sum of money (around £150/$225) in their possession when they enter the country. Contact the Kibbutz Program Centre: Volunteers Department; 18 Frishman Street, 3rd Floor, Cr. Ben Yehuda ☎Aviv 61030 (☎03-524-6156 or 03-527-8874; fax 03-523-9966; e-mail kpcvol@inter.net.il; www.kibbutz.org.il); it is open 9am-2pm, Sunday-Thursday. The centre advises people who do not pre-arrange a place before entering Israel that there might be a wait of days or even weeks before one is found, especially in the summer. However in the current political circumstances, there is a general shortage of foreign volunteers. All volunteers must be available for a minimum of 2 months, be between the ages of 18 and 35, speak a reasonable level of English and be in good mental and physical health.

The other major form of voluntary work in Israel consists of helping with archaeological excavations, often of Old Testament sites. The minimum stay for volunteers is normally two weeks. In the majority of cases volunteers must pay at least £15/US$25 a day for their expenses on a dig. British citizens wishing to find voluntary work in Israel can obtain placements through Concordia.

Those wanting to know more about not only work on kibbutzim and moshavim, but also all other forms of short-term work in Israel should consult the book *Kibbutz Volunteer* (see *Useful Publications*).

Placing an advertisement in the English language paper *The Jerusalem Post* may also lead to an offer of a job. They can be contacted at the *Jerusalem Post* Building, (PO Box 81, Romena, Jerusalem 91000 (fax 2-377646; www.jpost.com).

# RED TAPE

**Visa Requirements:** to work in Israel you must have a Foreign Worker's Visa for Israel which has to be arranged before arriving in Israel. This is the only visa that allows a visitor to work (other than for voluntary work e.g. kibbutz) in Israel. For volunteer work a work visa is not normally required prior to arrival by citizens of the UK, USA and some Western European countries.

**Residence Permits:** on entering the country, a visitor is likely to be given permission to stay for up to three months. Permission for a longer stay should then be obtained from the Ministry of the Interior, Hakirya Ruppin Road, no.2, Jerusalem.

**Work Permits:** your prospective employer should obtain the necessary permit from the Ministry of the Interior in Israel. You should have the permit with you when you enter the country.

**Voluntary Work:** a B4 Volunteer Visa is required of participants doing voluntary work (which includes kibbutzim and moshavim). The fee is NIS75 ($17) which covers 3 months. If you have pre-arranged your stay before arrival and have a letter of invitation you can obtain the B4 at the point of entry: otherwise, you can obtain it within 15 days of beginning voluntary work, provided you obtained the position through official channels. The B4 can be renewed only once.

# Kibbutzim and Moshavim

**KIBBUTZ PROGRAM CENTER:** 18 Frishman St. (corner of Ben Yehuda St.),

☎ Aviv 61030, Israel (☎ 03-524 8874/03-524 6156; fax 03-523 9966; e-mail kpc@ volunteer.co.il; www.kibbutz.org.il). The Kibbutz Programme Center is the only office officially representing all the 250 kibbutzim. The center is responsible for their volunteers and provides for them from arrival until they leave the kibbutz.

**Kibbutz Volunteers** required all year round, to work 7-8 hours per day over a 6 day week. Period of work 2 months (minimum) to 6 months. Volunteers receive full board and accommodation, free laundry and £60 pocket money per month. Volunteers are also entitled to three free days of their choice days per month.

Volunteers need to pay a registration fee of £40, and be able to converse in English. To apply contact the centre with details of your name and date of birth, date of arrival, passport number and a covering letter describing yourself.

*Applications* are accepted all year round, but apply at least one week in advance of your arrival in Israel.

# Voluntary Work and Archaeology

**DEPARTMENT OF CLASSICAL STUDIES:** Tel Aviv University, Ramat Aviv, Tel Aviv, Israel (fax +972 3-6406243; e-mail fischer@post.tau.ac.il; www.tau.ac.il/ ~yavneyam). Since 1992 five seasons of archaeological excavations have been carried out at the ancient port site of Yavneh Yam, with the help of hundreds of volunteers from about ten countries, offering them a unique possibility of both reconstructing the past and encountering the complexity of modern Israeli society. The participation fee of £470 for two weeks includes a full board accommodation at the modern Youth Village 'Ayanoth', a lecture series on archaeology, geography and history of the Holy Land, field trips, a wonderful swimming pool, the blue Mediterranean.

Volunteers (up to 40) needed to take part in **archaeological excavations**. Volunteers are recruited for two-week periods in July and August; it is possible to stay for more than one period. Volunteers must pay for their own food and accommodation (cost around £470 per two week period). Applicants should speak English, French or German: previous archaeological experience is an advantage but not essential.

For further details *contact* Prof. Moshe Fischer at the above address or visit; http:// itp.lccc.wy.edu/bibint2/articles/yavnehyam.htm.

**ELI SHENHAV:** JNF: 11 Zvi Shapira Street, Tel Aviv, Israel.
Volunteers (17) to work on an **excavation of a Roman theatre** three miles from Caesarea, a Roman Theatre in Shuni. Working hours are from 5.30am-noon, 5 days per week. Minimum period of work 1 week in July and August. Board and accommodation provided for around £10 per day.

For further details *contact* Eli Shenhav at the above address.

**FRIENDS OF ISRAEL EDUCATIONAL FOUNDATION 'BRIDGE PROGRAMME':** PO Box 42763, London N2 0YJ (☎ 020 8444 0681; fax 020 8444 0691; e-mail info@foi-asg.org; www.foi-asg.org). A British foundation established to promote an understanding of the geographies, histories, cultures and peoples of Israel, and to forge working links between the UK and Israel.

Scholarships are offered to 12 British applicants per year to enable them to take part in **kibbutz work and community action and do some teaching in a developing town.** The scholarships cover travel, insurance, board and lodging: there is no pay. 5-6 hours per day, 6 days per week between February and August. Applicants should be resident in the UK, prepared to work hard and to show initiative.

*Applications,* enclosing a stamped addressed envelopeand anInternational Reply Coupon, must be made to the above address by 1 July for the following year.

**UNIPAL:** BCM Unipal, London WC1N 3XX (e-mail info@unipal.org.uk; www. unipal.org.uk). Written enquiries preferred. Unipal (Universities' Trust for Educational Exchange with Palestinians) runs a summer programme of **teaching in the West Bank, Gaza and Lebanon**.
Volunteers to teach children, aged 12-15 from mid-July to mid-August. Volunteers must be native English speakers, based in the UK and at least 20 years old. Cost approx. £500.
   *Closing date for applications* is the end of February.

**WEIZMANN INSTITUTE OF SCIENCE:** PO Box 26, Rehovot 76100, Israel (fax 972-8-9344492; e-mail greta1.rosenberg@weizmann.ac.il; www.weizmann.ac.il/ acadaff//students.html).
**Undergraduate Research Students** to join a research project involving the Life Sciences, Chemistry, Physics and Mathematics and Computer Science. A small stipend is provided. Projects last for between 10 weeks and 4 months in the summer. Applicants must have finished at least 1 year at university and have some research experience.
   *Application forms* for Israeli students only are available on the Internet at the Weizmann Institute homepage (www.weizmann.ac.il/acadaff//students.html) and should be sent to the Academic Affairs Office the Summer Program for undergraduate students, at the above address; they must arrive by 31 December, of each year.

**YOUTH TRAVEL BUREAU:** 1 Shazar Street, PO Box 6001, Jerusalem 91060, Israel (☎972-2 655 84 00: fax 972-2 655 84 32; e-mail iyha@iyha.org.il; www.iyha. org.il).
Can help groups of Youth Hostel Association members to participate either in archaeological excavations for a minimum period of 2 weeks, or other educational tours for a minimum of 2 months.
   *Apply* to the above address for details.

# Kenya

Chances of finding a paid summer job in Kenya are minimal, but there are opportunities to participate in voluntary work with the following organisations. In addition, Concordia and UNA Exchange can place British, and Service Civil International, American nationals in voluntary work in Kenya: see the *Worldwide* chapter for details. For short-term teaching assignments in rural areas of Kenya, Americans can apply to Global Citizens Network/Harambee (www.globalcitizens. org/Kenya.html).

## RED TAPE

**Visa Requirements:** according to the Kenyan High Commission in London (www. kenyahighcommission.com), all non-Kenyan citizens have to be in possession of an Entry/Work Permit issued by the Principal Immigration Officer, Department of Immigration, PO Box 30191, Nairobi, before they can take up paid or unpaid work.

**AFRICA INLAND MISSION:** 2 Vorley Road, Archway, London, N19 5HE (☎020-7281 1184; fax 020-7281 4479; e-mail enquiry@aim-eur.org; www.aim.eur.org)

Africa Inland Mission is a Christian organisation that sends volunteers with strong Christian commitment to **teach in rural secondary schools** in East Africa including Kenya, Uganda and Tanzania. There are opportunities for qualified teachers, secretaries and doctors. Usually 30-50 volunteers are taken on annually. The age limits are 18-70 and volunteers must be in good health. Vacancies are year round but for teaching applicants the deadline for applications is usually the end of March.

Volunteers must raise all their own finances and although accommodation is usually provided, rent may have to be paid. Costs for 12 months range from £4000 to £5,500, depending on the country. Africa Inland Mission produces a quarterly magazine. A-Levels or above are the minimum qualification requirement needed for teaching in rural schools.

Applicants should *apply* directly to the Assistant Personnel Director at the above address.

**KENYA VOLUNTARY DEVELOPMENT ASSOCIATION:** PO Box 48902 - 00100, GPO Nairobi, 4th Floor Gilfilian House, Room 411, Kenyatta Avenue, Kenya (tel/fax 254-02-225379, or 254-02-247393; e-mail kvdakenya@yahoo.com; www.kvdakenya.com). Kenya Voluntary Development Association is an indigenous / non political / membership organisation which is non-sectarian and non-profit-making which started in 1962 as a work camp organisation. In 1993, KVDA was registered as a non-governmental organisation by the establishment of the NGO coordinating act.

Volunteers to work on projects in remote villages aimed at improving amenities in Kenya's rural and needy areas, working alongside members of the local community. The work may involve **digging foundations, building, making building blocks, roofing, awareness campaigns etc.** Short-term camps take place throughout the year, and there are normally 20-25 volunteers per camp with six hours of work per day, six days per week. The long-term programmes take place all year round, entailing placements of three or more months, in Kenyan communities on a professional basis as social workers, agriculturalists etc. Recent projects have included: awareness campaigns on HIV/Aids and other diseases, renovation of primary schools, construction of radio stations and volunteering in hospitals.

Accommodation is normally provided in school classrooms or similar buildings; foreign participants are expected to adapt to local types of foods, etc. Minimum age 18. There is a registration fee to be paid on arrival, of approximately £130/£220 for July and August. Projects can last anything from a 3 week camp up to one year volunteering and cost can range from $260 (USD) (approx £145) to $900 (USD) (approx £500).

For further details send three International Reply Coupons/ to the Director at the above address. British volunteers should apply through Concordia or another UK organisation.

**SKILLSHARE INTERNATIONAL:** 126 New Walk Street, Leicester LE1 7JA (☎0116 254 1862; fax 0116 254 2614; e-mail recruitment@skillshare.org' www.skillshare.org).

Skillshare recruits professionals to share their skills and experience with local communities for further economic and social development in Botswana, Kenya, Lesotho, Mozambique, Namibia, South Africa, Swaziland, Tanzania, Uganda, India and Nepal. Its vision is a world without poverty, injustice and inequality where people, regardless of cultural, social, and political divides come together for mutual benefit living in peaceful co-existence.

Projects cover a wide-range of activities and general management, agricultural, technical, educational and medical skills are all required. Applicants should be aged 21, have relevant qualifications and experience, particularly in training others.

Placements are usually for two years. Skillshare offers a modest living allowance, flights/travel to the placement and return, medical cover, and pre and post placement grants to assist with relocation. The living allowance is adequate to cover your living costs whilst in the country of placement but not adequate for savings or meeting other costs you may have in your country of residence.

An *information pack* is available from the above address.

**TAITA DISCOVERY CENTRE:** The Tsavo Kasiagu Wildlife Corridor, PO Box 48019, 00100 Nairobi, Kenya, (☎254-(0)2-331191 or 254-(0)2-222075; fax 254-2-330698 or 254-(0)2-216528; e-mail discoverycentre@originsafaris.info or info@ originsafaris.info; www.savannahcamps.com). Surrounding the unique Mount Kasigau are a number of relatively small and isolated rural communities. With the assistance of The African Wildlife Foundation's programme, these communities have committed themselves to participating in a conservation project to retain the unparalleled biodiversity of the region and preserve its currently untouched landscape.

**Volunteers** (max 20 at any time) live in basic conditions in the village, and are left to complete their chosen projects independently, although support is available 'on request' and in an emergency.

**Community Service Projects** Teachers needed for art, music, sport and drama.

**Community Based Micro Enterprises** Projects to develop the use of edible and useful plants of the bush, develop herbal remedies, and a Bonsai tree enterprise. There are also projects in elephant dung paper and other products, and aquaculture, sericulture and apiculture enterprise.

**Conservation Data Collection** Volunteers to take part in data collection, inventories of invertebrates, birds, plants, etc. Volunteers also needed for ecological plot sampling and behavioural studies of birds.

**Other Projects** include putting oral accounts of the Taita people onto paper, rural health programmes, primary school infrastructure development, economic studies and the development of alternative fuels.

Projects costs start at US$191 (approx £106) per person per week, plus the cost of getting to/from Tsavo. Minimum stay 4 weeks. In each week, volunteers will spend 5 nights working on community projects from their base at the Kasigau Bandas. The concept here is that the biggest threat to wilderness and wildlife in Africa is that of local people. Conservation is not only about looking after animals - but is also about changing attitudes, habits and concepts of the local people. By addressing the communities needs the project should inherently affect the various conservation issues. Then for the balancing 2 nights per week volunteers can if they wish go over to The Taita Discovery Centre for a bit of recreational game viewing, and possibly participate in the wildlife conservation and research activities.

*Contact* the above address for further details.

# Madagascar

Opportunities for paid temporary work in Madagascar are rare. The following organisations can arrange voluntary placements there.

**AZAFADY:** Studio 7, 1A Beethoven Street, London W10 4LG (☎020-8960 6629; fax 020-8962 0126; e-mail mark@azafady.org; www.madagascar.co.uk). Azafady is a registered UK charity and Malagasy NGO working to alleviate poverty, improve well-being and preserve beautiful, unique environments in southeast Madagascar. Has an award-winning team that works alongside rural communities on integrated conservation and development projects helping communities to build a better future for themselves.

**Pioneer Madagascar** is a ten-week volunteer scheme, run by Azafady, departing four times a year in January, April, July and October. Pioneers gain first hand experience of frontline development and conservation work. Volunteers live work and travel in one of the most beautiful and remote parts of southeast Madagascar. Living under canvas with basic facilities, the types of projects that pioneers will be involved with include: **building wells to provide clean water which helps protect villagers from cholera, monitoring endemic and endangered lemur species; assisting with GPS and other data-collection for forest management plans or establishing community market gardens and beehives to improve nutrition and provide villagers with alternative incomes.**

As part of the scheme, volunteers are asked to collect through fundraising a minimum donation of £2,000. This goes directly to support Azafady's charitable work, with only a small portion used to cover the volunteers' food, safe water, in-country travel, orientation and language training. Full support and advice is given to applicants on fundraising, international travel, visas, insurance and medical preparations before the expedition. Groups of 10-15 pioneers are accompanied by dedicated staff whilst in Madagascar. Pioneer is open to people over 18 of reasonable fitness. No special qualifications needed, but enthusiasm and flexibility to take part in ongoing projects is essential.

For more information and an *application form* visit www.madagascar.co.uk or call the London office at the telephone number above.

**REEFDOCTOR:** 14 Charlwood Terrace, Putney, London SW15 1NZ (☎0208-7886908; fax 0208-7892732; e-mail info@reefdoctor.org; www.reefdoctor.org). Reefdoctor is a young organisation which started a volunteer research assistant programme in reef conservation in Madagascar in 2004. Four volunteers are taken on at a time to spend a minimum of two and a maximum of three months as **reef research assistants**. Volunteers researchers need to be qualified up to PADI Advance Diver. Courses for this can be arranged in Madagascar. Volunteers also need to bring their own diving equipment. Accommodation is in reed huts on the beach and heat, humidity and insects are the norm. Volunteers should also have an interest and enthusiasm for marine conservation though training in research techniques is given. Ages 21-40. Cost is £1,100 for a month, £2,200 for two months and £2,800 for three months, excluding travel to Madagascar and in-country personal expenses. Research is conducted conjunction with Madagascar's only marine research institute.

*Applications:* to the above address.

# Morocco

Work permits are necessary for employment in Morocco: they are generally only given to people who speak French and/or Arabic, and have some particular skill or qualification that is in demand (e.g. teaching or IT).

There are, however, possibilities of seasonal work in the expanding tourist industry, especially around the resorts of Agadir, Marrakesh and Tangier. Several European holiday companies operate in Morocco and employ summer staff. Knowledge of French will normally be expected: this is also the language most likely to be used in voluntary workcamps, although English should be understood.

In addition to the voluntary opportunities listed below, Concordia, International Voluntary Service, Youth Action for Peace and UNA Exchange can help UK nationals, and the CIEE and Service Civil International Americans, find voluntary work in Morocco: see the *Worldwide* chapter for details. Students can arrange places in work camps listed.

# RED TAPE

**Visa Requirements:** a visa is not required by citizens of most Western European countries, Australia, Canada, New Zealand, the USA, the Russian Federation, Turkey and Switzerland if they are entering Morocco as tourists for up to 3 months.

**Residence Permits:** those planning a stay of over three months must register with the police and be able to provide evidence of how they are supporting themselves.

**Work Permit:** any foreigner taking up paid employment in Morocco must have a valid work permit: this will be obtained by the prospective employer from the Ministry of Labour (or by applying directly to the Ministry of Labour if self-employed). Work permits (*Contrats de Travail*) can be obtained while in Morocco if a job is found.

**Au Pair:** not customary.

**Voluntary Work:** a foreigner does not need a work permit or special visa in order to take part in an organised voluntary work project in Morocco providing (a) the scheme lasts for less than three months and (b) the work is unpaid.

# Teaching English

**AMERICAN LANGUAGE CENTRE:** 4 Zankat Tanja, Rabat 10000 (☎ 037-767103; alcrabat@mtds.com). Commercial language school, largest of a chain of ten schools in Morocco. The Casablanca school employs mainly American graduates with TEFL certification.

**Teachers:** (50). Typically semesters start in September and January but shorter contracts may be available.

*Applicants* for Rabat must have an arts degree.

# Voluntary Work

**AFRICATRUST NETWORKS:** Africatrust Chambers, P.O Box 551, Portsmouth, Hampshire, PO5 1ZN ( UK ☎01873-812453; e-mail info@africatrust.gi; www.africatrust.gi). Africatrust Networks offers 3 to 6 month periods of tropical work experience in North and West Africa with disadvantaged young people in Cameroon (French/English speaking), Ghana (English speaking) and in the southern parts of Morocco (French and Arabic speaking).

Africatrust Networks is looking for volunteers who can work as part of a team, wish to learn as well as to give, can cope with limited resources and adapt their skills to a very different and difficult work situation overseas.

The UK office carries out the selection, interviewing, pre-departure briefings and helps with the fund-raising for self-funded volunteer programmes. Each in-country director then leads the post arrival and in-country two week induction course; acclimatisation, language, health, security, culture, music, history, geography, experimental living etc. Volunteers then choose from selected programmes and meet host their family. The in-country director then resides over the regular volunteer/host review meetings throughout the programme.

Donations raised by volunteers are grouped and then distributed by the same team of volunteers. One vote per person not per pound raised. There are no deductions unlike the 22% expense deductions made by organisations such as Oxfam.

Teams consist of 6 or 8 volunteers who are usually graduates, university gap year students, or students on placements – seeking supervised work experience in tropical development environments with the possibility of using French or Arabic. Such field experience might lead to careers with the British Council, UN, Save the Children, Oxfam, CNN/BBC or World Bank.

For more information visit www.africatrust.gi or *contact* Africatrust Network at the above address.

**LES AMIS DES CHANTIERS INTERNATIONAUX DE MEKNES:** PO Box 8, 50000 Meknes, Morocco (fax +212 5 5511645; e-mail acim_b@hotmail.com). International non-profit making organisation.

Volunteers and professionals are needed to take part in work camps throughout Morocco from July-August. Camps take either two or three weeks. The aim of A.C.I.M is **protection of the environment, to work with children and old people, heightening awareness of conservation projects through workshops, guided tours, lectures, courses of Arabic language for foreigners, courses of English and French for Moroccans and foreigners who are interested, elimination of illiteracy, formation work camps; pottery, decoration on wood etc.** Activities are aimed at 17-35 year olds. The camps include food and accommodation. Volunteers are insured by the organisation when they are in the camp.

*Applications to* Rachid Sokhal, International Secretary, at the above address.

**CHANTIERS SOCIAUX MAROCAINS:** BP 456, Rabat, Morocco (☎212 37 26 24 00; fax +212 37 26 23 98; csm@wanadoo.net.ma; www.gaia.org.mx/workcamps/ Marruescos2.html).

CSM organises workcamps in Morocco which concentrate on **projects intended to benefit the local community.** About 300 volunteers a year are involved, spending two or three weeks of the summer on the sites with fellow workers from many European and African countries.

Applicants should be between 18 and 30 years old, and in good health. Food and accommodation are provided, but the volunteer is responsible for all his or her personal expenses.

Those interested can either *apply through* their national branch of the CCIVS (which is International Voluntary Service in Britain), or directly to the President at the above address.

**MOUVEMENT TWIZA:** BP 77, 15000 Khemisset, Morocco (☎212 37 55 73 15; fax: 212 37 55 73 15; e-mail twiza@iam.net.ma).

Mouvement Twiza organises weekend and summer work camps for volunteers in Morocco. It recruits about 500 volunteers per year to participate in a range of **socio-cultural activities including work in the slums and in schools and construction work.**

Applicants of any nationality are accepted, but volunteers must speak French and English, and preferably be outgoing and sociable. The minimum age limit is 18 years of age, and applicants must be healthy, willing and able. Volunteers are required in the summer for a maximum of three weeks. Accommodation is provided but pocket money is not.

Those interested should *apply* to the above address.

# Nigeria

Opportunities for paid temporary work in Nigeria are rare. However, the charity organisation VSO runs volunteer projects in many countries worldwide including Nigeria, for more information visit their website www.vso.org.uk. African Legacy (☎01202-554735; e-mail explore@africanlegacy.info) organises fieldwork adventure holidays to survey the remains of remote ancient civilisations in conjunction with the School of Environmental Services of Bournemouth University. The following organisation can also arrange voluntary placements there.

**NIGERIAN CONSERVATION FOUNDATION (NCF):** Lekki Conservation Centre, Km 19 Lagos-Epe Expressway, Lekki, P.O. Box 74638, Victoria Island, Lagos. Nigeria, West Africa (☎+234-(0)1-2642498; fax +234 –(0)1-8923717; ncf@ hyperia.com)
NCF promotes conservation through the management of protected areas, advocacy, research and education/awareness programmes. Volunteers not only assist in these areas, but with publications, communications and fund raising too. The period for which a volunteer stays and the the the time of year are flexible. Good verbal and oral communication in English is essential; knowledge of a Nigerian language is a distinct advantage. Volunteers must be in good health. Volunteers will be responsible for their food and accommodation costs.

NCF produces a variety of publications, a list of which can be found on their website.

*Applications* to the head of education unit using the above address.

**VOLUNTARY WORKCAMPS ASSOCIATION OF NIGERIA:**, G.PO Box 2189, Lagos, Nigeria (☎0803 712 8307; 01 8171168 4750508); email vwoan@yahoo. com.
VWAN organises workcamps centred on community projects for youths of different cultural backgrounds and nationalities throughout Nigeria. Between 120 and 150 volunteers per year participate in the workcamps; the work is mainly unskilled manual labour. This includes **bricklaying, carpentry, sport, games, excursions, debates and discussions.** VWAN also undertakes short and medium term programmes in the year.

Applicants of any nationality are welcome, but a knowledge of English is required. Volunteers must also be physically fit. The usual length of placement is between one and two months (i.e. July to September). Volunteers must pay a registration fee of approx £130 while feeding, board and lodging are provided for selected volunteers throughout the duration of the camps.

There is a charge of $20 (approx £11) for an application form, brochure and placement for the camps. Only applications received with the prescribed fee before the month of May will be treated each year.

*Contact* Kolawole Aganran or contact Service Civil International (www.sci-ivs. org/).

# South Africa

The government is (understandably) not keen to hand out work permits to Europeans and other nationalities when so many of their own nationals (40% at times) are unemployed. Work permits are granted only in instances where South African citizens or permanent residents are not available for appointment or cannot be trained for the position. The weakness of the land has lead to a 'brain drain' out of the country and positions exist for professionals.

Most people who do casual work have only a three-month tourist visa, which must be renewed before it expires. A 90-day extension can be obtained from the Department of Home Affairs in Johannesburg or Cape Town for a fee. After you have done this a few times, the authorities will become suspicious.

One solution to the problem is to consider BUNAC's work and travel programme in South Africa. Full-time students or those within 12 months of graduation aged 18 or over may be eligible for a 12-month working holiday permit (see entry) which allows them to look for work on the spot. Unfortunately for summer job seekers, the time when jobs are likely to be found is the high season of October to March.

Voluntary work is organised for British citizens in South Africa by UNA Exchange and Youth Action for Peace. See their entries in the *Worldwide* chapter for details. Work can be found in South Africa through the organisations below.

**SKILLSHARE INTERNATIONAL:** 126 New Walk Street, Leicester LE1 7JA (☎0116 254 1862; fax 0116 254 2614; e-mail recruitment@skillshare.org' www. skillshare.org)

Skillshare recruits professionals to share their skills and experience with local communities for further **economic and social development** in Botswana, Kenya, Lesotho, Mozambique, Namibia, South Africa, Swaziland, Tanzania, Uganda, India and Nepal. Its vision is a world without poverty, injustice and inequality where people, regardless of cultural, social, and political divides come together for mutual benefit living in peaceful co-existence.

Projects cover a wide-range of activities and general management, agricultural, technical, educational and medical skills are all required. Applicants should be aged 21, have relevant qualifications and experience, particularly in training others.

Placements are usually for two years. Skillshare offers a modest living allowance, flights/travel to the placement and return, medical cover, and pre and post placement grants to assist with relocation. The living allowance is adequate to cover your living costs whilst in the country of placement but not adequate for savings or meeting other costs you may have in your country of residence.

*An information pack* is available from the above address.

**WORK SOUTH AFRICA/VOLUNTEER SOUTH AFRICA:** BUNAC, 16, Bowling Green Lane, London EC1R OQH (☎020-7251 3472; fax 020-7251 0215; e-mail volunteer@bunac.org.uk; www.bunac.org).

BUNAC administer the *Work South Africa* programme that enables students who are to graduate this year and who are aged at least 18 to take up legally any job anywhere in South Africa: BUNAC can provide help in arranging work on arrival. Many participants work in hotels and restaurants or in jobs within the tourist industry. Many also take up shop-based or office work or community developmental work. The work visa is valid for up to 12 months and departures from the UK are year round. BUNAC arranges flights, visas, insurance and the first six nights' accommodation.

BUNAC has also offers the new placement programme, *Volunteer South Africa*, which enables applicants with suitable skills to become involved with volunteer projects in one of four main areas: the environment; tourism; education; and social welfare. Placements last for two months and accommodation and meals are included in the programme fee: participants may then stay for another month in South Africa travelling. Departures are available on a year-round basis.

For further details *contact* BUNAC at the above address or visit their website www.bunac.org.

## Voluntary Work and Archaeology

**SANCCOB – THE SOUTH AFRICAN NATIONAL FOUNDATION FOR THE CONSERVATION OF COASTAL BIRDS:** PO Box 11116, Bloubergrant 7443, Cape Town, South Africa (☎+27-21-557 6155; fax 21-557 8804; e-mail info@ sanccob.co.za; www.sanccob.co.za).

**Volunteers** required to help with the cleaning and rehabilitation of oil-soaked coastal birds. The main tasks involve **keeping the hospital clean (scrubbing pools and pens), feeding the birds and checking that the centre is prepared for a major oil spill.** The coastal waters of South Africa are a major shipping route and oil pollution is a recurrent problem, the main bird types dealt with are African penguins, gulls, gannets, terns and cormorants.

Volunteers must be willing to work in hard conditions with wild and difficult birds. Help is given with finding Bed & Breakfast accommodation and volunteers must meet their own living costs (approx. US$30-40) (approx £16-£22). The period May-October is the busiest but spills can happen at any time, the minimum stay is two weeks and applicants must be at least 16 years old.

*To apply* contact SANCCOB at the above address.

# Tanzania

In addition to the following entry, Concordia and UNA Exchange can offer short-term volunteer projects to Britons wishing to work in Tanzania for a few months, while Americans may be able to apply through Service Civil International; their entries in the *Worldwide* chapter give more details. There are other organisations which operate in a similar way to Volunteer Africa (below), i.e. you pay the organisation for your voluntary work placement of four weeks or longer: try also the UK-based Frontier (www.frontierconservation.org) and Madventurer (www. madventurer.com).

## RED TAPE

**Visa Requirements**: All visitors wishing to enter The United Republic of Tanzania need to obtain a visa, which must be obtained before entering Tanzania. A tourist or visitor visa is valid for up to 3 months (90 days).

**Work Permits**: One of three types of work Permit must be applied for, an 'A Class' permit is for self employed foreigners, a 'B class' is for other foreign employees and a 'C Class' permit is for students and missionaries etc.

**AFRICA INLAND MISSION:** 2 Vorley Road, Archway, London, N19 5HE (☎020-7281 1184; fax 020-7281 4479; e-mail enquiry@aim-eur.org; www.aim.eur.org) Africa Inland Mission is a Christian organisation that sends volunteers with strong Christian commitment to **teach in rural secondary schools** in East Africa including Kenya, Uganda and Tanzania. There are opportunities for qualified teachers, secretaries and doctors. Usually 30-50 volunteers are taken on annually. The age limits are 18-70 and volunteers must be in good health. Vacancies are year round but for teaching applicants the deadline for applications is usually the end of March.

Volunteers must raise all their own finances and although accommodation is usually provided, rent may have to be paid. Costs for 12 months range from £4000 to £5,500, depending on the country. Africa Inland Mission produces a quarterly magazine. A-Levels or above are the minimum qualification requirement needed for teaching in rural schools.

Applicants should *apply* directly to the Assistant Personnel Director at the above address.

**SKILLSHARE INTERNATIONAL:** 126 New Walk Street, Leicester LE1 7JA (☎0116 254 1862; fax 0116 254 2614; e-mail recruitment@skillshare.org' www.skillshare.org) Skillshare recruits professionals to share their skills and experience with local communities for further **economic and social development** in Botswana, Kenya, Lesotho, Mozambique, Namibia, South Africa, Swaziland, Tanzania, Uganda, India and Nepal. Its vision is a world without poverty, injustice and inequality where people, regardless of cultural, social, and political divides come together for mutual benefit living in peaceful co-existence.

Projects cover a wide-range of activities and general management, agricultural, technical, educational and medical skills are all required. Applicants should be aged 21, have relevant qualifications and experience, particularly in training others.

Placements are usually for two years. Skillshare offers a modest living allowance, flights/travel to the placement and return, medical cover, and pre and post placement grants to assist with relocation. The living allowance is adequate to cover your living costs whilst in the country of placement but not adequate for savings or meeting other costs you may have in your country of residence.

*An information pack* is available from the above address.

**VOLUNTEER AFRICA:** PO Box 24 Bakewell Derbyshire DE45 1YP e-mail support@volunteerafrica.org; www.volunteerafrica.org). Providing volunteers and fundraising to community-based organisations working in Tanzania, VolunteerAfrica is run largely by volunteers to keep down running costs. There are three programmes: Mwanza orphanages, Singida rural development and Tabora resource centre. Volunteers can participate for 4-12 weeks depending on which programme they choose.

The cost of participating during 2007 is £950 for 4 weeks, £1,330 for 7 weeks, £1,710 for 10 weeks. Of these fees, approximately 60% goes to the host organisations to support development work in Tanzania. Fundraising advice is given and the first week is spent in language and cultural training. Participants also need to budget around £600 for flights and medical insurance.

*Applicants* must be aged 18 or over when they are due to travel overseas and *applications can only be made through the organisation's website.*

# Uganda

The following organisations can arrange voluntary placements in Uganda

**AFRICA INLAND MISSION:** 2 Vorley Road, Archway, London, N19 5HE (☎020-7281 1184; fax 020-7281 4479; e-mail enquiry@aim-eur.org; www.aim. eur.org)
Africa Inland Mission is a Christian organisation that sends volunteers with strong Christian commitment to teach in rural secondary schools in East Africa including Kenya, Uganda and Tanzania. There are opportunities for qualified teachers, secretaries and doctors. Usually 30-50 volunteers are taken on annually. The age limits are 18-70 and volunteers must be in good health. Vacancies are year round but for teaching applicants the deadline for applications is usually the end of March.

Volunteers must raise all their own finances and although accommodation is usually provided, rent may have to be paid. Costs for 12 months range from £4000 to £5,500, depending on the country. Africa Inland Mission produces a quarterly magazine. A-Levels or above are the minimum qualification requirement needed for teaching in rural schools.

Applicants should *apply* directly to the Assistant Personnel Director at the above address.

**SKILLSHARE INTERNATIONAL:** 126 New Walk Street, Leicester LE1 7JA (☎0116 254 1862; fax 0116 254 2614; e-mail recruitment@skillshare.org' www. skillshare.org)
Skillshare recruits professionals to share their skills and experience with local communities for further **economic and social development** in Botswana, Kenya, Lesotho, Mozambique, Namibia, South Africa, Swaziland, Tanzania, Uganda, India and Nepal. Its vision is a world without poverty, injustice and inequality where people, regardless of cultural, social, and political divides come together for mutual benefit living in peaceful co-existence.

Projects cover a wide-range of activities and general management, agricultural, technical, educational and medical skills are all required. Applicants should be aged 21, have relevant qualifications and experience, particularly in training others.

Placements are usually for two years. Skillshare offers a modest living allowance, flights/travel to the placement and return, medical cover, and pre and post placement grants to assist with relocation. The living allowance is adequate to cover your living costs whilst in the country of placement but not adequate for savings or meeting other costs you may have in your country of residence.

*An information pack* is available from the above address.

**UNITED CHILDREN'S FUND INC:** PO Box 20341, Boulder, Colorado, 80308-3341, USA (☎+1-303 469 4339 or toll-free 1-800-615 5229; e-mail united@ unchildren.org; www.unchildren.org).
United Children's Fund, places volunteers on projects in Uganda including health care, working in village clinics, teaching in local village schools, assisting teachers, school construction, working with women's groups on income-generating projects and more.
**Volunteers** Volunteers are needed to work on projects where they think they can make the biggest difference. Special skills are not prerequisite. The minimum age for volunteers is 18. Placements last one or two months at any time of year.

*Applicants* pay a programme fee: $1,850 (onemonth), $2950 (two months). This

covers all food, transportation and local fees when in Uganda.
*For further details* check the website above.

**UGANDA VOLUNTEERS FOR PEACE (UVP):** PO Box 3312, Ki Wooya House, 256 Kampala, Uganda (☎+256-77 40 22 01; fax +256-41 53 07 65; e-mail uvpeace@yahoo.co.uk). UVP is now a member of ICYE Federation in Berlin hosting both long and short-term volunteers on various projects in Uganda. The UVP works towards peace, development and much needed solidarity in Uganda. It organises international **work camps** in January, March, April, June, August, October and December for 3-week periods. Age limits 15-35 years. Languages required: English, Swahili and French. Accommodation is provided free. There is a participation fee of US$200 (approx £111) and international membership costs US$100 (£55.75) per year.
*For further details contact* the above address.

# The Americas

## Canada

The employment of foreigners in either short or long-term work in Canada is strictly regulated. Even with Canada's relatively strong economy (unemployment currently at 6.7%), it is illegal to work in Canada without a work permit; with some exceptions, a job must be obtained from outside the country, and even then the employer will face difficulty in obtaining permission to employ you unless they can show that they are not depriving a Canadian citizen or permanent resident of the job.

Anyone seeking employment in Canada should write directly to Canadian employers before arrival to enquire about employment prospects. Information on jobs in Canada can also be obtained from Canadian newspapers or trade journals, which are available at larger newsagents. Addresses of potential employers can also be found in the *Canadian Trade Index* or the *Canadian Almanac and Directory*, both of which can be found at large libraries.

Teachers from British Commonwealth nations may be able to arrange exchange placements by contacting The League for the Exchange of Commonwealth Teachers, Commonwealth House, 7 Lion Yard, Tremadoc Road, London SW4 7NQ (☎020-7819 3938; fax 020-7720 5403; e-mail emily-ann.bowden@lect.org. uk; www.lect.org.uk).

To work legally in Canada, you must obtain a Work Permit from a Canadian High Commission or Embassy before you leave your home country. The exceptions are the special schemes for different categories. The other and more flexible option is to obtain an Open Work Authorisation through BUNAC's Work Canada programme which offers about 3000 students and non-students the chance to go to Canada for up to a year and take whatever jobs they can find. Participants on this programme can depart at any time between February and December. The great majority of participants go to Canada without a pre-arranged job and spend their first week or two job-hunting. The Canadian High Commission in London administers the scheme for British and Irish passport holders. There are similar schemes for Australians and New Zealanders.

Interested students should check the website www.canada.org.uk/visa-info or obtain the general leaflet 'Student Temporary Employment in Canada' by sending a large s.a.e. with a 50p stamp and marked 'SGWHP' in the top right-hand corner to the Canadian High Commission (Immigration Visa Information, 38 Grosvenor St, London W1K 4AA, or you can telephohe 0207-258 6350 and give your fax number for a form). Note that if you applying to work in Québec, there are separate and additional immigration procedures.

Concordia arrange voluntary placements in Canada, and UNA Exchange can organise voluntary work in French-speaking Québec; the CIEE can arrange voluntary work in Canada for Americans. For details of all these see the *Worldwide* chapter.

## RED TAPE

**Visa Requirements:** citizens of the United Kingdom and most other countries in

Western Europe, of UK dependent territories, Australia, New Zealand, the United States and Mexico do not normally require a visa for a visit to Canada. Citizens of other countries may need to obtain one. No matter what the length or purpose of the proposed stay, permission to enter and remain in Canada must be obtained from the Immigration Officer at the port of entry. If the purpose is any other than purely for a tourist visit to Canada, you should consult the Canadian High Commission or Embassy abroad before departure.

The length of stay in Canada is decided at the port of entry. Normally entry is granted for six months.

**Work Permit:** in almost all cases it is necessary to have a valid work permit. Authorises an individual to work 'at a specific job for a specific period of time for a specific employer'. It must be applied for before arrival. Some details of the work authorizations available through special schemes processed through BUNAC (16 Bowling Green Lane, London EC1R 0QH; ☎ 020-7251 3472; www.bunac.org.uk) are given above.

**Student General Working Holiday Programs :** see www.canada.org.uk. are open to full-time students aged 18-35 from the UK, Ireland, Sweden and Finland. Citizens of the latter four countries can apply directly to the immigration section of their local embassy, providing a letter of university acceptance and a letter confirming return to studies or proof that they have completed their studies within the previous 12 months and sufficient funds must be proven for voluntary work). Citizens of the UK, Ireland, Sweden and Finland can also make applications through local organisations: these are BUNAC for the UK (see above); CIMO PO Box 343 Hakaniemenkatu 2 SF 00531, Helsinki (www.cimo.fi) for Finland; and The International Employment Office, Kristinegatan 21, SE 791 60 Falum, Sweden (☎ 46 23 93700) for Sweden. There are also Student Working Holiday Programmes available for Australian and New Zealand citizens.

**General Working Holiday Program:** non-students aged 18-35 may be eligible for a 12-month working holiday permit. All enquiries from Irish citizens should be directed through USIT (9 Aston Quay, O'Connell Bridge, Dublin 2; ☎ +353 1 677 8117).

**Student Work Abroad Program** (SWAP) is available to full-time students aged 18-35 from Australia and New Zealand and is coordinated through STA (travel) offices in Australia and New Zealand. Prospective SWAP applicants must contact the STA office for information on the programme for that year.

**Voluntary Work:** a special category of work permit covers voluntary work which takes about two to four months to process if you have found a placement through a recognised charitable or religious organisation.

**Work Abroad Schemes for US Citizens:** the CIEE has a work placement scheme in Canada for Americans (www.councilexchanges.org).

# Agricultural Work

**AGRICULTURAL LABOUR POOL:** www.agri-labourpool.com. Seasonal and permanent agricultural jobs in the USA and Canada.

**WILLING WORKERS ON ORGANIC FARMS (CANADA):** 4429 Carlson Road, Nelson, British Columbia, Canada VIL 6X3 (☎/fax 250-354 4417; e-mail ; wwoofcan@shaw.ca; www.wwoof.ca). Hundreds of young people, from 30 different countries, every year go 'wwoofing' in Canada. 600 hosts available from the east to the west coast of Canada.

**Volunteers** to work on 600 **organic farms** in Canada ranging from small homesteads to large farms. Duties include general farm work and may include going to market, working with horses, garden work, milking goats, etc. No pocket money but board and lodging provided free of charge. Opportunities may be available all year round. Minimum age 16. Only EEA nationals with valid tourist visas need apply.

*Applications,* enclosing c.$50/£26(cash) includes postage, for a farm list and description booklet, should be sent to the above address.

## Voluntary Work and Archaeology

**FRONTIERS FOUNDATION/OPERATION BEAVER:** 419 Coxwell Avenue, Toronto, Ontario, Canada M4L 3B9 (☎416-690-3930; fax 416-690-3534; e-mail frontiersfoundation@on.aibn.com; www.frontiersfoundation.ca). Frontiers Foundation is a non-profit voluntary service organisation supporting the advancement of economically and socially disadvantaged communities in Canada and overseas.

Volunteers are recruited from across the world to serve in native and non-native communities across Canada for a variety of **community construction and educational projects.** The organisation works in partnership with requesting communities in low-income rural areas. Projects help to provide and improve housing, to provide training and economic incentives and to offer recreational/educational activities in developing regions.

Volunteers must be 18 or older and available for a minimum period of 12 weeks. Skills in carpentry, electrical work and plumbing are preferred for construction projects; previous social service and experience with children are sought for recreational/educational projects. The greatest need for volunteers is in June, July and August. Group size is usually between 2 and 8.

All accommodation, food and travel, within Canada is provided. Travel to and from Canada is the responsibility of the volunteer. Accommodation is normally provided by the community; volunteers must be prepared to live without electricity, running water or roads in some communities. Long term placements of up to 18 months are possible provided that the volunteer's work is deemed satisfactory after the initial 12 week period.

*Application kits* and information are available from the above address; please provide 3 International Reply Coupons. Once an applicant has sent in application forms there can be a delay of 3-12 weeks as references come in and possible placements are considered. Acceptance cannot be guaranteed.

## Other Employment in Canada

**INTERNSHIP CANADA PROGRAMME:** IST Plus Rosedale House, Rosedale Road, Surrey TW9 2SZ (☎ 020-8939 9057; fax 020 8939 9090; e-mail info@istplus.com; www.istplus.com). Assisting over 1500 students undertake practical training in North America each year, IST Plus is a worldwide organisation helping people develop skills and acquire knowledge for working in a multicultural, interdependent world.

The programme enables students who hold *British or Irish passports* to complete a period of work experience of up to one year in Canada. Minimum age 18. Applicants must be enrolled in full-time further or higher education (HND level or above) or a recent graduate within 12 months of finishing, or a gap year student with an unconditional offer of a university place. Before applying applicants must have secured a full-time work placement in Canada directly related to their studies.

Programme costs start at £200 for a two month stay which includes IST Plus insurance cover for the length of their stay. Official documentation and assistance with visa application are provided, as are orientation materials covering taxes, housing, Canadian culture and transportation; plus 24-hour emergency assistance with any problems whilst in Canada.

*Applications* can be made at any time of year, but should be made at least two months before the desired date of departure.

**WORK CANADA:** BUNAC, 16 Bowling Green Lane, London EC1R 0QH (☎020-7251 3472; e-mail canada@bunac.org.uk).
There are approximately 3,000 places on the Work Canada programme.The Work Authorisation is valid for one year and enables participants to work and travel anywhere in Canada.

Approximately 90% of participants go to Canada without a pre-arranged job and take an average of six days to find one. BUNAC also offers advice on job-hunting, various travel deals and on-going support services whilst in Canada.

For *further details* contact the above address or visit the website www.bunac.org.

# Colombia

The following organisation has vacancies for suitably qualified employees in Colombia.

## RED TAPE

**Visa Requirements:** EU nationals, with the exception of The Republic of Ireland, do not require a visa to enter Colombia as a Temporary Visitor. They will be granted a 180-day permit upon arrival.

**Work Permits:** This visa is granted to those foreigners who have been hired by a Colombian company and are going to work in Colombia. It will also be granted to foreigners going to work with the subsidiary of a foreign company in Colombia.

**CENTRO COLOMBO AMERICANO:** Cra. 45 No. 53-24, Medellín, Colombia (☎574-513-4444; fax 574-513-2666; e-mail info@colomboworld.com; www.colomboworld.com).
**TEFL Teachers** (140) in the programme, preference of nationality: U.S., Canadian or British. Six US/UK teachers hired. Other countries also welcome, conditions may vary. Applicants must have BA or MA (Education, Language teaching, TESOL, TEFL or related qualifications). Teachers are employed on one-year contract (renewable), 30 contact hours per week including Saturdays. English for children and adults. Salary: 1,500,000 2,200,000 pesos (£445-£535 approx.) per month, plus round trip ticket and all visa expenses paid. Assistance in finding housing. Pre-service and in-service training provided. Medical benefits and Spanish lessons provided.

Candidates should apply directly to the school; selection is made through references and phone interview. Send CV and three letters of recommendation to Lai Yin Shem, Academic Director.

# Costa Rica

Under Costa Rica law it is illegal for foreigners to be offered paid work, but the organisations listed in this chapter offer voluntary work. US nationals may be able to obtain voluntary work through the CIEE allowing for yearly changes in their project planning. Britons may find opportunities arranged by UNA Exchange.

## RED TAPE

**Work Permits:** For paid employment of one year or less, foreigners may apply for a Temporary Working Visa. The application should be made to the Department of Temporary Permits and Extensions at the General Directorate of Migration (GDM) while you are staying in Costa Rica. For longer stays in Costa Rica, you need to apply for Residency in Costa Rica.

**AGROPECURIA BALVE S.A.:** Am hohlen Stein 54, D-58802 Balve, Germany (☎/ fax +49-2375 21 70).
or Finca Bella Vista, Raizal Colorado de Abangares, Guanacaste, Costa Rica (☎+506-6780464; fax +506-6780467; e-mail balvesa@racsa.co.cr; http:/homepages. compuserve.de/RicaUrlaub).
Volunteers are needed to help run and work on a tropical ecological farm in Costa Rica. Typical work duties include **small-scale agriculture, gardening, construction, carpentry, fishing and maintenance work.** Relevant skills and experience are useful, but not essential, though it is recommended that volunteers have some basic knowledge of Spanish. An interest in ecology and biological farming is a plus. Applicants over 16 years are accepted. The minimum stay is one month, and there is no upper limit.

Volunteers are expected to pay $100/£55 a week to cover food and lodging in rooms usually rented to tourists. Wages cannot be paid, but volunteers can enjoy a lot of privileges like use of the swimming pool, horse or cycle riding, excursions, and working and living with Costa Ricans to learn Spanish rapidly. Those wishing to learn Spanish whilst they are there are encouraged to apply.

Those interested should *contact* Rudolf Micknass, President, at the above address, preferably by e-mail. Alternatively, contact Am Hohlen Stein 54, D-58802 Balve, Germany (☎/fax 0049 2375-2170). Please note only Spanish speakers should telephone the Costa Rica number.

**IYOK AMI:** PO Box 335-2100, San José, Costa Rica, Central America. (☎+506-387 2238 or +506-254 1822 (Spanish is preferred); fax 506-771 200 or 506-223 1609; e-mail iyokbosque@yahoo.es or ciprotur@rasca.co.cr; www.ecotourism.co.cr/iyokami).
An extensive private reserve that includes both tropical cloud and tropical rain forests, and an Indian reserve. These wild areas have been set aside to protect flora, fauna and water resources, and also to serve as areas of scientific and research study.
Volunteers' help is needed to **build and maintain trails** and for **reforestation, help with labelling and transplantation of flowering plants around the trails, making topographical and pictorial maps of the area, constructing signposts, teaching English in schools, protecting and stimulating the Quetzal bird reproduction.** Volunteers also help with the **classification of plants, birds and fungi,** and other work depending on the volunteer's interest and specialist knowledge.

Volunteers will receive a free daily hour of basic Spanish teaching. Anyone is welcome to apply. Iyok Ami is a private organisation that receives no funding and so volunteers pay $650 per month, to cover board, laundry and accommodation (overlooking the forest, the Irazu, and Turrialba volcanoes). Volunteers are expected to work five hours per day, Monday to Friday. Weekends are free for visiting other places (the beach etc.).

*Applications* to the above address.

**RAINFOREST CONCERN:** 8 Clanricarde Gardens, London, W2 4NA (☎020 7229 2093; fax 020 7221 4094; e-mail info@rainforestconcern.org; www.rainforestconcern. org).
Rainforest Concern is a non-political charity dedicated to the conservation of vulnerable rainforest and the biodiversity they contain. Volunteers are encouraged to help out with research and reserve maintenance and are invited to sponsor acres of forest for protection.
**Volunteers for reforestation/trail maintenance and the establishment of organic agriculture (18)** required at any time. The work involves an element of monitoring and of physical labour, such as reforestation or compiling species lists, or trail maintenance depending on the projects being undertaken at the time. Current volunteer opportunities are in the cloud forests of western Ecuador and in Amazonian Ecuador (minimum period of work 7 days). For costs and availability please see the website for individual project contact details. No special skills are required, although Spanish would be helpful. Applicants must have a sincere interest in conservation, be over 18 and generally fit.

*Applications* can be sent to the above address at any time of year.

**VOLUNTEER COSTA RICA:** BUNAC, 16 Bowling Green Lane, London EC1R OQH (☎020-7251 3472; e-mail volunteer@bunac.org.uk).
This placement programme run by BUNAC allows participants to spend 3-6 months working as a volunteer in Costa Rica. Placements can be in areas such as **agriculture, conservation, small business development or teaching**. Accommodation is provided as part of the programme fee however participants will be expected to make a contribution towards their food costs. Applicants are expected to speak Spanish confidently to GCSE level or equivalent and must be either a current university level student or a graduate aged 18-32.

For *further details* contact BUNAC at the above address or visit www.bunac.org.

# Cuba

The following organisation recruits people for a working holiday scheme in Cuba.

## RED TAPE

**Visa Requirements**: any person wishing to enter Cuba as a tourist must apply for a Tourist Visa-card. This card is valid only for tourism and recreational purposes.

**THE CUBA SOLIDARITY CAMPAIGN:** c/o Red Rose Club, 129 Seven Sisters Road, London N7 7QG (☎020-7263 6452; fax 0207-561 0191; e-mail office@cuba-solidarity.org.uk; www.cuba-solidarity.org.uk).
The Cuba Solidarity Campaign (CSC) works in the UK to raise awareness of the illegal US blockade of Cuba, and to defend the Cuban people's right to self-

determination. It publishes a quarterly magazine 'Cuba Si', in addition to organising meetings, cultural events, and specialist tours to Cuba.

**Volunteers** are needed to take part in a scheme in Cuba involving 3 weeks work on a self-contained camp near Havana. The work involves light agricultural work approximately 4 mornings per working week, a programme of guided visits to schools, hospitals and community projects, with excursions arranged and transport to Havana provided during time off. There are many opportunities to meet Cubans, and enjoy vibrant Cuban culture first hand. There are two working holidays organised each year, one in the summer and one in the winter.

Costs including flights, accommodation, full board, full programme of guided visits and 3 days of rest and relaxation in another part of the island. Summer brigade: £875. Winter Brigade: £950. The Campaign organises the necessary visa.

*Contact* the above address for application deadlines and further information.

# Ecuador

As well as the following organisations, Concordia, UNA Exchange and Youth Action for Peace offer short-term international volunteer projects to Britons in Ecuador, while the CIEE can do the same for US citizens. See their entries in the *Worldwide* chapter for more details.

**BENEDICT SCHOOLS OF LANGUAGES:** PO Box 09-01-8916, Guayaquil, Ecuador (☎593-4-2444418; fax 593-4-2441642; e-mail smacchiavello@ benedictschools.com; www.benedictguayaquil.com).

**TEFL Teachers: (15)** required for several schools in Guayaquil (Urdesa, Centro, Garzota, Centenario, Entrerios). Applicants should ideally be British, American, Canadian or Irish, hold a teaching certificate or college degree and be proficient in English.

Minimum period of work 6 months (two courses), although the school prefers it if teachers can stay at least 10 months. Help is given with finding accommodation and the salary is US$5.50/$6.50 (approx £3/£3.50) per hour.

Applications accepted and work available all year round, to *apply* contact Mercedes de Elizalde, General Director at the above address.

**FUNDACION GOLONDRINAS/ THE CERRO GOLONDRINAS CLOUDFOREST CONSERVATION GROUP:** c/o Calle Isabel La Catòlica N24-679, Quito, Ecuador (☎593-2-2226 602; e-mail manteca@uio.satnet.net (subject: volunteer); www.fundaciongolondrinas.org/).

Volunteers required to help conserve 25,000 hectares of highland cloud forest on the western slopes of the Andes. The project's work involves the introduction of **sustainable agro-forestry techniques, soil conservation, research and the reintroduction of tree species.** Volunteers will be involved in these activities in two field sites; some general labouring also required.

Minimum stay 1 month. Some experience of horticulture/permaculture, and advanced Spanish are prerequisites, and a contribution to costs of c. $310/£172 per month. Special financial arrangements will be made by the group for those with advanced skills in gardening, agro-forestry, permaculture and those who wish to stay more than 3 months.

Volunteers accepted all year round, but contact Fundacion at least 2+ months in advance of desired dates of placement. Volunteers must arrange their own travel, visas and field kit.

For details of work and kit requirements *contact* the above address.

**RAINFOREST CONCERN:** 8 Clanricarde Gardens, London, W2 4NA (☎020 7229 2093; fax 020 7221 4094; e-mail info@rainforestconcern.org; www.rainforestconcern. org).

Rainforest Concern is a non-political charity dedicated to the conservation of vulnerable rainforest and the biodiversity they contain. Volunteers are encouraged to help out with research and reserve maintenance and are invited to sponsor acres of forest for protection.

**Volunteers for reforestation/trail maintenance and the establishment of organic agriculture** (18) required at any time. The work involves an element of monitoring and of physical labour, such as reforestation or compiling species lists, or trail maintenance depending on the projects being undertaken at the time. Current volunteer opportunities are in the cloud forests of western Ecuador and in Amazonian Ecuador (minimum period of work 7 days). For costs and availability please see the website for individual project contact details. No special skills are required, although Spanish would be helpful. Applicants must have a sincere interest in conservation, be over 18 and generally fit.

*Applications* can be sent to the above address at any time of year.

# Mexico

Paid employment is difficult to find in Mexico and must be approved by the Mexican Government before a visa will be issued to enter Mexico. Permits are generally issued to people who are sponsored by companies in Mexico. Visitors entering Mexico as tourists are not permitted to engage in any paid activities under any circumstances though this does not stop private language schools employing English teachers who have tourist visas. This is illegal.

There are a growing number of opportunities for voluntary work in Mexico. British applicants can find voluntary work in Mexico through Outreach International (www.outreachinternatinal.co.uk), Concordia, UNA Exchange or Youth Action for Peace, US nationals through the CIEE; see the *Worldwide* chapter for details.

## RED TAPE

**Work Permits:** A Mexican firm or company must apply on the employee's behalf. Further details can be found at the Mexican Consulate website www.mexicanconsulate. org.uk and www.mexconnect.com.

**Voluntary Work:** a Non Immigrant Visitor carnet (FM3) is necessary for anyone entering Mexico wishing to perform activities of social assistance or voluntary work in private or public institutions. The FM3 is not available to all nationalities.

**AMERICAN FRIENDS SERVICE COMMITTEE:** 1501 Cherry Street, Philadelphia, Pennsylvania 19102, USA.

Volunteers to work in indigenous villages in Mexico learning from an intercultural exchange while contributing to communities with work projects and cultural workshops. Work generally lasts for 7 weeks from early July to late August. Applicants should be 18-26 years old and speak Spanish. Limited scholarships available some years.

Participants are responsible for their own travel costs and must make a contribution to cover orientation, food and accommodation and health and accident insurance. Please note that no paid jobs are available in Mexico or US through the AFSC or SEDEPAC.

For details *American applicants should write* to the above address enclosing an International Reply Coupon before 1st March or apply via the websitewwwlafsc.org/ mexicosummer. *European applicants should apply directly* to SEDEPAC, Apartado Postal 27-054, 06760 Mexico DF, Mexico (fax 52-5-584 3895; e-mail sedepac@ laneta.apc.org)

**CONCORDIA:** 19 North Street, Portslade, Brighton, BN4 1DH (☎01273-422218; fax 01273-421182; e-mail info@concordia-iye.org.uk; www.concordia-iye.org.uk). Concordia offers volunteers aged 20+ the opportunity to join an international team of volunteers working on community-based projects ranging from **restoration and construction, to art/culture and social projects including work with adults or children with special needs, children's play schemes and teaching.** Projects last for 2-4 weeks and run year round.

Generally no skills or experience are needed, although Concordia runs a preparation weekend for applicants. Volunteers pay a registration fee of £120, plus an extra fee payable to the in-country host of approx. £140, and fund their own travel. Board and accommodation are free of charge.

For further information on volunteering or coordinating please check the website or *contact* the International Volunteer Coordinator at the above address.

# Teaching and Language Schools

**AHPLA INSTITUTE:** Juan Escutia No. 97, Colonia Condesa, C.P. 06140, Mexico, D.F (☎+52 5 211 2806, ext. 112); fax: +52 5 211 2806, ext.119); e-mail kallen@ ahpla.com or ahpla@ahpla.com; www.ahpla.com).
**English teachers (35)** Applicants must be educated, flexible, willing to work with a team and travel. People skills and personality are a must. Teachers are expected to work a minimum of 6 months. Hours are mainly 7-9am and 5-7pm. Wages are 122 pesos per hour (approx £5.88). Alpha Institute offers no help with accommodation or flights, however help is given with working papers when teacher has shown a commitment to AHPLA.
*Applications* to Karen Julie Allen, Operations Manager.

**CULTURLINGUA LANGUAGE CENTER:** Morelos 636 Sur, C.P. 59680 Zamora, Michoacàn (tel/fax 351-512 3384; e-mail info@culturlingua.com; www.culturlingua. com).
**English teachers** with TESOL, ESL or any teacher's certificate. Native English-speaker essential. Must be adaptable to teach children, adolescents or adults. To work 30 hours a week with 6 daily classes Monday to Friday. Accommodation can be provided.
*Applications* to the above address/e-mail at any time.

**DUNHAM INSTITUTE:** Avenida Zaragoza 23, Chiapa de Corzo, Chiapas (☎291-60 961; fax 61-61498; e-mail dunhaminstitute@yahoo.com).
**English teachers (3)** required with ESL certificate, must be a native English speaker. To work minimum 5 months, 3-4 hours in the afternoon teaching. Study Spanish in the mornings. No salary is provided. Accommodation with a local family and 2 hours

of Spanish tuition a day. Work permits not required.
*Applications* to Joanna Robinson, Academic Coordinator at above address.

# Peru

The following organisations have vacancies for paying volunteers/suitably qualified employees in Peru.

## RED TAPE

**Visa Requirements**: British, Irish and EU nationals do not need a visa when travelling to Peru. Once in Peru visitors are allowed to remain for 90 days. However anyone hoping to take up paid employment in Peru requires a visa.
**Work Permits**: Resident working visas have to be requested by the employers in Peru.

**KIYA SURVIVORS:** 38 Hove Park Villas, Hove, East Sussex BN3 6HG (☎01273-721092; fax 01273-732875; e-mail ukinfo@kiyasurvivors.org; www.kiyasurvivors. org).
Kiya Survivors' unique Rainbow Centre, in Peru's sacred Valley is just an hour's drive from Cusco, the center provides invaluable help for children who have been abused, neglected or who have special needs.

Kiya Survivors is a registered Peruvian charity set up to **help special needs children in Peru** for whom there is virtually no help. Volunteers aged from 18-80 are needed for placements of two, four or six months' duration starting in September, January and May. Cost ranges between £900 and £2,700, depending on the length of stay. On average a full placement of four months costs £2,350 and includes flight Lima to Cusco, two nights in Lima, transfer to project, six-week Spanish course, accommodation in a volunteer family house or home, a two-day Inca trail and trip around the Sacred Valley; a horse-riding excursion and tourist ticket with access to all local ruins and museums. Volunteers buy their own insurance and food. The volunteer house has cooking facilities and local markets provide cheap fresh food.
*Contact* Jan Sampson at the above address or e-mail.

**TAMBOPATA JUNGLE LODGE:** PO Box 454, Cusco, Peru (tel/fax +51-84-245695; e-mail operaciones@tambopatalodge.com or tplcus@terra.com.pe; www.tambopatalodge.com).
**Nature Guides** to lead nature walks for tourists and accompany them during their stay at a jungle lodge in the rainforest of Southern Peru within the Tambopata National Reserve. Working hours required may be any time between 4am and 8pm, as the tour programme dictates. Those taken on will be qualified students and scientists. The exchange programmes are: people who participate in 20 days per month of guiding will receive in exchange return air travel between Lima or Cusco and Puerto Maldonado per 90 days and £100 per month, or guide 10 days per month and receive in exchange a return air ticket for each 90 days worked and the remainder of the month free for research, etc. Applicants can also combine these two programmes.

The minimum stay is 180 days at any time of year. Applicants will ideally stay for six months, have a background in nature studies, speak English and Spanish; knowledge of French and German would be an advantage.

Those interested should *contact* the above address including a curriculum vitae.

**VOLUNTEER PERU**: BUNAC, 16 Bowling Green Lane, London, EC1R 0QH (tel: 020-7251-3472; e-mail volunteer@bunac.org.uk). This programme run but BUNAC allows participants to spend 2-3 months working as a volunteer in Peru. There is a great need for volunteers with specific practical skills for example IT, placements can also be education or based on manual/unskilled labour. Accommodation is provided with a host family as part of the programme fee as are all support services in the UK and in Peru for the duration of your trip. Applications are expected to have Spanish Language skills to approximately GCSE level or equivalent. The programme is open to students, non-students and graduates.

For further details *contact* BUNAC at the above address or visit www.bunac.org.

# USA

Despite a slowing economy relative to most other countries the USA has low unemployment (4.6% in 2006) and there is still a strong demand for workers to fill a wide variety of specialised summer jobs. Opportunities for summer work in the United States are so numerous that apart from those listed below, there are thousands on websites including www.j1jobs.com, www.coolworks.com, www.apexusa.org, www.greatcampjobs.com and www.seasonalemployment.com/summer.html to name but a few. National and state parks in the USA list their recruitment needs on their sites. The website www.nps.gov/parks.html gives a list of all such parks from A to Z and their contact details.

Placing an advertisement in an American paper may lead to the offer of a job. The New York Times (www.nytimes.com) is published by A.O. Sulzberger, of 229 West 43rd Street, New York, NY10036. It has a UK office at 66 Buckingham Gate, London, SW1 6AU (☎020-7799 2981/7592 8325).

Au pairing in the US differs from au pairing in Europe since the hours are much longer and, if the au pair comes from the UK, there is no language to learn. The basic requirements are that you be between 18 and 26, speak English, show at least 200 hours of recent childcare experience and provide a criminal record check.

Voluntary work in the USA can be arranged through the Winant-Clayton Volunteer Association (entry below), Youth Action for Peace, UNA Exchange, Concordia, International Voluntary Service, the CIEE, and Service Civil International. See the *Worldwide* chapter for details.

# RED TAPE

**Visa Requirements:** since the introduction of the Visa Waiver Program, the tourist visa requirement is waived in the case of 28 nationalities, including British and Australian citizen passport holders. Nationals of the 28 VWP countries may enter the U.S. for up to 90 days for tourism or business, provided they meet all of the regulations for visa free travel. Note: Certain travellers are not eligible to travel visa free, for instance those who have been arrested and/or convicted of an offence. The Rehabilitation of Offenders Act does not apply to U.S. visa law. For a full list of the 29 visa free countries, including the criteria which must be met to travel visa free, and further information on those not eligible to travel under the VWP, contact your nearest Embassy or Consulate, or visit the Department of State's website at http://travel.state.gov or www.usembassy.org.uk.

Since Oct 1st 2004 visitors from 27 countries including Britain have been digitally photographed and electronically fingerprinted by US immigration before being given permission to enter the USA.

Anyone entering the United States to work requires the appropriate work visa. Under no circumstances can a person who has entered the U.S. as a tourist take up any form of employment paid or unpaid.

**Residence Permits:** Anyone seeking to take up permanent residence in the U.S. requires the appropriate immigrant visa. In general immigration is family or employment based. For further information, contact your nearest Embassy or Consulate, or visit the Department of State's website as above.

**Work Permits:** Anyone taking up temporary employment, whether paid or unpaid, requires the appropriate work visa. There are a number of possible visas for temporary workers, au pairs, exchange visitors and cultural exchange visitors on EVPs (recognised Exchange Visitor Programmes such as BUNAC and Camp America. Most of the opportunities listed in this chapter are covered by the J-1 Exchange Visitor visa, which is arranged by the organisations with entries. Employment-based H-2B visas are available through major employers of seasonal workers (as in ski resorts) only after the employer receives Labor certification from the Department of Labor (which takes 3-6 months).

**Au Pair:** J-1 visa available through officially approved exchange visitor programmes overseen by the Public Affairs Division of the Department of State. The au pair placement programme allows thousands of young Europeans with childcare experience to work for American families for exactly one year on a J-1 visa. They apply through a small number of sponsoring organisations (the au pair agencies), which must follow the guidelines, which govern the programme, so there is not much difference between them. They will issue the IAP-66 application form, which is sent to the Visa Branch of the US Embassy.

**Voluntary Work:** Individuals participating in a voluntary service program benefiting U.S. local communities, who establish that they are members of and have a commitment to a particular recognised religious or non-profit charitable organisation may, in certain cases, enter the United States with business (B-1) visas, or visa free, if eligible, provided that the work performed is traditionally done by volunteer charity workers, no salary or remuneration will be paid from a U.S. source other than an allowance or other reimbursement for expenses incidental to the stay in the United States, and they will not engage in the selling of articles and/or solicitation and acceptance of donations. Volunteers should carry with them a letter from their U.S. sponsor, which contains their name and date and place of birth, their foreign permanent residence address, the name and address of their initial destination in the U.S., and the anticipated duration of the voluntary assignment.

## Agricultural Work

**AGRICULTURAL LABOUR POOL:** www.agri-labourpool.com. Seasonal and permanent agricultural jobs in the USA and Canada.

## Industrial and Office Work

**TREK AMERICA:** PO Box 159, Rockaway, NJ, 07866, USA (☎001-973-983-1144; fax 001-973-983-8551; e-mail personnel@premierops.com or info@trekamerica.com;

www.trekamerica.com). A small group adventure camping tour operator offering treks throughout North America's National Parks and Indian lands.

**Sales Representatives (1-2)** to work inside and outside an office. Duties involve handling incoming calls, orientation for clients, greeting participants. Past sales experience and travel experience in the States is preferred. Must be friendly, and willing to do public presentations. To work 40-45 hours per five day week. Minimum of two months' work between July and September. A wage is provided but no accommodation. The successful applicant may be entitled to a free tour. No other languages required.

*Applications* to the above address.

# Summer Camps

**CAMP AMERICA:** Dept. SDA, 37A Queen's Gate, London SW7 5HR. Camp America is one of the world's leading summer camp programmes, offering its counselors over 40 years of experience placing people from Europe, Asia, Africa, Australia and New Zealand at American summer camps. Camp America is looking to recruit skilled people for a variety of job choices available all over the USA, form Camp Counsellor roles to Camp Power or Resort America positions; it takes pride in evaluating the background, training and main skill areas of applicants to help them find the right placement.

**Camp Counsellors**: required to undertake childcare and/or teaching sports activities, music, arts, drama and dance. Experience and qualifications in sport coaching, religious counselling, teaching, childcare, healthcare and life guarding is preferable. Applicants must be available to leave the UK between May 1 and June 27 for a minimum of 9 weeks.

Counsellors are offered return flights from London and other selected airports worldwide to New York and transfers to particular camp, free accommodation and meals, up to 10 weeks travel time after camp, plus 24-hour support and medical insurance, Cultural Exchange U.S Visa sponsor and pocket money, which ranges from $525 to $1,100 (depending on age and experience)

Early application is advised. Camp America host recruitment fairs allowing participants to meet face-to-face with Camp Directors. For the latest event information and to request a brochure, please *visit* www.campamerica.co.uk or call 020-7581 7373.

---

## Be a Camp Counselor in an American Summer Camp

If you are:
18+ years of age
Available from at least June 15 to August 25
Patient with a good sense of humour
Adventurous and enjoy the outdoors
Able to be away from home for more than 9 weeks

We offer you:
Free round-trip to USA (open return ticket)
All Visa administration
Comprehensive travel insurance
Pocket money

*the best Summer of your life!*

**CCUSA**
CAMP COUNSELORS USA

CCUSA
27 Woodside Gardens
Musselburgh EH21 7LJ
TEL: 0131 665 5843
www.ccusa.com

or

CCUSA
Devon House,
171/177 Great Portland Street
London W1W 5PQ
TEL: 020 7637 0779

---

**CAMP COUNSELORS USA:** UK Offices: Devon House, 171/177 Great Portland Street, London W1W 5PQ (☎020-7637 0779; e-mail info@ccusa.com; www.ccusa. com) and 27 Woodside Gardens, Musselburgh, nr. Edinburgh EH21 7LJ (☎0131-665 5843; e-mail ccusascotland@yahoo.co.uk; www.ccusa.com). US Office: 2330 Marinship Way, Suite 250, Sausalito CA 94965, USA.
Camp Counselors USA is a high quality programme that places young people at American Summer Camps. Counselors are only placed at camps that have a good reputation with CCUSA. Each year CCUSA staff inspect the camps and interview Counselors, so that improvements can be made if necessary. CCUSA require people with sports and/or arts and crafts qualifications or willing to assist with the physically and mentally handicapped.

In addition CCUSA require well-motivated young people who are willing to be role models for the camps (to look after the children whilst they are at camp). In the coming year Camp Counselors will also be recruiting support staff, who must be full-time students. All applicants must be available for interview in Europe.

For further information *contact* the above addresses.

**CAMP POWER:** Dept. SDA, 37a Queen's Gate, London SW7 5HR.
Camp Power, a programme of Camp America, is open only to full-time students who want to work in general maintenance roles at American summer camps. Applicants must be available to leave the UK between 1 May and 27 June for a minimum of nine weeks. Typical job roles involve assisting in kitchen/laundry duties, administration and general camp maintenance. This supportive role represents an ideal camp alternative for those not wishing to work directly with children. Experience in administrative roles, maintenance, health care and catering is preferable.

Participants are offered free return flights from London and other selected airports worldwide to New York and transfer to their camp, free accommodation and meals, up to 10 weeks of travel time after camp, 24 hour support and medical insurance, Cultural

Exchange US visa sponsor, and pocket money which ranges from $850 to $1,300 (dependant on age and experience). Early application advised. Camp America host recruitment fairs allowing participants to meet face-to-face with Camp Directors.

For the latest event information and to request a brochure, please *visit* www.campamerica.co.uk or call 020-7581 7373.

**KAMP:** BUNAC, 16 Bowling Green Lane, London EC1R 0QH (☎020-7251 3472; fax 020-7251 0215; e-mail camps@bunac.org.uk).

KAMP is a low cost fare-paid programme for summer camp staff who are not afraid of two months' work in an ancillary capacity. Working in the kitchen and maintenance areas, staff do not look after children and have access to many of the camps' facilities during time off.

BUNAC places applicants, arranges the special work/travel visa, flight and travel to camp. In addition, participants are given free board and lodging at camp, a salary and up to six weeks of independent travel afterwards. The programme is open to those who are currently enrolled at a British university, studying full-time at degree (or advanced tertiary or postgraduate) level; gap year and final year students are not eligible. The programme fee is approximately £69.

*Applications* to the above address.

**SUMMER CAMP USA:** 16 Bowling Green Lane, London EC1R 0QH (☎020-7251 3472; fax 020-7251 0215; e-mail camps@bunac.org.uk).

A low-cost, non-profit camp counsellor programme run by BUNAC (the British Universities North America Club), placing over 5,000 people in US summer camps. Provides job, work papers, flights, salary, board and lodging, and a flexible length of independent holiday time after the 9 week work period.

Applicants must be aged 18-35, have experience of working with children *and be living in the UK at the time of making their application.* The programme fee is approximately £69.

For details contact the above address or visit the website www.bunac.org.

# Voluntary Work and Archaeology

**ANDY'S ORGANIC:** PO Box 1729, Pahoa, HI 96778, USA (☎808 937-9806; e-mail andysorganic@hotmail.com). A certified organic farm striving to become a school for tropical agriculture, specialising in yellow ginger, Thai ginger and turmeric but also growing diverse tropical crops. The farm is located in a rural and beautiful agricultural area on Hawaii's largest island. Tide pools, hot ponds, a small lake and a healing centre where one can take yoga classes can be found nearby.

Voluntary farm hands with extensive experience who wish to deepen their understanding of sustainable agriculture in the tropics. Farm work includes **planting, cultivating, harvesting, washing and packing as well as other tasks that may arise.** Apprentices are required to work 20 hours a week in exchange for room and food from the garden, and are expected to contribute to community chores as well. Applicants should be prepared to stay for one to three months.

*Applicants* can apply to the above address at any time. Please enclose postal and e-mail address and a résumé would be helpful.

**GIBBON CONSERVATION CENTER:** PO Box 800249, Santa Clarita, CA 91380 (☎661-296 2737; fax 661-296 1237; e-mail gibboncenter@earthlink.net; www.gibboncenter.org). This non-profit organisation houses the largest group of gibbons in the Western Hemisphere. It is devoted to the study, preservation, and propagation of this small ape.

Voluntary **primate keepers** (up to 3 at any one time) to work with gibbons at the centre. Duties include **preparing food and feeding, changing water, cleaning enclosures, observing behaviour (if time permits), entering data into computer (Apple Mac), maintaining grounds** etc. To work from approx. 6.30am-5pm, 7 days a week; opportunities for time off depend on the number of volunteers. Volunteers must make their own travel arrangements and buy their own food locally; accommodation is provided.

Applicants must be aged at least 20, well motivated, love animals, be capable of retaining unfamiliar information, get along with a variety of people, be in good physical condition and able to work outside in extreme weather conditions. They will need to have the following medical tests: stool cultures, ova and parasite stool test, standard blood chemistry and haematology, tuberculosis (or written proof from a doctor certifying that they have been vaccinated against tuberculosis) and Hepatitis B. Also required are vaccinations against tetanus (within the last 5 years), rubella, measles and Hepatitis B (if not already immune).

*Applications* to Erin Bell or Patricia Dahle, Volunteer Coordinators at gibboncenter@earthlink.net or ☎661 296 9495 or to the above address.

**THE INTERNATIONAL VOLUNTEER PROGRAMME:** San Francisco Bay Area Office, 678 13<sup>th</sup> Street, Suite 200, Oakland, CA 94612, (☎510-433-0414; fax 510 433 0419; email ivpsf@swiftusa.org; www.ivpsf.com). The International Volunteer Programme was founded in 1991 by La Société Française de Bienfaisance Mutuelle with the assistance and cooperation of the French Consulate in San Francisco, the University of California at Irvine, and le Comité de Jumelages de Troyes. The IVP is a non-profit organisation that promotes volunteering in Europe, the US and Latin America.

Volunteer programmes are designed to facilitate a hands-on service and international exchange opportunities, with the aim of fostering cultural understanding at the local and global levels. IVP currently offers volunteer positions in France, Spain, the UK, the US and Costa Rica.

Further information including costs of programmes can be obtained from our website www.ivpsf.org or *contact* at the above address.

**KALANI OCEANSIDE RETREAT:** RR 2 Box 4500, Pahoa, Beach Road, Hawaii 96778 (☎+808 965-7828 (business) +800 800-6886 (registration); fax +808 965-0527; e-mail kalani@kalani.com; www.kalani.com). Kalani Oceanside Retreat is a non-profit inter-cultural conference and retreat centre located on an island with twenty acres of pristine land, surrounded by tropical forest and the Pacific Ocean.

The retreat centre operates with the assistance of approximately 40 resident volunteers who **help to provide services to the guests of the Retreat.** To participate in the programme volunteers must stay a minimum of three months. In exchange for thirty hours of volunteer time per week participants receive mainly vegetarian meals, shared lodging, and a week long vacation during the three-month placement. Opportunities for volunteering exist in food service, grounds/maintenance, and housekeeping. The cost of the Resident Volunteer Programme is $1200/£815 for the three-month term. Volunteers must be at least 18 years old and in good health; experience in the area for which the applicant volunteers is preferred.

*Application* form and free brochure are available from the above address.

**WINANT-CLAYTON VOLUNTEER ASSOCIATION (WCVA):** St Margaret's house, 21 Old Ford Road, Bethnal Green, London E2 9PI (☎0208 983 3834; fax 020-

7377 2437; e-mail wcva@dircon.co.uk; www.winantclayton.com). WCVA operates an annual exchange of volunteers between the UK and USA. It hopes to promote friendship and understanding between the two countries as well as to provide valuable life experiences.

Volunteers **(20)** for **work with the homeless, the elderly and children, psychiatric rehabilitation, drug rehabilitation and helping on HIV/AIDS programmes.** Placements are in New York. Pocket money, board and accommodation provided while working, but volunteers must pay for their own airfare and other travel expenses. However, some bursaries are available for volunteers from Ireland and East London. Period of work 8 weeks from the middle/end of June to the beginning of September, followed by a two/three week period for independent travel.

*Applicants must be UK or Irish passport holders.* No particular qualifications are essential, but previous experience of voluntary work is useful.

For further details send a large s.a.e. to the above address; *applications* must be received by 31<sup>st</sup> January as interviews are held in February.

**WWOOF HAWAII** (Willing Workers on Organic Farms): 4429 Carlson Road, Nelson, British Columbia, Canada V1L 6X3 (tel/fax 250-354 4417; e-mail wwoofcan@shaw. ca; www.wwoofhawaii.org). US youths and hundreds of people from all over the world go 'wwoofing' every summer. Farm Hosts are available in most states and on four of the Hawaiian islands.

Volunteer experiences range from small homesteads to large farms. **Duties include general work, milking goats etc.** Pocket money is not usually provided, but board and lodging are provided free of charge. Opportunities may be available all year round. Minimum age of sixteen. If not a US citizen, *only EEA nationals with valid tourist visas* need apply. Hawaii membership is $15 plus postage. Cash or cheques (made payable to John Vanden Heuvel) are accepted. WWOOF will then send you the booklet of host farms.

*Applications* can be made online, or send full name, mailing address and registration fee.

**WWOOF USA** (Willing Workers on Organic Farms): PO Box 510 Felton, CA 95060, USA, (☎+1 831 425-3276; e-mail info@wwoofusa.org; www.wwoofusa.org) WWOOF USA publishes an organic host farm directory with hosts in all 50 states, including Alaska and Hawaii. WWOOF USA has a number of separate organisations in the USA, included those listed below. North East Workers on Organic Farms (NEWOOF USA) supplies a list of farms in the north east of America only. It can arrange full season apprenticeships. It can also supply a list of other US farm apprenticeships programmes. Southeastern Willing Workers on Organic Farms (SEWWOOF), PO Box 134, Bonlee, North Carolina, 27213, USA; e-mail sewwoof@ crosswinds.net. SEWWOOF is a correspondence service linking organic farmers in the southeast of America with apprentices. It publishes the SEWWOOF Farm List that describes each farm operation, compensation etc. Apprentices may obtain the Farm List by contacting the above address, or download an application directly from the website. Apprentices should then contact the farmer in order to establish a farming work relationship.

# Other Employment in the USA

**BRITANNIA SOCCER USA:** 10281 Frosty Court, Suite 100, Manassas, Virginia 20109, USA (☎703-330-2532; fax 703-330-6850; www.britanniasoccerusa.com). **Football Coaches:** qualified coaches with coaching certificates from recognised national soccer associations are required to teach football throughout the USA including Hawaii and the Caribbean.

Applicants should have a playing background and dynamic personality as well as UEFA coaching qualification and coaching experience. Period of work is between June and August. 9-month contracts also available. Wages are $100-$300 per week. Homestay accommodation and transport provided including airfares. Longer contracts come with an apartment.

*Applications* to the above address.

**INTERNATIONAL EXCHANGE CENTER:** 89 Fleet Street, London EC4Y 1DH (☎020-7583 9116; fax 020-7583-9117; e-mail isecinfo@btconnect.com; www. isecworld.co.uk). The International Exchange Center works to promote positive, enjoyable cultural exchanges. Overseas work is offered in various countries for various types of work. See their website for full details.

**Work and Travel in the USA Programme:** Choice of various entry-level jobs around the US in cities, resorts and national parks. From ride operators at amusement parks to waitresses in Cape Cod. Working hours around 40 a week, pay £2.80 ($5.25+) per hour. Subsidised accommodation arranged. Applicants must be university students aged 18+. Enthusiasm and commitment the key to great time. The programme runs from May-July.

To *apply* contact the above address.

**INTERNSHIP USA PROGRAMME:** IST Plus Rosedale House, Rosedale Road, Surrey TW9 2SZ (☎ 020-8939 9057; fax 020 8939 9090; e-mail info@istplus.com; www.istplus.com). Assisting students to work in America each year.

This scheme enables students and recent graduates to complete a period of **course-related work experience/training** for a period of up to eighteen months in the US, with an optional travel period preceding or following placement. Minimum age 18. Applicants must be enrolled in full-time further or higher education (HND level or above) returning to full-time education. Students may participate after graduation as long as the application is submitted shile still studying. Participants must find their own training placements, related to their course of study, and either through payment from their employer or through other means, finance their own visit to the United States.

Participants pay an administrative fee of £340 with £30-£35 increments for each additional month of stay. IST Plus' US partner provides the legal sponsorship required to obtain the J-1 visa, as well as orientation materials covering issues such as social security, taxes, housing, American culture and transportation; plus 24-hour emergency assistance with any problems whilst in the United States and comprehensive insurance. See www.istplus.com for more details.-

*Applications* can be made at any time of year, but should be made 8-12 weeks before desired date of departure.

**GOAL-LINE SOCCER INC:** PO Box 1642, Corvallis, Oregon 97339, USA (☎541-753-5833; e-mail info@goal-line.com; www.goal-line.com).

**Football Coaches:** qualified coaches with coaching certificates from recognised national soccer associations are required to teach football to American children and play exhibition games against local teams. Coaches stay with American families and are offered opportunities. Placements are mainly in the West Coast states of Washington and Oregon. There are opportunities to take part in other recreational sports such as water-skiing and golf.

Applicants should be over 21. Interviews are held in the UK. There is a registration fee of $200. A 4-day orientation at Oregon state university is given prior to commencing placement. Placements are from the beginning of July and last 5 weeks; or longer if participant wishes. Payment is at the rate of $300+ per week.

*Applications* to Tom Rowney at the above address.

**PORTALS OF WONDER:** 212 East 83rd St – 4D, New York, NY 10028, USA (☎212 861-1638; e-mail contact@portalsofwonder.org; www.portalsofwonder.org).
**Artistic Helpers and Performers** for a company engaged in programs, exhibitions and training for the performing arts – illusion, comedy, song and dance.

*Applications* should be made to Sandra Nordgren at the above e-mail address.

**RESORT AMERICA – CAMP AMERICA:** Dept. SDA, 37 Queen's Gate, London SW7 5HR.
Resort America, a programme of Camp America, is open only to full-time students who want to work in supportive roles including catering and administration at holiday resorts or hotels in the USA. Applicants must be available to leave the UK between 1 May and 27 June for a minimum of 12 weeks. The application process for this programme closes in December. Experience in leisure and hospitality management, food and beverages supervision and entertainment is preferable.

Participants are offered free return flights from London and other selected airports worldwide to New York and transfer to the camp where the applicant is placed, free accommodation and meals, up to 10 weeks of travel time after camp, 24 hours support and medical insurance, Cultural Exchange US visa sponsor, and pocket money of $1,375 (dependant on age and experience). Early application advised. Camp America host recruitment fairs allowing participants to meet face-to-face with Camp Directors.

For the latest event information and to request a brochure, please *visit* www. campamerica.co.uk or call 020-7581 7373.

**WORK AMERICA:** BUNAC, 16 Bowling Green Lane, London EC1R OQH (☎020-7251 3472; fax 020-7251 0215; e-mail workamerica@bunac.org.uk).
**Work America** is a general work and travel programme open to students through BUNAC. The programme enables participants to take virtually any summer job in the US and provides the opportunity to earn back living and travelling costs. A special work and travel visa allows students to work and travel from June to the beginning of October.

BUNAC provides a Job Directory, which is packed with jobs from which to choose and arrange work before going. The programme is open to those who are currently enrolled at a British University or college studying at degree (or advanced tertiary or postgraduate) level; unfortunately gap year and final year students are not eligible. The programme fee is about £125. Early application is strongly advised.

*Visit* www.bunac.org for more details.

**WORK & TRAVEL USA:** IST Plus Rosedale House, Rosedale Road, Surrey TW9 2SZ (☎ 020-8939 9057; fax 020 8332 7858; e-mail info@istplus.com; www.istplus. com). IST Plus is a worldwide organisation helping students and young professionals to participate in casual work, internships and teaching positions across the world.
The Work and Travel scheme enables full-time university students to work and travel anywhere in the USA from early June to mid-October. The age minimum is 18 and applicants must be in full-time education and returning to full-time education. The programme includes sponsorship, insurance, registration into SEVIS (Student and Exchange Visitor Programme), pre-departure orientation materials and 24-hour emergency back-up while in the USA.

*Application* forms can be downloaded from IST Plus's website.

**WORK EXPERIENCE USA:** c/o Camp Counselors, UK Offices: Devon House, 171/177 Great Portland Street, London W1W 5PQ (☎020-7637 0779; e-mail info@ ccusa.com; www.ccusa.com) and 27 Woodside Gardens, Musselburgh, nr. Edinburgh EH21 7LJ (☎0131-665 5843; e-mail ccusascotland@yahoo.co.uk; www.ccusa.com). US Office: 2330 Marinship Way, Suite 250, Sausalito CA 94965, USA.
Work Experience USA work and travel programme is a US government authorised programme which runs between June and September. Applicants for this programme must be full-time students between the ages of 18 and 28.
   The only work limitations are that you cannot work as a domestic help or as a nanny; other than that the sky's the limit and the job is arranged before you leave the U.K. Wages will generally be at entry level and equivalent to those of Americans doing the same work.
   For further information *contact* the above address.

# Au Pairs, Nannies, Family Helps and Exchanges

**AU PAIR IN AMERICA:** 37 Queens Gate, London, SW7 5HR; (☎ +44 (0)20 7581 7322; fax 020 7581 7345; e-mail info@aupairamerica.co.uk; www.aupairamerica. co.uk).
**Au Pair In America** offers a visa-supported one-year stay to applicants aged 18-26. Au Pairs also have the opportunity to extend their year for another 6, 9 or 12 months. Applicants must hold a full, valid driving licence and have at least 200 hours of recent childcare experience. Benefits include a full round trip airfare, medical insurance and part-time college course, plus two weeks paid holiday. Salary is up to $200 (approx £111) per week for qualified nannies and a minimum of $139.05 (£77) per week for standard au pairs. Choose from a wide range of approved families from across the USA. A four-day orientation is provided on arrival in the USA. Full local counsellor support is provided throughout the year to introduce friends and give guidance with every aspect of the stay.
   Contact the above address for further details.

**CHILDCARE AMERICA/AU PAIR IN AMERICA:** Childcare International Ltd., Trafalgar House, Grenville Place, London NW7 3SA (☎020-8906 3116; fax 020-8906 3461; e-mail office@childint.co.uk; www.childint.co.uk).
**Au Pair** and **Nanny** stays in the USA. Childcare America offer a visa-supported one year stay to applicants aged 18-26 with good childcare experience. Applicants must drive. Families provide full round trip air fare, medical insurance and part-time college course plus two weeks paid holiday. Salary up to $200 (approx £111) per week for qualified nannies and a minimum of $139.05 (£77) per week for au pairs. Choose from a wide range of approved families from across the USA. Four days' orientation is provided in the USA. Full local counsellor support is provided to introduce friends and give guidance with every aspect of the stay.
   *Applications* to the above address.

**EDUCARE AMERICA:** Au Pair in America, 37 Queens Gate, London NW7 3SA (☎020-751 7322; fax 020-751 7345; e-mail info@aupairamerica.co.uk; www. aupairamerica.co.uk).
The Educare Program offers the opportunity to work and study in the United States. It provides the opportunity for young people aged 18-26 to spend a year in the States caring for school-aged children for 30 hours a week while attending an American college. Families provide air fare, medical insurance, two weeks paid holiday and a salary of $105 (approx £58.50) per week. Full year-round local counsellor support is

also available. Full driving licence is essential.

For programme information *please contact* the above address.

**RICHMOND & TWICKENHAM AU PAIRS:** The Old Rectory, Savey Lane, Yoxall, Burton-on-Trent, Staffs DE13 8PD (☎ 01543-473828; fax: 01543-473838; e-mail vicki@aupairsnationawide.co.uk; www.aupairsnationwide.co.uk).

An established agency running since 1992, run by Vicki, who has herself been a Nanny/Au Pair. Placements via the Au Pair America scheme.

*Applications* to the above address.

# Asia

## Bangladesh

The following organisation offers the opportunity of voluntary work in Bangladesh.

**BANGLADESH WORK CAMPS ASSOCIATION (BWCA):** 289/2 Workcamp Road, North Shajahanpur, Dhaka-1217, Bangladesh (☎+880-2-9358206/9356814; fax +880-2-956 5506/5483; e-mail bwca@bangla.net; www.mybwca.org). Bangladesh Work Camps Association (BWCA) promotes international solidarity and peace through organising community development, which takes the form of national/international workcamps for volunteers in rural and urban areas of Bangladesh. The projects organised include **environmental and health education, literacy, sanitation, reforestation, community work, development and construction, etc.** Volunteers work 30 hours a week on placements, which last from 1 to 6 weeks from October to February. A RTYP (Round The Year Programme) is also available to medium-term volunteers staying for a minimum period of three months. At least 30 volunteers a year are recruited onto one of the three international workcamps and 20 volunteers through RTYP.

Volunteers ages 18-35, must be able to speak English, be adaptable to any situation and be team-spirited. Accommodation and simple local food is provided for a charge of $20 per day and volunteers must pay all other expenses including insurance and travel.

*Applications* to BWCA three months in advance of scheduled Camp/Programme date. Applications must come through a BWCA partner organisation in the applicant's country; if this is not possible individual, direct applications may be accepted and should be accompanied by a payment of US$25 (approx £13.95). Apply in the first instance for the address of the nearest partner organisation.

## China

British nationals can find voluntary work in China through the UNA Exchange see the *Worldwide* chapter for details. Americans can check programmes such as Volunteers in Asia (VIA, Stanford University; www.viaprograms.org) which sends volunteer teachers to China and Vietnam and Princeton in Asia (pia@Princeton.edu) though these programs are likely to be for longer than a summer. However, VIA in particular is looking for ways to expand volunteering in China. The following organisations offers the opportunity to work in China.

**EARTHCARE:** GPO Box 11546, Hong Kong, China (☎+852-25780434; fax +852-25780522; e-mail care@earth.org.hk; www.earth.org.hk).
Earthcare, a local Chinese charity, aims to promote the concepts of benevolence

and compassion in traditional Chinese teaching to establish a green lifestyle, environmental conservation, humane education and the protection of animals. About 150-200 volunteers are recruited annually to help in the following areas: **fundraising, computer/data processing/maintenance, administration, clerical work, campaigning, animal care/treatment, publishing/printing, photography and filming, multimedia design and application, public relations and education.** Campaigns include: banning bear farming and advocating herbal alternatives to animal derived remedies in Chinese medicines. Minimum period of voluntary work is two weeks at any time of year. Applicants must be able to speak English, any knowledge of Cantonese would be a bonus. Very simple accommodation can be provided but all other expenses must be met by the volunteer.

*Applications* to the above address.

**ENGLISH FIRST:** 26 Wilbraham Road, Fallowfield, Manchester M14 6JX (☎0161 256 1400; fax 0161 256 1936; e-mail recruitment@englishfirst.com). English First is part of EF Education and is a world leader in language learning with over 200 schools worldwide. EF Education is a multi-national company group with some 20,000 employees at work in 48 countries. EF English First's Teacher Recruitment and Training department trains and recruits English language teachers to work both at home and abroad.

**English Language Teachers (75)** to teach English to children, teenagers and university students in various locations all over China. English First is looking for enthusiastic and committed teachers to teach EFL to mono-lingual Chinese students aged between 8 and 25 and to participate in the students' activity programme. 40 hours a week with 24 contact teaching hours, 5 days a week. EF offers a competitive salary (paid in local currency), free accommodation, working visa, health insurance and a generous flight allowance. The minimum contract term is for 2 months during the Chinese school summer holidays. Candidates must have or be willing to undertake a TEFL/TESL Certificate (EF can provide training in 10 European cities). All academic staff are recruited through EF's Online Recruitment Centre. Candidates are requested to register their details via www.englishfirst.com.

Closing date for applications 31[th] May.

**INTERNATIONAL CHINA CONCERN (ICC):** PO Box 20, Morpeth, NE61 3YP, UK (☎01670-505622; e-mail uk@intlchinaconcern.org; www.intlchinaconcern.org) ICC is a China based charitable organisation involved in projects in China's government orphanages. By bringing care and improvement of conditions ICC aims to make a difference to the lives of China's orphans. ICC is a bridge between China and the West to channel finances and people resources.

Twenty to thirty volunteers are recruited annually to perform one of the following roles: administration assistant (correspondence), accounts assistant (book-keeping), physical or occupational therapy co-ordinator, special education teachers, special needs nursing carer. Knowledge of Mandarin Chinese is helpful but not essential. Volunteers are required from 6 months to 2 years and must be self-supporting.

For more *information*, please visit the website.

**TEACH IN CHINA:** IST Plus Rosedale House, Rosedale Road, Surrey TW9 2SZ (☎020-8939 9057; fax 020 8332 7858; e-mail info@istplus.com; www.istplus.com). Sending more graduates to China than any other organisation, IST Plus is a worldwide organisation helping people develop skills and acquire knowledge for working in a multicultural, interdependent world.

Teach in China offers an opportunity for graduates to spend 5 or 10 months teaching

English in a university, college or school in China. There is no age limit, and teaching/ TEFL qualifications are not required in order to apply. Successful applicants attend a one-week training course on arrival in Shanghai; focusing on learning Chinese, understanding Chinese culture and giving an insight to TEFL. Host institutions in China provide private accommodation (usually a teacher's apartment on or near the campus), and a monthly salary, which is generous by Chinese standards. Participants are responsible for paying their outward air fare and programme fee to IST Plus to cover the costs of arranging the placement, processing all paperwork required for visas and work permits, visa fees, the training centre and 24-hour emergency support while in China. Return fare is paid by the host institution on completion of a 10 month contract.

IST Plus sends participants on this programme in late August and early February in accordance with the Chinese semester system, and *applicants* are encouraged to return forms and application materials at least 3 months beforehand in order to ensure that a suitable placement is found. US applicants should apply to the CIEE in the US (for address see the *Worldwide* chapter).

**OVERSEAS WORKING HOLIDAYS:** Level 1, Fife Road, Kingston, Surrey, KT1 1SF (0845 344 0366; fax 0870 460 4578; e-mail info@owh.co.uk; www.owh.co.uk)
Working holidays in various countries. Summer resort work in Canada and France and paid English teaching placements in Thailand, China, Poland and Korea.
Placements are for gap years or shorter placements. All jobs, visas and accommodation are arranged. Programme fees are from £299 to £599. Also available, African Experience Volunteer placements. Job interviews for all programmes are carried out pre-departure.
*Applications* through the website above or telephone 0845-344 0366.

# India

Despite its vast size India offers few opportunities for paid temporary work, particularly for those without any particular skill or trade to offer an employer: there are untold thousands of Indians who would be delighted to do any unskilled job available for a wage that would seem a pittance to a westerner. Anyone determined to find paid employment there should explore the possibility of working for tour operators who specialise in organising holidays to India, and they would normally only consider applicants who are familiar with the country.

There are, however, a number of opportunities for taking part in short-term voluntary schemes in India. The worldwide fame of *Mother Teresa's Missionaries of Charity* in Calcutta means it has no shortage of volunteers to take on part-time work to care for and feed orphaned children, the sick and dying, mentally or physically disabled adults and children or the elderly at its children's home in Calcutta (Shishu Bhavan, 78 A.J.C. Bose Road), in the Home for Dying Destitutes at Kalighat and other houses run by the Missionaries of Charity in Calcutta and other Indian cities, but no accommodation can be offered. To register, visit the Mother House at 54A A.J.C. Bose Road, Calcutta 700 016. Further information is also available from their London office at 177 Bravington Road, London W9 3AR (020-8960 2644).

Council: International Volunteer Projects and Service Civil International can place Americans on voluntary schemes in India, and Concordia and UNA Exchange can offer similar placements for Britons: see the *Worldwide* chapter for details. Please note that as is normal with short-term voluntary opportunities, those taking part must pay for their own travel expenses, and will often be required to put something towards the cost of board and lodging, though generally in India this is a modest amount. The organisation Aid India (www.aidindia.org) carries volunteer requests on its website.

## RED TAPE

**Visa Requirements:** a tourist visa is required by all non-Indian nationals entering India for a visit as tourists.

**Residence Permits:** those planning a stay of over 3 months must register with the Foreigners Regional Registration Office within 14 days of arrival and be able to provide evidence of how they are supporting themselves. It is not possible to change a tourist visa to a long stay visa within India.

**Employment Visas:** any foreigner taking up paid employment in India must have a valid work permit before they enter the country: they should apply (ideally in person) to the nearest Indian consulate, enclosing a copy of their contract.

**Au Pair:** not customary.

**Voluntary Work:** details of the voluntary work to be undertaken should be sent to the Indian consulate when applying for a visa at least 2 months in advance as they have to be forwarded to India. If you do want to attach yourself to a voluntary organisation for more than three months, you should aim to enter India on a student or employment visa (see Indian Embassy website www.hcilondon.org).

# Voluntary Work

**BHARAT SEVAK SAMAJ (BSS):** Nehru Seva Kendra, Gurgaon By-pass Road, Mehrauli, New Delhi 30, India (☎+91 11 66644761,6642215; e-mail bssranny@ vsnl.com).

The Samaj was founded by Shri Jawahar Lal Nehru, the first Prime Minister of India, as a non-political national platform for mobilising people's spare time, energy and resources for development and reconstruction. It has a network of branches all over the country, with a membership of over 750,000, 10,000 members working on projects, and about 20 foreign volunteers helping each year. Any person who offers his services for a minimum of two hours a week can become a member of the Samaj.

Its normal programme includes the **organisation of urban community centres in slum areas, night shelters, child welfare centres, nursery schools, training camps for national reconstruction work, family planning camps and clinics, and publicity centres. The work also encompasses relief and reconstruction work after natural calamities, such as famine, drought, cyclones and earthquakes as well as the construction of houses for the Schedule Caste (lower caste) and tribes and low cost latrines in villages.**

Both skilled and unskilled workers are welcomed. Foreign volunteers, who can serve for between 15 days and three months, should be prepared to live in simple accommodation and respect local customs and traditions. They must finance their own stay, and it is preferred that they speak English.

*Applicants* should contact the General Secretary at the above address for further details; IRCs should accompany all letters.

**CONCORDIA:** 19 North Street, Portslade, Brighton, BN4 1DH (☎01273-422218; fax 01273-421182; e-mail info@concordia-iye.org.uk; www.concordia-iye.org.uk). Concordia offers volunteers aged 20+ the opportunity to join an international team of volunteers working on community-based projects ranging from **restoration and construction, to art/culture and social projects including work with adults or children with special needs, children's play schemes and teaching.** Projects last for 2-4 weeks and run year round.

Generally no skills or experience are needed, although Concordia runs a preparation weekend for applicants. Volunteers pay a registration fee of £120, plus an extra fee payable to the in-country host of approx. £140, and fund their own travel. Board and accommodation are free of charge.

For further information on volunteering or coordinating please check the website or contact the International Volunteer Coordinator at the above address.

**DAKSHINAYAN:** F-1169, Chittaranjan Park, 1st Floor, New Delhi – 110019; INDIA (☎ +91 982 427 4370; e-mail info@dakshinayan.org; www.dakshinayan.org).
Volunteers to work with a registered trust engaged in **providing education assistance to tribes in the Rajamhal Hills and the surrounding plains.** Education is of primary level and volunteers are expected to assist in teaching English or arts and crafts, sports, poetry or singing. No formal teacher training is needed. Volunteers normally work 4-6 hours a day, 6 days a week for between 4 weeks and 6 months. Help is needed throughout the year. No expenses are paid. Dakshinayan charges a fee of $300 per month that includes food and accommodation while at the project, and no additional fee is charged. Volunteers are expected to cover all expenses to and from the project.

All applicants must be at least 18 years old, socially sensitive and willing to work in remote locations. Living conditions on most rural development projects are very basic. Knowledge of Hindi an advantage. Participants must arrive in Kolkata in the first week of the month where they group and travel together to the project.

*Applications*, at least 30 days in advance of desired departure date, to Siddharth Sanyal, Executive Trustee, at the above e-mail address.

**DORE:** (Devoted Organisation for Reforming Environment), 196-b Khari Bazar, Ranikhet 263645, Dish, Almora (Uttaranchal), India (☎+91 5966-20458; e-mail dore_7@rediffmail.com).
DORE recruits **15-25 volunteers** a year to help in the areas of **natural resource management, child health and education, socio-economic development of rural villages, introduction of appropriate technology, and eco-tourism** in India. Volunteers can stay from one to two months but preferably in the summer. No special skills or qualifications are required but a very basic level of conversational Hindi is advisable. All expenses (accommodation, food, airfares, local travel etc.) must be met by the volunteer.

*Applications* to the Secretary at the above e-mail, including information about the volunteer's particular environmental speciality and interests.

**JAFFE PUNNOOSE FOUNDATION:** Kunnuparambil Buildings, Kurichy, Kottayam 686549, India (☎+91-223 200 41; fax +91-2322547; e-mail jaffeint@sify.com).
**Voluntary teachers to teach in traditional village schools** all over India. Subject areas include: Beauty Therapy, Creative Writing, Cooking, English, French, Gardening, Journalism, Music, Painting, Photography, Travel and Tourism. Due to foreign currency restrictions, no salary is paid but free board and lodging is provided. Hours of work are flexible; minimum 3 hours a day, Monday to Friday. Volunteers required from 1 January to 31 December; minimum period of work 4 weeks. Applicants must have at least an undergraduate degree in the subject of specialisation and proficiency in the English language.

Applications minimum eight weeks before the expected start date, to the address above.

**JOINT ASSISTANCE CENTRE (JAC):** PO Box 60082, San Pablo CA, USA, (e-mail jacusa@juno.com; www.jacusa.org). JAC offers a unique opportunity of an exciting and challenging nature carrying out humanitarian works in close unison with local agencies as well as the UN and other international groups.

Volunteers can join 'learn while you travel' scheme and perform various jobs for a voluntary action group (registered as a charity) concerned with furthering disaster preparedness through training programmes, exhibitions and seminars. It also has cultural schemes, fund raising, camps, digs, workcamps and related publications. **Tasks include helping with office work, editing, writing, teaching, social work, joining youth workcamps, helping run seminars and giving demonstrations and lectures, etc.** on first aid, camping, trekking, rock climbing etc. There are opportunities for learning natural cures (chromopathy), yoga, meditation, Indian language and about Indian life philosophy through cheap travel and visits to several other projects through the JAC travel scheme.

Any number of volunteers are accepted, but for specific projects, to suit personal applicant profile, volunteers must be able to work for a minimum of three months. Working hours are 8 hours a day and 5 days per week with free days or weeks by mutual arrangement. Simple but safe and secure accommodation is provided in a rural camp style in huts or tents, in the slum or rural areas. Longer term placements in other projects according to skills/interests are also arranged. Three day long orientation programmes about India, its history, culture and thought, are organised every month. Students wanting to do internships or study and research in any field can also be accepted.

No special qualifications required but some experience of first aid, typing or scouting would be helpful. Minimum age 18 years. Help is needed from volunteers for periods of from 4-26 weeks, around the year. Participants are required to send a processing fee of £30 with their application. They must then contribute a further £150 for the first month to cover food, accommodation, administration, and airport pickup).

*Contact* the above address for application forms, enclosing 3 International Reply Coupons for reply by Airmail.

**NOMAD TRAVEL:** (☎01707-659510; e-mail katherine@nomadtravel.co.uk; www.nomadtravel.co.uk). Help is needed on the West Bengal/Sikkim borders, in the foothills of the Himalayas, approximately three hours from Darjeeling. This is a small clinic set up in Karmi Farm to help the indigenous population with day-to-day health care and child care. Funds are raised in the UK to pay for nurse, board and lodging and pharmaceuticals.

**Volunteer Nurse/Doctors** to help in rural communities. The clinic currently caters for 210 families from the surrounding area. There is also outreach work. Situated in the foothills of the Himalayas, transport is all on foot. The main illnesses are skin disorders, chest problems, dehydration, childhood illnesses. Midwifery plays a big part. People turn up at the clinic any time night or day. However, there are long spells when it is quiet. Minimum period of work for applications – 6 weeks. Work is available all year round. Comfortable accommodation and organic food provided

*Applications* should be made to Cathy Goodyear on the above details at any time.

**RURAL ORGANISATION FOR SOCIAL ELEVATION:** Social Awareness

Centre, Kanda Bageshwar 263631, Uttaranchal, India (☎+91 5963 241081; mob. +941 134 7867; e-mail jlverma_rosekanda@yahoo.co.in; www.rosekanda.info). ROSE is a small charity, based in a beautiful location at the foot of the Himalayas. It provides volunteers with the opportunity of experiencing true rural Indian life while providing education and improving local sanitation and health care facilities. ROSE offers many opportunities for students to conduct research in various subjects such as geography, anthropology, development, conservation and environmental studies as well as in the education development programme. Facilities include a library and learning participation. ROSE received the First Choice Responsible Tourism Award for Best Volunteering Programme in 2005.

**Volunteers (1-10)** to carry out **work in rural areas** including teaching English to children, construction, poultry farming, environmental protection, organic farming, agricultural work, recycling paper to make hand-made greetings cards, office work, compiling project proposals, reports and health care. Groups of volunteers can be organised into work camps lasting 10 to 30 days, but individuals are also welcome to apply. Volunteers work 5 hours a day, five days a week. Accommodation in a family house provided in addition to three delicious meals a day. Volunteers must pay their own travel costs and about £4.50 (350 Rupees) a day towards board and lodging costs, administration, guide, telephone, internet, rent and ROSE's school expenses.

Application/registration fee of £45 by British postal order, with the application, or 3500 rupees on arrival.

*Applications* should be addressed to Mr Jeevan Lal Verma at the above address.

**SKILLSHARE INTERNATIONAL:** 126 New Walk Street, Leicester LE1 7JA (☎0116 254 1862; fax 0116 254 2614; e-mail recruitment@skillshare.org' www. skillshare.org)

Skillshare recruits professionals to share their skills and experience with local communities for further economic and social development in Botswana, Kenya, Lesotho, Mozambique, Namibia, South Africa, Swaziland, Tanzania, Uganda, India and Nepal. Its vision is a world without poverty, injustice and inequality where people, regardless of cultural, social, and political divides come together for mutual benefit living in peaceful co-existence.

Projects cover a wide-range of activities and general management, agricultural, technical, educational and medical skills are all required. Applicants should be aged 21, have relevant qualifications and experience, particularly in training others.

Placements are usually for two years. Skillshare offers a modest living allowance, flights/travel to the placement and return, medical cover, and pre and post placement grants to assist with relocation. The living allowance is adequate to cover your living costs whilst in the country of placement but not adequate for savings or meeting other costs you may have in your country of residence.

An *information pack* is available from the above address.

Please enclose 3 International Reply Coupons and a large envelope.

# Japan

The range of short-term casual jobs open to Westerners in Japan is extremely limited, even with unemployment in Japan having rapidly fallen in recent years; it is now about 4.2%. However, longer-term opportunities do exist, particularly in the area of teaching English: it has been estimated that 11% of all Japanese people attend English 'conversation classes'. A native English-speaker therefore possesses a marketable skill if he or she has a degree; experience or qualifications in teaching

English as a foreign language are added advantages. One way of getting a teaching job is to advertise in the English-language *Japan Times* (www.japantimes.com. jp).

For further information on teaching work in Japan see *Teaching English Abroad*. Anyone who is serious about wanting to spend some time in Japan should read *Live and Work in Japan*, a thorough guide for anyone hoping to live and work there. See the *Useful Publications* chapter for details of these books.

CIEE and Service Civil International can help US residents, as can Concordia, Youth Action for Peace, UNA Exchange and International Voluntary Service UK residents, to find short term voluntary work in Japan; see their entries in the *Worldwide* chapter for details.

# RED TAPE

**Visa Requirements:** nationals of the UK, USA, Ireland, Germany, Switzerland and Austria can visit Japan as tourists without a visa for up to 3 months and extend this to 6 months. Most other nationalities can visit for up to 3 months, as long as they have a return or onward ticket and sufficient funds.

**Work Permits:** A position must be secured and working visa obtained before you enter the country. Applicants for working visas must submit their application to the Consulate in person. If the person obtains a certificate of eligibility from Japan a visa can be issued in three days.

**Working Holiday Visas.** Holders of British, Australian, Canadian and New Zealand passports can apply for working holiday visas: these must be applied for at the Japanese Embassy of their home country. The rules are generally the same, but full details can be obtained from the nearest Japanese Embassy or consulate.

For British citizens, working holiday visas may be granted provided they are:

(1) British citizens resident in the United Kingdom;
(2) intend primarily to holiday in Japan for a period of up to one year from date of entry;
(3) aged between 18 and 25 years inclusive at time of application, except where the competent authorities of the Government of Japan agree to extend the limitation upwards to 30 years;
(4) unaccompanied by children or spouses, except where the spouse also possesses a working holiday visa;
(5) in possession of a valid passport, return travel ticket or sufficient funds to purchase such reasonable funds for normal maintenance purposes during the initial part of the proposed stay in Japan;
(6) in good health;
(7) willing to leave Japan at the end of their stay;
(8) able to confirm that they have not previously been issued with such a visa.

There is a small, non-refundable processing fee for a working holiday visa. Working Holiday Visas are available to British citizens between April and the following March, applications are accepted from April. To apply for one each of the following must be supplied to the Japanese Embassy or Consulate-General in addition to a valid British passport: visa application form, a 35mm x 45mm photograph, a typed CV or personal history, a proposed itinerary for the first six months in Japan to include details of any prearranged employment, a typed reason for applying, evidence of travel tickets/reservations and evidence of funds (for ticket holders this is £1,500, confirmed reservation holders £2,500). Application forms and explanatory material can be obtained from the Japanese Consulate-General in London (wwwluk.emb-japan.go.jp) or Edinburgh.

There is a support organisation – the Japanese Association for Working-Holiday Makers with offices in Tokyo, Osaka and Kyushu (Tokyo office: Sun Plaza 7th Floor, 4-1-1 Nakano, Nakano-ku, Tokyo 164-8512, Japan; ☎03-3389-0181) which can be found on-line: www.jawhm.or.jp.

Japanese Working Holiday visas are single entry, so if you have to leave Japan for any reason you must obtain a re-entry permit from the competent immigration authorities before leaving. Travellers who stay in Japan longer than 90 days have to register with the local municipal office, and keep them informed of any subsequent change of address. They can also register with their embassy or consulate on arrival or later during their stay but this is not obligatory, merely advisable. For clarification of these points and news of any changes in the regulations please contact the nearest Japanese Embassy or consular mission.

**Voluntary Work:** a Volunteer Visa Scheme allows British nationals to undertake voluntary work in Japan, working for charitable organisations for up to a year. Work should be unpaid but pocket money and free board and lodging are permitted. Details and application forms are available from the Consulate General of Japan in London (101-104 Piccadilly, W1J 7JT; ☎020-7465 6565) and Edinburgh (2 Melville Crescent, EH3 7HW; ☎0131-225-4777).

# Teaching and Office Work

**THE JAPAN EXCHANGE AND TEACHING (JET) PROGRAMME:** JET Desk, Embassy of Japan, 101-104 Piccadilly, London WIJ 7JT (☎020-7465 6668; e-mail info@jet-uk.org; www.jet-uk.org).

In its 20th year, the Japan Exchange and Teaching (JET) programme has placed over 44,000 participants from over 44 countries into positions in Japan. to the JET programme, the official government scheme, sends graduates to promote international understanding at a grass-roots level and to improve foreign language teaching in schools. UK applicants from any degree discipline can apply through the website (www.jet-uk.org) between September and November for departure the following July/August. Participants receive remuneration of 3,600,000 yen (approximately £18,000 to £19,000) per year and a return air ticket to Japan. Orientation programmes are provided both pre-departure and post-arrival, as well as assistance with finding accommodation.

JET applicants in the USA should contact the Embassy of Japan at 2520 Massachusetts Avenue NW, Washington DC 20008 (☎202-939-6772). Graduates from Australia, Brazil, Canada, China, France, Germany, Ireland, Israel, Italy, New Zealand, Mexico, Peru, Portugal, the Republic of Korea, the Russian Federation, Spain and other countries should contact the Japanese Embassy in their country of origin, for information on whether they run the JET Programme.

*Contact* the above address or email for more information.

**SHIN SHIZEN JUKU (NEW NATURE SCHOOL):** Tsurui-Mura, Akan-Gun, Hokkaido 085-1207 Japan (☎0154 642821). SSJ belongs to UNESCO movement for Peace on earth.

Volunteers (up to 4) required: kind, honest, responsible and enthusiastic applicants wanted to teach English to Japanese people. Free food and accommodation are provided, in return for **teaching and gardening** work; minimum period of volunteering 6 weeks. Hours and programme vary from day-to-day but there is plenty of time for recreation. An interest in learning Japanese is encouraged. Applicants with an international driver's licence essential.

Six month paid contracts available for those who can make a contract to stay and teach for six months (with working holiday visa – Australia, New Zealand, Canada, UK and France).

*Applications* with photo to Hiroshi Mine, Manager, at the above address.

# Korea

## RED TAPE

**Visa Regulations:** Most countries particularly in Europe and the US may travel to South Korea without a visa. However the length of time that a visitor may stay varies from 1 month to 3 month, with special status of 6 months awarded to Canadians. Young Australians and New Zealanders are eligible for a working holiday visa for Korea. The Ministry of Education in Korea administers the English Program in Korea (EPIK) through its embassies in the UK, the USA, Canada and Australia. EPIK. Details of the scheme are given below.

**Work Permits:** if possible, you should obtain a work visa (E2) which is available only to graduates with a 4-year BA or BSc. The E2 is valid only for employment with the sponsoring employer. You can obtain the permit in advance or you can enter on tourist visa, find a job and then leave the country while the permit is being processed. As this takes about six weeks, it may not be worthwhile for a summer job.

## Teaching and Office Work

**ENGLISH PROGRAM IN KOREA (EPIK):** Education Director, Korean Embassy, 60 Buckingham Gate, London SW1E 6AJ (☎020-7227 5547; fax 020-7227 5503; in Korea 43-233 4516/7; e-mail www.epik.knue.ac.kr). Americans should contact one of the dozen Korean consulates in the USA. Other nationalities can apply to the EPIK office in Korea (Center for In-Service Education, Korean National University of Education, Chongwon, Chungbuk 363-791).

Working starting dates are staggered over the summer with application deadlines between April and June. Note that contracts are for a year (52 weeks).

*Applications* to the above address. Americans should contact one of the dozen Korean consulates in the USA. Other nationalities can apply to the EPIK office in Korea (Center for In-Service Education, Korean National University of Education, Chongwon, Chungbuk 363-791).

## Voluntary Work

**CONCORDIA:** 19 North Street, Portslade, Brighton, BN41 1DH (☎01273-422218; fax 01273-421182; e-mail info@concordia-iye.org.uk; www.concordia-iye.org.uk). Concordia offers volunteers aged 18+ the opportunity to join an international team of volunteers working on community-based projects ranging from **nature and wildlife conservation, restoration and construction, to art/culture and projects that are socially based including work with adults or children with special needs, children's play schemes and teaching.** Projects last for 2-4 weeks and run mainly in the summer months.

Generally no skills or experience are needed, although real commitment to a project is a must. Volunteers pay a registration fee of £110 depending on the country and fund their own travel. Board and accommodation are free of charge.

For *further information* on volunteering or coordinating please check the website or contact the International Volunteer Coordinator at the above address.

# Nepal

Nepal is one of the most promising destinations for young people who want to spend a few months as a volunteer in a developing country. People who find voluntary openings in Nepal may face a visa problem. The first tourist visa will be issued for 60 days (£20 single entry and £55 multiple entry from the Nepalese Embassy in London – near Notting Hill Gate tube station). Processing takes a few days. A tourist visa can be extended from the Department of Immigration and Pokhara Immigration Office for a total of 120 days. An additional 30 days visa may be granted on reasonable grounds from the department.

Over the course of a visa year, a tourist cannot stay in Nepal more than cumulative 150 days. People who overstay their visas have in the past been fined heavily or even put in prison. More information is available at www.nepembassy.org.uk. This applies to all except Indian nationals who do not require a visa to visit Nepal. An impressive range of non-governmental organisations makes it possible for people to teach in a voluntary capacity. Although volunteers must bear the cost of travel and living expenses, the cost of living is very low by western standards.

Concordia, UNA Exchange and Youth Action for Peace can arrange short-term voluntary work placements in Nepal. See their entries in the *Worldwide* chapter for more details. The following organisations are also looking for volunteers to work in Nepal.

**GLOBAL ACTION NEPAL:** Baldwins, Eastlands Lane, Cowfold, West Sussex RH 13 8AY (01403-864 704; e-mail info@gannepal.org).
Volunteers are taken for six months to work with GAN in poor Nepalese communities. GAN runs programmes for people of all ages and all nationalities between November and April. Volunteers are engaged in a **wide range of fields**, most specifically, working with children's clubs in activities as diverse as drama, dance and debating, and in developing the English skills of Nepalese teachers. GAN works in areas where volunteers can be of most long-term benefit to Nepal, where sustainability is fundamental to the projects' existence.

Basic cost to the volunteer is £1, 650 (excluding flights) which includes a three-weel training programme once in Nepal, as well as visa costs, insurance, full borad and lodging, and transport in-country.

*Enquiries* by email to enquiries@gannepal.org.org or telephone 0800 5877138 for further information.

**NEW INTERNATIONAL FRIENDSHIP CLUB NEPAL:** (NIFC-Nepal)
PO Box 11276, Maharajgunj, Kathmandu, Nepal (☎+977-1 427406/429176; fax +977-1 429176; e-mail nifc@mos.com.np; www.unarec.org/nepal). Friendship Club Nepal is a small Nepali-run NGO organising regular workcamps to assist rural communities. A long-term project in Chitwan district will establish a co-operative farm demonstrations.

Volunteers are required to participate in both research and physical workcamps. Research work usually involves investigating and **writing a report on the development situation** (health, education, environment or agriculture etc.) in a rural area. A physical workcamp might involve **construction or agriculture**. **Teacher** also needed for schools.

Volunteers should be aged between 17 and 65. Proficiency in English is essential. Working hours are approximately 36 hours, a six day week. Workcamps last 15 days, medium-term placements 2-6 months. No wages or fare paid but basic Nepali style board and lodging provided. Work camp fee US$150; medium-term volunteers should contribute US$150 per month. Registration fee US$30. Volunteers should arrange their own travel, visa and insurance.

*Recruitment* throughout the year; preferably apply at least 2 months in advance of intended departure date enclosing CV.

**KATHMANDU ENVIRONMENTAL EDUCATION PROJECT (KEEP):** PO Box 9178, Tridevi Marg, Thamel, Kathmandu Nepal (☎+977-(0)1 4413018; e-mail keep@info.com.np; www.keepnepal.org).
Volunteers are sought to go to various trekking villages in Nepal to **teach English** language **to lodge owners, trekking guides and porters** and also as teachers in government schools for a minimum of two months. Keep also sends volunteers to NGOs operating in the field of conservation or health and commuity development according to the interest and experience of the volunteers. Volunteers are required to be totally self-funding. Accommodation is with mountain families. Registration fee is $50.

*Applications* to the above address.

**INSIGHT NEPAL:** PO Box 489, Zero KM, Pokhara, Kaski, Nepal (☎+977-61-530266; e-mail insight@mos.com.np; www.insightnepal.org.np). Insight Nepal was established with a view to providing an opportunity to those who are interested in gaining a unique cultural experience by contributing their time and skills for the benefit of worthwhile community service groups.
Volunteer **Teachers (15) to teach various subjects in primary, secondary and vocational schools or development projects in Nepal**. To work 5 to 6 hours per day, 5 or 6 days per week. Insight Nepal organises homestays for the volunteers, and the host family provide accommodation and all meals. Work available all year round.

Applicants should be aged between 18 and 60 and be educated to at least A level standard. Experience of teaching is advisable but not essential. Applicants with games, sporting and artistic skills preferred. Short-term volunteer placements also can be arranged upon request.

*Applications* to the above address.

**PEOPLE'S WELFARE COMMITTEE:** G.PO 12137, Kathmandu, Nepal (fax 0977-1-412997; e-mail jbardewa@wlink.com.np)
Volunteer **agriculturalists (5 per month)** and volunteer **teachers (10 per month) to teach English in primary schools** needed to work for 60 hours per month.

For further details send an International Reply Coupon to Mrs Srijana Bardewa at the above address.

**SAVE THE WORLD:** PO Box 5947, Kathmandhu, Thamel, Nepal (☎+977 1 222939; fax +977 1 4250319; e-mail savetheworldnepal@hotmail.com; www.savetheworldnepal.org)
STW works to raise public awareness for peace, human rights and sustainable

development activities. Detailed information is provided on the website. 6-8 volunteers are taken on annually to work in the areas of **education, health and environment** related social organisation. Volunteers are normally recruited for three months and are provided with food and lodging.

*Apply* direct to the VWOP address below.

**SKILLSHARE INTERNATIONAL:** 126 New Walk Street, Leicester LE1 7JA (☎0116 254 1862; fax 0116 254 2614; e-mail recruitment@skillshare.org' www. skillshare.org)

Skillshare recruits professionals to share their skills and experience with local communities for further economic and social development in Botswana, Kenya, Lesotho, Mozambique, Namibia, South Africa, Swaziland, Tanzania, Uganda, India and Nepal. Its vision is a world without poverty, injustice and inequality where people, regardless of cultural, social, and political divides come together for mutual benefit living in peaceful co-existence.

Projects cover a wide-range of activities and general management, agricultural, technical, educational and medical skills are all required. Applicants should be aged 21, have relevant qualifications and experience, particularly in training others.

Placements are usually for two years. Skillshare offers a modest living allowance, flights/travel to the placement and return, medical cover, and pre and post placement grants to assist with relocation. The living allowance is adequate to cover your living costs whilst in the country of placement but not adequate for savings or meeting other costs you may have in your country of residence.

An *information* pack is available from the above address.

**VOLUNTARY AND SUPPORT PROGRAM IN NEPAL:** GPO Box 11969, Kathmandu, Nepal (fax +977 1 416144; e-mail vwop2000@hotmail.com).

**VSP-Nepal** was started in 1999 by local people in Nepal. It provides volunteer jobs and internships programmes in remote and urban areas of Nepal, including **school teaching, farm work, environment, health and research, hospitality, travel management**, etc. all year round. VSP-Nepal also helps volunteers plan travel, trekking and sightseeing expeditions within Nepal. Volunteers may implement their own ideas, activities and programmes to help the community.

Qualifications and experience are not essential except for health programmes. However, volunteers must speak English and be willing to stay with a local family during the placement sharing their home, food and amenities. The initial application and administration fee is US$200; volunteers must contribute US$100 per month to the host family for food and accommodation.

Interested volunteers should *email* vsp_Nepal@yahoo.com

**VOLUNTEER NEPAL:** c/o Anish Neupane, PBN 10210 KTM, Bagmati Zone, Nepal or 84 De Beauvoir Road, Reading, Berkshire, RG1 5NP, England (☎+977-1-6613724; e-mail info@volnepal.np.org or volunteer@volnepal.np.org; www. volnepal.np.org).

Volunteer Nepal, National Group is a community-based, non-governmental, non-profit organisation that coordinates local and international workcamps with community groups or institutions in need of voluntary assistance. Volunteers are needed to **teach in schools and be involved in health, agriculture, engineering, research** and other programmes. 2-4 weeks. Workcamps take place in February, May, August and November. There are 6-20 volunteers per workcamp. There is 4 hours of physical work in the mornings Monday to Friday and the afternoons are for seminars, lectures and discussions. Travel and tours in Nepal also arranged. There are also longer projects

needing 2 to 6 months commitment.
For further details and costs, contact the above address.

# Sri Lanka

## RED TAPE

**Visa Requirements**: British Nationals travelling to Sri Lanka as tourists need not obtain a prior visa. A visa will be for a period of 30 days on arrival at the port of entry in Sri Lanka. If they so wish they may obtain, before the expiry of initial period of visa, an extension of the duration of their stay at the discretion of the Department of Immigration & Emigration in Colombo by paying an appropriate fee. As volunteers are used informally to help with social, economic and technical development activities in villages, this works reasonably well for both parties. Volunteers usually pay something towards their keep while volunteering. This also applies to the nationals of most EU countries, USA, Canada, New Zealand and China.

**SAMASEVAYA:** National Secretariat, Anuradhapura Road, Talawa NCP, Sri Lanka (☎+94-25 2276266; +94-25 76266; samasev@sltnet.lk).
Samasevaya works towards peace through organising **development programmes.** About 10 volunteers a year are recruited to assist with the work on these projects. Minimum age 18 and volunteers must be in good health and prepared to work in rural areas. Placements are available all year round and normally last one month but this period can be extended. Simple accommodation is provided and volunteers are requested to pay US$90 per month for their food; all other expenses, including entry visa must be met by the volunteer also.
*Applications* to the National Secretary at the above address.

**VESL** (Volunteers for English in Sri Lanka): 68 Derinton Road, London SW17 8JB (☎07900-477096; e-mail info@vesl.org; www.vesl.org) VESL send volunteers throughout the year to run educational programmes in rural Indian and Sri Lankan communities, and trained UK teachers to run workshops for local teachers. Placements range from 2 weeks to 3 months or longer. The summer programme is the most popular, where volunteers run four week summer schools in July and August. **Volunteers (English Teachers): (20)** required to run a summer English programme in Sri Lanka and India. Involves 2 to 4 hours teaching per day 5 days a week. Projects starting throughout the year with summer schools starting in July. Costs are covered by fundraising; no volunteer should need more than £850 to cover project set-up, food, accommodation, insurance, training, backup and support costs.
Applications details can be obtained from the website or by emailing enquiries@vesl.org.

# Thailand

In addition to the conservation project listed below Concordia, UNA Exchange and Youth Action for Peace (see Worldwide section) offer British volunteers the chance to work in Thailand. English teaching jobs can be found at www.bangkokpostjobs.com.

# RED TAPE

**Visa Requirements**: as a general rule any foreigner wishing to enter Thailand must apply for a visa from a Thai Embassy or Consulate General. A tourist visa permits the holder to stay in Thailand for 60 days. A foreigner holding a Thai tourist visa is not permitted to work as an English teacher in Thailand, even on a voluntary basis. Applicants from English speaking countries wanting paid employment in Thailand must apply for a type B non-immigrant visa. With this visa it is possible to stay for up to 90 days; on arrival a work permit must be applied for at the Ministry of Labour. For voluntary work, a Type O visa is required; the applicant will be permitted to stay for a maximum of 90 days. Any person wishing to exceed that time must apply to the Office of Immigration Bureau. Most foreign nationals must apply for their visa before entering the country; however there are a few countries whose citizens may apply for a 15-day visa once inside Thailand.

## Teaching and Language Schools

**BAAN PASA (NES):** Nimmarnhemin: 10 Nimmarnhemin 17 Road, T. Suthep, A. Muang, Chiangmai 50200, Thailand (☎+66 53 221362/894807; fax: +66 53 222361). Somphet: Chaiyapoom Road, T. Changmoi A. Muang, Chaingmai 50300 (☎+66 53 233050/233550). Chiangrai: 162 Banpaprakarn Rd., T. Wiang A. Muang, Chiangrai 57000 (☎+66 53 712244; fax +66 53 752447; e-mail baanpasa@loxinfo.co.th).
Nes-Baanpasa is a well known chain of independent language schools in the north of Thailand. There are 3 schools in Chiangmai as well as schools in Chaiangrai, Lamphun and Tak Province, BAAN PASA are also registered with the Thai Ministry of Education. Teachers are highly sought after to teach various kinds of classes which run throughout the year. These include courses in: Kindergarten English, Young Learner English, Teenager English skills, Adult Conversation as well as academic/ exam courses (TOFL, IELTS, TOEIC or writing). Their Study Abroad Department (New Zealand Education Services or NES) provides counselling and placement for students who would like to do further study in New Zealand.

All English teacher applicants must be native English speakers who have achieved a reasonable degree of education and should possess an English teaching qualification (degree, diploma or certificate) with some teaching experience. If the applicants are also available to teach not only the academic/exam courses but also other subjects such as Maths or Science, whether at primary or secondary level, please indicate. Minimum stay 3 months with the option of a renewable contract. Teachers are contracted to teach a minimum of 20 hours. Part-time teachers are also needed. Work permits can be offered to teachers contracted for one year, with the appropriate documents. Salary package offered on qualifications and experience. Help provided in finding accommodation.

Applicants should *contact* Ms Tan Woraphant, Assistant Director, via the above e-mail address or apply in person at the Head Office on Nimmarnhemin 17 Road, Chiangmai.

**KING'S ENGLISH LANGUAGE SCHOOLS:** 58 Braidley Road, Bournemouth, Dorset BH2 6LD, UK (☎01202-293535; fax 01202-293922; e-mail info@ kingsschool.uk.com; www.kingsgroup.co.uk). Leading English language schools in Thailand and England.
King's Bournemouth is ideal for teachers who like the bustle of a busy summer and who enjoy working with teenagers and young adults. There are a variety of positions

available. King's is an accredited school.

**English as a Foreign Language Teachers.** Suitable qualifications will be expected.

*Applications* should be made to Danielle Watts or the Marketing Department at the above address.

**TEACH IN THAILAND:** IST Plus Rosedale House, Rosedale Road, Surrey TW9 2SZ (☎ 020-8939 9057; fax 020 8332 7858; e-mail info@istplus.com; www.istplus. com). Sending more graduates to Thailand than any other organisation, the IST Plus is a worldwide organisation helping people develop skills and acquire knowledge for working in a multicultural, interdependent world.

Teach in Thailand offers an opportunity for graduates to spend 5 or 10 months **teaching English in primary and secondary schools** in or around Bangkok. There is no age limit, and teaching/TEFL qualifications are not required in order to apply. Successful applicants attend a one-week training course on arrival in Shanghai focusing on the language and culture and giving an insight to TEFL. Host institutions provide private accommodation (usually a teacher's apartment on or near the campus), and a monthly salary which is generous by local standards. Participants are responsible for paying their outward air fare and a programme fee to IST Plus to cover the costs of arranging the placement, processing all paperwork required for visas and work permits, visa fees, the training centre and 24-hour emergency support while in Thailand. Return fare is paid by the host institution on completion of a 10-month contract.

IST Plus sends participants on this programme in late October and early May in accordance with the Thai semester system, and *applicants* are encouraged to return forms and application materials at least 3 months beforehand in order to ensure that a suitable placement is found. US applicants should apply to CIEE in the USA (for address see the *Worldwide* chapter).

**OVERSEAS WORKING HOLIDAYS:** Level 1, Fife Road, Kingston, Surrey, KT1 1SF (0845 344 0366; fax 0870 460 4578; e-mail info@owh.co.uk; www.owh.co.uk) Working holidays in various countries. Summer resort work in Canada and France and paid English teaching placements in Thailand, China, Poland and Korea.

Placements are for gap years or shorter placements. All jobs, visas and accommodation are arranged. Programme fees are from £299 to £599. Also available, African Experience Volunteer placements. Job interviews for all programmes are carried out pre-departure.

*Applications* through the website above or telephone 0845-344 0366.

**YOUTH HOSTELS ASSOCIATION OF THAILAND:** Giving English for Community Service programme, 25/14 Phitsaulok Road, Si Sao Thewett, Dusit, Bangkok 10300 (☎2-628 74 13 5; contact@tyha.org; www.tyha.org).

The Youth Hostels Association of Thailand recruits volunteers with some basic English teaching experience to spend three to five months **teaching English to classes of low-paid workers in the hospitality industry**. In exchange for teaching up to four hours a day, volunteers receive all living expenses including travel between the provinces in which they work.

*Applications* to the above address.

# Voluntary Work

**THE WILD ANIMAL RESCUE FOUNDATION OF THAILAND:** 65.1 3rd Floor, Sukhumvit 55, Klongton, Wattana, and Bangkok 10110, Thailand. (tel/fax (662) 712-9515, 712-9715; fax 662-712 9778; volunteer@warthai.org; www.warthai. org). The Foundation is dedicated to the protection and provision of welfare to all wild animals in need and operates two sanctuaries in the south of Thailand. The Gibbon Rehabilitation Project was set up in 1992 and deals exclusively with Gibbons many of which have been rescued from situations of abuse and cruelty. The aim of the project is to release selected gibbons from the sanctuary into the wild and to provide on-going care to those who through their association with humans are now unfit for release.

The second sanctuary in the province of Ranong provides a home to all wild animals common to Thailand which have suffered at the hands of humans. The project is still under development but already houses many gibbons, a large colony of macaques and many other species.

At both projects, volunteers are involved in the day-to-day operation of the unit including **food preparation, cage cleaning and maintenance, assisting with health inspections, behavioural observation and informing people who call at the visitors' centre of the work of the Foundation.**

Volunteers should be in good physical condition and be able to live and function in field station conditions. Enthusiasm and an ability to live and work with people of different cultures are essential. The minimum stay period is three weeks.

**For current placement rates and opportunities**, please contact preferably by e-mail.

**SEA TURTLE PROJECT PHRATHONG ISLAND:** CHELON, Viale val Padana 134B, I-00141 Rome, Italy (☎+39-06-8125301; e-mail chelon@tin.it). CHELON an Italian based research group, works to obtain in-depth knowledge of the biology of marine turtles and aid their conservation. They work in collaboration with the Marine Biological Centre in Phuket.

Volunteers to help researchers studying Olive Ridley, Green, Leatherback and Hawksbill turtles in the south of Thailand between December and May. Volunteers will assist in **gathering data on nesting behaviour, tagging turtles for observation and taking part in raising conservation awareness among tourists and local people.**

The presence of volunteers helps deter poaching of turtle eggs and young as well as involving the local community in the project. The work often involves long walks patrolling the three beaches to estimate the number of nests and the species of turtle nesting there. Visits to villages are used to involve the locals and to collect information on trade in turtle eggs, and talks given in the evenings at the Golden Buddha Beach resort increase understanding of turtle conservation amongst tourists.

Volunteers are accommodated in huts at the Golden Buddha beach resort, this and meals at the resort clubhouse are covered by the registration fee of £375, per two weeks. The minimum stay is two weeks, but volunteers can stay longer subject to approval. Travel and insurance expenses are met by the volunteer.

*Contact* CHELON at the above address for further information and an application form.

# Australasia

## Australia

The short length of this chapter does not bear any relation to the vast range and number of temporary opportunities available in Australia: there are many, even with unemployment running at the level of about 5% as unemployed Australians don't want to do the jobs that working holiday visa visitors are willing to do. However, there are a few factors to bear in mind when considering Australia as a destination for a summer job. The first factor is the reversal of seasons: the Australian summer takes place in what is winter to much of the rest of the world and so jobs on their fruit harvests and at the peak of their tourist industry occur at the wrong time of year for anyone hoping to find work between July and September. There is also the financial factor: the cost of a return ticket to Australia makes going there for a paid job for just a few weeks very uneconomic – even though in real terms the cost of getting to Australia is at its cheapest ever, the cost is still such that it makes better financial sense to stay for months rather than weeks.

Luckily for the foreigner, Australia has a reciprocal working holiday scheme with certain countries that can ease the formalities for those going there to pick up casual work. Some guidelines for those hoping to do so are given below, but working holidays in Australia are covered in greater depth in, *Work Your Way Around the World* (see *Useful Publications* section), in the information available from Australian High Commissions and Embassies or through the Australia Government Immigration Website at www.immi.gov.au. A third point to consider is that Australia is one of the most popular destinations for working travellers, and you need to begin the application process well in advance of your intended travel: 88,000 (and rising) people apply for visas every year and the processing usually takes at least 5 weeks. The fee at present is £70. It is important to remember that your Working Holiday Maker visa can only be obtained in your country of origin, you cannot apply for a WHM visa once you are in Australia.

Although Australia now has a declining unemployment rate, job-seekers must be prepared to devote time and energy to the job hunt. One tip is to look for work away from the big cities, where other new arrivals from overseas may be competing for the same jobs. A valuable source of rural jobs is Employment National (EN), the government's privatised job agency. Enquiring in one office will allow you to uncover harvest work near one of the more than 200 other offices across the country. Employment National encourage working holidaymakers to contact their specialist fruit and crop-picking department on 1300-720126 or to check their website (www.employmentnational.com.au) which has details of the EN offices all over the country and the types of work that these may offer.

The fruit harvests of Northern Victoria employ a massive 10,000-12,000 people in the Australian summer (January –March). The city of Shepparton is in the Goulburn Valley, about two hours north of Melbourne with easy accessibility via rail or bus services. From Sydney, catch a train to Albury and from there take the bus to Shepparton. Information can be obtained from the Northern Victoria Fruitgrowers' Association Ltd. (NVFA), PO Box 612, Mooroopna, Vic 3629 (03-5825-3700;

fax 03-5825-5029; e-mail administrator@nvfa.com.au and The Victorian Peach and Apricot Grower's Association (VPAGA) PO box 39 Cobram, Vic (03-5872-1729; fax 03-5871-1612). When sending for the information leaflet *Guide to Your Working Holiday* from NVFA, you must include an International Reply Coupon (IRC) obtainable from the post office to ensure a reply. Additional information relevant to the fruit harvest in the Goulburn Valley can also be obtained from the NVFA website www.nvfa.com.au. Go to 'Harvest Labour' on the menu. There is also a National Harvest Hotline number of 1300 720 126. This number gives the option of states and areas within Australia where current seasonal work is available. By following the prompts, callers are able to obtain accurate updated information to a particular area or are able to speak directly with a person in a particular area.

Searching the web for employment leads is especially productive in Australia. There are dozens of routes in to finding out about job vacancies. A wide search can be done by looking at Employment under Google's regional directory at http://directory. google.com/Top/Regional/Oceania/Australia/. Before leaving home, you might like to register (free) with www.gapwork.com which is updated regularly and lists employers who hire working holidaymakers. The relatively new www.jobsearch. gov.au is a government source of information with details of the National Harvest Trail. One of the best sites is a free service by the Wayward Bus Company (www. waywardbus.com.au/seaswork.html) which has an index of actual employers, hostels and pubs recommended for job-seekers and agents. EN's website has useful links (www.employmentnational.com.au).If in Queensland check the adverts in *Queensland Country Life* magazine (www.queenslandcountrylife.com). The magazine also has an online jobs guide (www.jobsguide.com.au). Some properties also function as holiday ranches and they often take on domestic staff and guides.

A publication called *Workabout Australia* shows areas where fruit picking and other seasonal work is available. It also gives times, transport information, accommodation information and contacts for jobs on arrival; this book is available from by Vacation Work (www.vacationwork.co.uk 01865-243311) price £10.99.

Hard-working travellers can earn A$100 a day doing harvest work, although AS$9 an hour would be more typical. The cost of living in Australia is a lot lower than in Britain so those wages go further than it sounds if you convert them into sterling at the current rate (£1 is worth A$2.50 at the time of writing).

Anyone who is serious about earning their way over a long period by fruit picking should consider obtaining the small format specialist booklet Fruit Picking around Australia which is available in Australia for A$10 from Pickpack (11 Coral St, Saunders Beach, Queensland 4818; payable to L. Hutchinson) or from campsites and bookshops in the relevant areas. Details can be found on www.cix.co.uk/~yama. fruit.

Some city-based employment agencies deal with jobs in outback areas, primarily farming, station, hotel/motel and roadhouse work. In Western Australia Pollitt's (13th Floor, 251 Adelaide Terrace, 13th Floor, Perth 6000; ☎08-9325 2544) who said that experienced farmworkers and tractor drivers are paid £4.50-£5 (A$12-$14) an hour for 10-12 hour days, seven days a week at seeding time (April to June) and harvest time (October to December). Housekeeping, nannying and cooking positions are available for two to three months at a time throughout the year. The standard wage is £105 (A$300) a week after board, most of which can be saved. For work in outback roadhouses and hotels, previous experience in kitchen, food and beverage service is essential to earn £140 (A$400) a week after lodging. The three-month commitments enable travellers to experience the regional country towns while saving most of their earnings.

In urban areas the usual range of jobs exists (bar, restaurant, office and factory work) available through the many private employment agencies such as Bligh, Adecco and Drake Personnel. It is also worth investigating tourist areas such as the coastal and island resorts of Queensland for jobs in hotels, restaurants, etc. especially during the Australian winter from June to October.

One of the best sources of job information for working holidaymakers in Australia is the extensive network of backpackers' hostels, some of which employ young foreigners themselves and all of which should be able to advise on local possibilities. One such is Brook Lodge Backpackers (3 Bridge Street, Donnybrook, WA 6239; ☎08-9731 1520; e-mail info@brooklodge.com.au; www.brooklodge. com.au) in Western Australia, which provides accommodation and can arrange hourly or weekly contract seasonal work including seasonal work in the apple harvest between November and May. Details of lodges like this can be found on the internet at http://backpackingaround.com, a website set up by backpackers which carries job and visa information as well as links and info on accommodation around Western Australia. Another useful source is the work exchange called Workstay Australia which is based in Western Australia and can be found at www. workstay.com.au. There is a membership fee and members are guided to a network of hostels when work is available. The group HNH Travellers Australia (Gabba Guesthouse, 18 Withington St, East Brisbane, Queensland 4169; ☎+61-7-3411-5955; www.hnh.net.au) primarily arranges accommodation for paying clients with host families, though it can also arrange fruit-picking in some areas. They offer a Travellers Discount Card for Aus $5 which will enable travellers a 10% discount at restaurants along with corporate car hire rates etc.

Either before you leave or once you are in one of the major cities, get hold of the free 200-page booklet *Australia & New Zealand Independent Traveller's Guide* published by the London-based travel magazine *TNT* (14-15 Child's Place, London SW5 9RX; ☎020-7373-3377; www.tntmagazine.com); send £2.95 postage. It includes a section on work and some relevant advertisements as well as travel advice.

Most newspapers advertise jobs on one or two days each week - varying from paper to paper and state to state. The *Sydney Morning Herald* is based at 201 Sussex Street, Sydney, NSW 2000 (www.smh.com.au). *The Australian* can be contacted at 46 Cooper Street, Surrey Hills, NSW 2010, and *The West Australian* at Newspaper House, 50 Hasler Road, Osborne Park, Western Australia 6017.

Copies of the above newspapers, plus information and application forms for visitor and working holiday visas may be obtained in the UK from the High Commission's designated agent, Consyl Publishing. For an application form and a free copy of *Travel Australia*, a newspaper aimed at those planning a working holiday in Australia, write to Consyl Publishing, 3 Buckhurst Road, Bexhill on Sea, East Sussex TN40 1QF (☎01424 223111; e-mail consylpublishing@btconnect. com; www.consylpublishing.co.uk); enclose an A4 stamped addressed envelope bearing at least 66p worth of stamps.

# RED TAPE

**Tourist Visa Requirements:** All intending visitors require either a visa stamped in their passport or an Electronic Travel Authority (ETA) which is a paperless visa. Tourist visas are issued for 6 or 12 months. ETAs are obtained through the Australian immigration office, airlines, travel agents or specialist visa agencies. An ETA is valid for 12 months and covers multiple entries into Australia for no more than three months each. Private visa agencies and delegated travel agencies can issue an ETA over the phone for varying fees, usually between £10 and £25.

Major airlines may offer a free ETA service if you purchase an air ticket through their reservations offices. Three of the many agencies are Visas Australia Company (PO Box 1, Nantwich, Cheshire CW5 7PB; 01270 626626; www.visas-australia. com) and Australian Visas Ltd (PO Box 170, Ashford, Kent TN24 0ZX; 01233 211800) and www.ausvisa.iborders.com (01270 626626). Those with ETAs and visitor visas are not permitted to work.

**Working Holiday Visas** The Australian Government operates a working holiday scheme for passport holders of the following countries: United Kingdom, Republic of Ireland, Belgium, Canada, Cyprus, Denmark, Estonia, Finland, France, Germany, Italy, Japan, Republic of Korea, Malta, Netherlands, Norway, SAR Hong Kong and Sweden. To be eligible for the granting of a 12 month, non-renewable working holiday visa you must satisfy the following criteria: be aged over 18 and under 31, have no dependent children have not previously entered Australia on a working holiday visa or applied for one, intend to travel and holiday in Australia with the option of taking incidental work to supplement your holiday funds but are prohibited from working for one employer for more than a total of three months, are in possession of reasonable funds (currently £2,000 in the UK and €3,200 in Europe) for normal maintenance purposes for the initial part of the proposed holiday period and sufficient for airfare.

There is a non-refundable processing fee for a working holiday visa, currently £70 in the UK (subject to change). Current information is available by calling the Australian Immigration and Citizenship Information Line on 09065-508900 (calls are charged at £1 per minute).

During those 12 months of the visa's validity you may leave and re-enter the country as many times as you wish. Most WHM applicants have been able to lodge their visa applications electronically over the internet via www.immi.gov.au. Visa Specialists such as Visas Australia (www.visas-australia.com) charge an extra £15. Either way the 'e-visa' or e-WHM will be processed within 48 hours. This initiative is a great improvement in visa service delivery.

# Agricultural Work

**PLUNKETT ORCHARDS**: 255 McIsaac Road, Ardmona Victoria 3629, Australia (☎ +61 3 5829 0015 (business hours only) fax: +61 3 5829 0324; e-mail info@ plunkettorchards.com.au; www.plunkettorchards.com.au). Plunkett Orchards is a friendly, professional, family-owned business that employs travellers each year to work on the annual harvest of apples, pears and peaches. Plunkett Orchards is 2 hours north of Melbourne and temperatures can reach up to 40 degrees during harvest time.

**Fruit Pickers (40):** to harvest pears, apples and peaches. Fruit picking is strenuous so applicants need to be in good physical condition. On-the-job training is provided, no previous experience necessary. Wages $28 (AUD) (approx £10.50) per bin harvested. New pickers may pick between 2 and 4 bins a day while developing their technique. More experienced pickers may harvest up to 10 bins. Hours of work are 6.30am – 3 pm, 6 days a week. Harvesters wanted 25 January to 25 March. Minimum period of work 1 week.

**Fruit Graders (10):** involves visually assessing the quality of pears passing over a conveyor belt. Wages $15.07 (AUD) (approx £5.80) per hour. Fruit grading lasts approximately 7 weeks, 6 days a week. Shifts last 7 to 9 hours at variable times. Minimum period of work 4 weeks.

Board and lodging is available for $70 (AUD) (approx £27) per week.

*Applications* invited from 1st November.

**RJ CORNISH**: RMB 2024, Cottons Road, Cobram, Victoria 3644, Australia (☎+61 (0)3 58 72 2055; e-mail jobs@rjcornish.com; www.rjcornish.com). RJ Cornish and Co is a family-owned and operated business located at Cobham on the Murray River on the border of Victoria and New South Wales. As one of Australia's largest producers of apples, pears and canned peaches approximately employment is also fruitful; 200 fruit pickers are required.

Pickers generally work 6 days per week from 7.30am to 4.00 pm (weather and crop permitting). Australian Workers Union rates are paid per bin of fruit harvested. Accommodation (two or three persons per room) and meals are available for approximately A$115 (£45) per week. Campsite and caravans are also available. Work period is from late January to mid-March. Please see website for further details and online application. For further enquiries contact Doug McKean at above e-mail address.

*Apply* in December to Doug McKean using online application form.

**OUTBACK INTERNATIONAL:** PO Box 8042, Allenstown, QLD 4700, Australia (☎+61-74927 4300; fax +61-74922 6923; e-mail admin@outbackinternational. com; www.outbackinternational.com). Outback International is an Australia-wide rural employment agency; they have jobs for farmers, tractor drivers, cotton workers, cooks and seasonal staff; and provide on-going support and back-up during your time working in Australia. The experience of working within the primary industries overseas aims to broaden your knowledge of technology and work practices.
**Farm Staff:** numerous vacancies for personnel to operate farm machinery, drive tractors/harvesters, or work on irrigation schemes. Wages start at around £4-£5 per hour; applicants must have an agricultural background.
**Cooks, Housekeepers, Nannies** to work on outback farm stations. Wages between £120-£160 per week. Applicants should have experience with cooking, housework and childcare.

All positions work 8-12 hours a day over a 5 or 7 day week. Farm workers are required all year, while cooks are needed between February and October. Minimum period of work two weeks. Board and lodging is usually included, but this depends on the location. It is essential that applicants speak English.

*Applications* are invited at any time to the above address.

**TORRENS VALLEY ORCHARDS:** PO Box 1659, Gumeracha, SA 5233, Australia (e-mail tvo@hotkey.net.au; www.tvo.com.au). Farm business that has used a lot of student and backpacker workers over the last 16 years particularly during the cherry harvest. He has had German, English, Japanese, Korean and French people, the majority of them female. Provides hostel type accommodation for travellers. Owner Tony Hannaford says that anyone who stays at TVO should be quick, polite, clean and look after the facilities provided. He organises trips to barbecues, football, beach etc. The farm is 30 minutes from Adelaide on the local bus run. **As well as picking, there is a lot of fruit packing work.**

*Apply* to Tony Hannaford at the above mail or e-mail address.

**VISITOZ:** Springbrook Farm, PO Box 69, Goomeri, 4601 Queensland, 4601 Australia (☎+61-741-686 106; fax +61-741-684-836; e-mail info@visitoz.org; www.visitoz. org).
VISITOZ offers an introduction to Australia for those with Working Holiday Visas. All those entitled to Working Holiday Visas find work in rural Australia as tractor drivers, stockworkers, horse riders, hospitality workers, on cattle and sheep stations, and as mothers' helps and teachers. Employment is guaranteed. Wages vary according

to the job being done, working hours, the State and the age of the worker; earnings are generally around $300 (approx £116) per week with free board and lodging but have been known to reach around $1000 (approx £390) per week for good tractor drivers.

Staff are needed around the year but working holiday regulations limit the time with any one employer to 3 months. Applicants must be aged 18-30 and all are assessed and/or trained for the job required. Participants in the scheme must pay for their own air fare, visa costs and the Visitoz training fee of $1680 (approx £700) which also covers being met at the airport on arrival, 3 days jet lag recovery, 5 days on the training farm and help with the red tape once in Australia.

For further details contact Adam and Robyn Moller at the above address by fax or e-mail; there are also two UK contacts; William on 07966-528664 or will@visitoz. org, and jules@visitoz.org.

**WILLING WORKERS ON ORGANIC FARMS (AUSTRALIA):** 2166 Gelantipy Road, W Tree via Buchan 3885, Victoria, Australia (☎+61-03-5155 0218; fax +61-03-5155 0342; e-mail hello@wwoof.com.au; www.wwoof.com.au).

WWOOF Australia offers the chance to learn about organic farming and Australian culture by giving practical help on over 1500 farms and properties around Australia. Jobs may range from weeding to building. Applicants should note that WWOOF **is not a source of paid employment**, but food and accommodation is provided in exchange for 4-6 hours work per day. Positions available all year.

Write for a brochure, or send £26 if single (£30 for a couple), for the list and insurance.

# Sports, Couriers and Camping

**THREDBO RESORT:** Kosciusko Thredbo Pty Ltd, PO Box 92, Thredbo, NSW 2625, Australia (☎+61-2-6459 4100; fax +61-2-6459 4101; e-mail info@thredbo.com.au; www.thredbo.com.au). Thredbo is Australia's premier ski resort, with a season from mid-June to the end of September. They employ over 700 staff in winter, and have a ski village population of over 4,400.

**Cashiering and Sales Staff: (5)** to sell ski lift passes, ski school products and assist in retail. Applicants should have sales and cash handling skills, accurate balancing and computer experience. Wages £853 per month.

**Ski Hire Staff (8)** to fit customers with skis and snowboards and hire out clothing and equipment. Should have some cash handling experience and be willing to work split-shifts. Wages £945 per month.

**Room Attendants:** to do all aspects of cleaning hotel rooms and apartments. Friendly and courteous disposition required. Wages approx £860 per month.

**Childcare:** trained and untrained staff who are prepared to assist in all aspects of caring for children 6 months to 5 years. Wages depend on qualifications, from approx £1,062 per month.

**Lift Attendants:** must be willing to work outdoors in all weather conditions. Some heavy work required. Good customer service skills. Wages approximately £943 per month.

**Chefs/Commis/Demis chefs:** to work for the Thredbo Alpino Hotel, including bistro, à la carte, fine dining and conferences. Wages approx. £1,200 per month.

Hours of work vary between 28-38 per week according to position. The period of work is from around 1 July to 28 September (depending on snow), with a minimum period of work of 12 weeks. Board and lodging is available for a cost of £57 per week.

*Applications* to the above address are invited from January and close in early-

April, with interviews in Sydney, Brisbane and Thredbo in early April.

# Voluntary Work and Archaeology

**AUSTRALIAN KOALA FOUNDATION:** GPO Box 3659, Brisbane, QLD 4001, Australia (☎+61-7 3229 7233; fax +61-7 3221 0337; e-mail akf@savethekoala.com; www.savethekoala.com). The Australian Koala Foundation (AKF) is a non-profit, non-government funded, conservation organisation whose central aim is the **conservation of Australia's unique koala habitat.**

Volunteers can also assist with **general office duties**, especially during the major public awareness and fundraising campaign – Save the Koala – held in July each year. Field trip participation costs begin at AU$1,000 per week, depending on location. Applicants should advise the AKF of any specialist areas of expertise or interest they may have. Details of field trips can be found on the website. Minimum age 18. Volunteers for office duties are generally required from March to October each year.

*Contact* Lorraine O'Keefe, Administration and Finance, at GPO Box 2659, Brisbane, QLD 4001, Australia, to discuss the voluntary opportunities available. Also check out the website for upcoming fieldtrips.

**BOB WHITWORTH:** 100 Deserio Road, Cedar, Pocket, Gympie, Queensland, Australia (☎07-54-886-147; e-mailforest@spiderweb.com.au; www.forest.spiderweb.com.au) Volunteer **farm workers** to assist with environmental work. Bob Whitworth also offers accommodation in a converted dairy, and in a small self-contained hut in a forest clearing (with wood stove, single bed and desk). The farm is surrounded by hills, a rainforest, and a creek. He invites visitors all year round (one or two at a time) of any nationality.

*Applicants* must speak some English. Accommodation is offered and usually food, although some visitors make a contribution. For more information look at the website or *contact* the above address for details.

**CONSERVATION VOLUNTEERS AUSTRALIA (CVA):** Head Office, PO Box 423, Ballarat, Victoria 3353, Australia (☎+61-3-5333 2600; fax +61-3-5333-2166; e-mail info@conservationvolunteers.com.au; www.conservationvolunteers.com.au). Conservation Volunteers Australia is Australia's largest practical conservation organisation. CVA welcomes everyone who is enthusiastic about the outdoors and hands-on conservation. Volunteers are part of a team of 6 to 10 people under the guidance of a CVA team leader. Projects undertaken by CVA include: **tree planting, native seed collection, endangered flora and fauna surveys, constructing and maintaining walking tracks in national parks.** Projects are run in every state and territory of Australia throughout the year and include some of Australia's most beautiful locations. CVA offers overseas volunteers the Conservation Experience six weeks package. Volunteering with CVA costs £8.50 (A$23) a night which includes all meals, project related travel and accommodation.

For more information *visit* the website or e-mail or write to CVA.

**CHRISTIAN WORK CAMPS AUSTRALIA:** PO Box K164, Haymarket, NSW 2000, Australia. Volunteers to take part in work camps, which are held for two to four weeks each January and July. The camps are currently held in New South Wales, the Northern Territory and Far North Queensland. Volunteers must pay camp registration fees of

approximately £23; additional expenses may include food and accommodation at a further £23, approx. per week. Volunteers are responsible for their own travel costs.
*For information* on forthcoming projects send an International Reply Coupon to the above address.

# Other Employment in Australia

**CAMP COUNSELORS USA:** UK Offices: Devon House, 171/177 Great Portland Street, London W1W 5PQ (☎020-7637 0779; e-mail info@ccusa.com; www.ccusa. com) and 27 Woodside Gardens, Musselburgh, nr. Edinburgh EH21 7LJ (☎0131-665 5843; e-mail ccusascotland@yahoo.co.uk; www.ccusa.com). US Office: 2330 Marinship Way, Suite 250, Sausalito CA 94965, USA.
Work Experience Down Under is a high quality programme that helps young people to work and travel in Australia or New Zealand for up to 12 months.
For details *contact* the above addresses; US citizens should *contact* CCUSA/Work Experience Down Under, 2330 Marinship Way, Suite 250, Sausalito, CA 94965; e-mail downunder@ccusa.com.

**WORK AUSTRALIA:** BUNAC, 16 Bowling Green Lane, London EC1R 0QH (☎020-7251 3472; e-mail downunder@bunac.org.uk).
BUNAC offers a work and travel scheme to Australia for up to a year. The package includes a working holiday visa, airport transfer. 2 nights' accommodation in Sydney, and orientation with guidance on jobs, housing, health, taxes, etc. plus back-up services. Participants have the option to travel on a BUNAC group flight with an organised stopover in either Hong Kong or Bangkok or arranging independent travel. Departures from the UK are year round.
Applicants must be aged 18-30 inclusive, *citizens of the UK, Ireland, Holland, Sweden, Denmark, Norway or Canada*, and will need to be able to show that they have reserve funds of at least £2,000. Programme costs are £450.
For further details *contact* Work Australia at the above address.

**WORK AND TRAVEL AUSTRALIA PROGRAMME:** IST Plus Rosedale House, Rosedale Road, Surrey TW9 2SZ (☎ 020-8939 9057; fax 020 8939 9090; e-mail info@istplus.com; www.istplus.com). IST Plus is a worldwide organisation placing people in casual work, internships and teaching positions across the world.
This programme allows participants to travel in Australia, taking up work along the way to support themselves. IST Plus offer assistance at every stage, from obtaining the visa, to helping find work and accommodation in Australia. Ongoing services include mail receiving and holding, 24 hour emergency support, and access to office facilities and free internet at their resource centre in Sydney.
*This programme is open to British, Canadian, Dutch and Irish passport holders resident in the UK*, aged 18-30, who have not been on a working holiday to Australia before. Programme fee starts at £320 (and rises in increments for every month's additional stay) and includes all services and 2 nights accommodation. Visa valid for 12 months from entry to Australia. Wide variety of work available, for up to 3 months per position.
*Applications* to the above address.

# New Zealand

New Zealand offers many job opportunities just as its massive neighbour Australia does. If you intend to work in New Zealand you will require a visa, but some visas such as Working Holiday visas are very easy and cheap to obtain; you don't need a visa if you go to New Zealand on holiday for up to 6 months and hold a UK passport.

The UK Citizens' Working Holiday Scheme allows Britons aged 18-30 to be employed in temporary jobs in New Zealand for up to two years. The scheme has proved so successful in allaying seasonal shortages of labour that the yearly ceiling of working holiday visas has been removed completely and applications are welcomed throughout the year to the New Zealand Immigration Service, Mezzanine Floor, New Zealand House, 80 Haymarket, London SW1Y 4TE (fax 020-7973 0370) via the internet at www.immigration.govt.nz/whs. Even if you are not in your home country you can apply online and pay by credit card (about £50) at the time of application. This entirely online application procedure was introduced in 2005 and keeps in touch with Working Holiday Makers by e-mail, sending them information about jobs and requesting feedback to keep the service up to scratch. You do not need a job offer when applying as the scheme allows you to pick up temporary work while holidaying in New Zealand.

Other working holiday schemes are open to Irish, Canadian, Japanese and Malaysian nationals who must apply in their country of nationality and whose visa is for up to a year. The expense of getting to New Zealand, means that many people who visit New Zealand to work are more concerned with the cultural than the financial aspects of their trip. Opportunities vary from region to region depending on the local employment situation. While wages are lower on average than in Australia, the cost of living is comparatively cheaper.

Worth reading is the *Independent Traveller's Guide – Australia & New Zealand* published bi-monthly by *TNT Magazine* which runs to around 200 pages of information, ideas and advice about travelling in Australia and New Zealand. To obtain a copy send an A4 S.A.E. (70p) to: TNT Travel Guides, TNT/Southern Cross, 14-15 Child's Place, Earl's Court, London SW5 9RX (☎020-7373-3377; www.tntmagazine.com).

If you want to place an advertisement stating that you are looking for work the *New Zealand Herald* is published by Wilson and Horton Ltd, PO Box 32, 46 Albert Street, Auckland (☎9-379 5050; fax 9-373 6410; www.wilsonandhorton.co.nz).

## RED TAPE

**Visa Requirements:** New Zealand has Visa Waiver agreements with 30 countries so citizens of the UK, Ireland, USA and most European countries do not need a visa for bona fide tourist or business visits of up to 3 months (6 months for UK citizens). On arrival, visitors must have valid passports, return tickets and evidence of sufficient funds (about £300 per month of stay). Renewals of permits will be considered to allow stays of up to a maximum of 12 months: approval is not automatic.

**Residence Visas:** People wishing to reside permanently in New Zealand can make a prior application to a New Zealand overseas post, or can apply while on a temporary permit in New Zealand.

**Work Visas & Permits:** Recent changes to immigration rules make it possible for people on working holidays to apply to extend their stay or even for residence without having to leave the country. Applicants with skills in demand may apply for a new work permit option that will be valid for up to six months at one of the seven Immigration Service offices in New Zealand. Permission may be given if there are no local residents available to take up the work offered.

The government of New Zealand has a programme enabling the young people (aged 18 to 30) of 30 countries to take working holidays in New Zealand, countries include UK, many other EU nations, Japan and USA. The Working holiday Permit must be obtained before applicant leaves their home country but it is not necessary to have already found employment.

American students are eligible to apply for a six-month work permit from the CIEE or BUNAC USA to work between April 1st and October 21st. CCUSA at 2330 Marinship Way, Suite 250, Sausalito, CA 94965 (1-800-999-CAMP; outbound@campcounselors.com/ www.campcounselors.com/australia.html) runs a three-month work experience programme (June to September).

**Au Pair:** Not customary. Work permit required.

**Voluntary Work:** Work permit required.

However, it should be noted that the above rules are liable to sudden change; all visas, including visitor visas, are charged for. There is a charge for all permit applications. For further information, contact the New Zealand Immigration Service: Immigration New Zealand (London Branch), 80 Haymarket, SW1Y 4TE, London, UK (☎020-7208 3886; fax 020-7973 0370); www.immigration.govt.nz.

# Agricultural Work

**FARM HELPERS IN NEW ZEALAND (FhiNZ):** 16 Aspen Way, Palmerston North, New Zealand, (tel/fax +646-355-0448; e-mail info@fhinz.co.nz; www.fhinz. co.nz).

FHINZ is a voluntary group of over 180 farms throughout New Zealand who offer free farm stays to visitors in exchange for 4-6 hours help per day. Board and lodging is provided in the family home in return for daily farm work dependent on season and type of farm. No experience is necessary and all equipment is provided. Most farms will collect visitors from the nearest town at no cost, and return them after the stay, which can be from 3 days to several months, depending on the needs of the farm. Visitors need to each have a membership booklet (revised every month), with full details of all the farms, the family and what kinds of work visitors will be helping with. These are $25 each, valid for one year and available either by mail order or through some agents.

For more information *contact* the address above.

**PUKENUI HOLIDAY PARK:** RD4, Kaitaia, Northland, New Zealand. (☎09 409 8803; fax: 09 409 8802; e-mail pukenuiholidays@xtra.co.nz; www.northland-camping.co.nz.). The Pukenui Holiday Park recruits for the **mandarin gangs** for Kerifresh, and **pickers for orchards** in the area. You can expect to earn $80-$100 per day. They organise accommodation, transport and work equipment. Pukenui is on SH1F en route to Cape Reinga, in the far North of New Zealand. There is a public bus that leaves daily from Auckland to Kaitaia and a bus is arranged from Kaitaia to Pukenui before each season starts.

Employees work 8 hours a day (weather permitting) 5-7 days a week, January to February, March to April and June to August, and August to November. Minimum period of work is 2 weeks. Board and lodging is available for $70 per week for camping or in a van and $98 per week for a bed with full facilities in a shared room. Both prices include transport to the orchard. For details of wages please contact Pukenui Holiday Park at above e-mail address.

Applications at anytime, preferably two to four weeks prior to commencement of work.

**WWOOF:** PO Box 1172, Nelson, New Zealand (tel/fax 03-5449890; e-mail support@wwoof.co.nz; www.wwoof.co.nz).
**Volunteer Farm Labourers** for unpaid work on organic properties including orchards, nurseries, farms etc. in New Zealand. It must be stressed that these positions are unpaid, and that participants must pay for their own travel expenses; they do, however, receive free food and accommodation. Positions are available at any time of year. WWOOF runs over 750 farms around New Zealand. Applicants must be aged over 16 and must not be from countries whose nationals need special invitations to enter New Zealand.

For further information *write to* Jane and Andrew Strange at the above address enclosing £12 membership fee or see the website.

# Voluntary Work

**INVOLVEMENT VOLUNTEERS NEW ZEALAND:** PO Box 153, Helensville, New Zealand (☎ +64-27 306 1818; e-mail ivnewzealand@volunteering.org.au and ivnz@xtra.co.nz).
Involvement Volunteers is an organisation that places volunteers in the areas of **social work, conservation, farming and education**. Board and lodging is sometimes provided free of charge but at other times a small fee is charged. Minimum period of work 2-6 weeks all year round. Knowledge of English is required. There is a fee for placement.
*Contact* the above address for further details.

# Other Employment in New Zealand

**BUNAC:** 16 Bowling Green Lane, London EC1R 0QH (☎020-7251 3472; fax 020-7251 0215; e-mail downunder@bunac.org.uk; www.bunac.org).
BUNAC offers a work/travel scheme entitled *Work New Zealand*, which enables participants to spend up to one year working and travelling in the South Pacific. The programme is open to students and non-students aged 18-35 *who hold a British or Irish passport*. Choose any type of job, anywhere in New Zealand. The package includes airport transfer on arrival, 2 nights' accommodation, a guaranteed job, arrival orientation and support services and resource centre are available throughout the stay. The programme cost is £450 plus visa.

For further information *contact* BUNAC at the above address or through their website www.bunac.org.

**CAMP COUNSELORS USA:** UK Offices: Devon House, 171/177 Great Portland Street, London W1W 5PQ (☎020-7637 0779; e-mail info@ccusa.com; www.ccusa.com) and 27 Woodside Gardens, Musselburgh, nr. Edinburgh EH21 7LJ (☎0131-665 5843; e-mail ccusascotland@yahoo.co.uk; www.ccusa.com). US Office: 2330 Marinship Way, Suite 250, Sausalito CA 94965, USA.
Work Experience Down Under is a high quality programme that helps young people to work and travel in Australia or New Zealand for up to 12 months.

For details *contact* the above addresses; US citizens should *contact* CCUSA/Work Experience Down Under, 2330 Marinship Way, Suite 250, Sausalito, CA 94965; e-mail downunder@ccusa.com.

**WORK AND TRAVEL NEW ZEALAND PROGRAMME:** IST Plus Rosedale House, Rosedale Road, Surrey TW9 2SZ (☎020-8939 9057; fax 020 8939 9090; e-mail info@istplus.com; www.istplus.com). This programme allows participants to travel in New Zealand, taking up work along the way to support themselves. IST Plus offer assistance at every stage, from obtaining the visa, to helping find work and accommodation. Ongoing services include mail receiving and holding, 24 hour emergency support, and access to office facilities and free internet at their resource centre in Auckland.

*This programme is open to British, Canadian and Dutch passport holders resident in the UK*, aged 18-30, who have not been on a working holiday to New Zealand before. Programme fee starts at £320 (and rises in increments for every month's additional stay) and includes all services and 2 night's accommodation. Visa valid for 12 months from entry to New Zealand. Wide variety of work available, for up to 3 months per position.

*Applications* all year round, at least 8 weeks before planned departure for New Zealand.

**WORK & TRAVEL NEW ZEALAND:** CIEE: (Council on International Educational Exchange), 7 Custom House Street, 3rd Floor, Portland, Maine 04101; (☎toll-free 1-800-40-STUDY; 1-207-553-7600; fax 1-207-553-7699; e-mail info@ councilexchanges.org; www.ciee.org or www.councilexchanges.org). This is the US address of the worldwide organisation placing people in voluntary work, casual work, internships and teaching positions across the world.

This is for *US citizens* aged 18-30; it allows employment in New Zealand for up to four months at any time of year, with the possibility of an additional tourist visa. The scheme includes documentation and assistance in country from a CIEE representative.

This is the equivalent to the above programme for US citizens aged 18-30; it allows employment in New Zealand for up to six months between April 1st and October 31st. The scheme includes documentation, assistance in finding work and housing through Council's partner organisation in New Zealand, orientation etc.

*For further details* call the above toll-free number in the USA or visit the websites.

# Useful Publications

**ARCHAEOLOGY ABROAD:** 31/34 Gordon Square, London WC1H 0PY; ☎ 0208-537 0849; fax 0208-5370849; e-mail arch.abroad@ucl.ac.uk; www.britarch. ac.uk/archabroad
Publishes bulletins twice a year (on CD ROM), which list a wide range of archaeological fieldwork opportunities worldwide, all easily accessible via live e-mail and web links. Fieldwork Awards are available to help subscribers with their expenses.

**CHRISTIAN VOCATIONS:** St. James House, Trinity Road, Dudley, DY1 1JB (☎01384-233511; fax 01384-233032; e-mail info@ChristianVocations.org; www. christianvocations.org).
Publishes the *Short-Term-Service Directory*, a comprehensive source of information about short-term service options with a Christian emphasis in the UK and abroad, at a cost of £4.00 plus £1 post & packing (overseas postage is extra). For further details and information on their other publications and services contact them at the above address.

**COORDINATING COMMITTEE FOR INTERNATIONAL VOLUNTARY SERVICE (CCIVS):** UNESCO, 31 rue Francois Bonvin, F-75732 Paris Cedex 15, France (☎+33-1-45-68-45-36; e-mail ccivs@unesco.org; www.unesco.org/ccivs).
CCIVS is an international non-governmental organisation created in 1948 under the aegis of UNESCO to promote and coordinate voluntary work worldwide. CCIVS has 140 member organisations present in more than 90 countries.
    Publishes *How to be a Volunteer* in Europe, Africa, Asia and America a guide and useful address book, costing €2.50 (£1.68)or two International Reply Coupons.

**JOBCENTRE PLUS:** International Job Search Advice Team, 6th Floor, Whitehall II, Whitehall Quay, Leeds LS1 4HR (☎0113 307 8090; e-mail international-jobsearch-advice@jobcentreplus.gsi.gov.uk).
The International Jobsearch Advice Team provides general information to assist customers in the UK and overseas who wish to relocate. The team produces a series of fact sheets, entitled *Working in....*, for each of the countries in the European Economic Area. These are available directly from the team at the above address, or via the website www.jobcentreplus.gov.uk (on the Customer pages, section entitled *Working or Training in Europe*). They also have access to information sheets on selected countries outside the EU, and can offer advice about volunteering, studying or working overseas and where they cannot help directly, can refer you to the relevant specialist organisation.

**WORLD SERVICE ENQUIRY:** 237 Bon Marché Centre, 241-251 Ferndale Road, London SW9 8BJ (☎0870-770-3274; fax 0870-770-7991; e-mail wse@cabroad.org. uk; www.wse.org.uk).
World Service Enquiry provides expert, impartial information and advice about working or volunteering overseas in the Third World. We provide a range of services suitable for both skilled and unskilled people seeking overseas placements. *The Guide to Volunteering for Development* outlines ways to be involved in development issues and lists over 300 agencies that take volunteers in the UK and overseas on short-term placements. WSE also provides career guidance and the monthly job magazine *Opportunities Abroad*,; further details can be found on the website above.

# Vacation Work Publications

**Vacation Work Publications, 9 Park End Street, Oxford OX1 1HH**
**Tel 01865-241978 Fax 01865-790885**

**Visit us online for more information on our unrivalled range of titles for work, travel and gap years, readers' feedback and regular updates:**
**www.vacationwork.co.uk**

**Books are available in the USA from the Globe Pequot Press, Guilford, Connecticut**
**www.globepequot.com**